W9-AAM-328

ATLAS OF
MILITARY HISTORY

First published by Parragon in 2013

Parragon
Chartist House
15-17 Trim Street
Bath, BA1 1HA, UK

www.parragon.com

Produced by Moseley Road Inc., www.moseleyroad.com

Design Philippa Baile and Duncan Youel, www.oiloften.co.uk
Art Director Tina Vaughan
Editorial Director Damien Moore
Editor Jill Hamilton
Indexer Nanette Cardon
Illustration Andy Crisp, www.andycrisp.co.uk

ISBN 978-1-4723-0962-4

Printed in China

ATLAS OF MILITARY HISTORY

AN ILLUSTRATED GLOBAL SURVEY OF WARFARE FROM ANTIQUITY TO THE PRESENT DAY

DR AARON RALBY

Bath • New York • Singapore • Hong Kong • Cologne • Delhi
Melbourne • Amsterdam • Johannesburg • Shenzhen

CONTENTS

ABOVE This *zun*, or wine vessel, dates to the early Spring and Autumn Period. It was excavated in Henan Province of China in 1956.

LEFT This coin depicts Roman Emperor Commodus (r. 180–192 CE) driving a two-wheeled chariot drawn by four horses.

BELOW The Great Wall of China was built and expanded to protect the empire's borders from the assaults of nomads and other enemies. Made of rammed earth and brick, the wall is one of the most impressive feats of construction in the medieval world.

RIGHT This clay tablet is from the reign of King Zimri-Lim of Mari. It is now housed in the Louvre, Paris.

CONTENTS

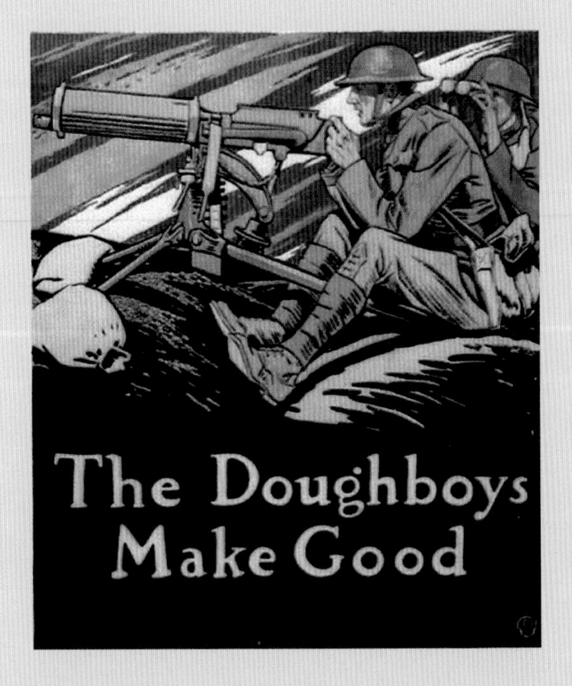

LEFT A wooden aboriginal shield from Queensland, Australia.

ABOVE A gold and copper ceremonial knife from the Sican culture of Peru, around 1000 CE.

RIGHT Magazine cover from 1917 showing American soldiers operating a machine gun.

EUROPE 220

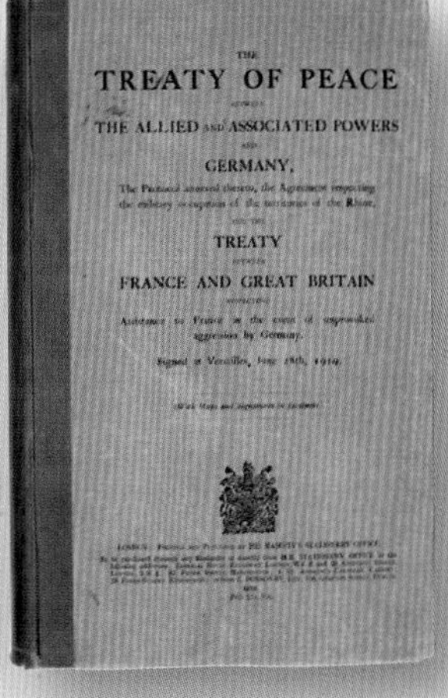

FAR LEFT British soldiers of the 13th Light Dragoons during the Crimean War, in 1855.

LEFT An English copy of the Treaty of Versailles that ended World War I.

INTRODUCTION

What we know about war in the Stone Age must be inferred from scant archaeological remains. How can we determine the purpose of weaponry? How can we tell when weaponry began to be used for hunting people instead of game? These are difficult questions to answer; we may never know for sure. We have a very biased picture of Stone-Age life on account of what survives: little other than stone and bone, and we must base a lot of theories on very little.

Stone-Age technology is actually more advanced than many people assume. The creation of stone tools by percussion and pressure flaking requires not only the right kind of stone, but also a significant amount of dexterity, skill, and knowledge regarding the properties of the stone. Extending the natural leverage of a human arm through the use of a sling or an atlatl takes no small amount of understanding of physics and mechanics. These seem like rudimentary devices to us now, but in the course of evolution, these are significant advances and served as basic building blocks on which we as a species were able to advance.

WHEN DID WAR BEGIN?

Conceptually, there is a big difference between using a spear to kill a boar and using a spear to kill a man. Practically, however, there is little difference. War, however, is not just

AGES OF MANKIND*

Lower Palaeolithic	2.5 million years ago
Upper Palaeolithic	40,000 years ago
Neolithic	11,000 years ago
Bronze Age	variable; 3300–300 BCE
Iron Age	variable; 1300 BCE –200 CE

*These dates are approximate, referring to Eurasia specifically: bronze and iron were not developed in all parts of the world.

ABOVE The distinction between tools and weapons is particularly blurred in considering early, Stone-Age implements.

LEFT Warfare requires organization of groups, not just combat.

BELOW Organized hunting of large animals may have provided a transition between individual combat and organized aggression between groups of people.

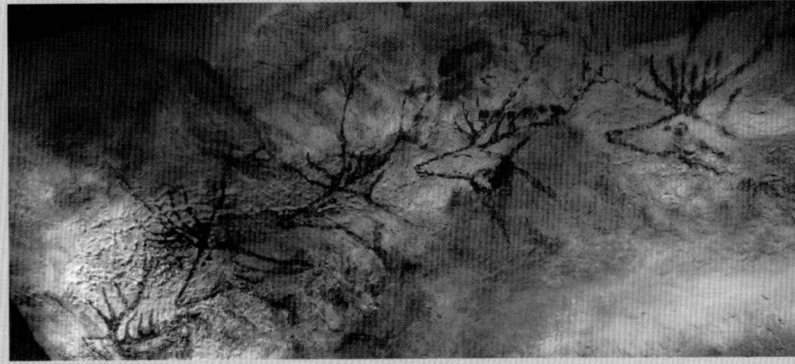

about killing: it is about systematically combining forces to combat another combined force. Some scholars may argue over whether "war" itself is a more recent invention, capable only with large-scale organization; but the principle of organizing one force against another must be very old. A 13,000-year-old mass grave from Egypt shows the earliest-known evidence of large-scale armed combat. When did individual combat transform into organized struggle?

The question of when it all began raises many other fascinating – albeit currently unanswerable – questions about human history and evolution. Many scholars speculate that war developed over territorial claims as a result of agriculture and fixed settlement. But bands of chimpanzees will march and fight against other bands, even using sticks as weapons. For this kind of organization, more advanced forms of communication are necessary. Is the development of warfare in human history tied to the development of language? Did our relatives, the Neanderthals, go extinct 30,000 years ago on account of war with Homo Sapiens? We may never know for certain, but in seeking answers to these questions we learn more about what makes us human in the first place.

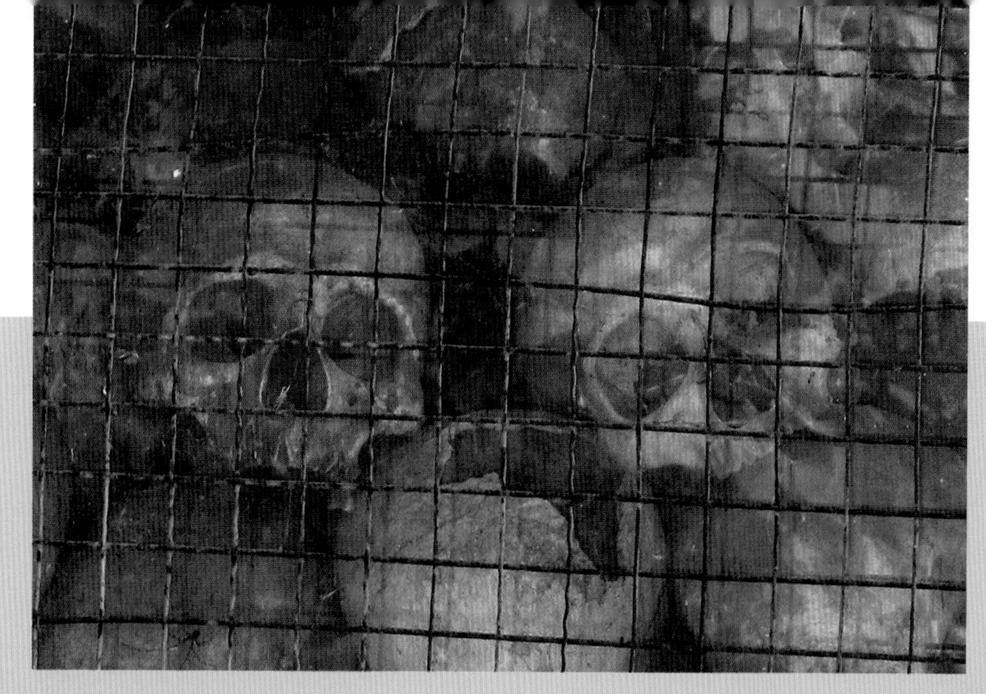

LEFT Skulls of those slain by the Khmer Rouge in Cambodia.

OPPOSITE Carthage falls to the Romans in 146 BCE. Two great civilizations pitted against each other during the Punic Wars.

THE HUMAN PASSION FOR WAR

General William Sherman coined the phrase 'War is hell' in 1879 in the speech he delivered to the graduating class of Michigan Military Academy. Most who have experienced the clash of battle, or its effects on those caught in its path, would agree that war is a terrible thing. Yet we as a species, regardless of our rational understanding of war's terror, are always drawn back to the allure of the fight. For many of you, that is why you are here, right now, reading this book on the great military exploits of the world.

Despite all the destruction and death caused in battle, there is something undoubtedly appealing about the great struggles of war. Perhaps it is our human desire to test and prove ourselves, requiring the greatest conditions of hardship. We long to compete, to match ourselves against our fellow man; and no competition is as great or as powerful as one that results in the death of one side. Human beings love to fight, whether with words, or on the playing field or on the battlefield. It is human nature to seek constantly to improve ourselves, and that is tested most definitively through conflict.

There are many types of wars we can wage in our lives, and the metaphor of battle extends across an array of disciplines and activities. In studying the strategies and tactics of great military leaders of days gone by, we can find inspiration for the various types of struggle and combat in our own lives, regardless of whether they in fact involve the physical death of ourselves or another human being. It is the transferability of the metaphor battle that allows us to see ourselves in the warriors of the past, and learn from them – both their successes and their failures – as we exercise the 'will to strive, to seek, to find, and not to yield'.

THE ROOTS OF WAR

However many thousands of times men and women have donned the trappings of war to march out into the field and do battle with one another, the roots and causes of war are almost always the same. We fight for resources, we fight for the freedom to exercise our will and sometimes we even fight for beliefs and ideas. Most of the time, however, we have fought with one another for control over a strip of land, or a waterway that will allow our family and kinsmen a better life and greater prosperity than the families and kinsmen of our opponents.

In Ancient Egypt and Mesopotamia, for example, only narrow strips of land surrounding the waterways of the Nile, the Tigris and the Euphrates were fertile enough to sustain agriculture and feed the populations of the great nations that developed in these regions. It is no wonder that people fought for such land and were willing to die for it; without it, they might be as good as dead anyhow.

From small familial bands fighting over control of a well, to the great armies of Alexander with their systematic organization and impressive logistics, war has existed on any number of scales. War has fragmented empires – as in the fall of Rome – and war has been the tool of great leaders – such as Harold Fair Hair or Oda Nobunaga – to unite a land divided. In every tale of military conquest and defeat, we see the same dichotomies of courage and cowardice, peace and struggle, threat and resistance. It is always the same, and yet, each conflict is unique.

ABOVE African Americans gather the bones of soldiers killed during the American Civil War.

ABOVE A US Army soldier aims a high-powered weapon. Carefully calculated camouflage has replaced the military uniforms of old.

ABOVE An intercontinental missile being transported in Moscow. Such weapons require significant supporting technologies to ensure proper storage, transport and – in the provision of their actual use – deployment.

THE CHANGING TIDES OF WAR

For thousands of years, the technology of war remained relatively constant. While significant technological advances, such as the use of stirrups or the high-backed saddle, afforded powerful military advantage, nothing has compared to the rapid development of firearms, missiles and other more intelligent forms of long-range weaponry over the last century and a half. Technology has changed society, and it has also changed the way we wage war.

Technological advances in weaponry have made the average modern soldier far more deadly than his ancient or medieval counterpart. Despite this, however, mortality rates of war have actually declined in recent years. While one could attribute some of this to advances in body armour and armoured vehicles, as well as in medicine, some must also be attributed to the changing nature of war. It is becoming increasingly targeted, increasingly focused, and the destructive capability of modern technology and weaponry is so massive as to place opponents in deadlock, neither side capable of harming the other without facing annihilation themselves. The shadow-boxing of the Cold War, or even the creation of widespread fear by terrorists, is emblematic of modern forms of conflict.

But technology has also had another important effect. With modern technology, we have new and improved ways of distributing and sharing the resources over which we fought so vigorously in the past. Along with technology, various media for transmitting ideas have spread across the world. Increased literacy rates and the availability of printed and now digital material have contributed to the popular uprisings of peoples from South America to the Arab Spring of North Africa. Nations are being shaped by whole populations in ways that would have been impossible in the past. We can only speculate how war, one of our most universal and, indeed, venerated traditions will continue to change as we advance.

LEFT Combining advances in radar with missile technology allows militaries to track and strike targets automatically, using computer-controlled systems.

HISPANIÆ PARS.
Estrecho de Gibralter
MARE ATLAN
BARBARIA
MARE MEDITER
Barca deser
ZANFARA REGNUM
GENEOA
REGIO
TOMBUTU REG.
Bangana
Zegzeg
Mandinga
Caragotes
Dauma
BENIN
BIAFARA REGNUM
Melli
Insulæ de Cabo Verde olim
Hesperides sive Gorgades
G U I
E
A
Kust van Benin
Tandt Kust
Oua qua Kust
Goudt Kust
ÆQUINOCTIALIS.
LINEA
OCEANUS
ETHIOPICUS

NOVA
AFRICA
DESCRIPTIO.
Auct. F. de Wit.
MARE
MULIER
ABISSINEA

AFRICA

Tigremahon
Bagamidri
Vangue
Malemba

EGYPT UNIFICATION C.3100 BCE

CHILD OF THE NILE

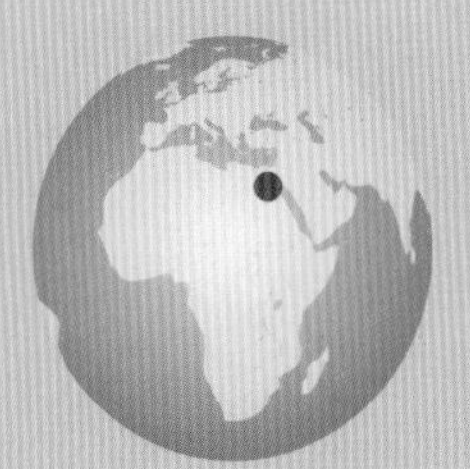

ANCIENT EGYPT IS CONSIDERED ONE OF THE GREATEST CIVILIZATIONS OF ALL TIME. BORN OF THE FERTILE LANDS OF THE NILE RIVER DELTA, THE GREAT KINGDOM OF EGYPT PROBABLY EMERGED THROUGH THE UNIFICATION OF SEVERAL SMALLER STATES.

While we do not know for certain how such unification came about, it is often speculated on the basis of an artefact known as the Narmer Pallete dating from the late Predynastic or early Dynastic periods (c. 3000–2686 BCE) that Egypt was united by King Narmer, depicted on the tablet brandishing a mace threateningly above a conquered opponent. Narmer is depicted on both sides of the tablet, on one side with the crown of Upper Egypt, on the other with the crown of Lower Egypt. This may mark the beginning of a unified Egypt, and unified Egyptian military.

ABOVE The Narmer Palette depicts the victorious King Narmer of Upper Egypt, who waged war against Lower Egypt, possibly unifying the empire. Some hold him to be the same as Menes, the first pharaoh of Egypt. The Palette dates to c. 3000 BCE.

LEFT Statue of King Thutmose III, who employed the khopesh in his military campaigns, a weapon brought to Egypt by the Hyksos along with the composite bow.

NAPOLEON OF EGYPT

The kingdom of Egypt rose to its greatest extent, expanding hugely, under the direction of King Thutmose III, Sixth pharaoh of the Eighteenth Dynasty. He expanded the territorial holdings of Egypt through 16 campaigns conducted as far away as Canaan and Syria, and Nubia in the south. Thutmose ruled for 54 years, 22 of which he ruled jointly with his stepmother as commander of her armies. At just 23 years of age, he led the Egyptians to a decisive victory against the combined forces of Canaan and Palestine. Later in his military career, Thutmose was able to take a Canaanite army by surprise and defeat them soundly at Megiddo, strategically taking the narrow pass of Aruna. He would also extend the power of Egypt south to the Fourth cataract of the Nile in Nubia. In total, Thutmose III conquered more than 350 cities through his military campaigns, and is widely regarded as one of the great military strategists of the ancient world.

TURNING TIDES OF BATTLE

Despite the power of the Egyptian pharaohs, Ancient Egypt experienced the pressure of foreign enemies many times during its 4,000 years on the Nile. Sometimes, it even caved in to that pressure. With the decided technological advantage of the composite bow and arrow, the Hyksos were able to subdue Egypt and bring the kingdom under their control in the Second Intermediate Period (1773–1550 BCE). The mysterious 'Sea People' would afflict the north during the twelfth century BCE. Nubia, which had been conquered by the Egyptians, would conquer Egypt during the Twenty-fifth Dynasty (760–656 BCE). Despite the various powers that did disrupt Egyptian rule, the empire maintained a consistency of culture and succession over thousands of years that is truly remarkable to behold.

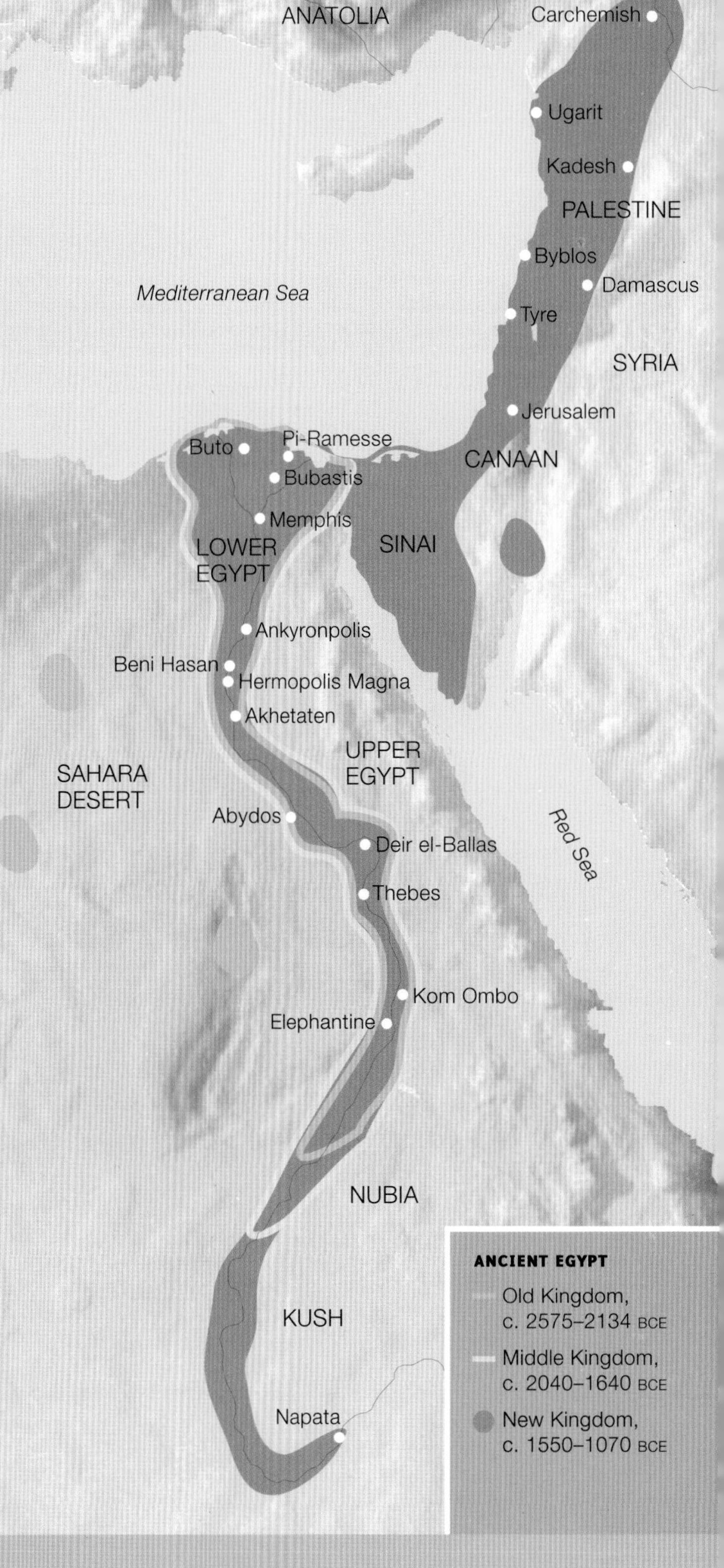

ABOVE This map shows the gradual expansion of Egypt outwards from the Nile Delta.

TOP LEFT Hunting provided an opportunity to practise and demonstrate bravery, particularly when the quarry was as fierce as a lion.

HORSES AND CHARIOTS

THE CART BEFORE THE HORSE

Despite the iconic association of the horse and rider as an essential component of battle, the mounted warrior is a relatively recent invention in the course of human history. In fact, compared to the earliest evidence of warfare, the use of horses at all in battle is itself relatively recent, beginning around 2000 BCE in Central Asia with the development of chariots.

The chariot created an instant and significant advantage on the battlefield, particularly when combined with the use of the bow and arrow. Rather than initially being used for charges, the chariot could be drawn along the breadth of an enemy, providing a swiftly moving, though stable and relatively secure platform, from which a warrior could pick off opponents from within enemy ranks, disrupting or even breaking formations to create openings for infantry. Chariots could also be used to carry men to and from the battlefield, relay messages and perform manoeuvres not possible simply on foot. Chariots often carried two warriors: the charioteer, who drove the chariot and guided the horses, and the archer in charge of taking down the enemy.

One may attribute some of the far-reaching spread of Indo-European languages across the world to the chariot. The technological innovation provided a military advantage that allowed Indo-Europeans originating in Central Asia to spread and conquer their neighbours with surprising force and power. This may have contributed to the early expansion of Indo-Europeans both to the west and to the east, which led to the development of peoples as diverse linguistically, culturally and geographically as Hindi speakers in India, Russian speakers in Russia and English speakers in the United Kingdom, Ireland, North America and beyond.

THE CHARIOT CREATED AN INSTANT AND SIGNIFICANT ADVANTAGE ON THE BATTLEFIELD, PARTICULARLY WHEN COMBINED WITH THE USE OF THE BOW AND ARROW.

ABOVE This coin depicts Roman Emperor Commodus (r. 180–192 CE) driving a two-wheeled chariot drawn by four horses.

RIGHT The chariots of the Egyptians were light and fast, allowing them to pursue their enemies, as at the Battle of Kadesh in 1274 BCE.

ABOVE This sand sculpture in Moscow commemorates the famous Russian king, Alexander Nevsky. Nevsky was a powerful king, but remained vassal to the Mongols, whose mastery of the horse was the foundation of their empire.

ABOVE LEFT A soldier with his horse during World War I, both wearing gas masks.

BELOW Cavalry charges became a powerful means of breaking enemy ranks, as depicted here in the charge of Napoleon's men at the Battle of Friedland in 1807.

THE HORSE AND RIDER

Two significant technological developments allowed for the rise of the mounted warrior during the Middle Ages in Europe, though mounted warriors had already existed on the steppes of Asia and in China. Indeed, one of those technological advances came out of China: the stirrup, allowing the warrior to stand in the saddle, and more effectively use weapons from atop his mount; the second innovation was the high-backed saddle, which provided the support necessary to prevent a warrior from falling off backwards as a result of frontal impact. Combining these two innovations, the mounted European knight was born, capable of using a lance in powerful frontal charges. So began the breeding of special warhorses, or chargers, who were larger and more powerful than horses had been before. The use of the horse in war throughout history has often been decisive, and horses have played central roles in conquests from the Mongols to the Americas.

NUBIA C.760 BCE

INVADERS FROM THE SOUTH

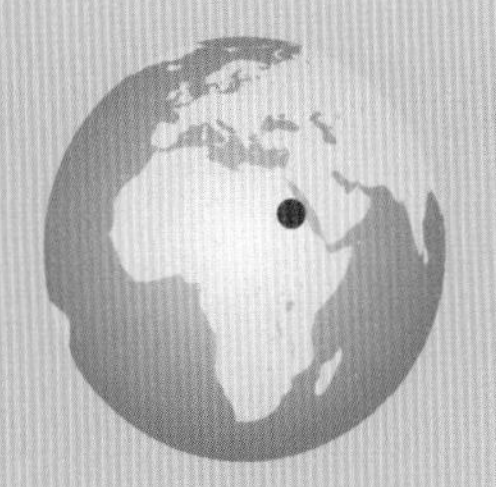

BY 800 BCE, EGYPT WAS CRUMBLING FROM THE INSIDE WITH THE BREAKDOWN OF UNIFYING POLITICAL AND MILITARY LEADERSHIP. THE FRAGMENTED EGYPTIAN KINGDOM PROVIDED AN OPPORTUNITY TO EGYPT'S NEIGHBOUR TO THE SOUTH, THE NUBIAN KINGDOM OF KUSH.

ABOVE This relief carving depicts Nubian soldiers bearing shields.

LEFT Painted wooden statuette of a Nubian woman, Middle or Early New Kingdom, c. 2030–1981 BCE.

BELOW The Kushite Pyramids of Nuri stand in what is now the Sudan.

Previously conquered by the Egyptians, the Kushites, under the rule of King Kashta, invaded Upper Egypt around 760 BCE, quickly taking Thebes and advancing further north. Despite the long relationship between Egypt and Nubia – including frequent intermarriage, as well as the shared tradition of pyramid-building – this was the first time Kush conquered Egypt.

THE HEIGHT OF THE KUSH

Kushite control of Egypt spread over the course of several generations. Although we know little of the conquest, we can be reasonably certain of several of its major events. Kashta first moved on Thebes and established his daughter as successor to the high priestess of Amun. Kashta's successor, Piye, whom we speculate to be his son, consolidated control of Upper Egypt and would defeat a challenge from the north from King Tefnakht, who had reunited Lower Egypt. Piye and the Kushites rose to the challenge, crushing Tefnakht and establishing control of all of Egypt, though Piye left Lower Egypt essentially as a tributary.

In 715 BCE, Piye's brother and successor, Shabaqo, brought the whole of Egypt back under the control of Kush. After moving the capital to Thebes, Shabaqo lay the foundation for a large revival of Egyptian art and architecture. The legacy of the Kushite kings can still be seen throughout the Nile River Valley in the form of the many temples and monuments they erected or restored. Rather than bringing and imposing Nubian culture in Egypt, the Kushite kings fostered the revival of Egyptian traditions, and even adopted the Egyptian writing system during this time themselves.

END OF A RENAISSANCE

In 690 BCE, Taharqa succeeded to the throne of the Kush Empire that encompassed Egypt. In the early part of his reign, the kingdom flourished, and Taharqa himself was responsible for much in the way of monument-building and restoration. Taharqa also worked to expand his influence into southwest Asia, but was eventually checked by Assyrian king Esarhaddon, who worked to remove Egyptian control from the Levant. Esarhaddon would attack Egypt in 671 BCE, defeating Taharqa and taking control of his capital Memphis. Though Esarhaddon withdrew, and Taharqa was able to reconquer Egypt, the Assyrians would return and break Kushite control of Egypt, sacking Thebes and establishing a new dynasty under Psamtik I.

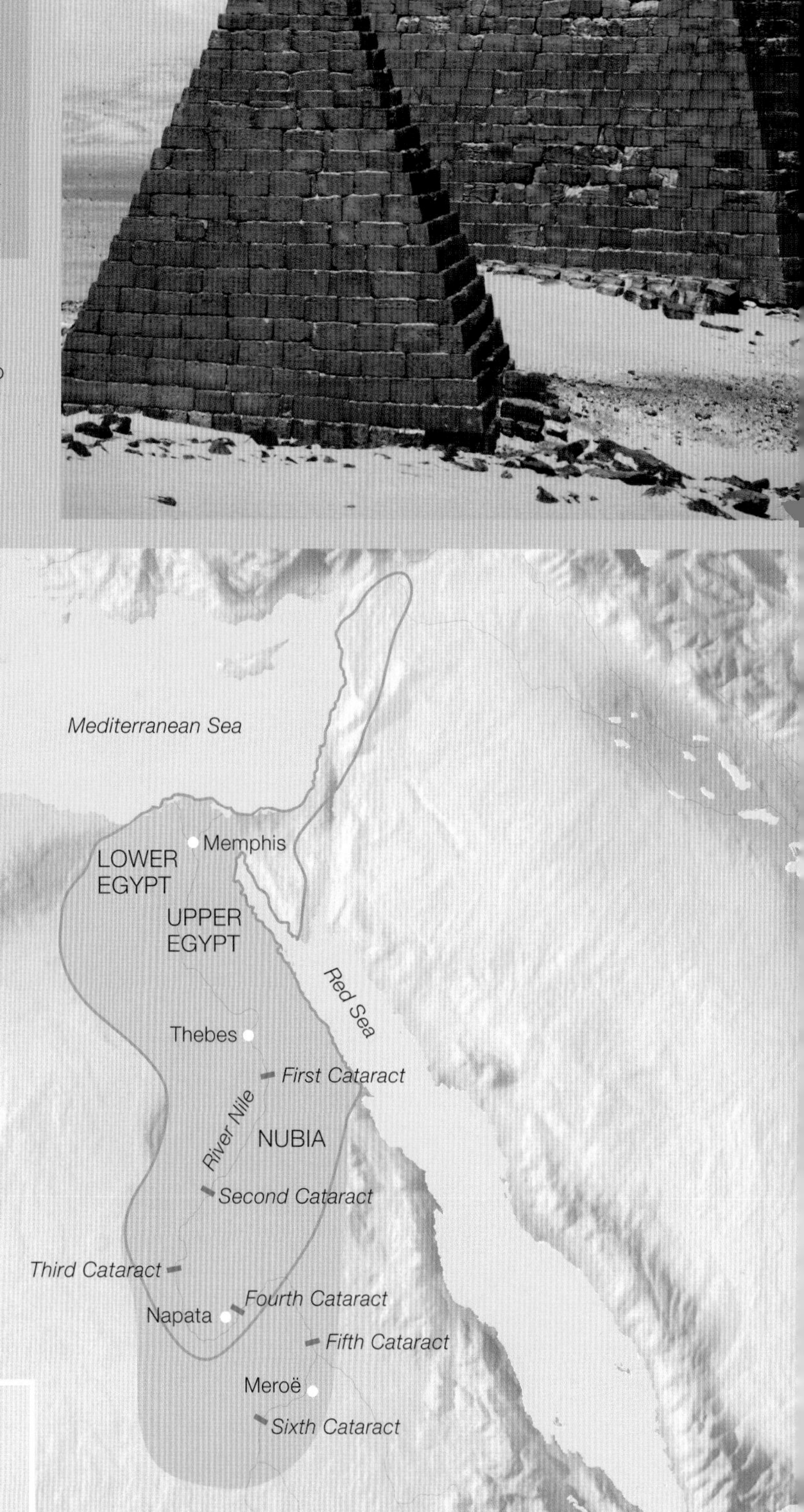

RIGHT Like their neighbours to the north, the Nubians built pyramids to house their dead rulers. More than 200 pyramids stand in Meroë, the capital of Kush.

BELOW The Kingdom of Kush, 700 BCE

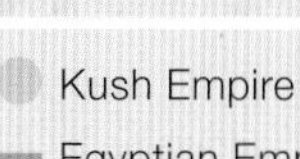

THE PUNIC WARS 264–146 BCE

EPIC PROPORTIONS

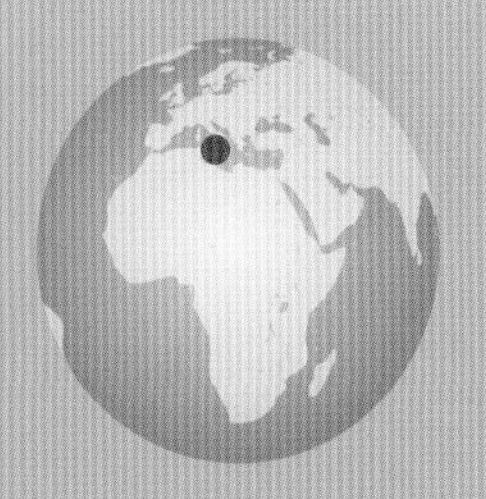

THE PUNIC WARS, A SERIES OF CONFLICTS BETWEEN THE POWERS OF CARTHAGE AND ROME, WERE AMONG THE LARGEST ARMED CONFLICTS THE WORLD HAD KNOWN AT THE TIME OF THEIR OCCURRENCE.

Two great powers of the Mediterranean, Carthage and Rome, kept expanding until conflict between the two became inevitable. A small quarrel over territory in Sicily rapidly escalated into one of the most famous series of battles in history.

The first war (264–241 BCE) was largely a naval war, favouring the superior naval capabilities of Carthage. The steep learning curve for Rome had significant demographic impacts on the Roman Empire, resulting in a loss of 17 per cent of the male population by 247 BCE. In an effort to play

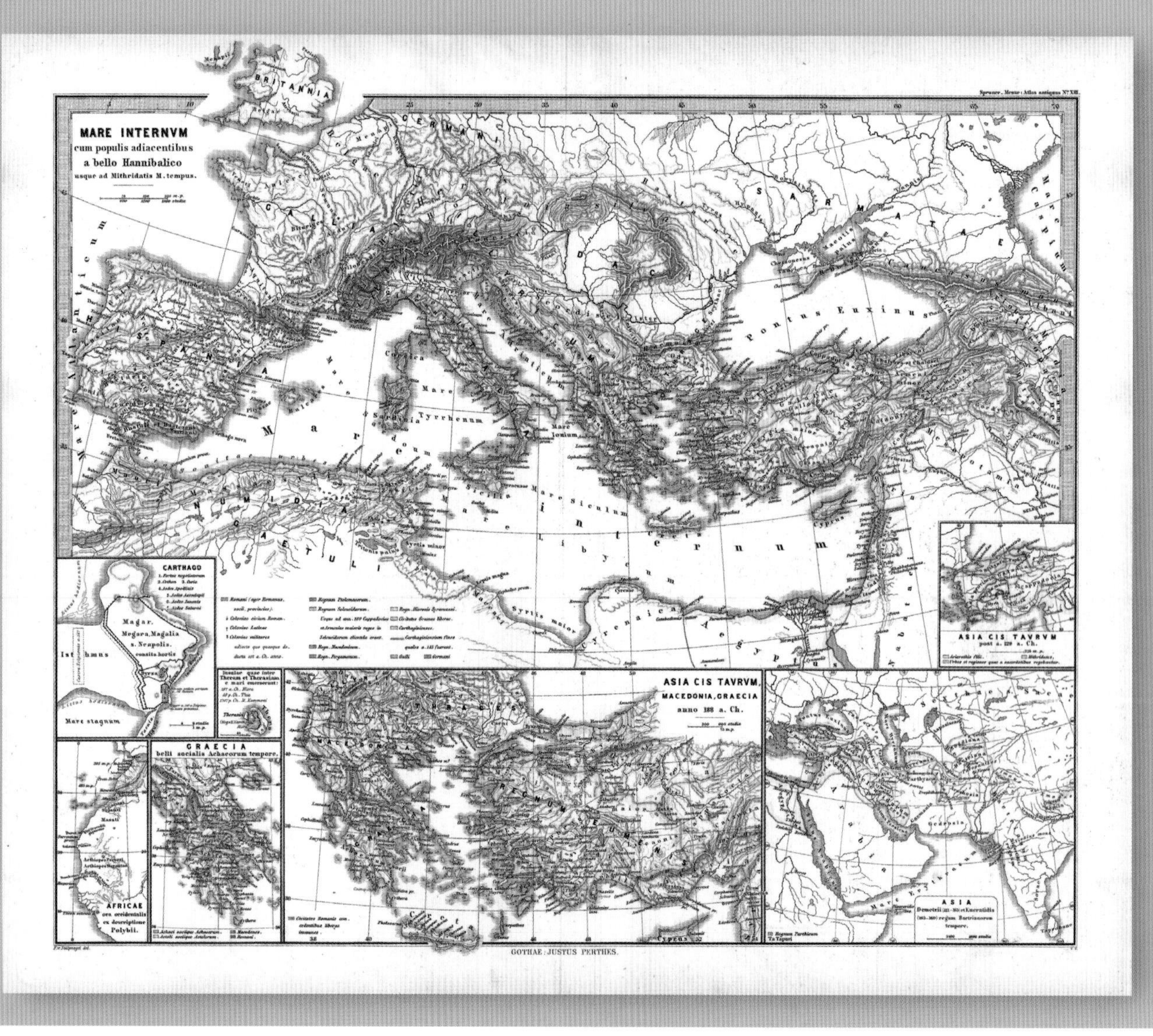

to their strengths, Romans developed a device called the *corvus*, a type of spiked plank used to connect Roman and Carthaginian ships at sea, to form a stable platform on which soldiers could fight hand-to-hand. Despite the power of Carthage, Rome would nonetheless eventually gain control of Sicily in 242 BCE.

ABOVE Virgil's *Aeneid* recounts the fate of Dido, queen of Carthage, who fell in love with the Trojan warrior, Aeneas. Here, she shows Aeneas the harbour at Carthage.

LEFT Hannibal won fame for trekking across the Alps with 24 war elephants. His surprise tactics and brilliant strategies put Rome against the ropes.

OPPOSITE This map depicts the territories under the control of Rome and Carthage, two giants of the Mediterranean.

THE STRATEGIES OF HANNIBAL

The Punic Wars are perhaps most famous for one of the key generals in the struggle: Hannibal. Hannibal was the son of Hamilcar Barca, one of the great Carthaginian leaders during the First Punic War. In 219 BCE, Hannibal effectively began the Second Punic War by attacking Saguntum, a city in Spain allied with Rome.

Hannibal is most famous for taking his troops, along with several war elephants, over the Alps, moving from Spain to attack Italy from the north. Surprising the Romans there, Hannibal was able to win a number of decisive victories, despite being vastly outnumbered. His brilliant strategies allowed him to achieve great success in the battles of Trebia, Lake Trasimene and Cannae, but the loss of his elephants to the cold of the Alps, as well as his lack of siege engines, meant that he did not have the strength to march against Rome itself. Roman attacks on North Africa led Hannibal to eventually return there, where he was at last defeated by Scipio Africanus at the Battle of Zama.

ABOVE This cartoon depicts Hannibal swearing his hatred for Rome, something the warrior is reputed to have done as a child.

OPPOSITE Carthage was utterly destroyed by the Romans and lay in ruins until the city was rebuilt in 49–44 BCE by Julius Caesar. The city would again face destruction in 698 by the Muslims.

RIGHT This statue from the Louvre shows Hannibal, counting the rings of Roman soldiers slain at the Battle of Cannae.

ROMAN SUPREMACY

After the defeat of Hannibal, Carthage had little choice but to sue for peace. The terms of settlement seemed harsh, with Rome exercising considerable control over the former power. Carthage was subsequently harassed by neighbouring state, Numidia. The treaty with Rome, however, prevented Carthage from retaliating against Numidia, as it was a Roman ally. Though the Carthaginians were defeated, Rome sought to impose strict demands on the city. Carthage's refusal led to armed conflict once again: Rome launched a final assault on Carthage, utterly destroying the city in 146 BCE.

SONGHAI EMPIRE 1468–1591

TO TIMBUKTU AND BACK AGAIN

THE SONGHAI PEOPLE HAVE INHABITED WEST AFRICA FOR OVER 1,000 YEARS, BUT ROSE TO PROMINENCE IN THE LATE FIFTEENTH CENTURY UNDER THE REIGN OF SUNNI ALI (1464–1492).

In 1468, Sunni Ali conquered the wealthy city of Timbuktu, which was then resisting the control of the Tuareg people. The Songhai had already declared independence in the fourteenth century from the disintegrating Mali Empire, and it was only a matter of time before they were ready to establish a dynasty of their own. Though often described as a tyrant, Sunni Ali founded an empire that would become one of the largest Islamic empires in history.

With Timbuktu under his control, Sunni Ali turned his attention to Jenne (modern Djenné, Mali), where he met staunch opposition. After a seven-year siege in which he effectively starved the inhabitants, he was at last able to subdue the city and incorporate this other important trading centre into his dominion.

IN WORD AND DEED

Sunni Ali received serious criticism for his apparently nominal profession of Islam. But at least it was nominal. Sunni Ali's son and successor, Sunni Barou, refused to declare himself a Muslim, which led to open rebellion. Songhai general, Muhammad Touré – or Askia – rose against Barou, defeating him and staking claim to the throne of the empire. Askia was pious not only in word but in deed as well, establishing Islamic schools and centres of worship. He fostered learning in his dominion, ushering in a time of great prosperity in Songhai and West Africa. Though he was not as strong a military commander as his predecessor, Askia was still a sound tactician and a strong leader of his people. His might extended far beyond his military campaigns, however,

LEFT Sankore Madrash, part of the university in Timbuktu. Askia the Great encouraged learning, initiating a revival of scholarship in Songhai.

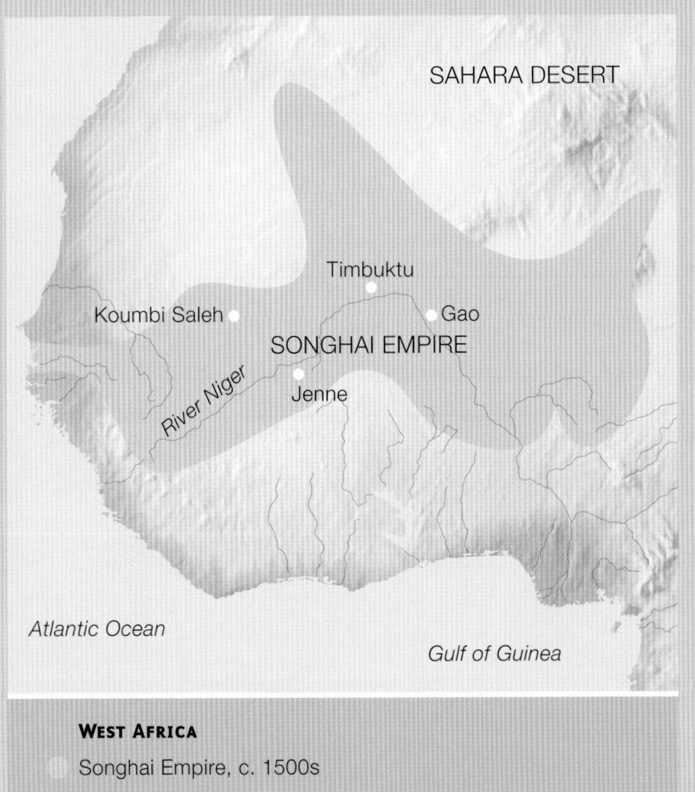

and his more lasting achievements are likely to be the creation of schools and promotion of scholarship and astronomy. He established Sankore University in Timbuktu, and brought scholars back to Songhai from Egypt and elsewhere in the Islamic world after making a pilgrimage to Mecca.

Songhai rose to prominence under the ruthless hand of Sunni Ali, and was expanded and flourished under the skilful leadership of Askia. But no lasting skillset of leadership was established or passed on, and the empire quickly became divided under the rule of Askia's sons and heirs. Civil war weakened the country, and the Saadi Dynasty of Morocco invaded, defeating the Songhai in 1591, in part aided by a stampede of cattle that tore through Songhai's troops.

ABOVE The Great Mosque at Djenné was originally built during the 13th century, but this massive adobe structure now stands on the same ground as the medieval mosque. The mosque at Djenné was a great centre of learning in Mali.

LEFT Map of the Songhai Empire at its height.

ASHANTI EMPIRE 1701–1896

LOGISTICS OF CONQUEST

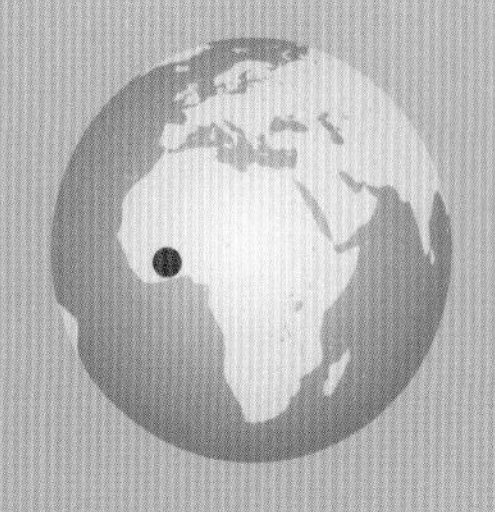

THE ASHANTI OF WEST AFRICA BECAME A DOMINANT POWER DURING THE EIGHTEENTH CENTURY IN PART DUE TO THEIR USE OF FIREARMS AND WEAPONRY FROM EUROPEAN COLONISTS, AND IN PART BECAUSE OF THE IMPRESSIVE LOGISTICS AND FORMATIONS THEY EXERCISED ON THE BATTLEFIELD AND ON THE MOVE.

LEFT This Ashanti gold mask attests to the wealth of gold in parts of West Africa.

BELOW This Ashanti gold disc would have been worn in ceremonies and is known as a 'soul-washer's badge'.

The Ashanti controlled a territory of more than 259,000 sq km (100,000 square miles) and a force of up to 200,000. Basing their movements on observations of ants – one of the only other creatures to wage war – the Ashanti organized their forces into narrow columns for travelling through the dense forests, and could quickly bring these columns together into an impenetrable force.

OPPORTUNITY IN CONFLICT

The Ashanti were united by chieftain Osei Tutu (r. 1801–1824) and found great strength through their unity. They even incorporated conquered enemies into their ranks to increase their own strength. As they rose to dominance in West Africa, the Ashanti began to capitalize on two major assets that would bring them great wealth: gold and slaves.

Led by the desire to sell gold to the British and European colonists, the Ashanti pushed southwards against the Fanti tribe from their homelands towards the coastal region known as the Gold Coast. At the same time, they found another profitable industry in raiding enemy tribes, hauling off captives and selling them to Europeans as slaves. European slave traders could thereby remain on the coast and rely on the Ashanti to bring out captives from the interior of Africa. The Ashanti traded gold and slaves for firearms, thereby increasing their military might and prominence in the region.

OPPOSITE This painting of the First Anglo-Ashanti War shows the defeat of the Ashanti at the hands of the British in July 1824.

ATTACKING IDENTITY

When Osei Tutu united the Ashanti, he created symbols to help forge that unification, and these became important elements of Ashanti identity and pride. One was a crown made of elephant skin and the other was a golden stool. The stool was a symbol of a chieftain, and this golden stool was supposed to hold the soul of the Ashanti. When Sir Frederick Hodgson, governor of the Gold Coast, demanded the stool be presented to him in 1900, he provoked the fury of the Ashanti once more. Though weakened greatly, and without much hope of success against superior British forces, the Ashanti rose under the direction of their queen, Yaa Asantewaa, to defend their honour in the War of the Golden Stool. The Ashanti were defeated, but they largely retained their independence and the stool remained theirs.

ABOVE The Ashanti Hall of Justice in Kumasi. The hall is shown here in the late 19th or early 20th century, falling into disrepair after the Anglo-Ashanti Wars.

TOO MUCH FOR TWO

In 1807, the British abolished the slave trade, cutting off one of the Ashanti's great sources of wealth. The other – its rich gold mines – became the object of envy and desire among British colonists. In 1824, the Ashanti soundly defeated the British in the First Anglo-Ashanti War, killing the British commander, Sir Charles McCarthy, and taking his head as a prize of battle.

Over the ensuing decades, the British and Ashanti continued to fight, through a series of wars known as the Anglo-Ashanti Wars. The British were able to check the Ashanti in 1831 and later defeated them soundly in subsequent engagements. The success of the British can be attributed in large part to advances in weapon technology, including the use of rockets developed in England based on ones used in India against British forces. When the Dutch sold territory to the British in the early 1870s that the Ashanti considered to be theirs, the Third and most decisive Anglo-Ashanti War kicked off, and the Ashanti were defeated and forced to accept harsh terms. A Fourth Anglo-Ashanti War lasted only a brief few months, spanning the winter of 1895–1896.

ANGLO-ZULU WAR 1878–1879

END OF AN ERA

THE ZULUS ROSE TO PROMINENCE IN THE FIRST HALF OF THE NINETEENTH CENTURY UNDER THE LEADERSHIP OF SHAKA, WHOSE BRILLIANT MILITARY INNOVATIONS ALLOWED HIM TO ACHIEVE DECISIVE VICTORIES AND MOBILIZE LARGE ARMIES.

Among Shaka's innovations was the use of short assegai spears for stabbing, rather than throwing, and the practice of going barefoot to increase the speed of his troops. Shaka was a brilliant but brutal leader, and he was eventually assassinated, but not until after he had already united a large Zulu kingdom covering about 29,785 sq km (11,500 square miles).

The Zulus were a large and powerful people, but they faced pressures from two colonial powers: the Dutch and the British. Though they fought a number of battles with the Dutch and the British, things came to a head late in 1878 when British High Commissioner, Sir Henry Bartle Frere, set an ultimatum for the Zulus with which they could not possibly comply. This had the desired effect of provoking war.

BELOW Zulu warriors attack the camp of Boer Voortrekkers in 1838. The Boers circled their covered wagons to form makeshift defences.

ABOVE The Battle of Isandlwana in 1879 was a powerful victory for the Zulus over the British.

JOY OF VICTORY, BITTERNESS OF DEFEAT

On 22 January 1879, a large force of Zulus surprised and attacked British troops at what is known as the Battle of Isandlwana. The Zulus were armed mostly with spears and shields made of animal hide; what firearms they possessed were largely older and not as advanced as contemporary British weaponry. Nonetheless, due to their numbers and swift, intelligent tactics, the Zulus were able to defeat the British soundly and take their weapons. Despite the victory at Isandlwana, the Zulus were unable to capture the garrison of Rorke's Drift on the same day, which was defended by a small, determined band of British soldiers. The Battle of Rorke's Drift has been famously retold in the film *Zulu*.

The Battle of Isandlwana was a crushing blow to the pride of British military superiority, and could not escape retaliation. Over the ensuing months, the British and Zulus fought in several engagements, and the Zulus put up staunch opposition under the leadership of their king, Cetshwayo. But on 4 July 1879, the British marched on the capital of Zululand, Ulundi. With characteristic discipline, the British attacked the main army of the Zulus; their superior weaponry and drilling allowed them at last to defeat the Zulus at the heart of their homeland. The British lost only 12 men in the engagement, compared to 1,500 Zulus. Cetshwayo was captured and, with him, Zulu independence. The British burned Ulundi to the ground.

ABOVE Despite their success at Isandlwana, the Zulus were unable to defeat the British at Rorke's Drift.

MAJOR ENGAGEMENTS

Battle	Date (1879)	Victor
Isandlwana	22 January	Zulu
Rorke's Drift	22–23 January	British
Hlobane	28 March	Zulu
Khambula	29 March	British
Gingindlovu	2 April	British
Siege of Eshowe	11 February–3 April	British
Ulundi	4 July	British

LEFT Portrait of King Cetshwayo (1826–1884), who led the Zulus during the Anglo-Zulu War of 1879.

FIRST ITALO-ETHIOPIAN WAR 1895–1896

THE LAND NEVER CONQUERED

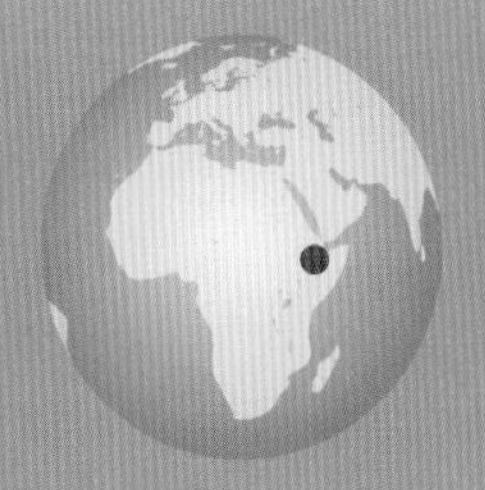

AMONG AFRICAN NATIONS, ETHIOPIA IS THE ONLY ONE TO BOAST TODAY THAT IT WAS NEVER CONQUERED BY A EUROPEAN COLONIAL POWER DURING THE 'SCRAMBLE FOR AFRICA'. THAT'S NOT TO SAY, HOWEVER, THAT EUROPEANS DIDN'T TRY.

Italy, a latecomer to the game, staked its territories on the eastern coast of Africa and the Red Sea, establishing Eritrea and Somalia in the late nineteenth century. Italy thought it would begin with such a foothold, and from there take on the Empire of Ethiopia; they were sorely mistaken.

FROM WORDS TO WAR

In 1889, Emperor Menelik II of Ethiopia signed the Treaty of Wuchale, recognizing Italian control of Eritrea and Somalia. But the treaty differed in its Amharic and Italian translations: a difference that accorded Italy control of Ethiopia in the Italian version. Real control, however, would be proven on the battlefield.

Over the next several years, tensions between Ethiopia and Italy mounted. In 1895, Italy defeated the Ethiopians at Coatit and proceeded to fortify the town of Makalla; but the success of this victory would be short-lived. The Ethiopians would defeat the Italian army at Amba Alagi on 7 December 1895, and successfully take Makalla by siege on 20 January 1896.

Emperor Menelik would win his decisive victory a few months later on 1 March, 1896. Seeking to surprise the Ethiopians, General Baratieri of Italy set out at midnight from Adowa, where Italian forces had gathered. During the night, the divisions of the Italian army were separated in the mountainous terrain. Poor maps meant they were unable to determine their positions reliably and could not converge as

LEFT Emperor Menelik II as portrayed in the French publication *Le Petit Journal* in 1895.

RUSSIAN ALLIES

Ethiopia's closest European ally was Russia, and Menelik was aided by Russian advisers in the Battle of Adowa. Russia also provided firearms and weaponry that proved essential for defeating the Italians. A troop of Russian volunteer soldiers even fought alongside the Ethiopians against the Italians at Adowa.

a single army. Meanwhile, Menelik, having risen early to pray, was informed of the advancing Italian army and prepared his troops. Outnumbering the divided Italians, Menelik dealt a crushing blow. Out of an estimated 20,000 Italian troops, roughly half were slain or wounded.

ABOVE Emperor Menelik II bravely led the Ethiopians in their resistance against the Italians. The defeat he dealt at Adowa in 1896 would live on in Italian memory for decades to come.

BELOW This painting depicts the Battle of Adowa in 1896. The Ethiopians on the left face off against the Italians on the right. Note the display of firearms and cannons alongside swords and shields.

SOUTH AFRICAN WARS 1880–1902

CONVERGENCE AND CLASHING

SOUTH AFRICA, WHICH TODAY BOASTS 11 OFFICIAL LANGUAGES, SAW THE CONVERGENCE OF SEVERAL DIFFERENT PEOPLES DURING THE NINETEENTH CENTURY. UNSURPRISINGLY, THERE WERE SEVERAL FIERCE ENGAGEMENTS BETWEEN INDIGENOUS PEOPLES AND EUROPEAN COLONISTS, EACH VYING FOR CONTROL AND TERRITORIAL EXPANSION.

Britain's annexation of Transvaal in 1877 sparked resentment among the Boers – farmers descended from Dutch settlers. Complex political and economic tensions mounted over the ensuing years, especially as Britain sought to control more of the diamond-rich land of South Africa. The Boers could not initially resist the British on one front because they faced attack from the Zulus on their other side.

Inspired by the success of the Zulus at the Battle of Isandlwana in 1879, the Boers rose up against the British in December 1880 in what is known as the First Boer War. Expert marksmen and hunters, the Boers had no formal military, but rather local militias organized into groups, or commandos. Shooting from behind rocks and any available cover, the Boers were able to devastate the British, whose

ABOVE The British defeated the Boers at the Battle of Belmont in November 1899. British forces outnumbered the Boers roughly 4 to 1.

infantry uniforms at the time were bright red: easy targets. At the clash of Bronkhorstspruit, the first engagement, a Boer commando unit quickly defeated 120 British soldiers, losing only two itself. The Boers went on to gain the upper hand at Laing's Nek, Ingogo and the Battle of Majuba Hill. At Majuba Hill, the Boers routed a force of 360 British soldiers, but only lost one Boer fighter.

THE FIGHT TURNS UGLIER

While the Boers were able to negotiate a degree of independence in the Transvaal in 1881 after their successes in the First Boer War, the discovery of large deposits of gold in the Transvaal in 1886 led the British to once more seek control of the territory. Eventually, the Second Boer War erupted in 1899 and quickly turned into an even uglier confrontation than the clashes of a decade earlier. The Boers of Transvaal and Orange Free State fought through ruthless guerrilla warfare, and the British burned farmlands, poisoned wells and slaughtered cattle to weaken the Boer opposition. The British, largely under the direction of Lord Kitchener, also set up concentration camps where Boer women and children were held prisoner and mistreated. With little food and terrible hygiene, many died in these camps, especially children. The British also sent more than 25,000 Boer male captives overseas in exile. This was one of the first uses of concentration camps and is often overshadowed by the later employment of concentration camps by the Nazis during World War II.

TOP The Indian Ambulance Corps assisted medically during the Second Boer War. Future leader of Indian Independence, Mohandas Gandhi, is featured in this photo (in the middle row, centre, his arms crossed).

ABOVE People celebrate in the streets of Toronto, Canada, upon the return of troops from the Second Boer War. The conflict was truly international.

AFRICA IN WORLD WAR II 1935–1945

A NEW ROMAN EMPIRE?

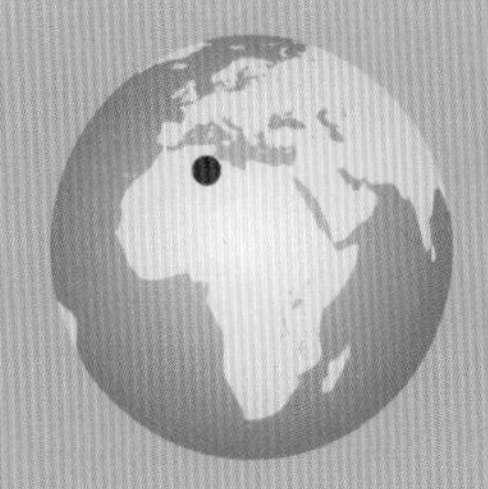

IN 1935, STILL EMBITTERED BY THE DEFEAT SUFFERED AT THE HANDS OF THE ETHIOPIANS AT ADOWA IN 1886, BENITO MUSSOLINI SENT TROOPS INTO ETHIOPIA, QUICKLY OVERRUNNING THE COUNTRY AND SEIZING CONTROL.

Under the leadership of Benito Mussolini, Italy began an aggressive imperialism in an attempt to establish a new kind of 'Roman Empire'. Since 1911, Italy had also maintained control of the Libyan coast and, in 1935, Mussolini sent his troops to invade Ethiopia. After forming a military alliance in 1939, Italy and Germany would fight vigorously to expand and hold territories in North Africa. Often overshadowed by the atrocities on the European continent, the African Theatre of World War II was an enormous battleground dominated by such military geniuses as Erwin Rommel, Bernard Montgomery and George Patton.

LEFT Erwin Rommel was one of the masterminds of World War II. His strategies turned Italian defeat into Axis victory in North Africa, earning him the nickname 'Desert Fox'.

BELOW Rommel defied orders to continue his advance in North Africa. Capitalizing on the situation, he moved his forces swiftly, winning several important victories for the Axis Powers.

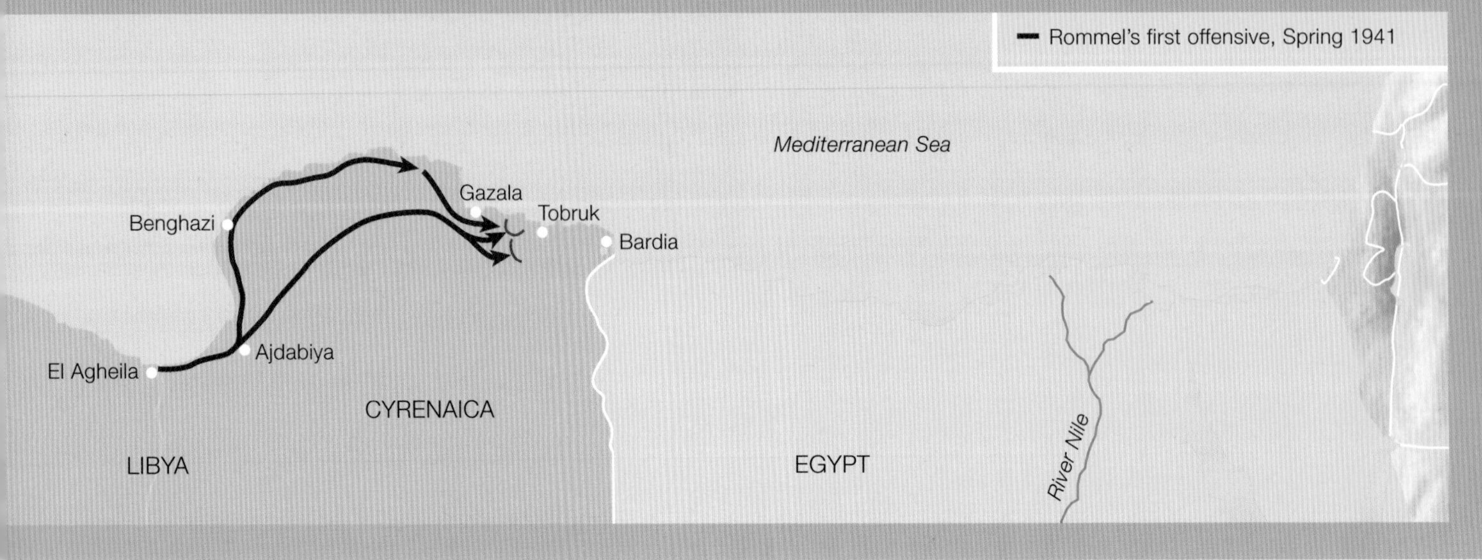

THE NATIONS CLASH

ABOVE Lieutenant-General Bernard Law Montgomery was a British commander in North Africa during World War II. He led several successful missions against the Axis Powers' forces, and would later lead the planning of the D-Day invasion at Normandy.

With Italians exercising control to the west in Libya and the east in Eritrea and Ethiopia, things soon came to a head in Egypt, where British forces responded vigorously against the encroachment. Should Italy have won control of the Suez Canal, it would have given the nation a serious advantage in controlling North and East Africa. But the Brits responded, and the Italians soon found themselves struggling to hold on.

To their aid came the Germans, and most notably the brilliance of military leader, Erwin Rommel. Rommel had already earned a stellar reputation as an officer in World War I, and successfully led the Seventh Panzer Division in 1940 when Germany invaded France. Rommel was then sent to North Africa, however, where he earned the nickname *Wüstenfuchs*, the 'Desert Fox', for this cunning ability to outmanoeuvre and outwit his opponents in the desert sands. Ignoring orders to maintain a defensive position, Rommel struck against British forces in Libya with a small force in March 1941. Encouraged by his success, he decided to advance to capture the whole of Cyrenaica, despite both Italian and German orders to halt. Rommel continued to succeed, but ran into trouble in besieging Tobruk in 1941.

ABOVE RIGHT The Second Battle of El Alamein in 1942 was a turning point for Allied forces in their fight against the Axis in North Africa.

RIGHT The Polish Carpathian Rifle Brigade board a ship at Alexandria to head to the Siege of Tobruk in 1941.

ALGERIAN REVOLUTION 1954–1962

FRANCE'S CRUMBLING EMPIRE

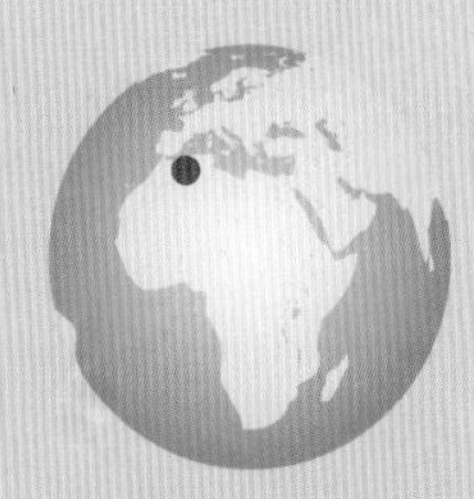

IN THE WAKE OF WORLD WAR II, MANY OF THE COLONIAL HOLDINGS OF EUROPEAN POWERS ROSE UP FOR THEIR INDEPENDENCE. INSPIRED BY THIS, ALGERIANS ORGANIZED A RESISTANCE MOVEMENT TO GAIN INDEPENDENCE FROM FRANCE.

ABOVE Women soldiers fighting for Algerian independence stand before the Algerian flag.

TOP A barricade set up in Algiers in 1960. The banner reads *Vive Massu*. Jacques Massu was a general leading efforts against the FLN, and is known for his use of torture.

In 1947, India – the gem of Great Britain's Empire – gained independence; in 1954, French Indochina defeated its colonial rulers at Dien Bien Phu on 7 May, ultimately leading to independence. Algeria would follow.

The *Front de Libération Nationale* (FLN) or National Liberation Front was established on the eve of 1 November 1954. A group of Algerians in the FLN launched a series of attacks against the police and military of French Algeria. The day is known as *Toussaint Rouge*, or 'Red All Saints' Day', because of the bloodshed caused on this Catholic festival. This was the beginning of a long and drawn-out conflict between Algerian Muslims and French Catholics as Algerians used guerrilla warfare to fight for their independence from France.

The losses were heavy on both sides. The FLN adopted a new approach in August 1955 when it expanded its targets to include civilians, not just military. Attacking Philippeville and massacring more than 120 civilians caused swift retaliation. Figures of FLN deaths range from 1,200 (reported by the French) to 12,000 (reported by the FLN). The FLN went on to use terrorism as a primary weapon, planting bombs in the capital, Algiers, in 1956. Torture was common, and the French used internment camps for resistance fighters. Eventually, France would end up sending 400,000 troops to attempt to regain control of Algeria.

ALGERIAN ALGERIA

Algerians of French descent, known as the *Pieds-Noirs* (literally 'Black Feet'), had held control of Algerian politics and government. Desperate to restore their position, they eagerly sought a solution, particularly as the bloodshed continued. They sought the aid of Charles de Gaulle, former leader of the Free French Forces during

ABOVE, LEFT TO RIGHT Charles de Gaulle; six leaders of the FLN in 1954; and Frantz Fanon, an influential Algerian author and member of the FLN who supported Algerian independence.

TOP Map of French Algeria, clearly marking the country as belonging to France.

World War II. Charles de Gaulle founded France's Fifth Republic in 1958. Addressing the situation in Algeria, he brought a swift resolution to the crisis by going against the wishes of his *Pieds-Noirs* supporters and granting Algerian Independence. The *Pieds-Noirs* felt betrayed and several revolted, but the hostilities did eventually come to an end, largely by 1961, and more officially by the ceasefire of 18 March 1962. While estimates vary considerably as to the total death toll, even the most conservative estimate of 350,000 Algerian dead marks the conflict as one on a grand scale. The French reported losses of around 25,000. Some estimates on the Algerian side go up to 1.5 million dead; the effects on the Algerian population were far-reaching and long-lasting.

RWANDAN CIVIL WAR 1990–1993

THE HORRORS OF CIVIL WAR

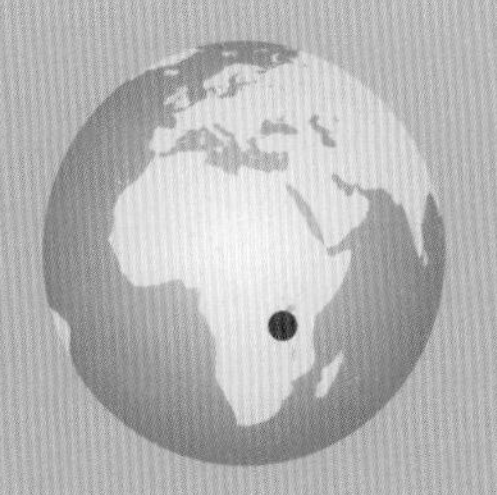

THE CENTRAL AFRICAN COUNTRY OF RWANDA WAS UNDER BELGIAN CONTROL FROM 1916 TO 1962. DURING THIS PERIOD, THE BELGIAN AUTHORITIES FAVOURED THE TUTSI ETHNIC GROUP, WHO WERE THE MINORITY. UPON LEAVING, HOWEVER, THEY CHANGED THEIR ALLEGIANCE, PROMOTING THE HUTU MAJORITY.

ABOVE Photo from The Rwanda Genocide Memorial.

LEFT Paul Kagame took over the RPF from Fred Rwigema and led an effective force of guerrilla warfare. Kagame would go on to become President of the Republic of Rwanda.

This helped stir the pot of ethnic tensions that would contribute to the Rwandan Civil War of 1990 and the later genocides of the mid-1990s.

Rwandan Tutsis living in exile began to unite, forming the Rwandan Patriotic Front (RPF) and invading Rwanda on 1 October 1990. Thus began three years of bloody conflict between the Tutsi RPF and the Hutu government of Juvénal Habyarimana, who at least nominally acknowledged the need for reconciliation between the two ethnic groups. Such reconciliation would be hard-won, however, after the RPF crossed over the border from Uganda and killed a customs guard.

The RPF was initially led by Fred Rwigema, but he was killed early in the conflict, and eventually Paul Kagame took over control. In 1991, Kagame withdrew RPF forces to the mountains where he reorganized the men and worked to expand their power by raising funds and purchasing more and better weaponry. He then launched a series of guerrilla offensives. Eventually, a ceasefire was signed on 12 July 1992, but the RPF struck hard once again on 8 February 1993, after hearing reports of Tutsi massacres. A tenuous peace was reached that year, but violence would erupt again within a matter of months.

MASS KILLINGS

On a trip back from Dar es Salaam, President Habyarimana's plane was shot down. This sparked a new wave of violence, targeted initially at prominent Tutsi leaders and officials, and then extending to all Tutsi. What began as a fight for the right of Tutsis to return to Rwanda disintegrated into a horrifying display of humankind's monstrous capabilities.

Mass killings, gang rape and the targeted murder of all Tutsis characterized the following months. Many people were even deliberately infected with HIV. Within the short span of a few months, hundreds of thousands of Tutsis were killed (most estimates are more than 800,000 killed in the genocide). The RPF, however, continued its fight and was able to put an end to the genocide, eventually defeating the Hutu government. Kagame went on to chase Hutu officials who fled to the Congo (then Zaire). He would also become Rwanda's new president, but he has not escaped criticism for war crimes apparently committed by the RPF under his command. These events led to massive wars in the Congo, lasting until 2003 and claiming the lives of between 4 and 5.4 million people.

ABOVE Mass killings and mass graves characterized the genocide of the 1990s. The evidence of the killings and their scale can be seen in the bones of the victims.

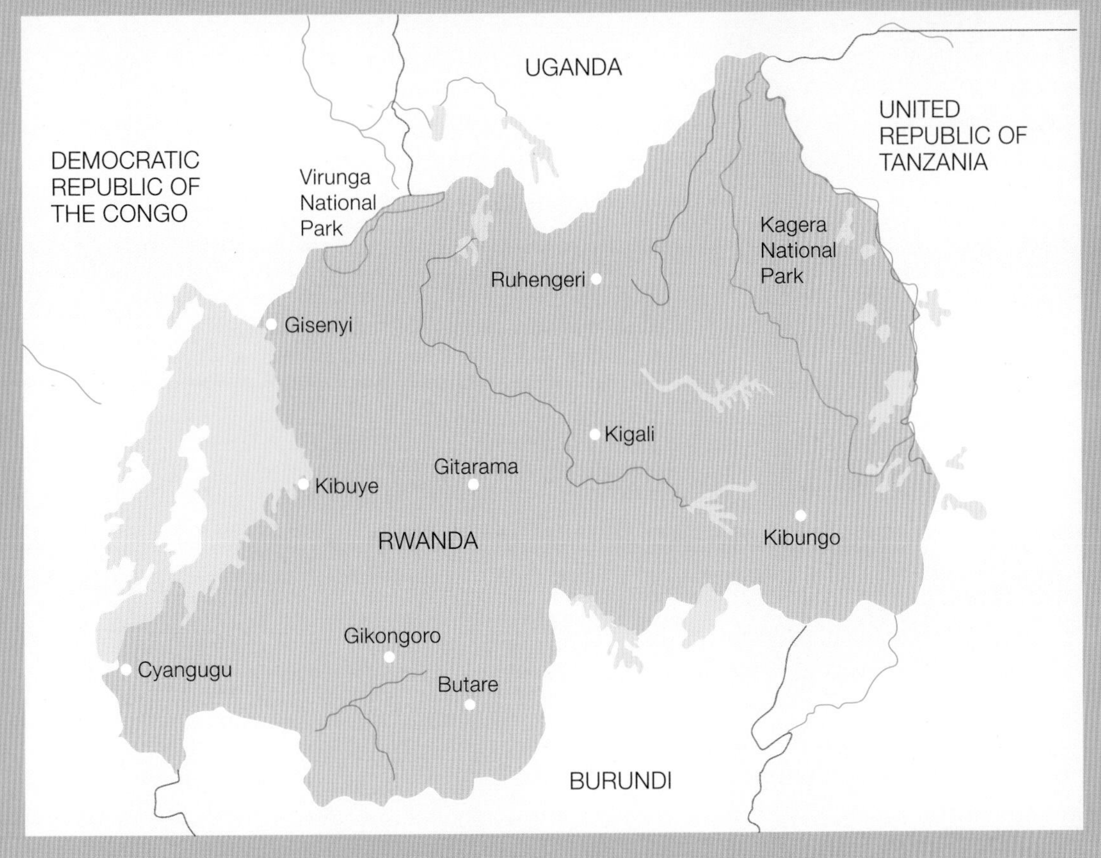

TOP LEFT Juvénal Habyarimana was president of Rwanda from 1973 until 1994, when his plane was shot down and he was killed. Habyarimana's death in 1994 contributed to the Rwandan genocide of the mid-1990s.

LEFT Rwanda is a small, mountainous country in Central Africa. Rwanda is known for its beauty and for being home to large populations of gorillas; but the country's beauty is often overshadowed by the ugliness of its violent past.

LIBYAN REVOLUTION 2011

LIBYA FOLLOWS EGYPT AND TUNISIA

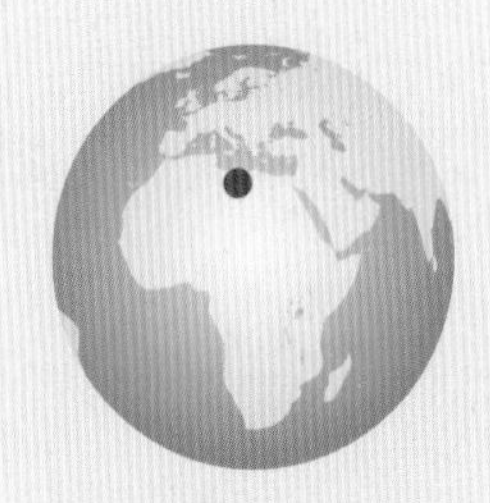

IN 1969, MUAMMAR QADDAFI TOOK OVER CONTROL OF LIBYA FROM KING IDRIS IN A BLOODLESS COUP. HE WOULD REMAIN IN POWER FOR THE NEXT 42 YEARS, HOLDING STRICT CONTROL OVER THE COUNTRY.

Qaddafi was known for sponsoring extremist militant groups internationally to carry out acts of terrorism against Western powers. He also supported the Irish Republican Army (IRA) and its bombings. In 1986, he supported the bombing of La Belle Discotheque in West Berlin. Despite international outrage, his tight hold on the reins of Libya appeared unbreakable.

His power remained unbroken until 2011, when the Libyan people found inspiration in the revolutions of their neighbours in Egypt and Tunisia. Protests began in Benghazi, particularly after the arrest of Fathi Terbil, a civil rights lawyer who represented hundreds of Libyan citizens whose kinsmen had been imprisoned and killed in Abu Salim in Tripoli. On 15 February 2011, the protests turned violent. With more arrests of public figures, the Libyan people needed little further urging to revolt.

Protests spread through Benghazi and on to Tripoli. With the two largest cities in uproar, it was not long before the whole country was in revolt. Relying heavily on mobile phones and social networks, the Libyans were able to organize quickly. In response, Qaddafi shut down the Internet and telephone, and sent security out in force, shooting and killing many of the protesters. The protesters continued to organize, however, and their ranks swelled with trained soldiers defecting from Libya's own army. They negotiated with the UN a no-fly zone over Libya and prepared for battle.

ABOVE LEFT Muammar Qaddafi, shown here in his military regalia. He was known for wearing stylized sunglasses and extravagant clothes.

LEFT A burning car marks the violence of the protests in February 2011.

Progress of the Libyan Civil War

- Libyan rebel holdings by 1 March
- Areas of contention between March and August
- Rebel offensive in August
- Territory gained by rebels by October
- Last loyalist pockets
- Major campaigns
- Battles

ABOVE Protests quickly spread throughout all the major cities, and were facilitated by the use of mobile phones and social media.

TOP Rebel protesters confront the armies of Qaddafi. Despite inferior weaponry, the rebels were able to achieve success through a combination of sheer numbers and through the aid of several defectors from the Libyan armed forces.

TYRANNY OVERTHROWN

Over the following months, the Libyan rebels continued to press on key areas of control, including Benghazi, Ajdabiya, Ras Lanuf and Bin Jawad. Tripoli was the big win, however, and it was not until 23 August that they were able to seize control of Qaddafi's palace in Tripoli, only to find that the dictator had already fled. It was nearly two months before he was discovered near his hometown of Sirte, after surviving an air strike by French forces on a convoy of his loyal soldiers. Qaddafi was reportedly found hiding in a drain; he was subsequently beaten and killed by his captors.

PONTUS EUXINUS
Heraclea
BITHYNIA
Bursa
NATOLIA
Amasia
Trabisonda
CURDIES
GEORGIA
Erserum
Turcomania
M. Ararat
ARMENIA
Rhodes
Cyprus
Candia
Aleppo
Antiochia
Tripoli
MARE
MEDITERRANEUM
SYRIA
Chaider
Damascus
Cair
Ierusalem
ARABIA
DESERTA
Balsara
Busseret
Cairoan
Alexandria
R. Nilus
Suez
Cairo
Benisuef
Eltor
Tschach Haffer
Sur
Chaibar
R. Chaibar
Negel
De Zee en Land-Reyse, van
JOH. MILDENHAL en CARTWRIGT
na PERSIEN en MOGOL,
op't Spoor gevolgd.
MARE RUBRUM
Medina
t'Alnabi
Cossir
Vadifatima
Dgebel
Harafat
Siden

MIDDLE EAST

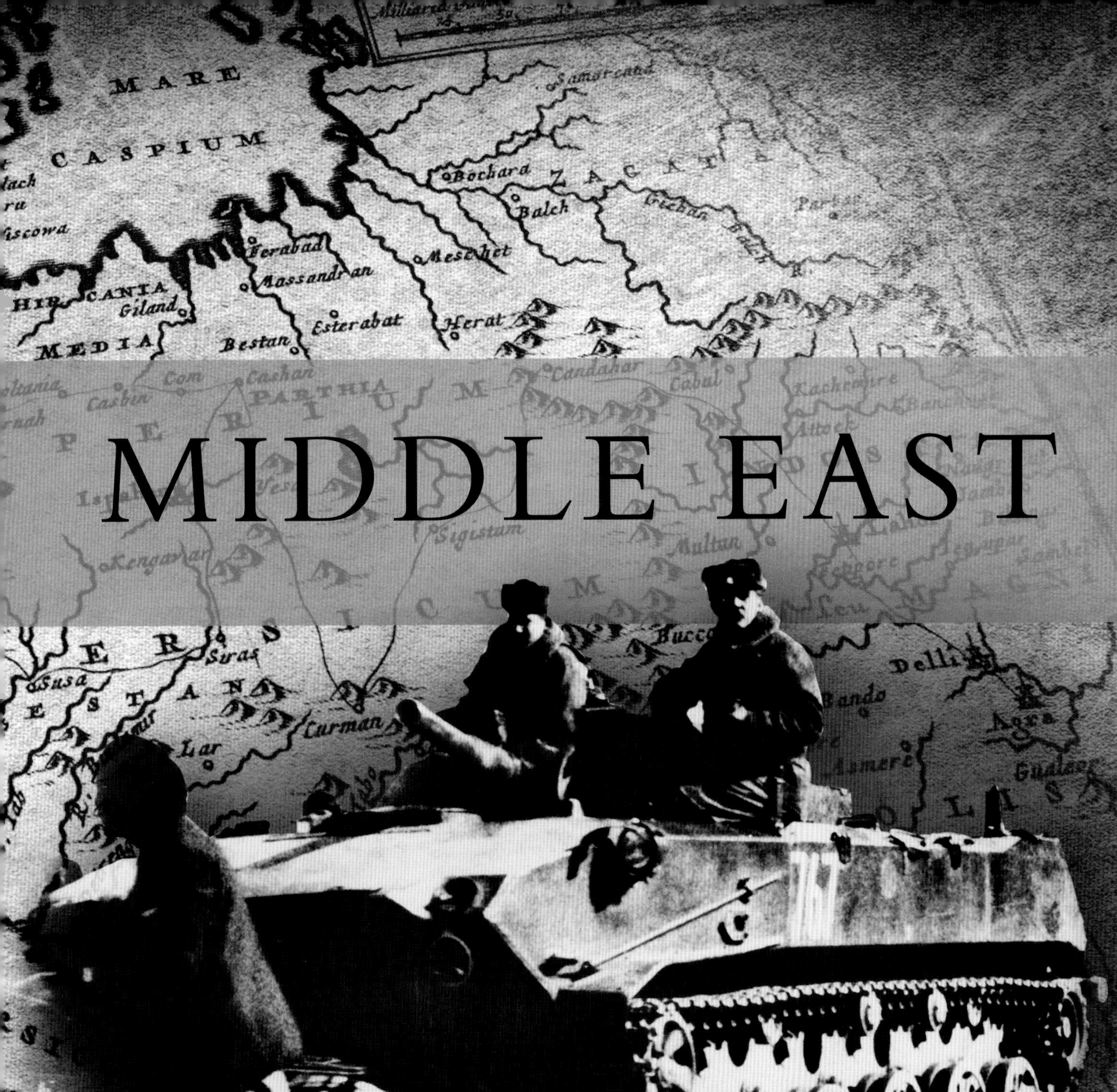

MARE
CASPIUM
Samarcand
Bochara
Balch
Meschet
Ferabad
Massandran
HIR CANIA
Giland
Esterabat
Herat
MEDIA
Bestan
Candahar
Cabul
Kachemire
PARTHIA
Sigistam
Multan
Kengavar
Bucco
Delli
Siras
Susa
Curman
Bando
Agra
Lar
Asmere
A R A B I
Masta
INDICUM
F O E L I X
Nageran

SUMER C. 2900–2270 BCE

RECORDED IN CLAY

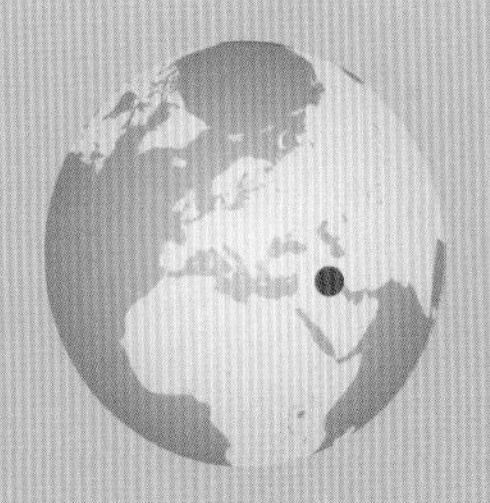

THE ANCIENT CIVILIZATIONS OF MESOPOTAMIA WERE AMONG THE FIRST IN THE WORLD TO DEVELOP BRONZE AND WRITING SYSTEMS, CREATING ADVANCED CIVILIZATIONS WITH SIGNIFICANT MILITARY POWER – AS WELL AS TEXTS RECORDING THESE CIVILIZATIONS.

The same cuneiform script came to be used for several different languages of the region, including Sumerian, Akkadian, Babylonian and Assyrian. Sumerian, the oldest recorded of these, would become a sacred and scholarly language during later periods when Akkadians rose to prominence. Hittite, the world's oldest recorded Indo-European language, was also written on cuneiform tablets. Sumerian, Akkadian and Hittite all stem from completely different language families.

The prevalence of writing and the preservation of many texts and artefacts afford us significant windows into the life and civilization of Ancient Mesopotamia. Sumer was organized in a series of city-states, each of which possessed its own agricultural resources and military. These city-states often fought with one another over territory and resources. The strong military culture – and the availability of bronze for manufacturing arms and armour – not only contributed to the growth of a powerful civilization, it also spawned some of the oldest literature of the world. The *Epic of Gilgamesh* tells the story of Gilgamesh, the mighty King of Uruk, and his adventures with his companion Enkidu, upon whose death Gilgamesh sets out on a quest for immortality. When he learns from the wise Utnapishtim the story of the flood and about immortality, he accepts the inevitability of his own death and returns to Uruk to rule his people. It is likely that Gilgamesh was a real king, who would have reigned around 2600 BCE. The earliest Sumerian versions of the epic date to the eighteenth century BCE.

Archaeological evidence confirms the existence and impressive scale of Uruk. Its famous walls, praised in the *Epic of Gilgamesh*, were roughly 10 km (6 miles) in length and

RIGHT Gilgamesh, King of Uruk, was one of the most famous legendary figures throughout Ancient Mesopotamia.

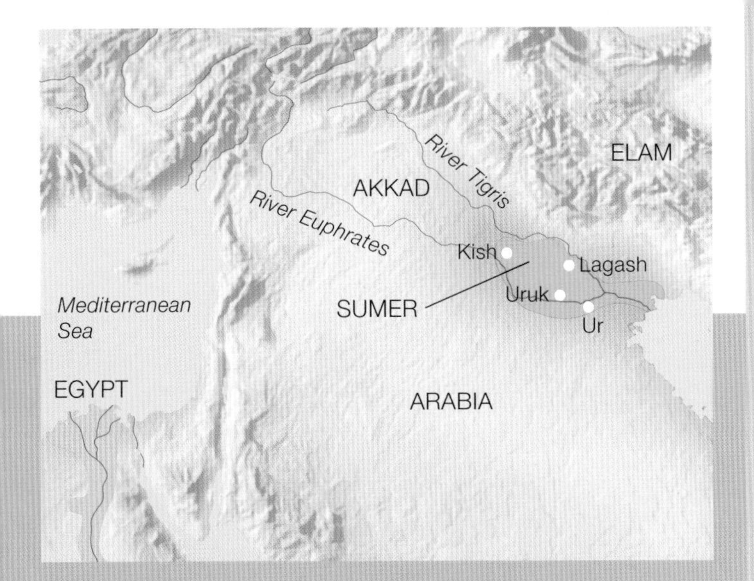

ABOVE Map showing the location of Sumer in relation to Ancient Egypt.

would have been 12–15 m (40–50 feet) tall, with 900 towers. The scale of this fortress reflects the intense militarism of the age and the necessity of such heavy defences to combat the type and scale of warfare waged in the day.

IMAGES OF WAR

Sumerian art reveals much of the nature of armed conflict in early Mesopotamia. Artefacts, including the famous Stele of the Vultures, depict warriors in tight formations carrying spears and large rectangular shields. Warriors wore metal helmets, and the kings and princes rode chariots and shot bows and arrows. Chariots early on were pulled by donkeys and only later developed into more powerful engines of war. The thick brick walls of the citadels would have also spawned a whole branch of siege warfare.

TOP The Stele of the Vultures is more than 4,500 years old and tells a story of battle and victory.

ABOVE This mace is inscribed with a dedication to Gilgamesh.

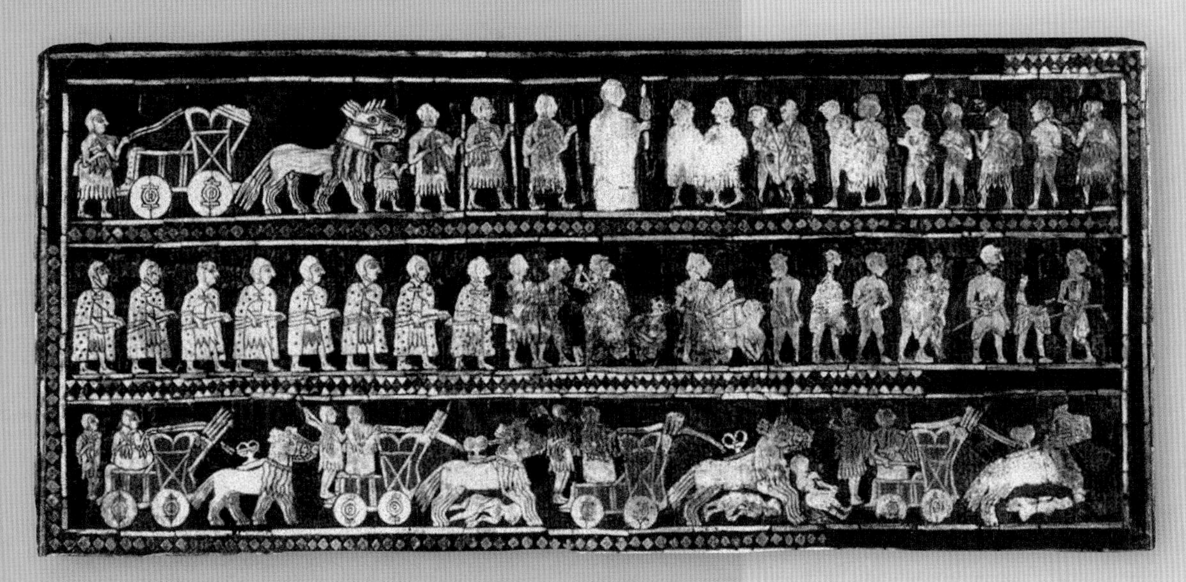

LEFT The Standard of Ur was discovered in a royal cemetery, south of Baghdad. It shows scenes of battle and the use of chariots.

SARGON THE GREAT C. 2300 BCE

THE FALL OF SUMER

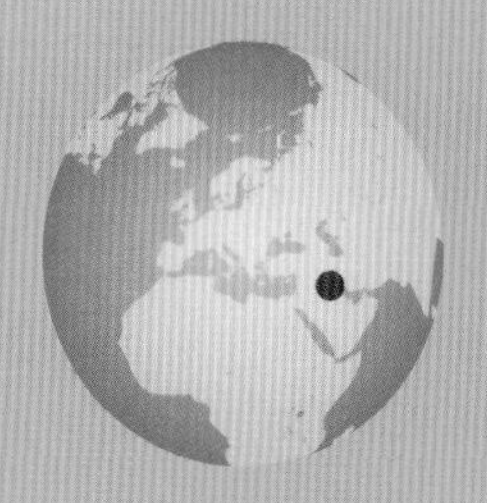

LIKE ALL THE WORLD'S GREAT CIVILIZATIONS, SUMER WAS NOT DESTINED TO LAST FOREVER. COMPRISED OF A NUMBER OF CITY-STATES, SUMER EVENTUALLY SUCCUMBED TO THE ATTACKS OF THE RULER OF AGADE, AN AKKADIAN KING KNOWN AS SARGON, 'THE RIGHTFUL KING'.

Sargon pushed southeast from Agade and defeated the rulers of Sumer, forging a great Akkadian empire and establishing the world's first-known standing army, comprised of 5,400 professional soldiers. At the height of his power, Sargon reportedly controlled areas as far west as Cyprus in the Mediterranean and as far east as Susa, the location of the modern town of Shush in present-day Iran. We cannot be certain of any of these geographies, as our recorded sources are limited, largely restricted to literary and legendary materials often fraught with exaggeration.

Though uncertain, Sargon's reign is usually fixed from 2334–2279 BCE. He reportedly fought 34 battles in Sumer, claiming Kish, Uruk, Ur and Lagash, as well as defeating 50 rulers, known as *ensis*. Archaeological evidence shows large battles fought during the time period of Sargon in places like the 'Cedar Forest' of modern Lebanon and the 'Silver Mountains' of Turkey. With Sargon's conquests, the Semitic Akkadian language replaced that of Sumer but, owing to the large amount of material already written in Sumerian, it became a kind of scholarly and religious language for many centuries. Akkadian, however, was spoken across the empire, which was linguistically and culturally diverse.

Sargon is listed in the Sumerian King List as having reigned for 54 years. Having extended the empire to the Mediterranean and the Persian Gulf, he was able to expand his dominion through trade as well as conquest. Rule passed to his sons after his death, and Sargon was held for centuries as the model of Mesopotamian kingship.

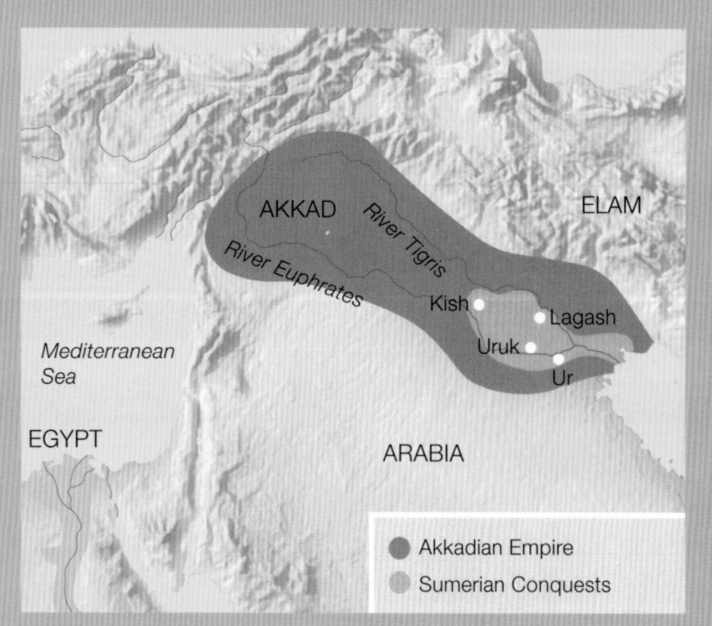

LEFT The Akkadians controlled a territory spanning the valleys of both the Tigris and Euphrates.

ABOVE Bronze mask of Sargon the Great.

ZIGGURATS

Some of the largest and most impressive structures of Ancient Mesopotamia were ziggurats, step-pyramid structures made of brick and serving as religious symbols and centres. Their high walls and fortress-like appearance would lead one to believe these were used for defensive purposes, but they seem to have been used solely for religious and ceremonial activities.

TOP Ziggurats were massive brick structures with high walls, but they were used for religious purposes only, and did not play a role in defence.

THE FIRST AUTHOR

Perhaps the world's first recorded author, Sargon's daughter's name, Enheduanna, appears attached to a number of hymns she composed. She was appointed by her father Sargon as High Priestess in Ur of the moon god Nanna. She is one of the first named women in all of history.

RIGHT Priestess Enheduanna was one of the world's first named authors.

OPPOSITE ABOVE The cuneiform writing on this clay tablet outlines the monthly rations of barley for adults and children.

HAMMURABI'S BABYLON C. 1792–1750 BCE

THE KING'S LAW

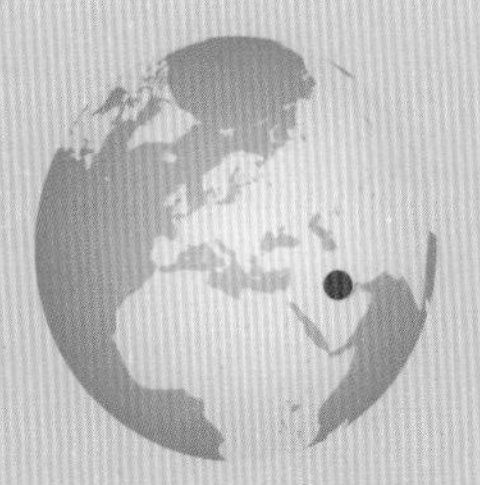

ONE OF THE MOST FAMOUS KINGS OF MESOPOTAMIA WAS THE BABYLONIAN KING, HAMMURABI, BEST KNOWN FOR HIS CODE OF LAW. HAMMURABI ASCENDED THE THRONE OF BABYLON IN 1792 BCE AMIDST POLITICAL TENSION AND INSTABILITY ACROSS MESOPOTAMIA.

King Shamshi-Adad of Upper Mesopotamia (Assyria) had died in 1776 BCE, leaving the region weak. Meanwhile, neighbouring states and tribes of Elam, the Fertile Crescent, Anatolia, Syria and the Zagros Mountains all mixed in an elaborate dance, each collaborating or clashing as they all vied for power. Hammurabi would be the one to capitalize on this discord, eventually establishing himself as the most powerful king in Mesopotamia.

After Syrian tribesman, Zimri-Lim, seized control of Mari from the Assyrian king at Eshnunna, in 1779, the king of Elam, Siwe-palar-huppak, formed a three-way alliance with Mari and Babylon. Together, they invaded Assyria, and Assyria fell to Elam in 1769. But capitalizing on the loss of one foe, Hammurabi convinced Zimri-Lim to join forces with Babylon and turn against their former ally of Elam, who had tried to start a war between Babylon and Larsa. Together with neighbouring Aleppo, they marched on Elam in 1764. Internal discord in Elam weakened the resistance, and the alliance was able to control the country.

Hammurabi continued his campaigns, consolidating control and taking Larsa in 1763. Against Larsa, Hammurabi is rumoured to have dammed the Euphrates, to withhold life-giving water and to release it in a flood. In 1761, he defeated a coalition that had formed to oppose him, and went on to

LEFT A statue of bronze and gold made to celebrate the life of Hammurabi.

ABOVE This clay tablet is from the reign of Zimri-Lim, King of Mari. It is now housed in the Louvre Museum, Paris.

take control of Mari from his former companion in arms, Zimri-Lim. With an empire loosely formed, Hammurabi turned his attention to quelling unrest in the northern region of Eshnunna. The armies of the day were likely large and well organized, employing spears, heavy shields, axes and various forms of body armour. Through strategy and might, Hammurabi was able to unite most of Mesopotamia.

THE CODE OF HAMMURABI

The Code of Hammurabi, one of the most famous texts of the ancient world, was a legal code outlining specific punishments for specific crimes. Among the most quoted is 'An eye for an eye, and a tooth for a tooth'. There are 282 laws inscribed on the stone tablet dating from 1772 BCE. The code is written in cuneiform in the Akkadian language.

BELOW Water was an all-important resource in Hammurabi's Babylon. Control of its flow meant control of life and death.

HATTI AND MITANNI 18TH–12TH CENTURIES BCE

A KINGDOM FOUND

PRIOR TO THE DECODING OF HITTITE CUNEIFORM TABLETS IN THE NINETEENTH CENTURY AND SUBSEQUENT ARCHAEOLOGICAL FINDS IN ANATOLIA, THE ONLY CLEAR MENTION OF THE 'HITTITES' WAS IN THE OLD TESTAMENT OF THE BIBLE.

ABOVE Map showing the relative position of the Hittites and Hurrians.

The Hittites, however, had a large and powerful kingdom based in Anatolia and later stretching south towards Babylon and Egypt. The Hittites referred to their own land as Hatti, and based their capital at Hattusas under King Hattusilis (r. c. 1650–1620 BCE). This is the modern city of Bogazköy in central Turkey.

The Hittites, whose language was known as *Nesili*, spoke an Indo-European language – the oldest recorded Indo-European language in the world. While many scholars suppose the Hittites to have settled after spreading westwards from Central Asia, recent genetic studies have placed the Indo-European homeland in Anatolia itself. This is still debated, however.

Under Hattusilis, the Hittites attacked Aleppo, sacking Alalakh, then taking Arzawa in western Anatolia. The Hittites used chariots and appear to have been one of the first peoples to work with iron, ushering in the Iron Age. In addition to butting heads against the Mesopotamian kings, the Hittites had to deal with their neighbours to the east – the Hurrians.

BELOW Alanya, Turkey, was once a part of the vast realm of the Hittites.

ANOTHER MYSTERY

The Hurrians, like the Sumerians, spoke a language unrelated to either the Semitic languages of Akkadian or Egyptian, or the Indo-European language of the Hittites. We do not know for certain where and how this people developed, but they established a powerful kingdom in the Zagros Mountains: the Mitanni Empire. The empire, which began around 1500 BCE, would conquer Assyria, Arrapha and Kizzuwatna, occupying a central position between Hittite, Babylonian and Egyptian kingdoms. Archaeologists have not found the Hurrian capital, known as Wassukkani, but it is believed to have been located near the source of the River Khabur – a tributary of the Euphrates in modern Syria.

The Hittites would end the Mitanni Empire under King Suppiluliumas I, who reigned in the middle of the fourteenth century BCE. Under his rule in the New Kingdom, the Hittites expanded the boundaries of their realm, taking the Mitanni capital of Wassukkani, then advancing to Kadesh, Damascus and Carchemish. The Hittites appear to have held their ground against the armies of Ramesses II at the Battle of Kadesh in 1274 BCE, which was probably the largest chariot battle of all time, with possibly more than 5,000 chariots deployed. For the next 175 years, until about 1200 BCE, the Hittite kingdom remained on a par with the kingdoms of Egypt and Assyria.

ABOVE An ingot inscribed with markings from the Hittite Kingdom.

RIGHT A Hittite vessel in the shape of a bull.

BATTLE OF KADESH C. 1274 BCE

CLASH OF EMPIRES

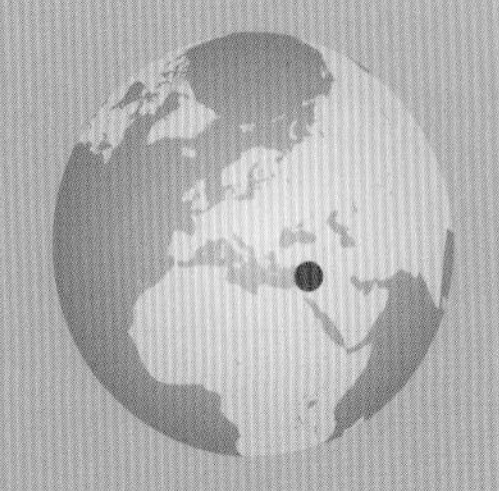

RAMESSES II OF EGYPT WAS A STRONG MILITARY LEADER WHO SOUGHT TO EXPAND EGYPT'S DOMINION TO ITS FORMER GLORY UNDER THE TUTHMOSIS KINGS OF A CENTURY PREVIOUSLY.

TOP Ramesses II shooting a bow from his chariot. Egyptian chariots were lighter and faster than the chariots of the Hittites.

ABOVE This Egyptian relief carving shows the spies of the Hittites being beaten after the Egyptians discovered them lying about the location of Hittite forces.

Ramesses II of Egypt took his military of some 20,000 men and pushed northwards along the Mediterranean coast, regaining control of large territories and contending for dominance in the Levant. Meanwhile, the Hittites under the direction of King Muwatalli pressed southwards. A clash was inevitable.

The Egyptians and the Hittites were both mighty empires with large and strong military forces. The Hittites favoured heavier armour and armoured chariots with teams of three men, while the Egyptians favoured lighter forces and chariots with teams of two men. Ramesses II knew the Hittites would prove a mighty adversary and he sought to control his position in the Levant carefully. Hittite spies, however, convinced Ramesses that the bulk of Hittite forces were far away in Aleppo, when they were in fact only a short distance away in Kadesh. Duped by the spies, Ramesses was at an early disadvantage. Eager to move, the young king split his divisions, weakening his position.

The Hittites attacked with a powerful offensive, breaking the ranks of Egyptians and routing their camp. But the Hittites rejoiced too early in their victory, and Ramesses was able to regroup the remnants of his forces and launch a counter-attack on the Hittites, who had already broken formation to plunder the Egyptian camp. The Egyptians put the Hittites to flight and – with their lighter, faster chariots – were able to catch many of the heavier Hittite forces. Losses were heavy on both sides, and many Hittite warriors reportedly had to swim across the River Orontes to safety, though many drowned in flight.

ABOVE This clay tablet is a copy of the peace treaty between Ramesses II and Hattusili III from 1259 BCE. The original was silver.

LEFT Egyptian relief showing Egyptians using ladders to attack the Hittites at the Battle of Kadesh.

WAR WITHOUT A VICTOR

The Battle of Kadesh is known for the large-scale deployment of chariots, probably more than 5,000 in total, making it possibly the largest chariot battle in history. It is also one of the earliest battles for which we have some understanding of the actual tactics used. Ramesses, for example, organized his troops into four main divisions: Amun, Re, Ptah and Sutekh. Their movements are described in Egyptian texts. Despites Ramesses II claiming victory in the battle, he was unable to take Kadesh and the Hittites retained control of the region. The outcome of the battle is disputed, both sides having suffered heavy losses, as well as having succeeded at different points on the field.

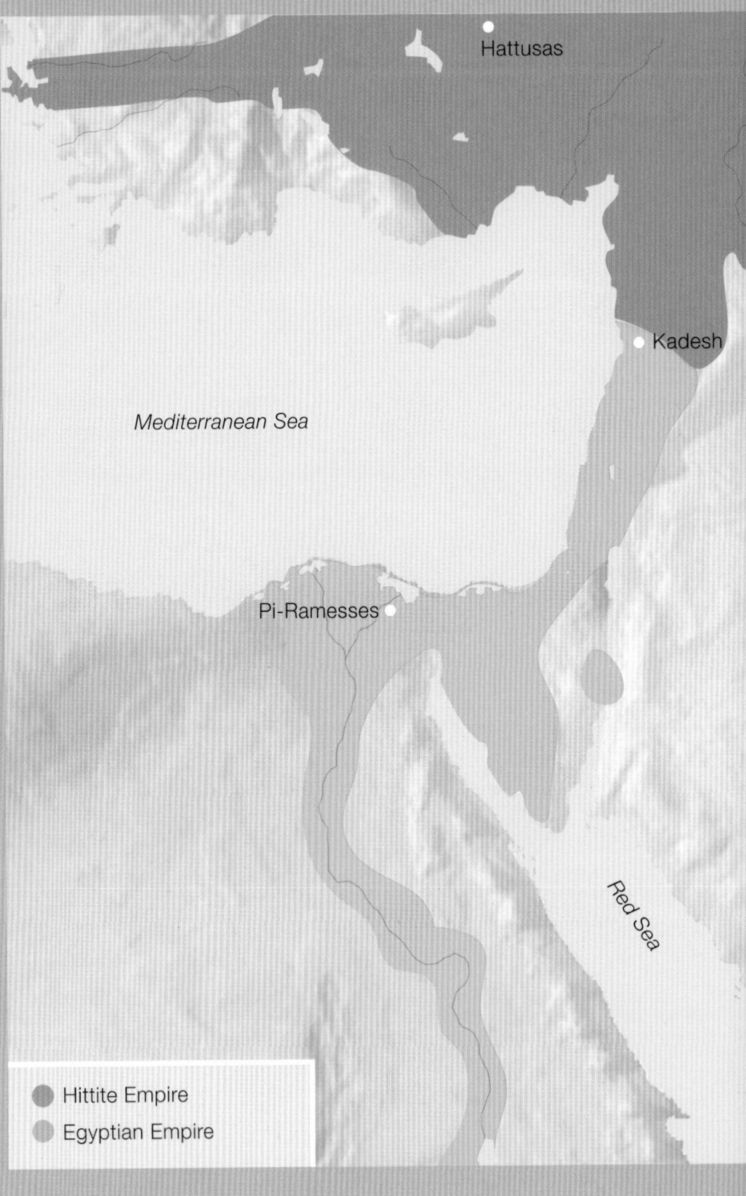

RIGHT As both the Hittites and Egyptians expanded their territories towards one another, a clash became inevitable.

ASSYRIAN EMPIRE C. 911–627 BCE

ASSYRIA REBORN

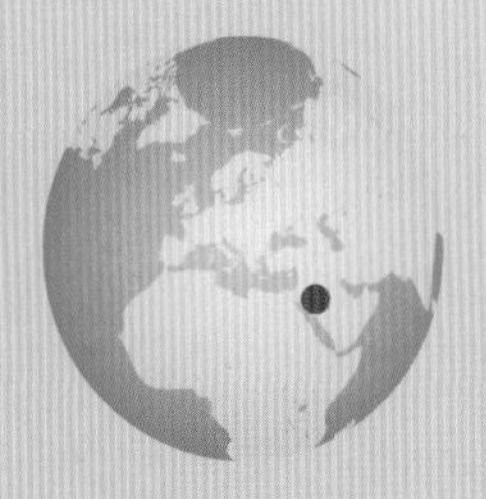

FROM AROUND 1100 BCE, ASSYRIA WEAKENED AND SHRANK IN SIZE AND INFLUENCE. HOWEVER, IN 911 BCE, ADAD-NIRARI WAS CROWNED KING AND QUICKLY LAUNCHED A SERIES OF CAMPAIGNS RESULTING IN CONQUESTS THAT EXPANDED THE ASSYRIAN DOMAIN AND STRENGTHENED THE POWER OF THE KINGDOM.

This was a new beginning for Assyria and is the start of the so-called Neo-Assyrian Empire, which would flourish under the military leadership of Adad-nirari's grandson, Ashurnasirpal II (r. 883–859 BCE). Although chariots had played an important and often decisive role in battle in the region for more than a thousand years, Ashurnasirpal II was one of the first commanders to use archers mounted directly on horseback. Essentially riding bareback, these horsemen must have possessed incredible skill, for they had saddles of only rough cloth and no stirrups. (Two centuries later, King Ashurbanipal [r. 668–627 BCE] was one of the first to have a whole division of cavalry in his military.) Ashurnasirpal II worked vigorously – and often ruthlessly – to expand the Assyrian dominion to its former glory of the thirteenth century BCE. He

ABOVE Relief of Assyrian warriors in a horse-drawn chariot.

RIGHT A clay brick with a cuneiform inscription from Ashurnasirpal II, now housed in the Metropolitan Museum of Art, New York.

secured the wealth of trade by expanding to the Mediterranean coast, and moved the Assyrian capital to Kalhu.

ABOVE This relief carving shows the capture of the city of Astartu by Tiglath-Pileser III around 730 BCE. It is now housed in the British Museum, London.

THE EBB AND FLOW OF EMPIRE

Shalmaneser III (r. 858–834 BCE) succeeded his father Ashurnasirpal to the throne and continued the expansion of the Assyrian Empire still further, though he was unable to achieve his goal of taking Damascus. For the next century, Assyria would weaken and decline until the reign of Tiglath-Pileser III (r. 745–727 BCE). Originally a general, Tiglath-Pileser overthrew the king and quickly began an aggressive campaign of expansion, doubling the size of Assyria's army and striking hard against his neighbouring foes. In 732 BCE he took Damascus, and Babylon fell to his might in 729 BCE.

In the following years, Assyria would butt heads with the might of the Nile, Egypt, conquering the land under the direction of Esarhaddon. Under Ashurbanipal, Assyria reached its height, stretching from the Caucasus Mountains in the north, to Nubia in the south, whose king Ashurbanipal swiftly and decisively defeated, securing Assyrian control of Egypt. Ashurbanipal also defeated Elam in the east, and put down a rebellion waged by his own brother in Babylon. After Ashurbanipal, however, Assyria fell into civil war and began to decline.

BELOW Tiglath-Pileser III was a great Assyrian king who helped usher in the prosperity of the Neo-Assyrian Empire.

NEBUCHADNEZZAR AND ISRAEL C. 603 BCE

BABYLONIAN DOMINANCE

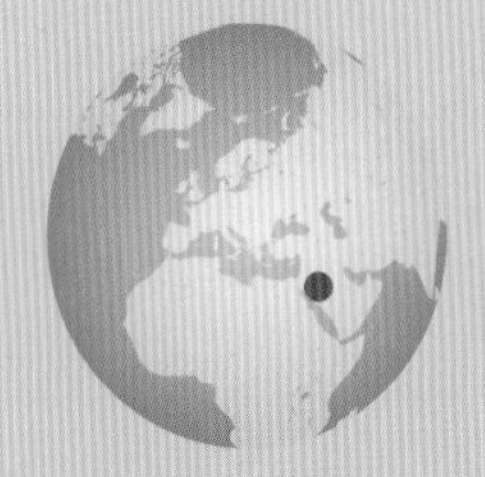

AFTER BECOMING VASSAL STATES OF ASSYRIA IN 738 BCE, THE JEWISH KINGDOMS OF ISRAEL AND JUDAH FACED CONTINUED THREATS FROM POWERFUL NEIGHBOURS IN ASSYRIA, EGYPT AND BABYLON.

Assyrians sacked Israel's capital, Samaria, in 722 BCE, destroying the seat of political power, so that Judah remained the only Jewish kingdom – and one under Assyrian control. After the Medes and Chaldeans of Babylon defeated the Assyrians, taking Nineveh in a campaign from 612–609 BCE, Judah launched an offensive under the direction of King Josiah to reclaim some of their former power and territory. The effort would be short-lived, however, as Egypt swept onto the scene under the direction of Pharaoh Necho in 609, who claimed Judah for Egypt.

Egypt, however, did not possess the might of its younger years and would not be able to hold onto its power or

ABOVE Map of the Holy Land by Nicholas Visscher, from 1657.

possessions in the face of the Chaldean Empire of Babylon, whose mighty king Nebuchadnezzar II (r. c. 605–561 BCE) threw his forces upon the Egyptians with shocking force. Babylon secured its dominance by defeating the Egyptians and Assyrians. Nebuchadnezzar continued his campaigns, taking control of Judah away from the Egyptians completely by 603. Judah now faced a new ruler, and its people were divided as to what they should do.

ABOVE A 17th-century painting depicting Nebuchadnezzar's forces burning the city of Jerusalem.

JUDAH EXILED

Some of the Judeans advocated an alliance with Egypt to overthrow the rule of Nebuchadnezzar. In 601, King Jehoiakim of Judah took this counsel and rebelled. The rebellion led to a protracted siege of Jerusalem, ending with decisive victory for Nebuchadnezzar in 597. By the end of the conflict, King Jehoiakim was dead and Babylon controlled all of Judah. Nebuchadnezzar burned the Temple of Solomon to the ground and installed Jehoiakim's uncle, Zedekiah, on the throne of Judah. Despite Nebuchadnezzar taking 10,000 Jewish captives back to Babylon, Zedekiah would rebel twice against the Babylonian king, who responded, unsurprisingly, with great force and determination. Judah was no more, and the Jews would not gain their own territory again for another four centuries until the Maccabean Revolt. This would have a lasting effect on the culture and traditions of the Jewish peoples.

ABOVE Babylon was a magnificent city in the ancient world and was allegedly home to one of the Seven Wonders of the Ancient World: the Hanging Gardens of Babylon.

Nebuchadnezzar, despite causing great destruction and being credited with the Babylonian Exile of the Jews, is also reported to have created the famous Hanging Gardens of Babylon, one of the Seven Wonders of the Ancient World. Whether these gardens actually existed is still debated, but even the legend attests to the perception of the scale of the Babylonian king's power.

CYRUS THE GREAT C. 575–530 BCE

A LEGENDARY KING

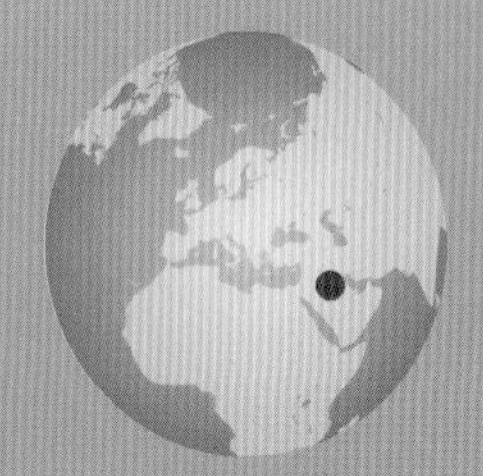

AROUND 575 BCE (IT IS NOT KNOWN FOR CERTAIN), CYRUS II WAS BORN. HE WOULD GO ON TO BECOME KNOWN AS CYRUS THE GREAT, FOUNDER OF THE PERSIAN, OR ACHAEMENID, EMPIRE.

Cyrus overthrew the Median king Astyages in 550 BCE and then expanded his realm through a series of conquests to include lands from Anatolia to the Indus and beyond. Later legends figure Astyages as Cyrus's grandfather, and Cyrus as having been exposed as a child by Astyages after having prophetic dreams that the boy would one day overthrow him. Cyrus did not die, however, and was found by a herdsman and his wife, who raised him. Little is known of Cyrus's actual early life; we know far more about his actions as king and emperor.

THE CAMPAIGNS OF CYRUS

After defeating Astyages, Cyrus mounted an offensive against the Kingdom of Lydia in western Anatolia. Croesus, King of Lydia, met Cyrus in battle at the River Halys in 547 BCE, where Cyrus easily defeated the Lydian forces and marched on to do battle again at Sardis, the capital of Lydia. According to later legend, Cyrus drove his riderless camels before him towards the Lydian cavalry; the Lydian

ABOVE A cylindrical cuneiform seal.

TOP The artwork of the Persian Empire was extensive and detailed.

RIGHT Magnificent ruins still stand from the old capital of the Achaemenid Empire.

horses panicked at the scent of the camels, and could not be controlled, granting a decisive advantage to Cyrus and his men. Lydia fell to Cyrus in 546 BCE.

Cyrus now moved south against the Babylonian king, Nabonidus. An unpopular ruler, Nabonidus was unable to inspire his people to a strong defence. Invading in 539 BCE, Cyrus handily defeated the Babylonian king at Opis. The Jews of Babylon, forced into exile by Nebuchadnezzar II, viewed Cyrus as a liberator and welcomed the Persian king.

Cyrus was eventually killed in his campaigns against the Massagetae, a tribe of the southern steppes related to the Scythians. He sent an offer of marriage to their queen, but she refused, and the two peoples squared off in battle. Cyrus gained the early upper hand, but Queen Tomyris retaliated and fought an enormous battle in which Cyrus himself was slain. Despite having suffered an untimely end in the southern steppes, Cyrus the Great's legacy would endure. He united and expanded the large empire of Persia, and is often credited as one of the first military leaders to use a true cavalry, rather than just chariots. He is also known for his bodyguard of highly trained warriors, known as the 'Immortals'.

ABOVE Apadana Palace in Persepolis, Iran.

ABOVE RIGHT Cyrus died fighting the peoples of the steppes. This painting shows his head being presented to Queen Tomyris of the Massagetae.

RIGHT The tomb of Cyrus the Great as it now stands in Iran.

DARIUS THE GREAT C.522–486 BCE

A NEW KING OF PERSIA

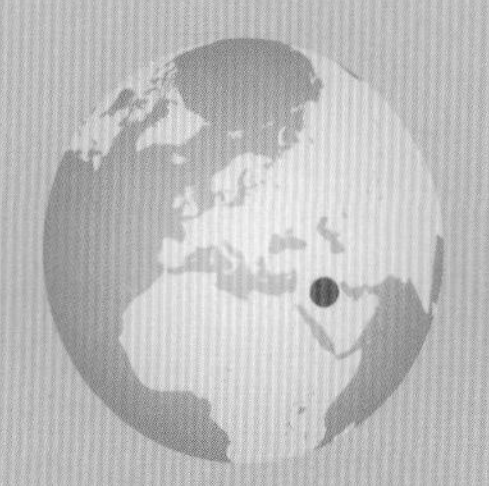

DARIUS I, OR DARIUS THE GREAT (R. 522–486 BCE), IS KNOWN FOR HIS MILITARY MIGHT AND HIS ENCOURAGEMENT OF ART AND ARCHITECTURE, WHICH FLOURISHED IN THE ACHAEMENID EMPIRE DURING HIS REIGN.

A self-styled 'King of Kings', Darius had no initial claim to the throne of Persia. He was the son of a provincial governor, but travelled to Media from Egypt upon hearing of the death of Cambyses, the true heir to the throne of the empire. Darius then killed the next surviving heir. According to Herodotus, there was a contest to see who would become king next: the nobles who staked a claim to the throne assembled at dawn with their horses. The owner of the horse who neighed at sunrise would become king. Through a cunning plot executed by Darius's slave, Oebares, Darius's horse was the one to neigh, and he was thus proclaimed king.

BELOW Detailed relief carvings provide some of the best evidence of the dress and weaponry of the time. Here, we see long daggers dangling from the men's belts.

PROVING GREATNESS

Darius's ascent to the throne did not sit well with everyone, and he spent the early part of his reign combating rebellions, particularly in Babylon, where he laid siege three times in a row. Darius was able to quell the rebellions, however, and turn his attention towards expanding the realm of the empire. With the trusted aid of his generals, Darius could mount attacks on several fronts simultaneously. Between 519 and 513 BCE he conquered Cyrenaica, Thrace and Samos. By 518 BCE, he had extended the Achaemenid Empire to the River Indus in the east. He was held as Pharaoh of Egypt, and controlled Anatolia. Organizing the empire into satrapies (provinces), Darius also initiated huge building projects and sponsored infrastructural

ABOVE Darius the Great's legacy was powerful and endurng. Here, Ardashir I (left) of the Sassanid Empire is crowned by the spirit of Darius (right).

development. He standardized currency and made the Semitic language, Aramaic, the standard language of the Empire.

Darius was unable to defeat the horse archers of the Scythian peoples, and he was defeated at Marathon in 490 BCE, when the Greek hoplites proved devastating against Persian forces. One of the legends of this battle is, of course, concerned with the soldier who ran from Marathon to Athens to announce the victory, and collapsed and died upon doing so. The story appears to be a variant, however, of a version in Herodotus, in which a man named Pheidippides ran from Athens to Sparta – a distance of 225 km (140 miles) – in a single day to request aid in the fight against the Persians. The distance we take for our modern marathon is thankfully the shorter of the two! The Battle of Marathon was a turning point for Greece in its wars with the Persian Empire, and would inspire later generations of Greek warriors.

ABOVE This beautiful mosaic from the palace of Darius the Great shows Immortals carrying long spears, and bows with large quivers. The Immortals were the elite fighting force of the Persian Empire.

ALEXANDER THE GREAT C.336–323 BCE

THE YOUNG GENERAL

ALEXANDER THE GREAT IS AMONG THE MOST FAMOUS GENERALS IN HISTORY, AND WIDELY REGARDED AS ONE MOST DESERVING OF THE APPELLATION 'GREAT'. HE ASCENDED THE THRONE OF MACEDONIA IN 336 BCE AT JUST 20 YEARS OF AGE.

ABOVE Detailed relief carving showing Alexander at the Battle of Gaugamela, a significant victory against the Persians. Gaugamela was also where Alexander first encountered war elephants.

RIGHT Alexander was tutored by the famous scholar Aristotle.

For the next 13 years until his death in 323 BCE, Alexander the Great would wage campaign after campaign, vigorously extending the territories under his domain until he had conquered lands all the way to India. The most lasting effect of his conquests was the spread of Hellenic language and culture throughout Persia and Central Asia.

After the Athenian victory at the Battle of Marathon, the Greeks started to gain a stronger position against the mighty Persian Empire of the East. Alexander first consolidated control of Thessaly, Thrace and Macedonia, blocking out attacks from Illyrian and Getae forces. He then began his long and impressive campaign eastwards. His first major test would come at the Battle of the River Granicus in 334 BCE – the first time he was to face the Persian army. With daring yet brilliant tactics, Alexander was able to command his forces with decisive swiftness, inflicting heavy losses on the Persian side and suffering fewer than 200 on his own. His use of cavalry was particularly noteworthy, and helped him win the day.

Alexander went on to demonstrate skill on the open battlefield, and similar mastery in siege warfare, taking Halicarnassus in 334 BCE – a city whose capture seemed impossible. In 333 BCE he won the Battle of Issus, and went on to lay siege to Tyre and Gaza in 332 BCE. Alexander was welcomed into Egypt, where, according to legend, he received an important prophecy at the Siwa Oasis.

THE PEAK OF POWER

Despite being vastly outnumbered by a Persian army of some 200,000 – compared to Alexander's 40,000 – Alexander nonetheless won a crucial victory against the Persian army of Darius III at Gaugamela on

31 October 331 BCE. It was at Gaugamela that Alexander first encountered war elephants, of which Darius deployed 15. Alexander was terrified of them, supposedly sacrificing to the god of fear before the battle, but the elephants were exhausted from a long march so were not deployed effectively. Alexander was so impressed, he took these 15 elephants and incorporated them into his forces, later swelling their numbers.

Alexander pressed on, taking Babylon, Susa and, finally, Persepolis and Pasargadae of Persia. He went on to defeat the Scythians, and pushed towards India, laying siege to Aornos and winning. But Alexander's own ambition and insane drive were checked when his men mutinied at the River Hyphasis, largely putting an end to his expansion of the empire.

Soon after the death of his close companion Hephaestion, Alexander met death himself in Babylon. He was only 33.

TOP Alexander has been the subject of literature and art ever since his great conquests. This 17th-century painting shows Alexander meeting the family of King Darius III after defeating the Persian ruler.

LEFT Ruins of what some believe to be the lost tomb of Alexander the Great.

ROMAN-PARTHIAN WAR 55–36 BCE

THE BEGINNINGS OF WAR

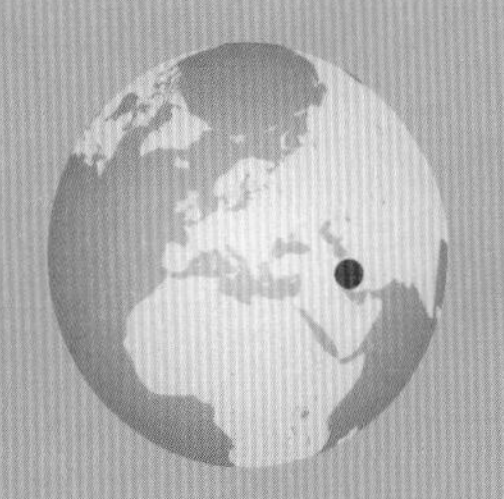

THE ROMAN REPUBLIC EXPANDED EASTWARDS AT THE SAME TIME THE PARTHIAN EMPIRE EXPANDED WESTWARDS. CONFLICT AROSE OVER THE BORDER BETWEEN THE TWO POWERS, PARTICULARLY THE LAND ALONG THE EUPHRATES.

Roman leader Pompey refused to acknowledge the Parthian king, Phraates III, as the 'King of Kings', further contributing to the mounting friction between the two powers. In 55 BCE, Marcus Licinius Crassus, a Roman triumvir, broke treaties with Parthia and invaded with a force of some 44,000 men comprised of seven legions plus cavalry. Crassus engaged the Parthian general Suren near Carrhae in what would become one of the most humiliating Roman defeats of all time.

Suren deployed a mere 9,000 horse archers and 1,000 cataphracts – heavily armoured cavalry – mostly comprised of nobility and highly trained warriors mounted on chargers with spears. Despite outnumbering Suren's forces, Crassus had just taken his men on a long march and was unfamiliar with the desert terrain and conditions he faced. Arranging

TOP The Parthian cataphracts were a dominant force on the battlefield. Here, one is shown killing a lion with a spear.

ABOVE Rome and Parthia were both expanding when wars between them began in the 1st century BCE.

LEFT Parthian bronze statue, now housed in the National Museum of Iran.

his infantry in a large square formation, Crassus deployed his cavalry against the Parthian forces. The Roman cavalry did not hold a candle to Suren's forces, and Crassus's infantry soon found themselves trying to withstand the iron rain of Parthian missiles. Hoping to withstand the siege, the Romans hunkered down, but Suren used camels as well to relay supplies, and the Parthians did not run out of arrows as the Romans hoped. Crassus and his son were killed, and many of the survivors were captured. Only a fraction of the original force made it back alive.

LASTING GRUDGES

The Romans did not suffer humiliation lightly, and it would not be long before they again sought to gain the upper hand against the Parthians. In the meantime, Rome underwent a civil war as it transformed from the Roman Republic into the Roman Empire. Parthia would lend support to certain factions within Rome, but the two powers found themselves at odds once again by 38 BCE. Roman general Mark Antony led the Romans in an effort to regain control of Syria and Judea, gaining victory against the Parthians and pushing them out. Mark Antony then led an offensive through the Armenian mountains into modern-day Azerbaijan, but the Parthians harried his supply chain and inflicted heavy casualties, particularly when Antony's Armenian allies failed to lend support. The Romans were eventually forced to withdraw.

A FLEXIBLE FORCE

The Parthians, like their neighbours to the north on the steppes (the Scythians), were able to succeed in battle often due to their use of horse archers. Capable of shooting in virtually any direction while riding at speed, these archers could inflict heavy damage while maintaining a position of relative safety themselves. Even when fleeing, the archers could turn and fire backwards at their enemies, a practice from which the term 'Parthian Shot' emerged. The term has come to be used for sharp words dealt while taking leave; one can easily see that the negative connotations of this phrase suggest a Roman origin, as they would have been the ones getting hit by those shots!

TOP These coins show General Mark Antony (left) and Emperor Octavian.

CENTRE RIGHT Parthian horsemen were famed for their ability to fire deadly arrow shots even while retreating or feigning retreat.

RIGHT Bust of Marcus Licinius Crassus, who died fighting the Parthians at the Battle of Carrhae in 53 BCE.

JEWISH-ROMAN WARS 66 CE–135 CE

MASSACRE IN ROMAN PALESTINE

IN THE FIRST AND SECOND CENTURIES CE, ROME SOUGHT TO EXPAND ITS HOLDINGS AND CONTROL OVER THE EASTERN SHORE OF THE MEDITERRANEAN. RATHER THAN SIMPLY IMPOSING POLITICAL AND MILITARY CONTROL OVER THE REGIONS OF MODERN-DAY PALESTINE AND ISRAEL, ROME SOUGHT TO MANDATE ROMAN CULTURE AND LAW.

The tension between Jewish and Roman populations mounted, particularly with the introduction of laws clearly afflicting the Jews, such as the banning of circumcision. In 66, tensions exploded in the massacre of some 20,000 Jews in Caesarea Maritima. The story of the massacre is famously told in *The Jewish War* by first-century historian Flavius Josephus. The massacre began a series of violent wars between the Jews of the region and the Roman Empire.

ABOVE Coins of Jerusalem from the First Jewish War.

ABOVE LEFT Dramatic painting depicting the destruction of Jerusalem under Titus.

LEFT Relief showing Romans carrying treasures out of the Temple of Jerusalem, including a large menorah.

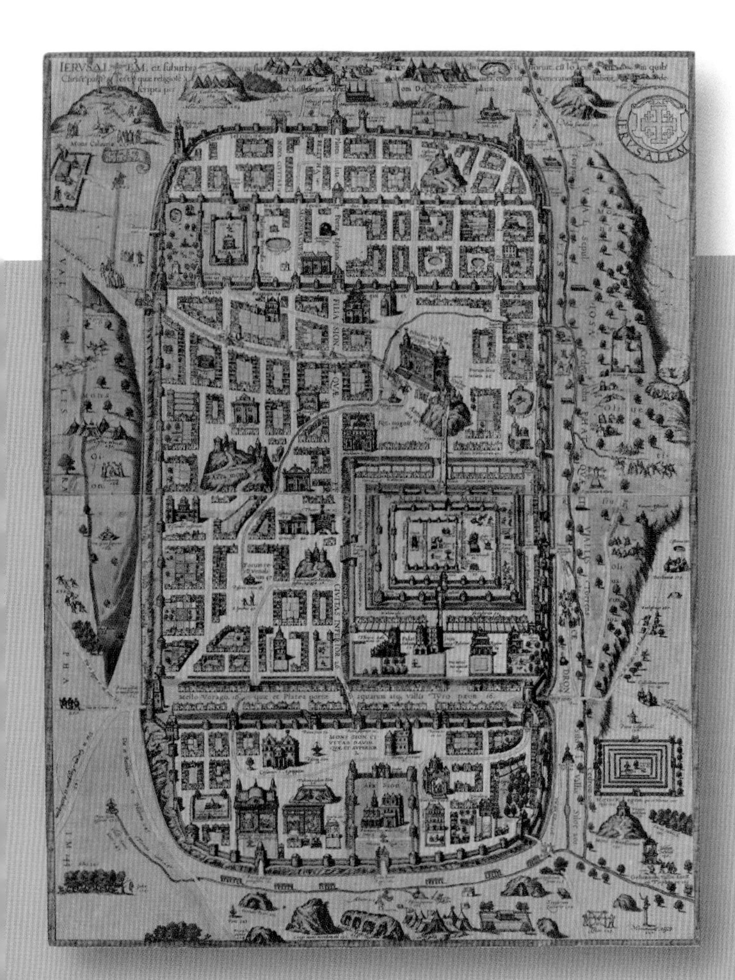

ABOVE Map of Jerusalem by 16th-century Flemish artist, Joris Hoefnagel.

ABOVE Ruins of Roman legionary camps – such as this one at Masada – can still be seen in Israel today.

INITIAL SUCCESSES

Initially, the Jews found success in their battles against the Romans. Stirred to action, they were able to retake Jerusalem and won the Battle of Beth-Horon, destroying an entire Roman legion and killing some 6,000 soldiers after ambushing them in the narrow pass of Beth-Horon. This was one of the worst defeats Rome had ever suffered at the hands of a rebellion. But Rome was proud – it would not be long before the empire struck back.

In the wake of their defeats, Rome regrouped and sent a force of 60,000 men under the command of General Vespasian to quell the rebellion. Beginning by taking Galilee in 68, Vespasian and his son, Titus, would decimate Jewish opposition over the coming two years. Vespasian took Yodfat and Gamla in quick succession, then Jotapata after besieging the fortress for 47 days. Titus would besiege Jerusalem for 134 days in 70, taking the Holy City by force. Upon his victory, he destroyed the Temple of Solomon, only provoking further anger and resentment by the Jewish opposition.

THE SECOND UPRISING

Jewish rebels continued to oppose Roman control, often massacring Roman citizens in the tens or even hundreds of thousands. Rome had stationed two legions in Judea to help put down the rebellions, but it was not enough. War broke out again in 115, known as the Kitos War after General Lusius Quietus. It took Trajan two years to subdue the rebellions, which raged throughout Judea, Egypt, Cyprus and beyond.

A third conflict erupted in 132, known as the Bar Kokhba Revolt, in part provoked by Emperor Hadrian's building of a temple to Jupiter on top of the ruins of the Jewish Second Temple. The Jews retook Jerusalem, Herodion and Betar under the direction of Bar Kokhba. The Romans struck again with a large army, retaking Jerusalem and banning Jews from entering, except for Tisha B'Av, one day a year. The Romans would crush what was left of the rebellion in 135 at Betar, killing Bar Kokhba. About half a million Jews died in the war, and the region then received its name of 'Palestina'.

SASSANID EMPIRE C. 226–651

PERSIA ONCE MORE

THE SASSANID PERSIAN EMPIRE WAS ESTABLISHED AFTER KING ARDASHIR DEFEATED THE PARTHIAN EMPEROR AT HORMIZDAGAN IN 226. THE SASSANID DYNASTY WOULD BECOME ONE OF THE MOST POWERFUL AND INFLUENTIAL IN HISTORY, LASTING UNTIL 651 WHEN ARAB INVADERS WOULD AT LAST BRING DOWN THE EMPIRE.

ABOVE Treasures such as this gold jug attest to the wealth and sophistication of the Sassanid Empire.

Ardashir, after his victory against the emperor, marched into Ctesiphon, the Parthian capital, and began consolidating control of large territories of modern-day Iran, Iraq, Afghanistan and Syria, seeking to emulate the dominance of his Achaemenid forebears. He established Zoroastrianism as the official religion, for example. On the battlefield, he reintroduced the famous 'Immortals'.

Over the centuries of its reign, the Sassanid Empire sought to expand and protect its vast borders from a number of hostile enemies. In the west, the Sassanid kings faced the Roman Empire, inheriting the animosity of its Parthian predecessor. Shapur II actually captured and imprisoned Emperor Valerian in 260. To the north and east, the Persians faced the Huns, Turks and nomads of the steppes. Despite constantly shifting borders, the Sassanid Empire maintained an enormous territory throughout its existence, expanding

RIGHT Ruins of the Sassanid palace, Taq-i Kisra, in Ctesiphon in modern-day Iraq.

OPPOSITE BELOW Warriors adorn the rock faces of Bishapur in Iran.

greatly in the early seventh century. The Sassanid armies took Armenia, Anatolia and even some territory in Mesopotamia under Byzantine control. Significantly, in 616, the Sassanid Empire also claimed control of Egypt.

THE BATTLE OF NINEVEH

Despite momentary weakness, the Byzantines found strength in General Heraclius, who defended Constantinople from a Sassanid attack in 626. Repelling the Sassanids, Heraclius pursued them east, facing off against a large Sassanid army at the Battle of Nineveh in 627. Outmanoeuvring the Sassanid general, Rhahzadh, Heraclius wore his opposition down while travelling through the country deep into Persian territory, leaving little for his pursuers to take in the way of food for man or beast. Beset by fog, the Sassanid army could not deploy its ballistas to best effect when the two armies met at Nineveh. Despite a hard battle that raged for 11 hours straight, Heraclius proved victorious. He travelled on to Ctesiphon, taking the Sassanid capital. The victory at Nineveh reestablished Byzantine dominance, swelling their borders once more to their former glory. But this revival would be short-lived, as the Arab kings would soon be sweeping out across the whole of the Middle East.

The Sassanid Empire, harking back to the glory of its Persian predecessors, had a lasting impact not just on the regions under its domain, but also on many of the civilizations of Eurasia. The influence of its wealth and art spread east into China and west into Europe, and the empire had lasting effects even after its demise in the middle of the seventh century.

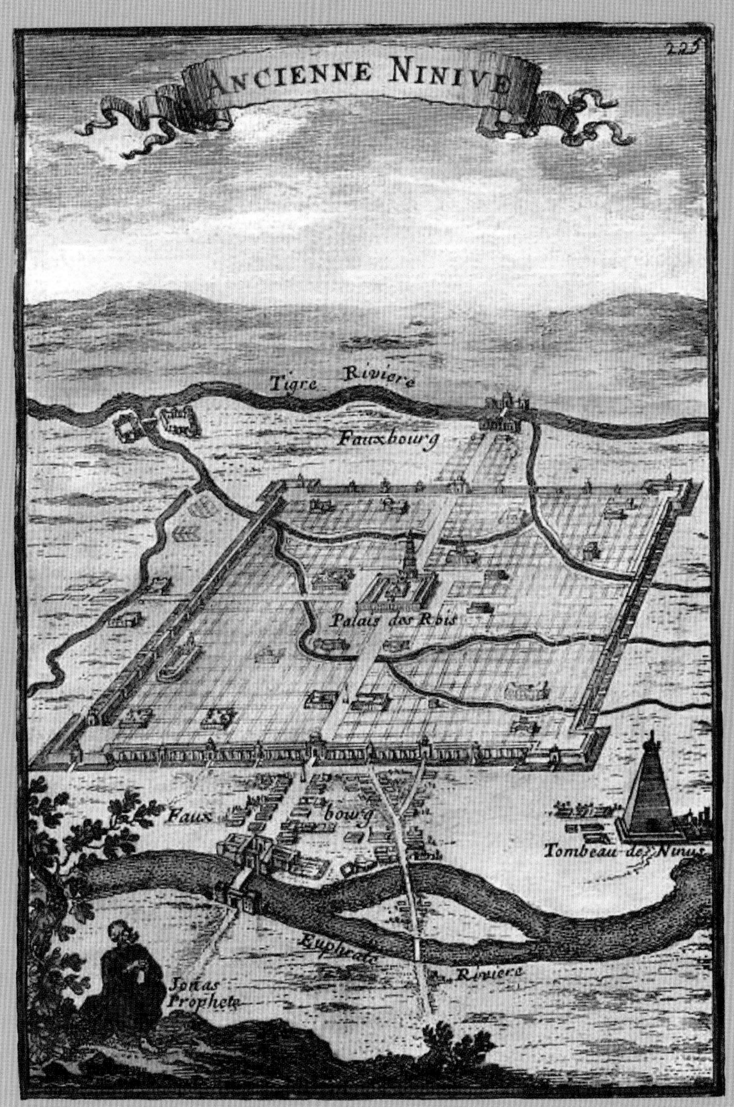

ABOVE A 17th-century depiction of the ancient city of Nineveh, where the Byzantines defeated the Sassanids in 627.

ISLAMIC EMPIRE-BUILDING 632–750

THE RISE OF ISLAM

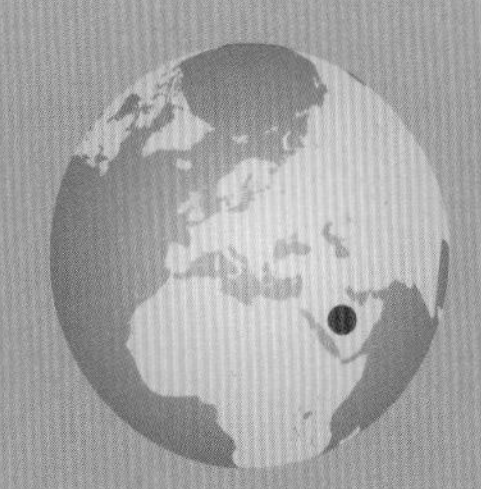

AFTER THE PROPHET MUHAMMAD FOUNDED ISLAM IN THE EARLY SEVENTH CENTURY, HE WAS ABLE TO UNITE MUCH OF THE ARABIAN PENINSULA BEFORE HIS DEATH IN 632.

ABOVE A 16th-century Turkish painting of Abu Bakr, father-in-law of Muhammad and Caliph of the Rashidun Caliphate.

OPPOSITE The Invocation to Muhammad, an engraving by 19th-century French artist, Gustave Doré.

Control of the caliphate passed to Abu Bakr, and thus began a new era of expansion that would result in the creation of an Islamic Empire, stretching from the Iberian Peninsula in the west to Central Asia in the east. The caliphates of Islam would become some of the largest, most powerful and wealthiest civilizations the world had known.

THE BLAZE OF CONQUEST

In 633, Abu Bakr quelled a rebellion of Arabs in what is known as the Ridda Wars, or Wars of Apostasy. He would then go on to fight against the might of Byzantium, at whose hands the Islamic armies had suffered defeat not long before. Despite the small size of his forces, Abu Bakr was able to gain victory against armies of both Byzantium and Sassanid Persia.

Abu Bakr, the first of the Rashidun, or four 'Righteous Caliphs', died in 634. Control passed to Umar, and the expansion of the empire continued. Despite being outnumbered six to one, the caliphate's forces were able to defeat the Sassanid army in 637 at the Battle of al-Qadisiyah in what is now Iraq, but which at the time was part of the Persian Empire. By 640, the Arabs controlled Iraq and Syria, having taken Damascus in 635 and having defeated the Byzantines at the Battle of Yarmuk in 636. The final victory against the Sassanids came at the Battle of Nahavand in 641, when the Muslim army outmanoeuvred the Persians, despite being outnumbered roughly three to one. Next came Alexandria and Egypt. By the end of the reign of the fourth Rashidun, the caliphate encompassed territories stretching from Tripoli in the west to Afghanistan in the east.

Dôms Sc
G. Doré

THE UMAYYAD EXPANSION 656–750

STRENGTHENING THE ISLAMIC EMPIRE

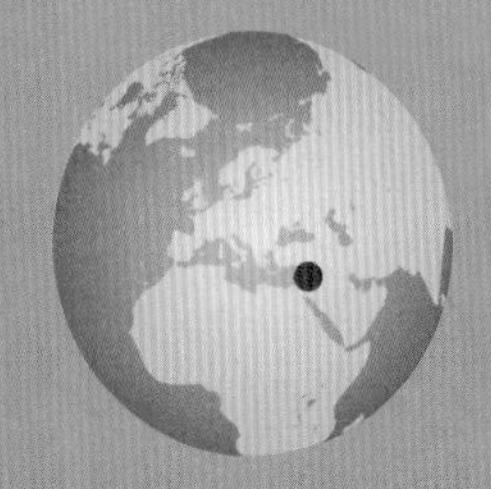

THE RASHIDUN CALIPHATE ENDED IN 661 WHEN RASHIDUN ALI WAS ASSASSINATED, JUST FOUR YEARS AFTER HIS PREDECESSOR, UTHMAN, WAS ASSASSINATED IN 656. THIS DID NOT STOP THE EXPANSION OF THE ISLAMIC EMPIRE, HOWEVER.

Internal discord was already beginning to weaken the empire, and Ali had nearly engaged in civil war, sending 90,000 men against the rebellion of Muawiyah, the governor of Syria and kinsman of Uthman. Though matters were settled peaceably at the time, Muawiyah would later seize control after Ali's untimely death. Muawiyah moved the capital of the empire from Mecca to Damascus and continued the expansion. Quarrels over succession continued, evidence of which we still see today in the differences between Sunni and Shia sects of Islam.

The Umayyad Caliphate expanded on the successes of its predecessors, branching out swiftly across North Africa, taking the city of Tunis, or Carthage, in 698 and continuing the push westwards. In 711, the Umayyads struck at Visigothic Spain, taking the country by storm. At the same time, Umayyad forces gained control in the east of the River Indus in 713 and of Transoxiana by 715. Eastward expansion would largely end here, and westward expansion was checked famously by Charles the Hammer at the Battle of Poitiers in 732.

The Umayyad Dynasty would come to an end in 750, having taken the already large Islamic Empire of the Rashidun and expanding it to include large portions of Europe, Africa and Asia. Though the dynasty came to an end in the mid-eighth century, Arab and Islamic control of this territory would continue for centuries to come.

TOP LEFT The Great Mosque of Damascus, one of the holiest places of Islam, built on top of the Basilica of John the Baptist.

LEFT Magnificent stone work from an Umayyad palace.

ABOVE Umayyad coin from around 700 showing caliph Abd al-Malik ibn Marwan, based on contemporary designs of Byzantine coins.

RIGHT Dome of the treasury at the Great Mosque in Damascus.

FORGOTTEN SIEGE

The Umayyads achieved unlikely successes in many of their battles, sweeping across the globe in a storm of swords and spears. Despite other victories against the armies of Byzantium, they were unable to capture the Byzantine capital of Constantinople. Besieging the city from 674–678, the Umayyad Caliphate sought control of the crucial waterway of the Bosphorus between the Black and Marmara Seas (and therefore the wider Mediterranean). Using the mysterious Greek fire, a chemical mixture that apparently burned even on water, the Greeks were able to defeat the Umayyad forces, both in the siege of 674 and again in a second siege from 717 to 718. Halting the Umayyad forces at Constantinople was critical for preventing their wider expansion into Europe, though this siege is often overshadowed by Charles the Hammer's victory at Poitiers. Constantinople and the Eastern Roman Empire would only fall centuries later to a different Islamic Empire: the Ottoman Empire, in the fifteenth century.

ABOVE An illustration showing the use of Greek fire. Scholars are still unsure of what exactly Greek fire was, or how it was used; we know from contemporary sources, however, that it was an incredibly effective weapon against those who sought to attack Constantinople.

THE CRUSADES 1096–1291

THE NINE CRUSADES

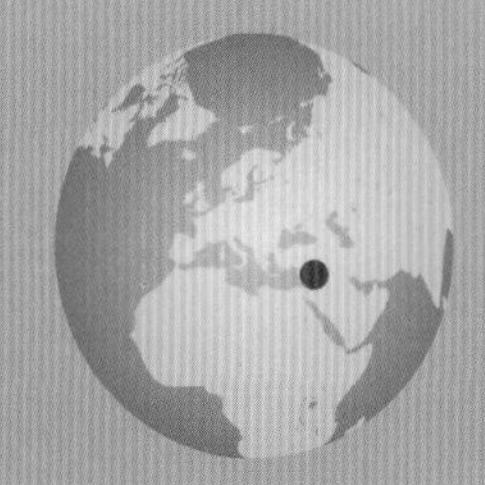

TRADITIONALLY, SCHOLARS RECOGNIZE NINE CANONICAL CRUSADES, FROM THE FIRST IN 1096–1099 TO THE NINTH AND FINAL ONE FROM 1271–1272. THESE WERE THE FAMOUS EXPEDITIONS OF EUROPEAN KNIGHTS TO THE HOLY LAND.

ABOVE Painting of Baldwin of Boulogne. Baldwin was the brother of Godfrey of Bouillon, both of whom led the First Crusade. Baldwin became Count of Edessa and later King of Jerusalem.

OPPOSITE TOP Map showing the routes of crusaders to the Holy Land.

OPPOSITE BELOW Dramatic rendition of the Siege of Antioch depicting the knights of Bohemond scaling the city walls.

When Pope Urban II preached the First Crusade in 1095, however, he began a series of armed conflicts that would last for centuries and could not be contained by nine distinct episodes in the chapters of history. The Crusades spawned a European culture of warfare in the Holy Land, which was passed down through several generations of warriors. The results of this cultural development were so strong that they can still be seen and felt in modern Western society.

DIVINE DUTY

The motivations of men travelling to the Holy Land on crusade were mixed, and many marched to war for purely economic reasons: they could not sustain themselves adequately at home, so took to conquest in the hopes of being able to return wealthy. Pope Urban II's call for crusade in 1095 included a call for reclaiming the Holy Sepulchre of Jesus Christ's tomb. This provided religious justification to a number of political and economic factors that made large expeditions to the Middle East desirable. At the time, the Middle East was known as a land of riches and splendour, possessing sophistication far beyond that of Europe.

Four armies rose to the call in 1096, led by Godfrey of Bouillon, Baldwin of Bourcq, Bohemond, Robert of Normandy, and Raymond of Saint-Gilles. As many of the men who swelled the ranks of these armies were opportunists who had not succeeded at home, the armies were often difficult to tame, and performed many atrocities, both along the way and after reaching the Holy Land. The troops were supposed to assist the Byzantines in their fights against the Muslim invaders, but caused so much trouble as to be unwelcome guests to the emperor of Byzantium.

FIRST SUCCESSES

Despite the unruly nature of the men, and despite internal struggles among the crusaders over who should exercise control of the armies and their strategies, the First Crusade was – at least militarily – a success. Defeating their opponents at Nicaca (modern Iznik) and Dorylaeum, the crusaders crossed Anatolia in five months, progressing to the Holy Land and beginning their siege of Antioch on 20 October 1097. The gruelling siege lasted until 2 June 1098, by which point many of the crusaders had deserted or died. Conditions were tough: starvation, disease and the unfamiliar climate claimed a heavy toll. But the crusaders took Antioch, leaving Bohemond in control there, and marched on to Jerusalem. With only 13,500 warriors left in their ranks, the crusaders attacked Jerusalem on 7 June 1099. Little more than a month and a half later, on 15 July 1099, the Holy City fell to the crusaders. They stormed in, pillaging and massacring the inhabitants of the city.

THE CRUSADES 1096–1291

Meanwhile, the Muslim world was in disarray. Division between sects of Islam, including the strong divide between Sunni and Shia Muslims, caused political instability as various fractions vied for power. The Abbasid Caliphate faced internal destruction in 1092 when Sultan Malik-Shah died. Malik-Shah was a Sunni Seljuk, while the Shia Fatimid Caliphate lay just a short distance away in Egypt. The politically tenuous nature of the Abbasid Caliphate allowed European crusaders to strike in 1096 with surprising efficacy. And even in the wake of their success, the Islamic rulers did not yet feel compelled to unite against the intruders from Europe.

RIGHT A brutal illustration of crusaders throwing the heads of Muslims at their enemies during the Siege of Maarat, in 1098. Crusaders supposedly resorted to cannibalism during the siege.

BELOW A manuscript illustration showing pitched battle between Saladin and Guy de Lusignan.

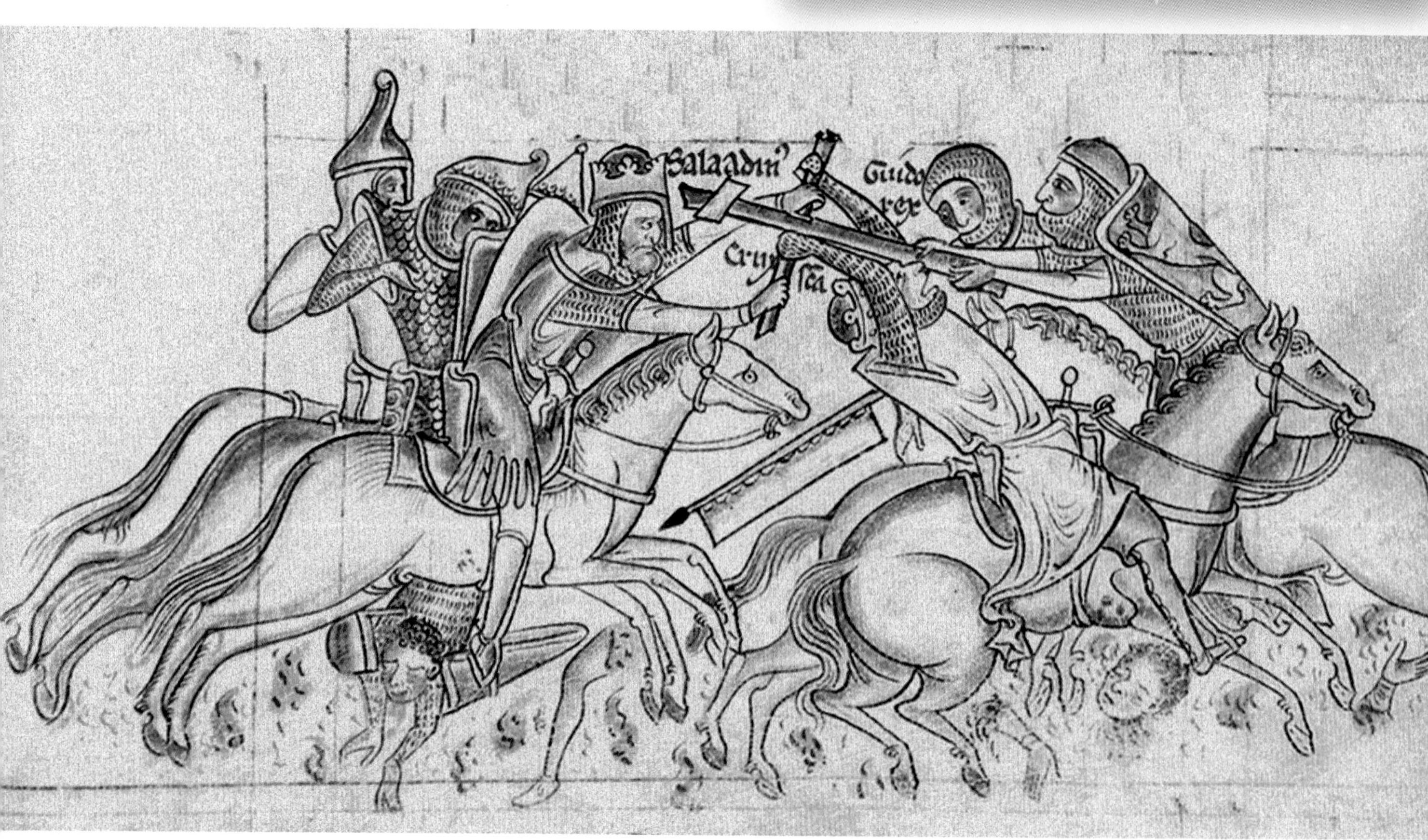

MUSLIMS UNITED

Continuing the work of the governor – or *atabak* – of Mosul, Nur al-Din, Salah al-Din (Saladin) would unite the Muslims once again into a powerful political and military entity. Nur al-Din conquered Edessa in 1144 and Damascus in 1154, then went on to take control of Egypt in 1169. This paved the way for Saladin, who took control of the Fatimid Caliphate in 1171, then returned to Syria after the death of Nur al-Din to re-establish an empire. For the next several years he set about consolidating his control and the power of his clan, the Ayyubids. In 1183, however, he began to address the issue of the crusaders who still threatened his empire.

On 4 July 1187, Saladin launched an attack on the crusaders of Jerusalem in what is known as the Battle of Hattin. Completely crushing the crusaders in battle and killing most of them in Jerusalem, Saladin continued his campaign by destroying crusader control of the neighbouring territories. The Byzantines, who had once sought the aid of the crusaders, now sided with Saladin. Saladin used relatively small, light forces, armed with leather and lamellar armour, and deploying cavalry and horse archers to great effect. News of the loss of Jerusalem nearly a century after its original conquest caused an upheaval in Europe and gave rise to the Third Crusade.

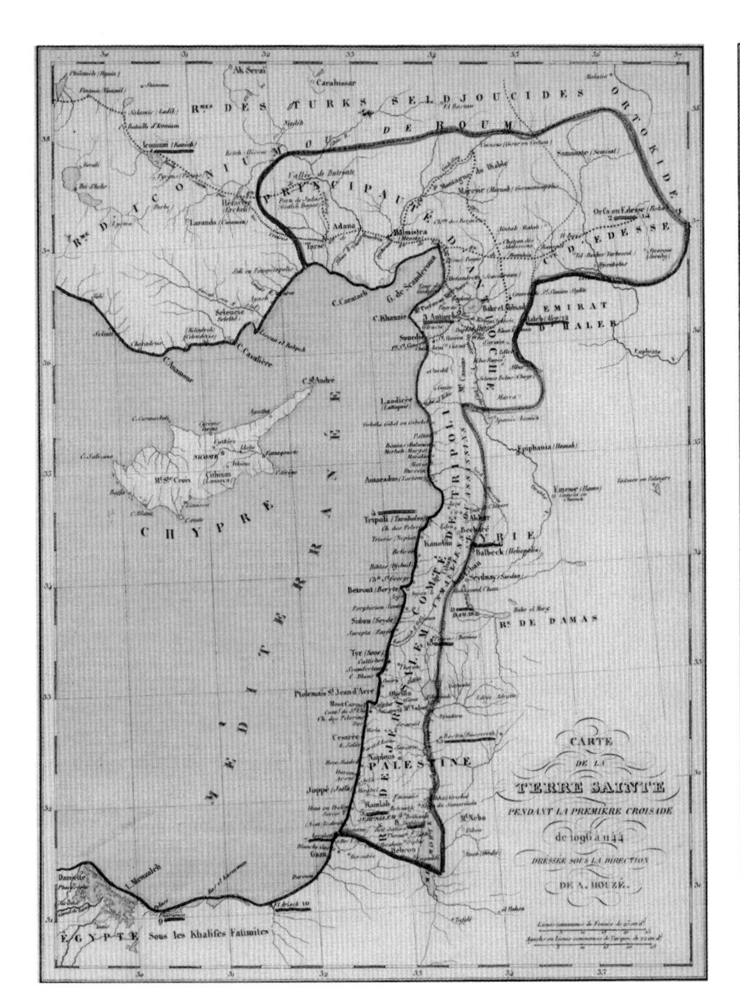

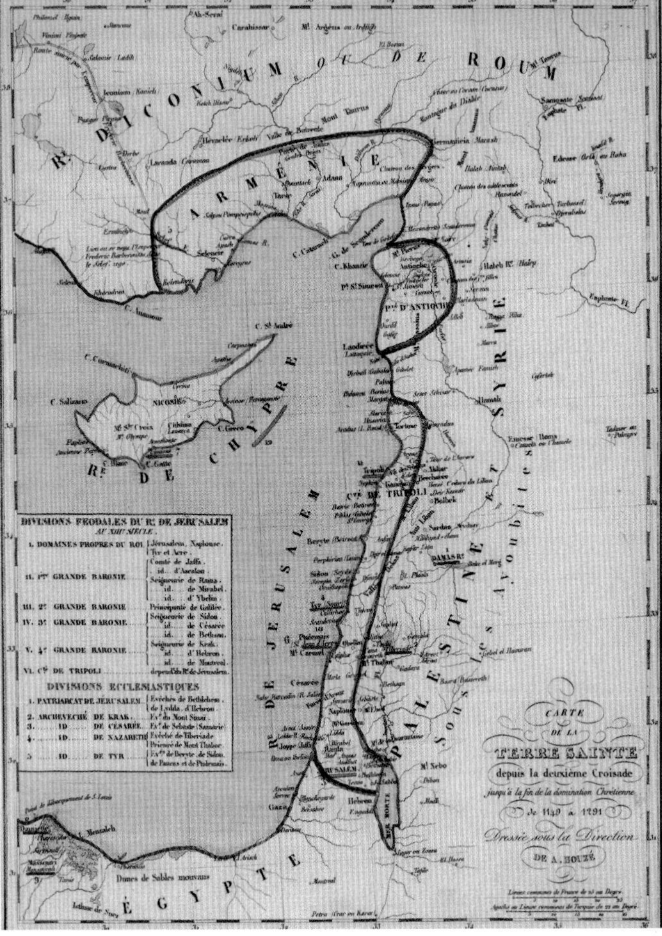

ABOVE These maps show the gains and losses of crusader control of territories in the Holy Land.

THE CRUSADES 1096–1291

The Battle of Hattin brought the Third Crusade to a close on 2 September 1192, with a peace treaty. The only real European victory was that of Richard the Lionheart (Richard I), who captured Cyprus, establishing a dynasty that would last for three centuries. Richard won victories at Acre and Arsuf in 1191. Saladin was unable to defeat Richard, but he nonetheless regained control of Jerusalem, though Christian pilgrims were permitted to visit the city by the terms of the peace treaty. Crusader failure to retake Jerusalem would lead to the Fourth Crusade some six years later.

A number of crusades followed in the thirteenth century, the nature of these expeditions changing considerably from their original iterations in the eleventh and twelfth centuries. Crusades were launched within Europe or on its borders. The Hohenstaufen Crusades of 1239–1268, for example, were directed at political enemies of the pope; the Albigensian Crusade of 1209–1229, on the other hand, was directed at supposed 'heretics'. While control of Jerusalem was reclaimed through negotiation between 1229 and 1244, the military efforts in the Holy Land were otherwise largely unsuccessful.

ABOVE With all the fighting in the Holy Land, it is easy to forget the Albigensian Crusade against heretics in France, which began in 1209.

RIGHT A 14th-century manuscript image of Conrad III of the Hohenstaufen leading his crusaders through Hungary.

Assuming that control of the Holy Land would come from victory in Egypt, the home of the Ayyubid power, King Louis IX of France launched an assault on Egypt in 1248, gaining the upper hand at Damietta and al-Mansurah. But he and many of the nobles who accompanied him were captured and ransomed for a hefty sum. When he attempted another assault in 1269, he died of illness. Two decades later, in 1291, a Mamluk force captured Acre, which was the last remaining crusader possession in Palestine. The crusaders were defeated and expelled, and the crusades essentially came to a close by the end of the thirteenth century. Their effects, however, would continue to be seen for centuries.

THE ORDERS OF GOD AND WAR

One of the consequences of the crusades was the creation of knightly orders, such as the Templars, Hospitaller and Teutonic Knights. Combing martial and religious duties, these orders functioned in their ideal versions as almost monastic orders, though in reality they did not always

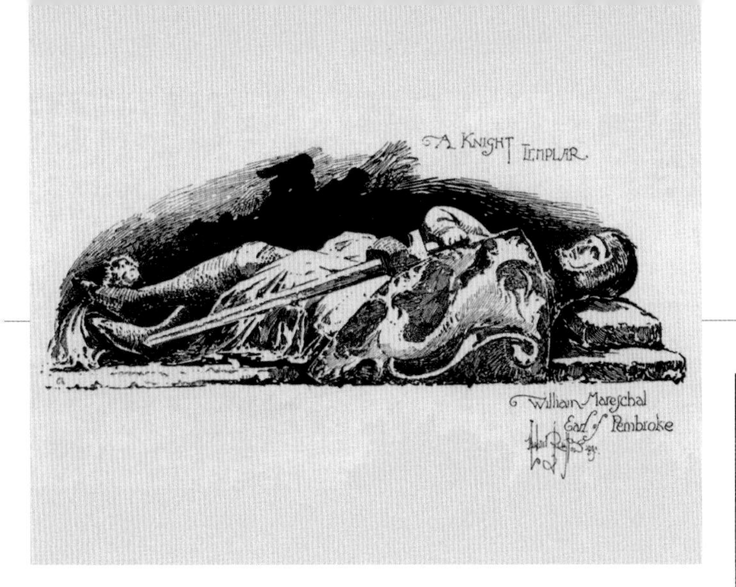

ABOVE The knightly orders, such as the Templars, would become the subject of legends and fantasies whose popularity lasts to this day.

BELOW Richard the Lionheart of England was one of the European heroes of the Third Crusade, and achieved legendary status for his leadership.

ABOVE A stained-glass window depicting King Louis IX carrying the crown of thorns. The French crusader king was canonized in 1297.

encapsulate the ideal combination of holy and military perfection. The subject of many legends today, these orders - and the crusades in general - had a profound impact on the culture back in Europe, spawning a whole body of vernacular literature in French and German about the adventures in the Holy Land. Among the most famous of these is Wolfram von Eschenbach's *Parzival*, which presents a holy order of knights assigned to protect the *graal* - the stone from heaven.

SIEGE OF BAGHDAD 1258

THE MONGOLS ADVANCE ON BAGHDAD

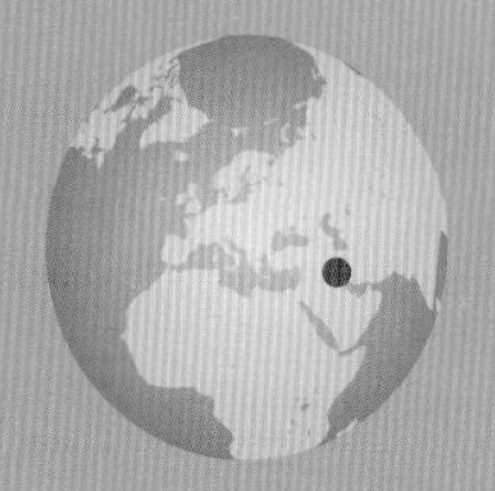

FOLLOWING IN THE FOOTSTEPS OF HIS GRANDFATHER, GENGHIS KHAN, HÜLEGÜ LED AN ARMY OF 120,000 SOUTHWARDS, CROSSING THE RIVER OXUS ON 1 JANUARY 1256, WITH THE INTENTION OF SUBDUING THE ABBASID CALIPHATE.

Despite the loss of Genghis in 1227, the Mongols continued their aggressive expansion under the direction of Genghis's heirs and descendents. Hülegü lived up to expectations, claiming victory in his initial campaigns against the Assassins of the Elburz Mountains and marching on to Baghdad.

THE MARCH TO BAGHDAD

Hülegü had under his command a series of Chinese engineers who assisted him in the construction and use of various siege weapons. These would play an important role in taking the fortresses of the Abbasid Assassins, a military order whose name provides the origins of our modern word 'assassin'. Hülegü's forces destroyed the base of the Assassins at Alamut, and many of the documents relating to the order were likewise destroyed. From Alamut, Hülegü advanced on Baghdad, reaching the capital of the Abbassid Caliphate in January 1258. The caliph did not respond in time.

From 30 January to 6 February, Hülegü's forces besieged Baghdad before the Mongol forces stormed the eastern wall. During the following week, the Mongols took more and more of the city until they had taken Baghdad completely by 13 February. The Mongol forces wreaked horrible

ABOVE The Mongols were masters of the bow and arrow, but also used large siege engines in their campaigns in the Middle East.

RIGHT Hülegü supposedly imprisoned the Abbasid Caliph with heaps of gold and treasure, but no food.

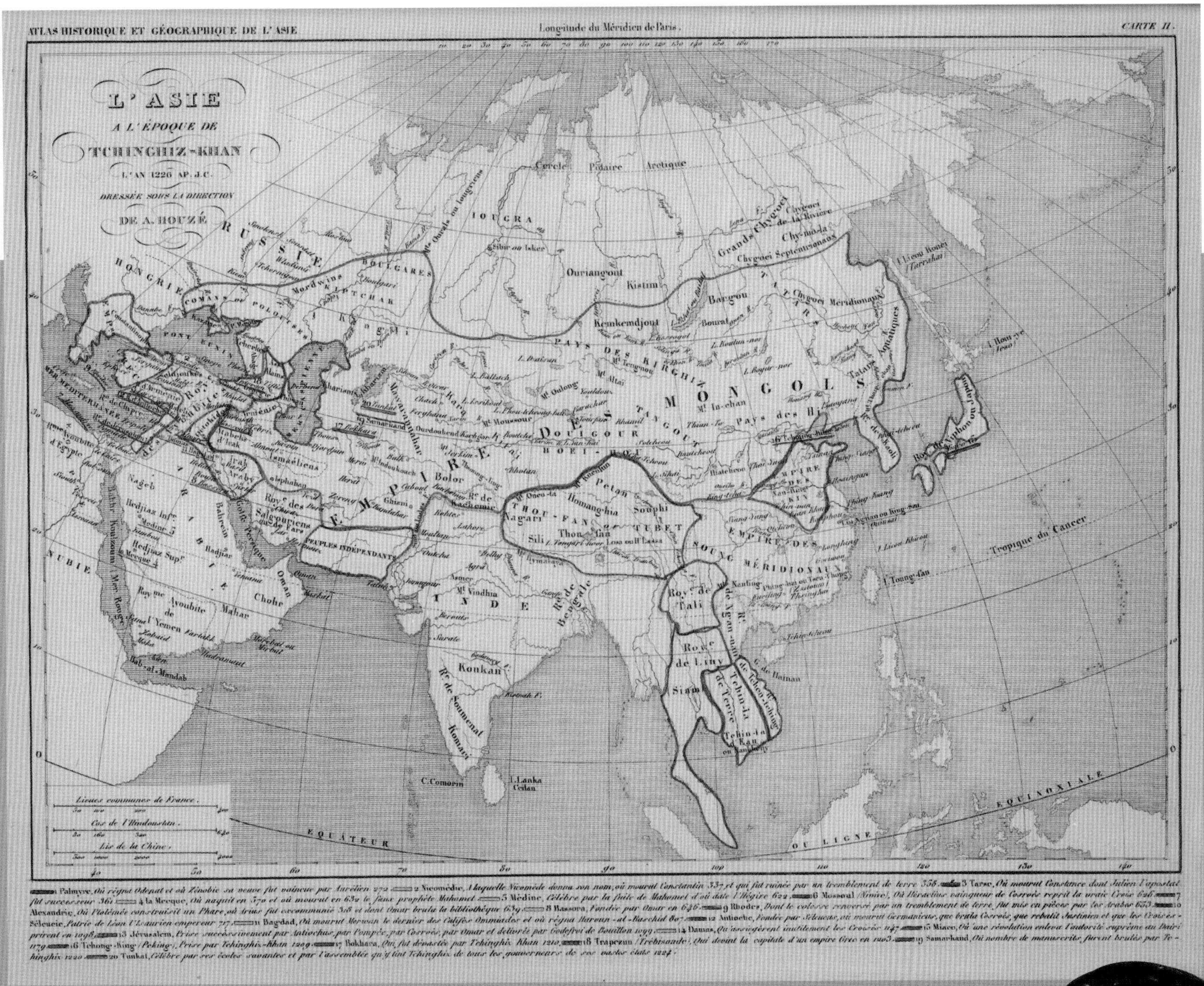

destruction on the city, once the jewel of the medieval world, massacring tens of, if not hundreds of thousands of people. They destroyed the irrigation system, as well as many of the textual and literary treasures of the city.

Hülegü moved on from Baghdad to conquer Syria. A Maluk army finally defeated him in 1260 at Ayn Jalut, but the devastation to the Abbasid Caliphate was complete.

THE HASHASHIN

The Hashashin was a military order founded shortly before the First Crusade. Little is known about their origins or operation, but they were known for eliminating key figures of opposition by assassination (hence the derivation of 'assassin' from 'hashashin'). The Hashashin often used daggers to perform the deed, and were reputed to use poison. Hülegü's thorough destruction of the fortresses of the Hashashin has contributed to the lack of knowledge of the order's workings, helping shroud them in mystery.

ABOVE A noble Mamluk warrior from Aleppo. The Mamluks in the Middle East were able to defeat the invading Mongols, notably at the Battle of Ayn Jalut, in 1260.

ABOVE RIGHT A hare adorns this coin of Hülegü.

TOP The Mongol Empire stretched from the Pacific in the east to central Europe in the west.

GUNPOWDER

EXPLOSION OF NEW TECHNOLOGY

Owing to differences in textual descriptions, it is difficult to determine when exactly gunpowder was invented. It may have been invented as early as the ninth century in China by Chinese alchemists; it was definitely in use by the eleventh century. The explosive powder soon began to be used in war and new devices were created to control the direction of the explosions. Soon they were used to propel missiles. Early firearms included bamboo tubes, reinforced with iron, used to shoot arrows. The development of devices such as the *hwacha* in Korea, which could send a cascade of arrows with a single charge, would become decisive in battle.

At the end of the thirteenth century, the Arabs, having brought gunpowder from China, used firearms against the invading Mongols. Bombs hurled at defensive works were among the most effective early uses of gunpowder. The Ottomans achieved victory over Constantinople in 1453 in large part because of their use of artillery. The Europeans, however, would be the ones to take the possibilities of gunpowder and turn them into the most advanced weaponry the world had ever seen. Firearms, which were used in the Hundred Years' War (1337–1453), eventually led to the demise of the armoured knight.

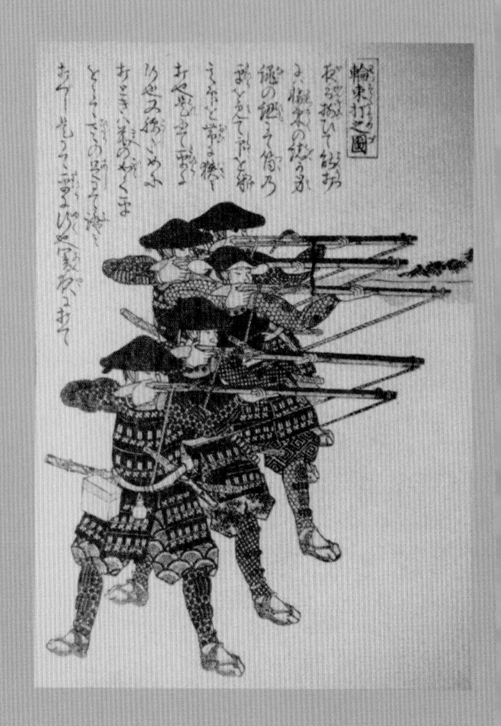

IN RESPONSE TO THE NEW FORMS OF WEAPONRY, NEW TYPES OF DEFENCES HAD TO BE BUILT TO WITHSTAND THE BLASTS OF BOMBS AND CANNONS.

TOP A 19th-century illustration of Japanese soldiers firing matchlock rifles.

LEFT Mehmed II leading his army towards Constantinople.

BELOW Gunpowder was a key ingredient in the Ottoman victory over Constantinople in 1453.

THE NEW DEFENCES

While early experiments with gunpowder focused on enhancing existing weaponry – such as propelling arrows – new artillery started developing quickly towards the end of the Middle Ages. In response to the new forms of weaponry, new types of defences had to be built to withstand the blasts of bombs and cannons. Among the most famous and most influential military engineers was Sébastien Le Prestre de Vauban (1633–1707). Vauban, a Marshal of France and adviser to King Louis XIV, was a brilliant strategist and engineer, who redesigned and refurbished fortresses to make them more impregnable and also capable of deflecting and defending the new gunpowder-based weaponry of the day. Excelling at building fortresses, Vauban was also an expert at taking them down and developed many novel methods to penetrate the walls of his opponents' defences. Among these techniques was 'ricochet fire', the practice of firing cannons at a low angle so that the cannonballs would skip across the ground and ricochet off multiple targets. Borrowing from the Turks, he also made use of parallel trenches in approaching a fortress – a canonical feature of European warfare.

ABOVE A painting of Shah Jahan, the Mughal emperor, using a matchlock rifle to hunt deer.

LEFT Edo Period (Tokugawa Period) firearms from Japan.

TOP Sébastien Le Prestre de Vauban revolutionized the construction, defence and attack of fortresses to meet the demands of new gunpowder weapons.

OTTOMAN EMPIRE C.1300–1922

KINGDOM OF THE TURKS

AFTER THE MONGOLS SHATTERED THE EXISTING POLITICAL AND MILITARY STRUCTURES OF THE MIDDLE EAST AND ANATOLIA, A NEW LEADER EMERGED IN ANATOLIA IN THE EARLY FOURTEENTH CENTURY.

Consolidating control over the peoples pushed westwards into Anatolia by the Mongol invasions, Osman I quickly established a strong force, founding an empire that would take his name and would last for six centuries until 1922.

The Ottoman Empire really started to take off under the direction of Osman's son, Orhan I. Osman died in 1324, and two years later his son had conquered Bursa, making it his new capital. Orhan went on to win battle after battle, taking Nicaea (Iznik) in 1331 and Nicomedia (Izmit) in 1337. The Ottomans grew stronger and stronger as their neighbours to the west, the powerful Byzantine Empire, grew weaker and declined. By the end of the fourteenth century, the Ottomans had asserted control over a large territory and were pushing into Europe. Two battles gave them a critical foothold in Eastern Europe: the Battle of Kosovo, in 1389, and the Battle of Nicopolis, in 1396, both of which resulted in Ottoman victories.

EMPIRE DELAYED

In 1402, the Byzantines, who suffered loss after loss to the Ottomans, found unexpected aid at the hands of Timur (or Tamerlane), a Mongol who fought victoriously against the Ottomans at the Battle of Ankara, in 1402. During the battle, Timur took the Ottoman sultan, Bayezid I, captive. Bayezid died a year later in captivity and his four sons fought against one another over the succession during a period of civil war that lasted until 1413. This Interregnum interrupted the growth of the Ottoman Empire, but it did not put an end to this rising power.

Mehmed I, one of Bayezid's sons, emerged victorious at the end of the civil war and took control of the Ottoman throne. He and his son, Murad II, strengthened the Ottoman territory, which was weakened by the years of civil war. Murad II would go on to attack Venice and Hungary, and his son, Mehmed II, led the Ottomans in the victorious campaign against Constantinople, in 1453. The end of the Byzantine Empire marked a new beginning for the Ottomans.

Over the next century, the Ottomans fought many battles, constantly working to expand and solidify their dominion. By 1517, they had defeated the Mamluks, thereby taking the territories of Syria and Egypt, as well as Mecca and Medina. In the 1520s, they campaigned in Hungary, crushing that country's forces at the Battle of Mohács, in 1526: 20,000 Hungarian soldiers were no match for the highly trained 100,000 troops fielded by the Ottomans. They went on to take Rhodes, Tripoli, Cyprus and Tunis, by 1574. By the end of the sixteenth century, the Ottomans controlled an enormous territory across three continents.

ABOVE The Kingdom of Hungary was defeated by the Ottomans at the Battle of Mohács, in 1526.

TOP The Holy League defeated the Ottomans at the Battle of Lepanto, in 1571.

ABOVE The Ottoman Empire is named after its founder, Osman I, who declared an independent Turkic state, in 1299.

RIGHT Mehmed II beheaded John Hunyadi, a Hungarian military leader who opposed the Ottoman advance into Eastern Europe.

DEFEAT OF CONSTANTINOPLE 1453

THE GREAT CITY

FOR 11 CENTURIES, THE BYZANTINE CAPITAL OF CONSTANTINOPLE HAD REMAINED A TANTALIZING TARGET OF ATTACK, YET ITS STRONG WALLS AND THE SKILLED SOLDIERS WHO GUARDED THEM HAD MANAGED TO REPEL ALMOST ALL ATTACKS.

With its control of the Bosphorus, Constantinople was a critical gateway into Europe, and one on which the Ottomans set their sights in the fourteenth century. The Ottomans had attempted to take Constantinople twice in the late fourteenth and early fifteenth centuries – from 1394–1402 and again in 1422 – but they failed. Byzantium, however, continued to weaken, as more and more of its former glory diminished. In 1453, the Ottomans – who meanwhile were getting stronger by the day – attacked Constantinople once again under the direction of Sultan Mehmed II. Mehmed had two key advantages. First, he outnumbered the 50,000 inhabitants of Constantinople with an army of between 80,000 and 150,000. Second, he had cannons. Only about 7,000 of the inhabitants of Constantinople were trained warriors.

ABOVE The Siege of Constantinople was celebrated for centuries to come by Ottoman historians, and immortalized by Ottoman artists seeking to capture the glory of the victory.

OPPOSITE LEFT Medieval map of Constantinople, showing the Golden Horn.

OPPOSITE RIGHT A portrait of the Ottoman emperor, Mehmed II.

PREVIOUS CONQUEST

Constantinople had resisted attack after attack during the course of its history, narrowly evading capture by a Viking fleet of 200 ships in the ninth century and again in the tenth. But the great city had been conquered before the Ottomans took it in the middle of the fifteenth century. During the Fourth Crusade (1199–1204), crusaders besieged and overthrew Constantinople, taking the city by force and pillaging brutally for three days straight. The assault represents the intense disparity between the eastern and western branches of the Christian church. Pope John Paul II formally apologized for the Fourth Crusade to Patriarch Bartholomew of the Eastern Orthodox Church in 2004, a full 800 years later.

THE SIEGE OF CONSTANTINOPLE

Mehmed launched his attack on 18 April 1453. The soldiers of Constantinople had the home-field advantage, and used a boom across the Golden Horn to keep Mehmed's fleet from reaching the city. After the first attack, however, Mehmed used his large force to carry ships overland on the night of 21 April and thereby get around the boom. Mehmed took 70 ships overland around Galata and built a bridge over the Horn. However, despite being able to deploy his fleet and having an overwhelmingly superior force, Mehmed was not able to gain an easy victory. For the rest of April and all of May, Mehmed and his men launched attack after attack, hammering the walls with cannon blasts. The elite fighting force of the Janissaries breached the walls at the Gate of St Romanus on 29 May. It was the third assault of the day, and the Ottomans poured in. Constantine XI himself rose to meet them, fighting to his last breath. He fell before the gates at the hands of the Ottomans, and with him fell the Byzantine Empire. The eastern half of the Roman Empire had finally met its end.

ISRAEL'S WARS 1948–PRESENT

POLITICS AND RELIGION

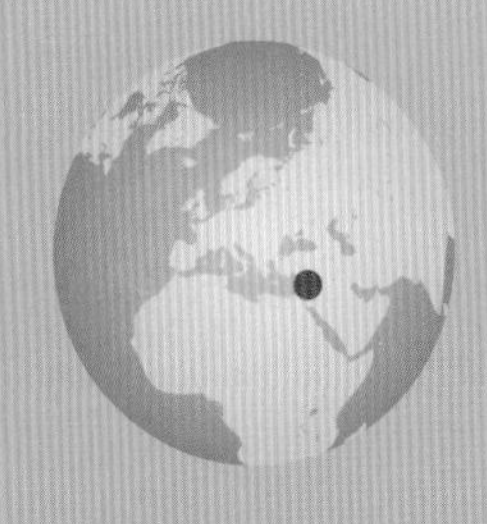

ON 14 MAY 1948, ISRAEL DECLARED ITS STATEHOOD, SPAWNING A SERIES OF CONFLICTS BETWEEN THE NEW NATION AND ITS SURROUNDING NEIGHBOURS. ISRAEL WAS NOW A POLITICAL ENTITY, BUT ITS DEMOGRAPHIC MAKE-UP WAS PREDOMINANTLY JEWISH BY ETHNICITY AND RELIGION.

TOP Israeli tanks during the Six-Day War, in 1967.

ABOVE Smoke billows into the sky after an Israeli air strike during the Six-Day War.

The countries surrounding Israel were (and still are) predominantly Arab by ethnicity and Muslim by religion. Tensions between religious and ethnic groups have manifested on political levels as vicious and violent wars for decades; the tensions and violence continue to this day.

WAR ERUPTS

Between 1948 and 1982, Israel fought at least five major battles with its Arab neighbours. The first was in 1948, when Israel declared independence. The United Nations sought to divide the territory of Israel in a way that would provide land for the Jewish people, but still allow Arabs living in Israel their own territory. When Israel declared independence, however, a large combined force from several Arab nations – including Egypt, Lebanon, Syria, Iraq and Jordan – invaded the newly formed country. The Jordanian troops swiftly took control of Jerusalem, but Israel fought back and was able to drive the invaders away, despite being outnumbered. They staked out a territory beyond what the UN had originally envisioned as belonging to Israel.

THE WAR WITH EGYPT

On 29 October 1956, Israel invaded Egypt and with shocking efficiency deployed its troops on the ground and in the air such that they had captured Sinai by 5 November. The UN brought a swift close to the engagement, and Israel returned Sinai to Egypt in exchange for rights to use the Straits of Tiran. Egypt had provoked the war by taking control of the Suez Canal. This deeply offended Britain and France, who

ABOVE A ceasefire was agreed in Jerusalem on 30 November 1948.

RIGHT Egyptian President Gamal Abdel Nasser in 1956.

BELOW RIGHT Israel's borders in 1947 and 1967.

in turn joined with Israel in hope of regaining control of the canal. Meanwhile, Egypt had already been blockading Israel's port of Elat and making other preparations that seemed to threaten Israel.

A DECADE OF PEACE, SIX DAYS OF WAR

Between 1956 and 1967, Israel and Egypt remained relatively peaceful in their relations, at least when it came to actual military action. Tensions, however, had not dissipated, and the peace was only possible with a UN force in Sinai designed to help form a buffer between the two nations. However, the peace was shattered in 1967 when President Nasser of Egypt sent his forces into Sinai, blocking the Straits of Tiran. Meanwhile, Egypt's ally, Syria, began bombing Israel in the north from the Golan Heights. When Israel struck back on 5 June, Jordan also invaded and marched on Jerusalem. Fighting on three fronts, Israel first devastated the Egyptian forces through skilful use of its air force. Repelling the attack on Jerusalem, Israel swiftly turned the Jordanian assault back, and a few days later focused its efforts against the Syrians in the Golan Heights. Within six days (by June 10) Israeli forces had repulsed three attacks and brought an end to the war.

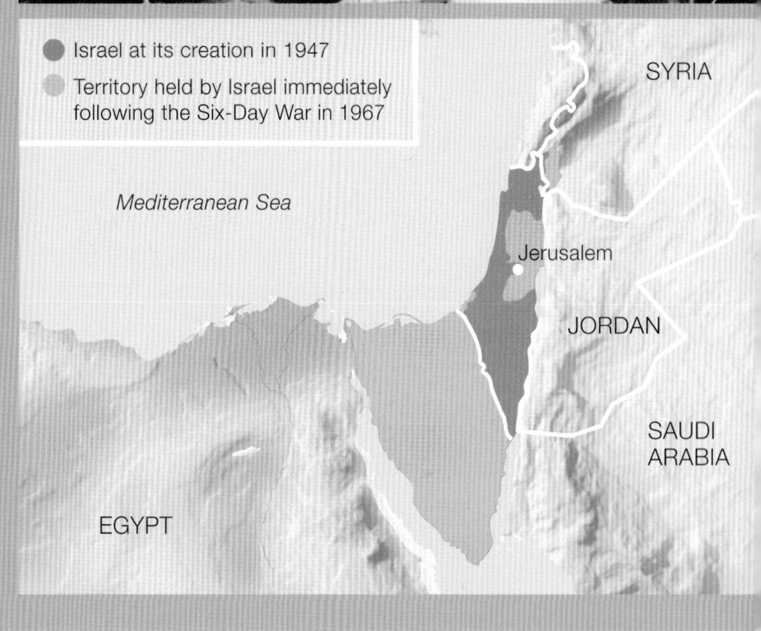

ISRAEL'S WARS 1948–PRESENT

On 6 October 1973, Egypt and Syria attacked Israel in unison, taking the nation by surprise on the Jewish holiday of the High Holy Day of Yom Kippur. With superior numbers and force, Egypt broke through the Bar Lev Line of Israeli fortifications along the Suez Canal and advanced into the country while Syria once again attacked the Golan Heights in the north. Despite being outnumbered on both fronts – Syrian forces outnumbered Israeli forces by eight to one – Israel once again struck back to defend its territory. Within four days after the initial attacks, Israel reclaimed its holdings in the Golan Heights. Another four days later, on 14 October, Israel defeated Egypt at the Battle of Sinai. Israeli forces more or less surrounded the Egyptian Third Army, rendering their superior numbers ineffective. This was the last major campaign of Egypt against Israel. Egypt agreed to a ceasefire on 18 January 1974, and signed the Camp David Accords five years later – a peace treaty that would bring greater stability to interaction between these two nations.

ABOVE Fortifications along the Bar Lev Line.

THE HOLY CITY

Jerusalem has been inhabited for thousands of years. After King David conquered the city in 996 BCE, he established its first Jewish kingdom there. The position of Jerusalem in the Bible and in the events crucial to the formation of all three Abrahamic religions – Judaism, Christianity and Islam – has made the city the focus of much attention and an object of desire for neighbouring kingdoms. In its history, the city has belonged to the Egyptians, the Assyrians, the Babylonians, the Persians, the Umayyads, the crusaders, the Ottomans and even Great Britain. It remains one of the most contested locales in all of Eurasia.

MORE WAR FOR ISRAEL

Despite Egypt's acceptance of peace, Israel was not finished with fighting. Israel bombed Beirut on 5 June 1982, and did not withdraw until 1985. Two years later, in 1987, the violent Palestinian riots, known as Intifada, began over control of the Gaza Strip and the West Bank. The Intifada lasted until the peace agreement of 1993, but this agreement did not settle the underlying disputes, and another Intifada began in 2000. Terrorist activity punctuated the next decade, as Palestinians sought to stake their claim to the West Bank, while Israelis moved into the region, establishing settlements. Mahmoud Abbas, the Palestinian president, urged the United Nations to recognize Palestine as an independent state in 2011, but was unsuccessful, in part because of opposition from Israel's ally – the United States. Fighting again broke out in 2012 over control of Gaza and the West Bank. The conflict continues and a peaceable solution may take many years to realize.

TOP Egyptian forces cross the Suez Canal during the Yom Kippur War.

ABOVE Palestinian leader, Yasser Arafat, in 1999.

AFGHANISTAN WAR 2001–PRESENT

TO THE HILLS ONCE MORE

FOLLOWING THE ATTACKS OF 11 SEPTEMBER 2001, A COALITION INCLUDING THE UNITED STATES, AUSTRALIA AND GREAT BRITAIN WENT TO WAR WITH AFGHANISTAN, FORMING AN ALLIANCE WITH THE UNITED FRONT, OR NORTHERN ALLIANCE, OF AFGHANISTAN.

ABOVE The mountainous terrain of Afghanistan provides ample hiding places for guerrilla fighters.

BELOW An Afghan member of the Mujahideen, here with a Soviet rocket launcher.

The objective was to defeat and dismantle the Taliban forces who had controlled Afghanistan since 1996 and who harboured the terrorist group, al-Qaeda, responsible for the September 11 attacks. The war began on 7 October 2001, and has lasted more than a decade. At the time of this writing, the war continues, making it America's longest-ever war. Afghanistan, the home of many epic battles throughout history, has been a crucial region connecting China, India and the Middle East. Many great nations and leaders have met defeat in its rocky hills, including Britain, but the United States and Britain decided the need was great enough to head once more into this tricky terrain.

DECEPTIVE SUCCESSES

The initial onslaughts of the war were very successful for the US and its allies. The assault – named Operation Enduring Freedom – consisted of four separate but coordinated attacks carried out on critical centres of Taliban and al-Qaeda control: two in the north – one on Kabul, the capital of Afghanistan, and one on Kandahar, the birthplace of the Taliban. With the help of Afghan forces opposing the Taliban, the main initial targets had been taken by 7 December, an important date in American history as it is the anniversary of the attack on Pearl Harbor in 1941. Fighting in Tora Bora, al-Qaeda's main territory, came to a successful close a week later. Things looked positive for the US and its allies, and they continued to have success, defeating the Taliban and al-Qaeda again in Operation Anaconda a few months later in March 2002. However, these early successes were just the beginning of a protracted struggle in the region that would continue for more than a decade.

LEFT Osama bin Laden stencil graffiti in Bucharest street, Romania.

TOP US Marines in Operation Enduring Freedom.

ABOVE Though the use of the horse in battle has largely faded into the past, American servicemen successfully used horses as means of transport during Operation Enduring Freedom; they provided the reliability and flexibility required on the roadless, rocky terrain of Afghanistan.

TIMELINE: OPERATION ENDURING FREEDOM AND OPERATION ANACONDA

19–20 October 2011	US troops raid Kandahar
21 October– 14 November	Battle on Shamali Plains
7 November	Battle in Darya Suf Valley
10 November	Victory at Mazar-e-Sharif
11 November	Victory at Taloqan
13–23 November	Battle for Khanabad
14 November	Capture of Kabul
16 November	Fighting begins near Kandahar
23 November	Kunduz surrenders without fighting
7 December	Kandahar surrenders; Taliban flees
Mid-December	Battle of Tora Bora
2–19 March 2002	Operation Anaconda at Shahi Kowt

STAYING TO BUILD

Despite the initial successes of coalition forces, the mastermind of 9/11, Osama bin Laden, escaped capture. Taliban and al-Qaeda forces fled to neighbouring Pakistan, where they regrouped and began a new offensive of guerrilla warfare. The Western powers who had led the offensive stayed in Afghanistan to rebuild the country and oversee the creation of a successful democratic nation. However, this proved more difficult than many expected. The country was damaged not only physically, but also in its mentality towards governance. No stable government had existed for years, and the Western nations had to combat many cultural norms in Afghanistan that were completely alien to the US and Europe.

The guerrilla warfare of al-Qaeda and the Taliban was extremely difficult to combat. Using improvised explosive devices (IEDs) and suicide-attack tactics, guerrilla fighters could not be beaten with conventional military tactics. In the first year of his presidency, Barack Obama sent an additional 33,000 troops to Afghanistan, accompanying an additional 32,000 NATO troops. This surge was intended to put an end to the resistance there, and was coupled with targeted attacks on al-Qaeda leaders. A team of Navy Seals were successful in taking out Osama bin Laden on 2 May 2011. However, despite these further successes, the violence continues in Afghanistan, and lasting peace and stable governance still seem a long way off. The best way to end the engagements in Afghanistan is still the subject of much debate.

WAR IN IRAQ 2003–2011

END OF A DICTATORSHIP

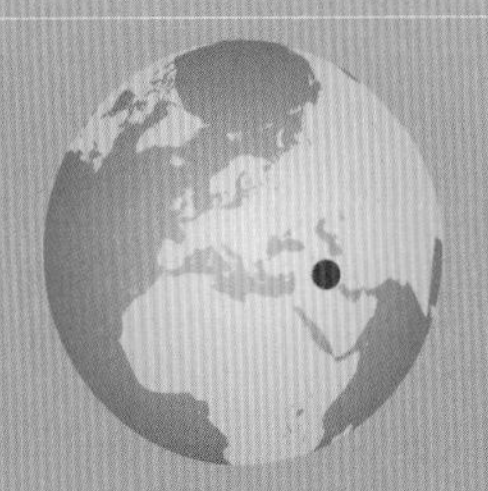

ON 20 MARCH 2003, AMERICAN AND BRITISH FORCES INVADED IRAQ WITH THE AIM OF TOPPLING THE DICTATORIAL GOVERNMENT OF SADDAM HUSSEIN, WHO HAD RULED IRAQ SINCE 1979.

Saddam Hussein was guilty of several crimes against his own people as well as his neighbours, invading Iran in 1980 and Kuwait in 1991, and repressing his own citizens, many of whom were Shia. He openly criticized Israel and Western nations. Two alleged crimes, however, tipped the scales and sparked the invasion of Iraq in 2003. The first was that Saddam was harbouring terrorists of al-Qaeda, who had been responsible for the September 11 attacks on America; the second was that Saddam Hussein had managed to acquire weapons of mass destruction, with which he would have been capable of even greater atrocities. Based on this justification, President George Bush and UK Prime Minister Tony Blair decided to invade, though the supposed source of information regarding these weapons of mass destruction is still the matter of some controversy – none were ever found.

LEFT Saddam Hussein held office in Iraq from 1979 to 2003.

BELOW High columns of smoke rise from burning oil wells in Baghdad, set alight to deter air strikes in April 2003.

OPERATION IRAQI FREEDOM

Following the initial invasion in March, the US and Britain launched their 'Shock and Awe' campaign. Designed to be the most impressive display of targeted military might to date, the campaign was supposed to cause the greatest damage to the enemy politically and militarily with minimal civilian casualties. It was hoped that the tactics would be so impressive they would inspire fear and instant capitulation. Baghdad and Basra fell on 9 April. Kirkuk, Mosul and Tikrit fell by 14 April. Only about 150 American and British casualties were reported during this initial phase of the war. President George Bush declared the mission accomplished on 1 May, but the fighting was far from over.

As in Afghanistan, where initial military successes were followed by difficulties in rebuilding a broken state, the

ABOVE Black Hawk helicopters move in during Operation Iraqi Freedom.

RIGHT The destructive force of modern weaponry creates chaos on the ground.

BELOW RIGHT Map showing Kurdish areas in Iraq. Saddam Hussein launched genocidal campaigns against the Kurds.

US and British forces ran into trouble when it came to helping establish a new democratic government in Iraq. Severely fractious relations between different ethnic groups within Iraq did not cease, but actually increased upon the removal of Saddam from power. These made it difficult to establish a strong new government. Sentiment towards American troops also began to change as they became guilty of more and more crimes in Iraq. Torture, rape and even murder at the prison of Abu Ghraib caused international scandal, though many of the American perpetrators escaped without punishment. These actions instigated further resentment not just from Iraqis, but from much of the Middle East and indeed the world. Crimes of US private contractors, affiliated with an American company then known as Blackwater, also added to the list of wrongs committed by Western forces against the Iraqis.

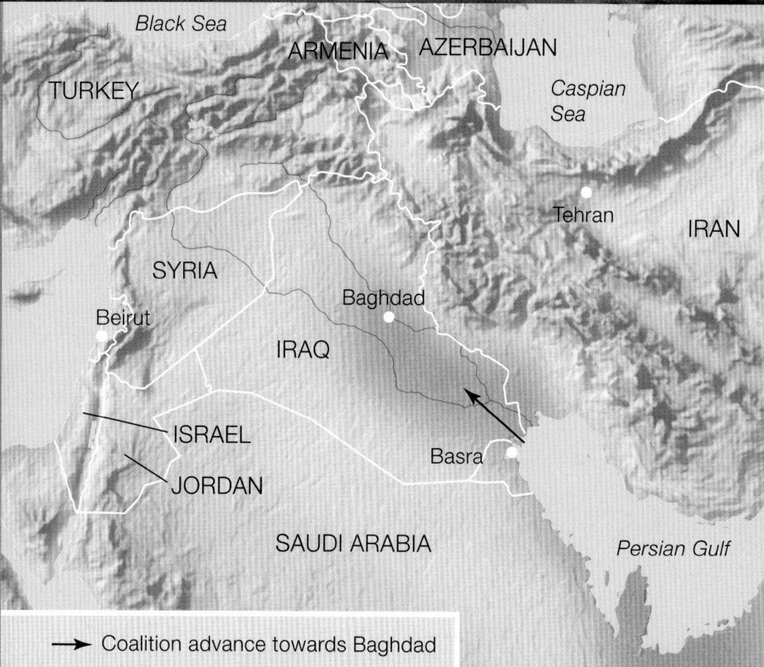

ABOVE The Coalition forces advanced from the Persian Gulf towards Baghdad during Operation Iraqi Freedom.

ABOVE A US Army Humvee burns in Baghdad in 2006 after being blown up by a car bomb.

The initial successes were easily forgotten in the quagmire that followed. Sunni and Shia groups contended in guerrilla warfare, and fighting continued with no clear end in sight. In 2007, President Bush sent in another 21,000 troops in a 'surge' to try to bring an end to the fighting. However, when President Obama took office in 2009, he made a commitment to withdraw from Iraq. The last American troops were brought out in December 2011. More than 4,000 US soldiers (not including contractors) and over 100,000 Iraqis had died in the war. The war had cost 3.2 trillion dollars, and no weapons of mass destruction were ever found.

ARAB SPRING 2011–PRESENT

THE GROWTH OF FREEDOM

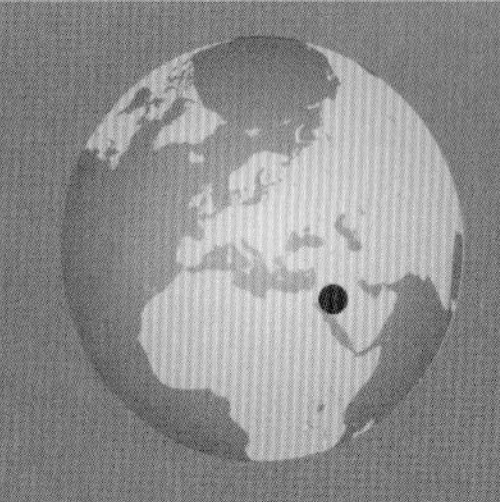

BY 2011, NORTH AFRICA WAS RIPE FOR CHANGE. IN JANUARY 2011, PROTESTERS IN TUNISIA SUCCESSFULLY FORCED THEIR PRESIDENT, ZINE AL-ABIDINE BEN ALI, TO STEP DOWN AND FLEE THE COUNTRY.

Ben Ali has since been sentenced in absentia for drug trafficking, violence and murder. The popular uprising in Tunisia sparked revolutions across North Africa and the Middle East in what is known as the 'Arab Spring'.

INSPIRING SUCCESS

Protests were already under way in Egypt when Tunisia successfully ousted their president. Having started in December 2010, the protesters took encouragement from the successes in Tunisia. The protests escalated in scale and intensity until President Hosni Mubarak was ousted in mid-February. Protests erupted across the region in Libya, Yemen, Bahrain and Syria. Relying heavily on the Internet and social media, protesters spread ideas and tactics quickly across the Arab world. These new technologies of communication also facilitated large-scale organization, allowing protesters to overwhelm the forces of the governments they sought to topple.

ABOVE Thousands take to the streets in Al-Bayda, Libya, in July 2011.

SPRING FROST

The relatively swift successes of Tunisia, Egypt and Libya did not translate everywhere in the Arab world. In Yemen, for example, a state of emergency was declared in March 2011, when protests turned violent and fatal after President Ali Abdullah Saleh failed to keep his promise of not returning for re-election. Protesters began organizing into a full armed rebellion, and Saleh himself was injured in a rocket attack in June 2011. Although Saleh formally stepped down in February 2012, he passed power on to his vice president, Hadi, who was the only candidate on the ballot in the new elections. Tensions continue in Yemen.

In Syria, protests met violent and deadly responses almost immediately after beginning in January 2011, when the people rose up against President Bashar al-Assad. The Assad regime was criticized internationally for human rights violations, and harsh, strict rule of its people. Though foreign journalists were expelled from the country, local protesters used phones, cameras and social media to broadcast the revolution to the rest of the world. By late 2012, the protests had escalated to the point of civil war in Syria.

ABOVE Protests spread throughout the Arab world with varying degrees of success. Here, protesters gather in Yemen.

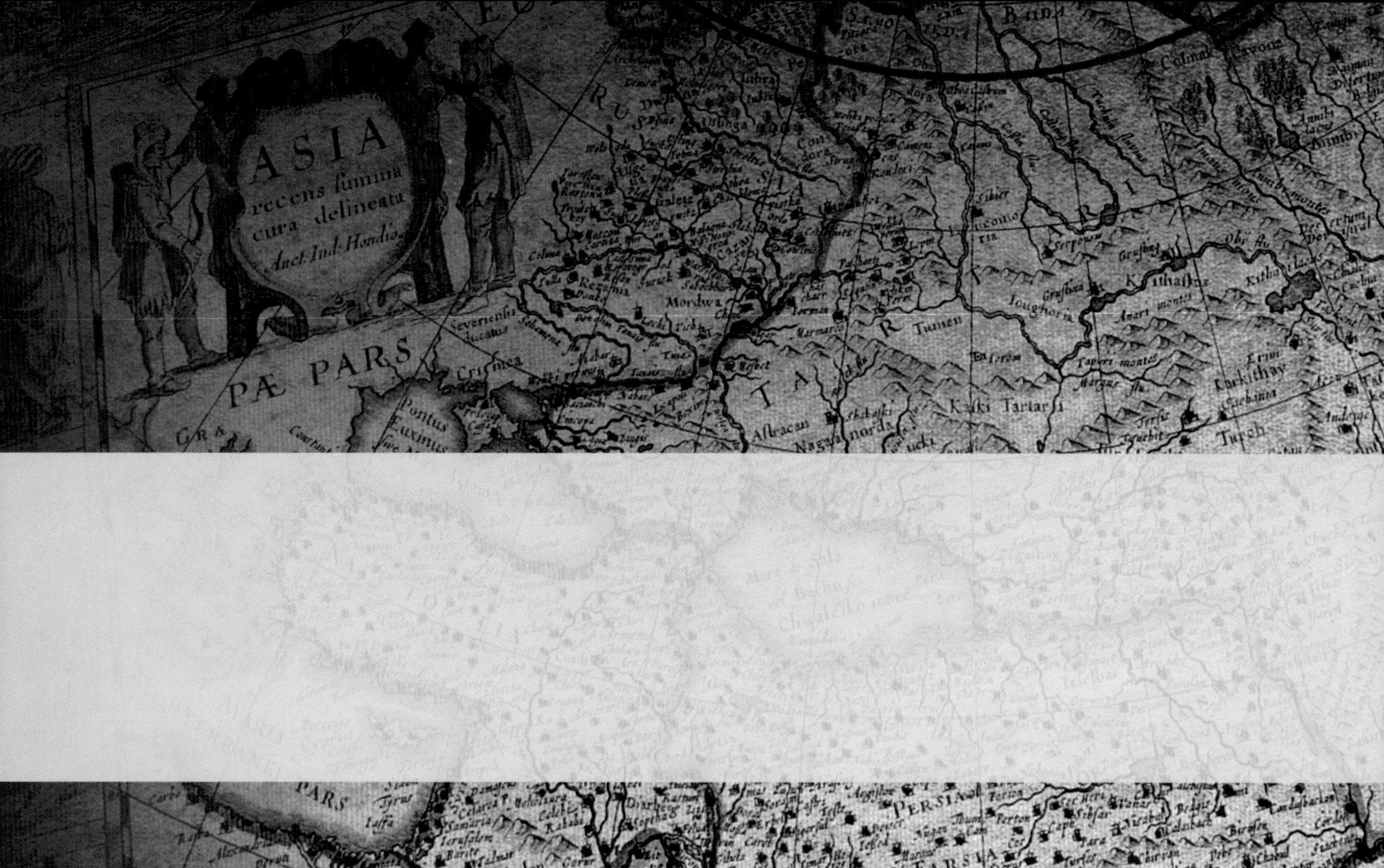
ASIA
recens summa
cura delineata
Auct: Iud: Hondio
PÆ PARS
Crimea
Pontus
Euxinus
Mordwa
Tumen
Kaki Tartari

PERSIA
FARSA
ARABIA DESERTA
Caldea
AYAMAN
olim
ARABIA
FELIX
MARE
ARABICUM
et INDICUM
AFRI
Aden
Zocotohora
OCEANUS
PARS
CÆ
ORIEN
Magadoxa

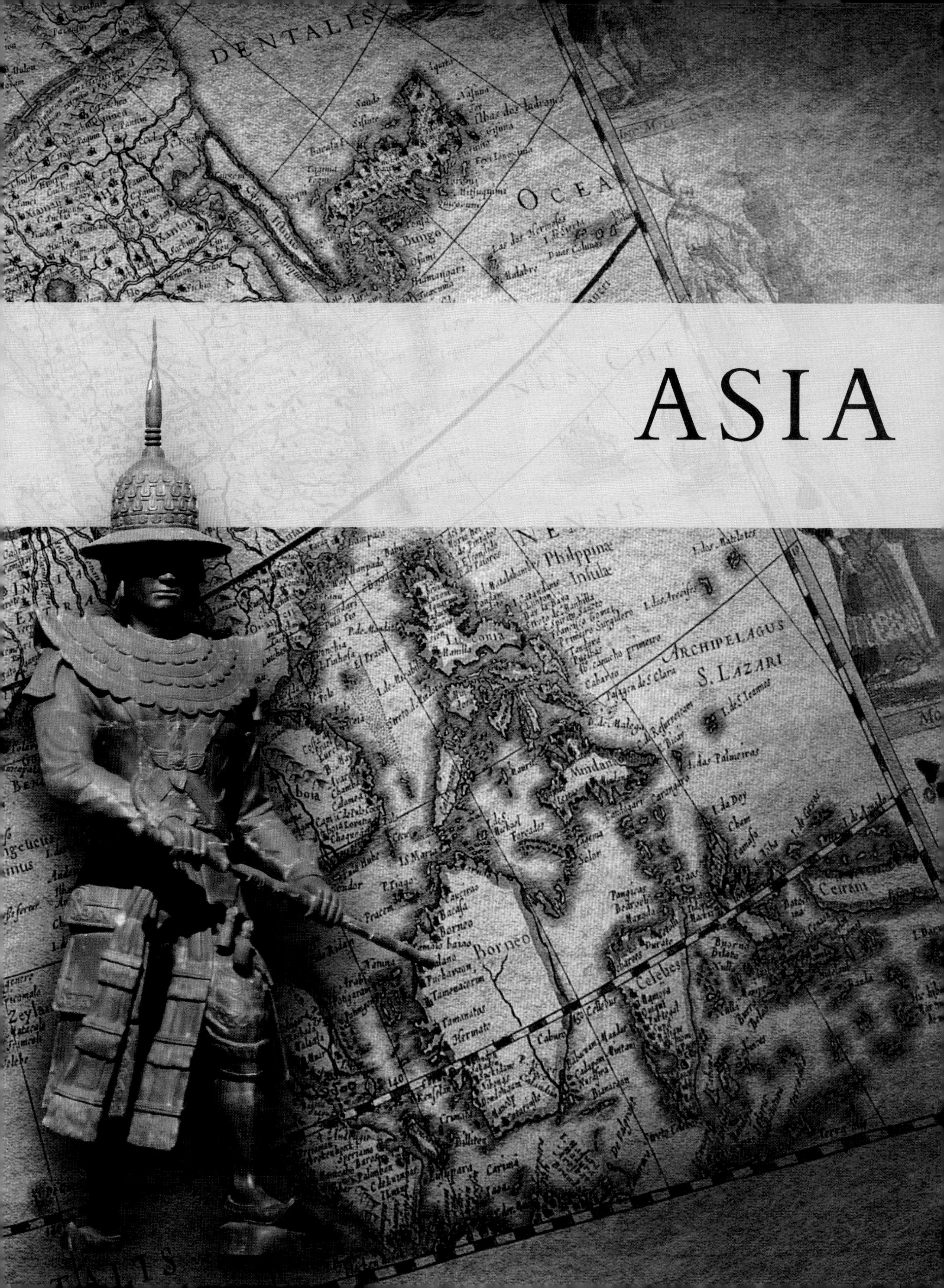
DENTALIS
Philippinæ Insulæ
ARCHIPELAGUS
S. LAZARI
Borneo
Celebes
Ceiram
Bungo

ASIA

SPRING AND AUTUMN PERIOD 771–476 BCE

THE CHRONICLES OF LU

THE SPRING AND AUTUMN PERIOD IN CHINESE HISTORY REFERS TO THE PERIOD BETWEEN 771 AND 476 BCE IN THE LANDS AROUND THE YELLOW RIVER BASIN. IT TAKES ITS NAME FROM THE *SPRING AND AUTUMN ANNALS*, A CHRONICLE COMPILED IN THE STATE OF LU.

ABOVE This elaborate bronze tripod, or *ding*, dates to the Spring and Autumn Period. It shows the high level of craftsmanship of the era.

Much of what we know about this time period comes from this central document. The beginning of the Spring and Autumn Period roughly corresponds to the beginning of the Eastern Zhou (770–256 BCE), when the capital of the Zhou Dynasty was moved to Luoyang by Emperor Pingwang.

The Zhou Dynasty controlled only a small territory and force around Luoyang itself; its feudal vassals exercised real power and control, despite the technical overlordship of the Zhou. These vassal states contended both with foreign powers and with each other, each vying for power in an elaborate dance between the various states. The constant fighting of the period resulted in significant advances in military technology and strategy, with the development of iron weaponry and crossbows, and the transition from chariots to mounted warriors.

THE TIDES OF BATTLE

Dominance shifted back and forth among the city-states of China during the Spring and Autumn Period. Four main powers, however, emerged from the 170 or so city-states under the Zhou Dynasty. These were the Qi, Qin, Jin and Chu.

One of the largest battles fought during the Spring and Autumn Period was the Battle of Chengpu in 632 BCE. The state of Chu had been pushing northwards after the death of Huangong (r. 685–643 BCE), a Qi leader who had kept the Chu neighbours in check. But despite the apparent opportunity in the north, opposition came not so much from the Qi as from the Jin.

LEFT Intricate bronze work from a royal tomb of the state of Chu.

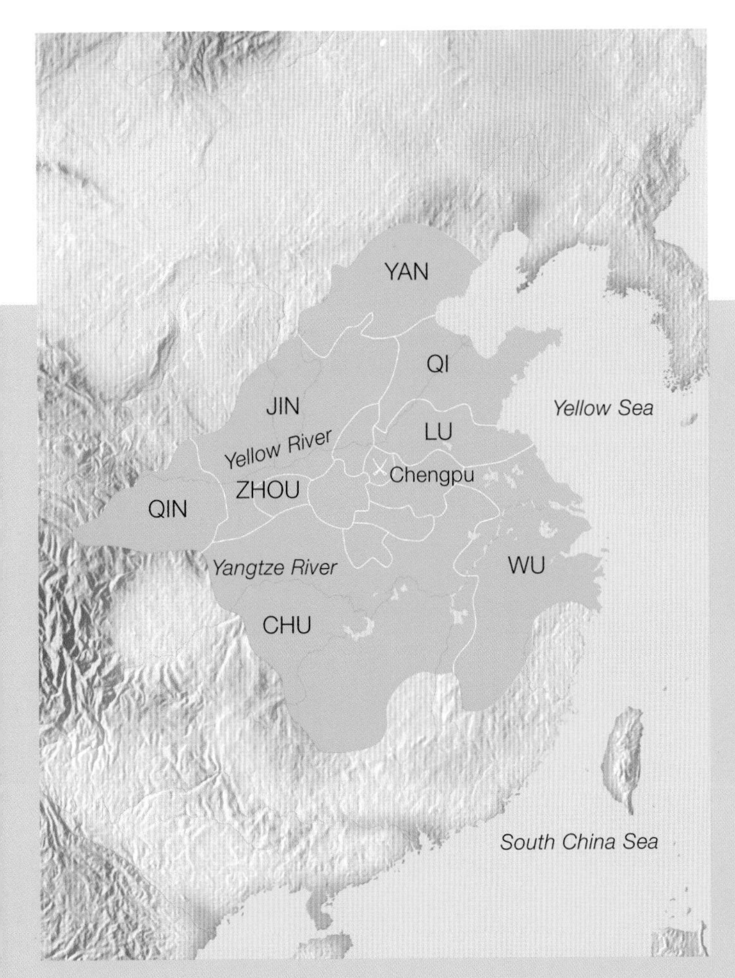

LEFT A number of small states all warred with one another during the Spring and Autumn period. Boundaries frequently shifted, so any map of the period is only a rough approximation.

Under the direction of General Wen, the Jin met the Chu army at Chengpu. Approximately 40,000 men filled the ranks of each camp, and the battle is known for its use of chariots. The armies were divided into three primary divisions, comprised of a central force with two wings. The left wing of the Jin forces quickly took out the weak right wing of the Chu. They pressed against the Chu central force, keeping it from turning against the Jin centre or the Jin right wing. Meanwhile, the Jin right wing feigned retreat and broke the ranks of the Chu left wing. This left the Chu centre force pinned in from three sides. Victory fell to the hands of the Jin.

ARMOURED VEHICLES

The chariots used during this time were heavy, armoured vehicles, typically carrying three men: a driver and two warriors. One warrior would have wielded a bow for longer-range targets, while the other would have commanded a halberd for direct clashes. The chariots were strong and fast, providing a higher vantage point from which to view the battle and effectively deploy formations. They were also effective in carrying banners and flags to organize the troops on the ground.

The Battle of Chengpu gave Jin the upper hand in China until the death of Duke Wen in 628 BCE, at which point power began to shift back to the Chu. The Chu defeated the Jin at the Battle of Mi in 598 BCE, but the balance would continue to swing to and fro as the states continuously vied for power. None, however, would achieve lasting dominance during the Spring and Autumn Period.

LEFT This *zun*, or wine vessel, dates to the early Spring and Autumn Period. It was excavated in Henan Province in 1956.

ABOVE Polearms were principle weapons in early Chinese warfare and developed into a variety of forms in later periods.

WARRING STATES CHINA 475–221 BCE

AN ERA OF WAR

THE CONTESTS FOR POWER THAT CHARACTERIZED THE SPRING AND AUTUMN PERIOD ONLY ESCALATED IN THE TIME THAT FOLLOWED. KNOWN AS THE 'WARRING STATES PERIOD', THIS ERA OF CHINESE HISTORY WAS, AS ITS NAME WOULD SUGGEST, ONE OF INTENSE CONFLICT.

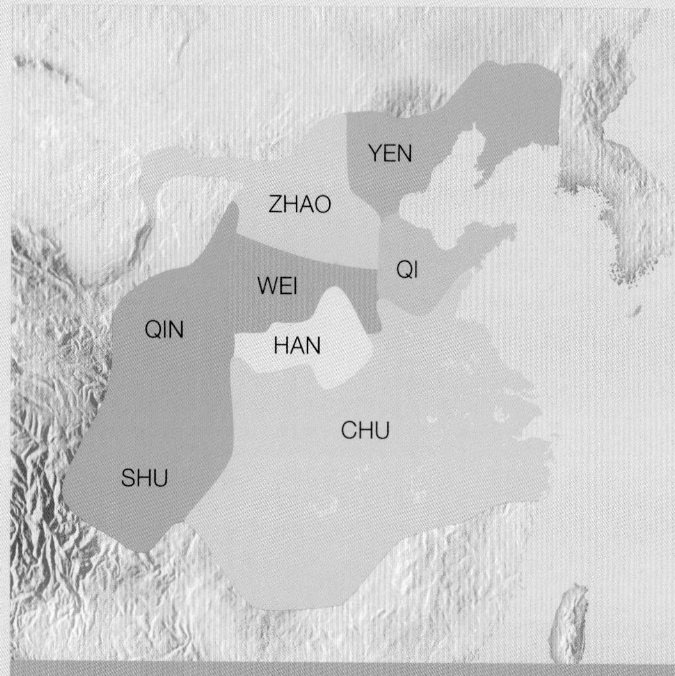

ABOVE This map shows the different states of China during the Warring States Period.

The Zhou continued to exercise nominal power, but in reality had no control over the territories or peoples of the various states that comprised the region. The state of Jin fragmented into three states in 453 BCE. Local rulers began to refer to themselves as *Wang*, or 'King', a title before only given to the emperor. Instead of a contest between four major states, the Warring States Period saw the contest for power play out among seven different states: Wei, Zhao, Han, Chu, Qi, Qin and Yan.

THE STRUGGLES AND FRUITS OF WAR

The nature of combat had changed considerably by the end of the Spring and Autumn Period, and would continue to change throughout the Warring States Period. Mounted warriors came to replace the heavy chariots of old. Infantry swelled to enormous sizes, expanding from armies of tens of thousands of highly trained soldiers to armies of hundreds of thousands, mixing trained warriors with armed peasants. Crossbows came into heavy use, including early versions of the repeating crossbow, which would later be refined during the Three Kingdoms Period. The construction of defences also saw new innovations, including the use of long walls to protect large territories and advances in fortress building. The era also produced great works of art and scholarship. The works of Confucius, who lived during the late Spring and Autumn Period, became widely popular, as well as the *Art of War*, written by Sunzi during the early Warring States Period (fifth century BCE).

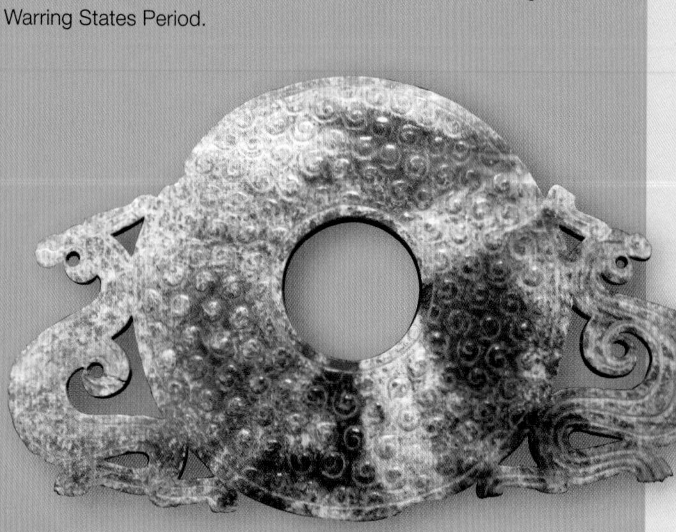

LEFT Jade *bi* depicting two dragons. The bi was a ceremonial object associated with heaven.

ABOVE Statue of Confucius, whose philosophies became popular during the Warring States Period.

CONSTANT FIGHTING

The period is characterized by an endless shifting of power back and forth among the states in wave after wave of bloodshed. The Qi invaded Yan in 380 BCE, but Yan gathered the support of neighbours to expel them without a fight; but Yan then invaded Qi in 373 along with Wei and Lu. While the Wei were taking apart the Zhao and besieging their capital, the Qi strategist, Sun Bin, called for an attack on the capital of Wei. Wei forces withdrew from attacking Zhao to protect their own capital, but this only made them easy targets along the road between states. Taking advantage of a civil war that broke out in Yan in 318 BCE, the Qi invaded again, this time nearly conquering the whole state; but they were at length driven out, in large part because of their mistreatment of the people of Yan. The great Confucian scholar, Mencius, criticized Qi for this transgression. Yan then banded with neighbouring states, and under the direction of King Zhao of Yan, nearly conquered Qi; but the Yan expedition faltered on the death of Zhao and the Yan forces were driven out. There was no end to the tide of war.

ABOVE An elaborate bronze mirror dating from the Warring States Period.

RIGHT Iron swords (bottom) began to replace bronze swords (top two) during the Warring States Period.

LEFT A later portrait of Confucius. The tradition of Confucius was continued by such great scholars as Mencius and Xunzi.

CHANDRAGUPTA MAURYA 321–297 BCE

A UNIFIED INDIA

WHEN ALEXANDER THE GREAT REACHED THE INDIAN SUBCONTINENT TOWARDS THE END OF THE FOURTH CENTURY BCE, HE FOUND IT INHABITED AND RULED BY MANY SMALL KINGDOMS. THAT WOULD CHANGE WITH CHANDRAGUPTA.

Born the son of a Mauryan chieftain, Chandragupta was left fatherless at a young age and became a cowherd. He was eventually bought by a Brahman named Kautilya. Chandragupta would soon see a change in his fortune. Kautilya recognized Chandragupta's intelligence and sent him to be trained in strategy in Taxila in modern-day Pakistan. Chandragupta met Alexander the Great, and must have taken inspiration from the man. After Alexander's death in 323 BCE, Chandragupta set about assembling an army of mercenaries, reconquering lands lost to Alexander, and establishing a single, unified government unlike any India had seen previously.

ABOVE This painting depicts a scene from the Sanskrit epic, the *Mahabharata*. Here, Arjuna and Bhishma attack each other in their chariots. The epic is a foundation of Indian culture and society.

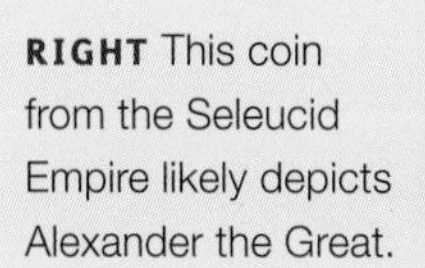

RIGHT This coin from the Seleucid Empire likely depicts Alexander the Great.

LEFT Sayings of Ashoka the Great are recorded on the Pillars of Ashoka. A fragment of the Sixth Pillar is shown here.

ABOVE Chandragupta Maurya supposedly starved himself to death as an ascetic in this cave after abdicating the throne.

A WORTHY STRATEGIST

Chandragupta did not simply benefit from the disorganized and mutinous state of the Macedonian army. He had some serious challenges to overcome, as well as experienced and capable generals to defeat. While few sources survive, it seems that Seleucus, who succeeded Alexander, attempted to reclaim what had been won by Chandragupta. Chandragupta appears to have defeated Seleucus handily, maintaining control of Punjab, and even extending his dominion westwards and northwards through Sindh, Kandahar and Kabul.

After controlling the Greeks, Chandragupta had to contend with the Nanda Dynasty of the Magadha kingdom. We have few sources of the encounter, and the scale of the battle is likely exaggerated, with the Nanda army estimated at 200,000, including 2,000 chariots, 3,000 elephants and 20,000 cavalry. Chandragupta defeated Bhaddasala, the Nanda commander, and went on subdue the whole Magadha kingdom. He then turned his attention south.

EMPIRE

Chandragupta pushed his forces south, conquering almost all of the Indian subcontinent before his death. He created the first national army, with a force recorded at approximately 600,000 strong. To support this force, he also established the first centralized administration system for an Indian government. He also appears to have created one of the first-known espionage forces. Chandragupta's mentor, Kautilya (also known as Chanakya) assisted the young general in creating an empire and is famous for having written the *Arthashastra*, a treatise on economics and politics still studied today.

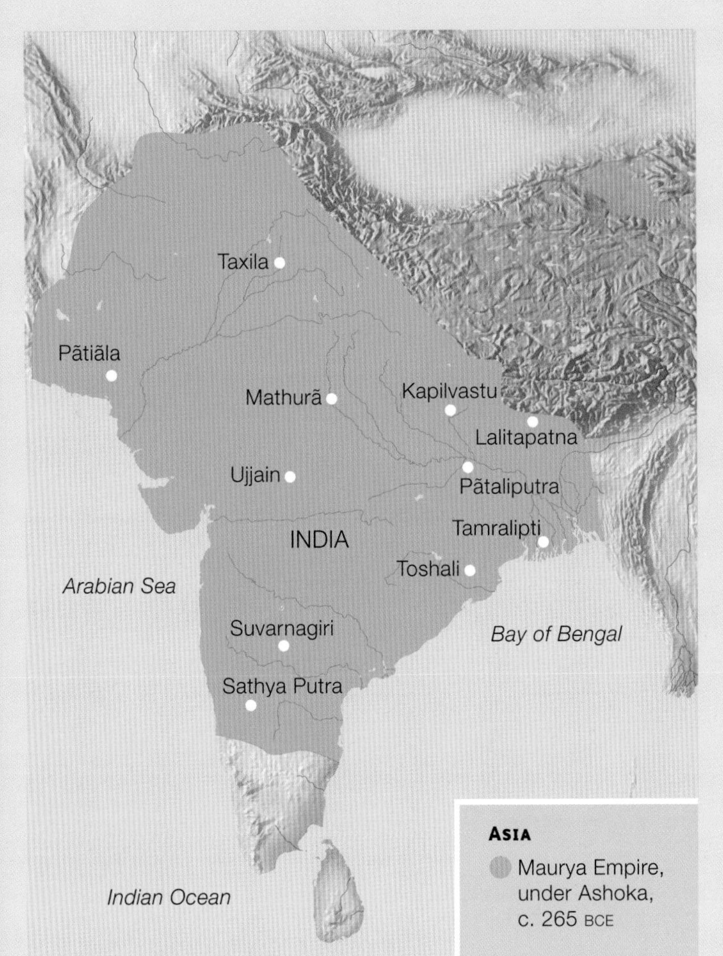

LEFT At its height, the Mauryan Empire covered a vast territory, extending from modern-day Afghanistan and Pakistan to almost the southern tip of the Indian subcontinent.

ELEPHANTS: NATURE'S WAR ENGINES

BEAST OF BATTLE

ABOVE An image by Henri-Paul Motte depicting Hannibal crossing the River Rhone with his elephants on large rafts.

As the largest land animal on earth, properly trained elephants could present a devastating force on the battlefield. Aggressive by nature, elephants can run fast, charge head on and use their long tusks to lethal effect. Their thick hides make them difficult to take down, and small wounds would only incite an elephant to inflict greater damage.

An artefact from Mesopotamia more than 4,000 years old suggests that people started riding and using elephants around the same time as they started using horses. While the horse became an important component of warfare most of the world over, the elephant was a far more powerful weapon in itself. It only took 15 war elephants to terrify Alexander the Great at the Battle

IT ONLY TOOK 15 WAR ELEPHANTS TO TERRIFY ALEXANDER THE GREAT AT THE BATTLE OF GAUGAMELA, AND HANNIBAL ONLY NEEDED 24 TO THREATEN ROME.

ABOVE This work by an anonymous Dutch painter shows the power of an elephant on the battlefield, with a large war tower built upon its back.

of Gaugamela, and Hannibal only needed 24 to threaten Rome. But elephants are much less adaptable than horses, and require significant attention, as well as large quantities of food. The amount of fodder necessary to sustain a large force of war elephants is astonishing, limiting the use of war elephants to certain regions. In India and Southeast Asia, the elephant occupies a revered position as one of the great engines of war that helped build and shape the world as we know it today. In Africa, use of elephants was more limited; Egyptians even hunted their elephants to extinction before using them in battle.

ABOVE Alexander the Great first discovered the use of elephants in war at the Battle of Gaugamela. Despite his fear of the beasts, fate was on his side during the battle.

BELOW This gruesome image shows the chaos elephants could wreak on the battlefield, leaving a trail of death and destruction in their wake. Only male elephants could be used in battle, as female elephants will instinctively flee when charged by a male.

BELOW This medieval Latin manuscript from around 1500 depicts an elephant trampling a man. Note the impressive tower on the elephant's back.

QIN DYNASTY CHINA 221–206 BCE

UNIFICATION OF CHINA

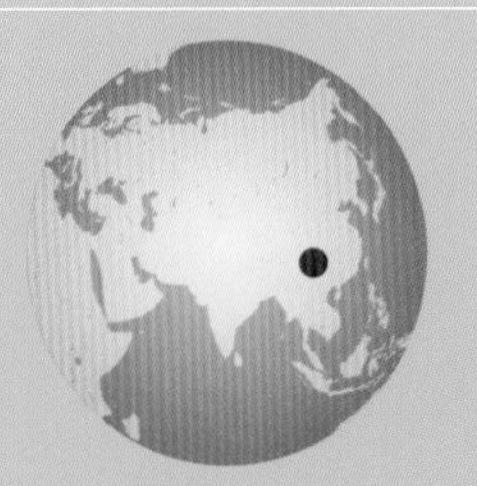

MORE THAN FIVE CENTURIES OF CONFLICT PRECEDED THE RISE OF QIN SHI HUANGDI, THE QIN EMPEROR WHO WOULD UNITE THE VARIOUS STATES OF CHINA, WHICH HAD SPRUNG UP UNDER THE ZHOU DYNASTY.

After centuries of battles, alliances, broken promises and backstabbing, a leader rose up in the state of Qin who would unite the states of China into a single empire in 221 BCE. Though his reign was short, Qin Shi Huangdi effected such great reforms that the results are still visible today. The unification of the various warring states established the first real semblance of 'China' as we know it today, more than 2,000 years later.

In addition to uniting China, 'emperor' Qin Shi Huangdi – who styled himself after the mythical Yellow Emperor, Huangdi – also built the first Great Wall of China, standardized the width of roads and cart axles, introduced a standardized currency and standardized the written language. It was also Qin Shi Huangdi who was entombed with the famous army of terracotta warriors.

LEFT Despite there being thousands of soldiers buried with Qin Shi Huangdi, each one possesses its own unique face.

BELOW Qin Shi Huangdi united the warring states of China into a single empire.

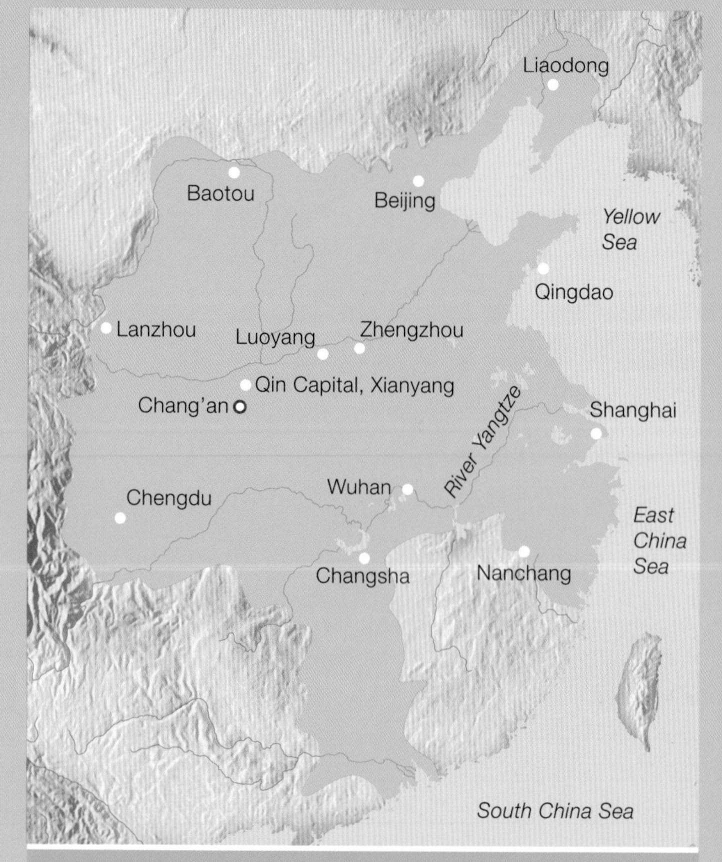

LEGALISM

One of the reasons the Qin were able to be so effective against the other states was the introduction of a concept called 'Legalism' by Shang Yang. The term refers to a cold pragmatism in war, shunning earlier forms of courtesy on the battlefield that were often crippling. It meant taking an advantage when presented with one, even if this seemed 'unfair' to the opponents. Take this one step further, and one begins to look for these particular kinds of advantages, and attack the opponent when he is weak or vulnerable. The adoption of this mentality in war contributed to the popular notion of the Qin as a brutal and ruthless state. While the Qin practice of Legalism earned the kingdom the contempt of its neighbours, it also gave the Qin a necessary advantage to actually unify the warring states. One by one they fell to Qin, Qi being the last to hold its independence.

RIGHT These terracotta warriors would have held spears or pikes. They face west, towards the historic enemies of the Qin.

THE CLAY ARMY

Many people are aware of the famous 'Terracotta Army' near Xi'an in China, but don't always realize the significance of the man for whom the statues were made. Eight thousand warriors accompany Qin Shi Huangdi in his tomb, all of them arranged in formation and facing eastwards into the Chinese interior, where the emperor's greatest enemies lay. Unearthed in 1974, the tomb provides not only a stunning example of the scale and expense of projects undertaken during the Qin Dynasty, but also tells us a great deal about military tactics of the day. We can study the formations, the depiction of armour, how the warriors held their weapons, the stance of the crossbowmen, the horses and chariots – the tomb provides a rare window into the armies of the past. Despite the regularity of the clay soldiers, each has his own face.

BELOW Qin Shi Huangdi unified China. Though various dynasties subsequently ruled the imperial court of China, the Qin legacy of unification lasted more than 2,000 years.

SINO-XIONGNU WARS 206 BCE–89 CE

BARBARIANS ON HORSEBACK

A MYSTERIOUS NOMADIC PEOPLE EMERGED ON THE STEPPES OF MONGOLIA AND CENTRAL ASIA IN THE FIFTH CENTURY BCE. KNOWN AS THE XIONGNU FROM CHINESE SOURCES, NO ONE KNOWS FOR SURE WHO EXACTLY THEY WERE.

There are several theories regarding who the Xiongnu were ethnically and linguistically. Some place them with the Mongols, the Turks, the Tocharians and even the Huns (there is a suggestion that the name 'Xiongnu' is cognate with 'Hun'). As the Xiongnu had no written record of their own, we must rely on the scant Chinese sources, which only present a few poorly transcribed words from the Xiongnu language. We may never know who they were or where they came from, but we know they caused a great deal of trouble for Han Dynasty China, which emerged after the short-lived Qin Dynasty in 206 BCE.

The Xiongnu were a nomadic horse people. Children started riding sheep almost before they could walk, and would learn to shoot simple bows not long after. Trained from such early years to both ride and shoot, the Xiongnu had an instinctive command of both horse and bow. They could mobilize very quickly, and could disappear into the steppes faster than any army could chase them. This made them an exceptionally difficult opponent to face.

BELOW The Great Wall of China was built and expanded to protect the empire's borders from the assaults of nomads and other enemies. Made of rammed earth and brick, the wall is one of the most impressive feats of construction in the medieval world.

ABOVE The Great Wall was begun during the reign of Qin Shi Huangdi but little of that original structure survives. The wall we know today was mostly built during the Ming Dynasty, roughly 1,700 years later.

LEFT This bronze statue shows people of Dian in modern-day Yunnan. Emperor Wu convinced Dian to submit to his power during the Han Dynasty in 109 BCE.

NOMADS UNITED

In 209 BCE, three years before the start of the Han Dynasty, a Xiongnu chieftain's son took the title of *shanyu* (leader) of the Xiongnu and quickly assembled the various tribes together into a single unified force. Perhaps Mao Dun, as the chieftain's son was called, had been inspired by the successes of Qin Shi Huangdi in unifying the various warring states of China. We can only speculate as to his motives, but we know for certain he turned this unified force against the Han only a few years later, taking the Ordos in 200 BCE, and advancing to Taiyuan. Han Emperor Gao opposed Mao Dun, but the Xiongnu's mobile forces were able to surround and trap the Han emperor with a supposed 400,000 mounted warriors. While he escaped with his life, the emperor had to pay tribute to the Xiongnu.

Realizing war with the Xiongnu was a bad idea and one likely to result in defeat, the Han largely sought to appease the Xiongnu. In 133 BCE, however, the Han changed stance and attacked the Xiongnu under the leadership of Emperor Wu. Despite initial failures, Wu persisted in his campaigns. Between 127 and 119 BCE, he effectively drove the Xiongnu north and west away from Han territory, taking the Ordos in 127 under the direction of General Wei Qing. The Han built fortresses and sought the favour of border peoples to aid in the protection of the empire from the nomadic warriors. By 108 BCE, Wu had not just fortified the west, but also conquered Choson in the east, in what is now modern Korea. Though not fully defeated, the Xiongnu split into two branches after a civil war in around 60 BCE and largely faded back into the steppes.

THREE KINGDOMS PERIOD 220–265

LEGENDARY GENERALS

THE THREE KINGDOMS PERIOD IN CHINESE HISTORY IS KNOWN FOR SEVERAL BRILLIANT GENERALS AND THEIR STRATEGIES. THE TALES OF THESE MASTERMINDS IS FAMOUSLY TOLD IN THE CLASSICAL CHINESE NOVEL, *ROMANCE OF THE THREE KINGDOMS*.

The three kingdoms from which this period derives its name were Wei, Shu-Han and Wu. After the Yellow Turban Rebellion of 184 CE, the Han Dynasty lost control and broke apart. The last Han emperor abdicated in 220, and several centuries of warfare and dynastic struggles followed. Six dynasties are known to have competed for power.

Cao Cao led the kingdom of Wei. A fierce general, he had his sights set on conquering all the lands of China. Shu-Han was led by Liu Bei, who was of humbler birth than his rivals and had extremely limited resources; he nonetheless was able to use his brilliant strategies to defend Xu province from Cao Cao in 194 and carve out the Shu-Han kingdom. The southern state of Wu was led by Sun Quan, a young and ambitious leader. While the interplay was already developing in the late second century, the Three Kingdoms were not yet fully formed.

Eventually, Wei conquered Shu-Han in 263, but Wei was overthrown and renamed Jin. The kingdom of Jin conquered Wu in 280. The Jin Dynasty, while presenting a single government once again, was beset by numerous struggles and violent conflicts, spawning the Sixteen Kingdoms in the fourth century. The Jin Dynasty collapsed in 420.

LEFT Though Liu Bei came from humble origins and had limited resources, he made up for any lack of material wealth through his brilliant strategies.

BELOW This painting depicts a scene from the Classical Chinese novel, *Romance of the Three Kingdoms*, which tells the tales of the great generals of the era.

ABOVE The repeating crossbow is said to have been refined and implemented by Zhuge Liang during the Three Kingdoms period. This photograph shows how bolts drop down onto the track from the top magazine, while the lever is used to draw the bowstring.

RED CLIFFS

One of the most famous events of the period – and indeed all of Chinese history – is the Battle of Red Cliffs, a battle likely fought on the southern Yangtze in the winter of 208–209. Sun Quan and Liu Bei joined forces to combat the 220,000 strong force of Cao Cao. Despite the alliance, Sun Quan and Liu Bei were vastly outnumbered. They had a couple of key advantages, however: Cao Cao's men were not accustomed to either the southern weather or to fighting on ships. Cao Cao is said to have lashed his ships together to form more stable fighting platforms. To combat the larger force, however, General Huang Gai feigned surrender, sailing towards Cao Cao's enormous fleet on ships laden with brimstone. At the critical moment, he set fire to the ships, sending the flaming vessels into Cao Cao's bound fleet while escaping overboard into the waters of the Yangtze.

ZHUGE LIANG

One of the most influential strategists of the time was a man named Zhuge Liang, who served Liu Bei. Zhuge Liang was the one responsible for forming the alliance with Sun Quan and Wu. He is also credited with many of the strategies that proved decisive against Cao Cao and in other battles. A learned man, Zhuge Liang is reported to have refined the design of the repeating crossbow and brought it into widespread use.

THE SIX LEGITIMATE DYNASTIES

Wu (222–280)
Eastern Jin (317–420)
Liu Song (420–479)
Southern Qi (479–502)
Liang (502–557)
Chen (557–589)

ABOVE This mask of Cao Cao dates to the Qing Dynasty, illustrating the popularity of the characters from the Three Kingdoms Period in later Chinese culture and society.

ABOVE Guan Yu and Zhang Fei were two of Liu Bei's loyal generals.

GUPTA EMPIRE 320–550

A PROSPEROUS KINGDOM

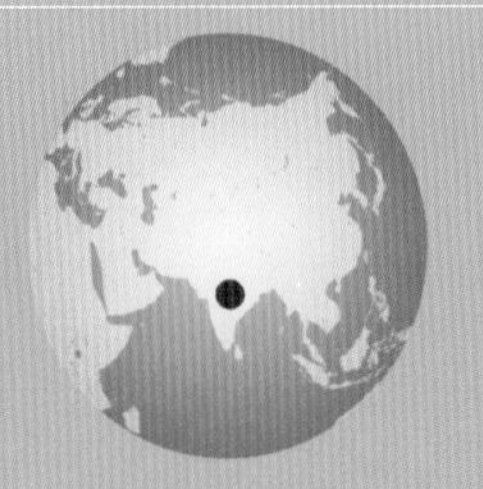

THE GUPTA EMPIRE, FOUNDED BY CHANDRAGUPTA I (R. 320–330) OF THE GUPTA DYNASTY, IS WIDELY REGARDED AS A GOLDEN AGE IN INDIAN HISTORY, A TIME OF GREAT ART, LITERATURE AND SCHOLARSHIP. THE PROSPERITY, HOWEVER, WAS BORN OF CONQUEST.

Chandragupta was the grandson of Sri Gupta, founder of the Gupta Dynasty, based in Magadha. He is not to be confused with the earlier Chandragupta who formed the Mauryan Empire in the fourth century BCE. Chandragupta married Princess Kumaradevi of Licchavi, and received a large territory along with her dowry. Capitalizing on this advantage, Chandragupta set about expanding his dominion and quickly consolidated the various independent states that adjoined his kingdom. He quickly amassed a kingdom spanning a large portion of the Indian subcontinent, and he took the title of *Maharajadhiraja*, 'The King of Kings'.

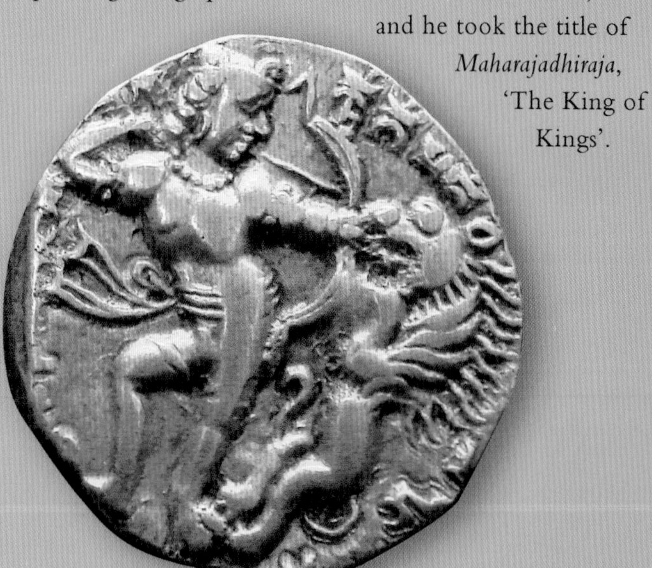

ABOVE Gold coin from the reign of Kumaragupta I (415–455). At the end of his reign, the Gupta Empire became threatened by invasions from the Hephthalites.

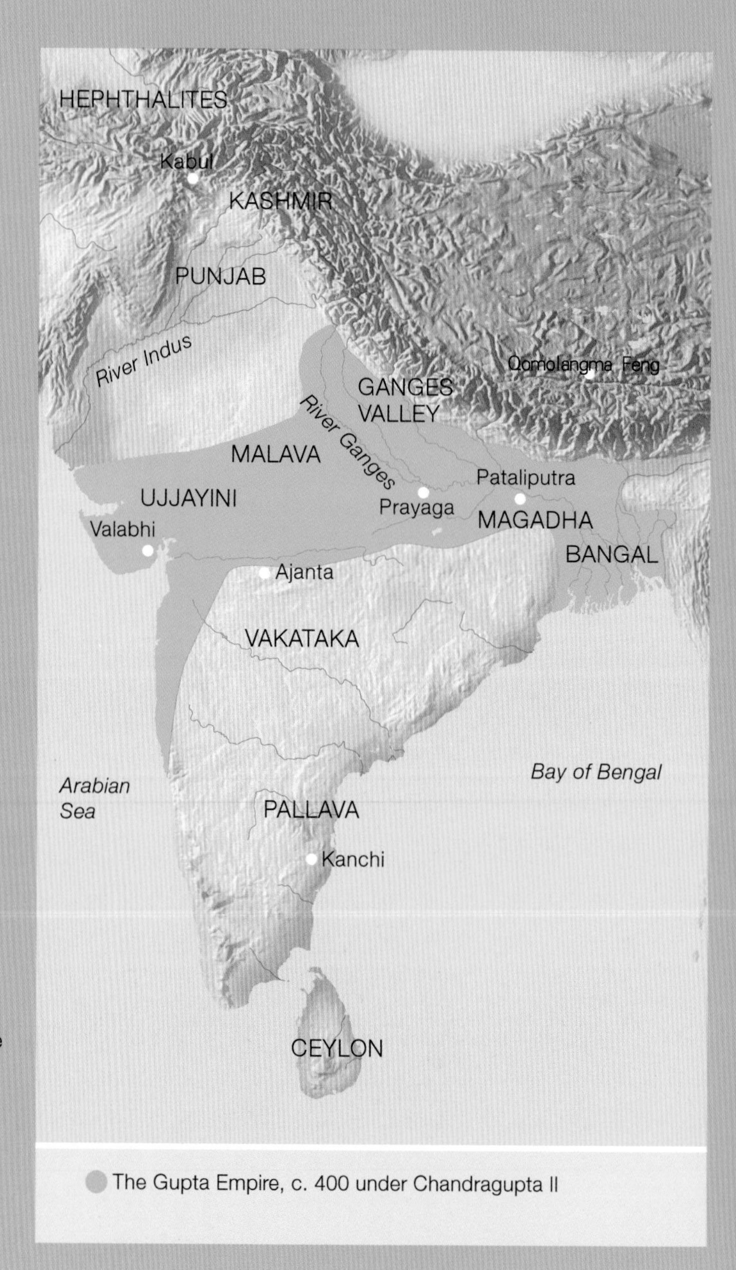

RIGHT The Gupta Empire controlled all of northern India. Art and literature flourished during the rule of the Gupta Dynasty.

ABOVE Terracotta head from northern India around the end of the Gupta Empire in the sixth century.

THE DYNASTY LIVES ON

Around 330, power over the empire passed to Chandragupta's son, Samudragupta, who took up the banner of his father and continued the efforts of expansion and consolidation. Samudragupta would prove an exceptionally able leader, and undertook the empire's greatest expansion. He conquered Ahichchhatra, near present-day Ramnagar, and Padmavati. Samudragupta then pushed southwards with his armies, conquering many kingdoms one after another. Although we know little about where these kingdoms actually lay and what kind of resistance they were able to field, we know of their existence from the Pillars of Ashoka, which bear their names. The Gupta emperor marched across the Deccan Plateau to Kanchipuram, conquering at least 12 different kingdoms. After defeating a king in battle, Samudragupta would take the lord captive, then make him into a vassal, free to return to govern his people, but now with a duty to the overlordship of the Gupta Dynasty.

UNSUSTAINABLE TERRITORY

Samudragupta united much of the Indian subcontinent and conquered parts of the Punjab, Rajasthan and Aryavarta. After some 45–50 years of reign, he died in 380 and was succeeded by his son, Chandragupta II. Chandragupta II was able to expand the empire to the Arabian Sea and is even reported to have defeated the Scythians, although this may be a spurious claim of later historians. A nomadic people, known as the Hephthalites, began to encroach on the territories in the northwest. In 480, they launched a full-scale invasion of the Gupta Empire, weakening it significantly. The empire shrank quickly, effectively disappearing in the sixth century.

BELOW A terracotta relief from the Gupta Empire depicting a scene from the *Ramayana*, one of the central epics in Indian Sanskrit literature.

KOGURYO'S WARS WITH CHINA C.400–668

A FRACTIOUS RELATIONSHIP

THE KINGDOM OF KOGURYO ON THE KOREAN PENINSULA ROSE TO THE HEIGHT OF ITS POWER UNDER KING GWANGGAETO (R. 391–413). GWANGGAETO WAS A REAL KING, BUT ONE WHO ACHIEVED LEGENDARY STATUS ON ACCOUNT OF HIS MILITARY CAMPAIGNS.

After ascending the throne in 391, Gwanggaeto quickly turned his attention to bolstering the armies of the nation and soon launched attacks against their southern neighbour, Baekje. A few years later, Gwanggaeto would focus more and more on the western border and the Manchurians. Gwanggaeto supposedly conquered 64 fortresses and 1,400 towns during his reign. His efforts were continued by his successor, King Jangsu (r. 413–491).

For several centuries, Koguryo contended with the Manchurians and peoples of northern China. It was not until the end of the sixth century that China returned in force and was able to start retaking ground from the Koguryo Kingdom.

ABOVE The tomb of Gwanggaeto the Great, the famous Korean king who ruled Koguryo from 391 to 413.

RIGHT Emperor Taizong of the Tang Dynasty ruled from 626 to 649. Credited with helping found the Tang Dynasty, Taizong is regarded as one of China's great rulers. He ruled well and ushered in a golden age in China.

CHINA ORGANIZES

In 589, China reunited under the Sui Dynasty. The Sui were not fated to last long, but provided an important precursor to the prosperous Tang Dynasty. In 598, Wendi, the first emperor of Sui, launched an expedition against Koguryo. With some 300,000 men and a fleet of ships to support the infantry, Wendi launched the offensive in July. But it rained so heavily during the expedition, that neither the infantry nor the fleet could make much progress, and the Koguryo forces were able to repel the attack. They were safe – for a brief time.

Wendi's son, Yangdi, returned in 612 with an even larger force. Though it is hard not to assume that sources from the time are vastly exaggerated, Yangdi is reported to have taken an army one million strong into Koguryo. Even if grossly exaggerated, the size of the expedition must have been an impressive feat of logistics and organization.

ABOVE The conquest of Korea was completed during the reign of Empress Wu Zetian (r. 690–705). One of few female rulers in Chinese history, Wu Zetian's reign was very successful.

Yangdi attacked the fortress at Liaotung in modern Liaoyang. Despite the siege, the inhabitants fought back with such force and aggression that Yangdi decided to split his forces and send an army to Pyongyang, the capital of Koguryo. General Yu led a force of roughly 300,000, but he never reached the city, for he was diverted and trapped by Koguryo general, Ulchi Mundok, along the way. Relatively few Chinese soldiers escaped the engagement, and Yangdi decided to abandon the ongoing siege. He returned a few years later, and though he was able to reach the capital, he was not able to subdue Koguryo. The battles with Koguryo had weakened the Sui tremendously, and the dynasty collapsed in 618. The Tang rose to take its place, however, and invaded in 645, and again in 647, both times not achieving the success they had hoped. Not until 668 under the leadership of Empress Wuhou did the Tang finally conquer Koguryo. The Tang formed an alliance with the Kingdom of Silla on the southern portion of the Korean Peninsula, and attacked Koguryo.

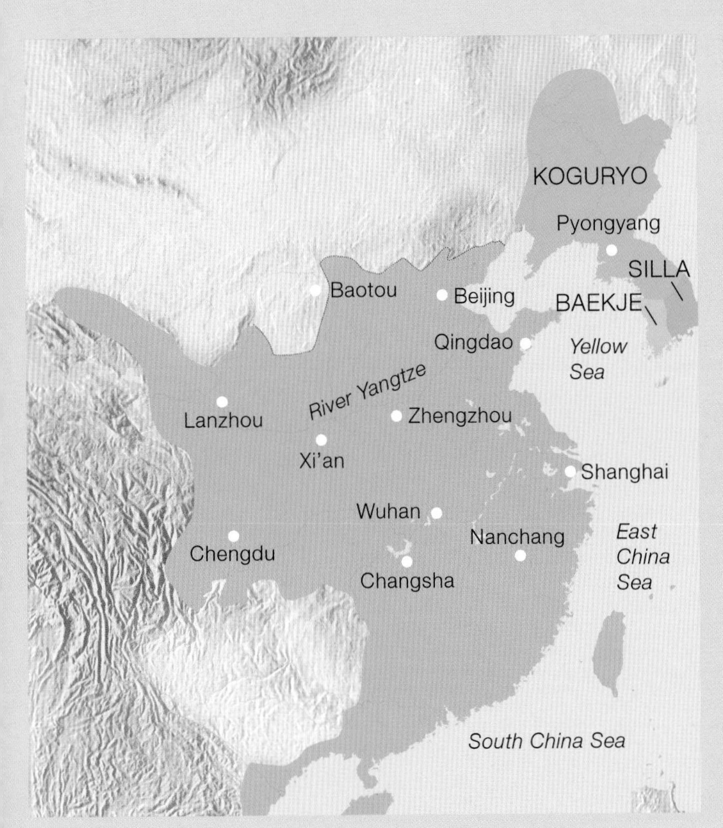

LEFT The short-lived Sui Dynasty reestablished a unified China and laid the groundwork for the prosperous Tang Dynasty, which is still heralded as a golden age of learning and culture. The Sui's wars against their eastern neighbor, Koguryo, were unsuccessful.

HEPHTHALITES AND HUNS 427–453

FURY OF THE STEPPES

FROM THE XIONGNU IN THE THIRD CENTURY BCE TO THE MONGOLS OF THE THIRTEENTH CENTURY, NOMADS OF THE STEPPES TERRIFIED THE PEOPLES OF ASIA AND EUROPE. AMONG THE MOST POWERFUL WERE THE HEPHTHALITES AND THE HUNS.

Perhaps two branches of the same people, the Hephtalites and the Huns spread in opposite directions in the late fourth and fifth centuries: the Hephthalites south and east, the Huns westwards into Europe. While lack of written records prohibits us from ascertaining their linguistic or cultural make-up, many believe both peoples are related to the earlier Xiongnu.

Both the Hephthalites and Huns shared similar principles of organization and military strategy. These were developed through the nomadic horse culture of the steppes, where every man was capable of riding a horse and shooting a bow, and therefore capable of riding to war. With an entire male population capable of mobilizing quickly and effectively, and with exceptionally high average levels of skill in archery, these horse peoples presented a lethal combination of force, mobility and sheer numbers.

ABOVE A Hephthalite coin depicting Napki Malka, a Hephthalite king from the 6th–7th centuries.

LEFT This 19th-century depiction of Attila shows the Hunnish King adorned in rich clothes and feasting in a grand hall. It is based on a Roman account.

LEFT Eugène Delacroix's portrayal of a windswept Attila on horseback above the bodies of slain soldiers.

HEPHTHALITES RIDE SOUTH

In the fifth century, the Hephthalites began to expand aggressively out of Central Asia. Their original homeland – according to Chinese sources – was in Dzungaria. In the 420s, they pestered the Sassanid Persian Empire, but were defeated in 427. In 469, however, the Hephthalites returned in force and defeated Peroz, emperor of the Sassanids, at the Battle of Herat in 484. Soon after, they turned their attention eastwards, and took Sogdiana, Kashgar and Khotan, and moved on into India against the weakening Gupta Empire.

UNSTOPPABLE

At around the same time the Hephthalites were attacking the Sassanid Empire, the Huns were achieving victory after victory against the eastern half of the Roman Empire, and quickly advancing on Europe. The most famous leader of the Huns is, of course, Attila, a man who led the Huns from 434–453. Known in various European legendary traditions of the Middle Ages, Attila would occupy a place in the traditional literature of northern Europe for a millennium to come. Known as 'Etzel' in Middle High German and as 'Atli' in Old Norse, Attila figures (albeit anachronistically) alongside other semi-historical heroes, such as Dietrich von Bern, Hildebrand and Sigurd/Siegfried the Dragonslayer.

When the western Roman Emperor refused to give Attila the hand of his sister, Honoria, in marriage in 450, Attila launched a violent campaign into Europe, killing its citizens and burning its villages. He and the Huns stormed westwards, advancing all the way to Thermopylae in Greece and into Germany, Austria and Italy. Visigothic king, Theodoric I inflicted Attila's one defeat at Catalaunum (modern Châlons-en-Champagne). The city of Venice was founded when Romans fled into the swamps from the nearby city of Aquileia upon the arrival of Attila's forces.

Attila died in 453, and the importance of his influence and strength as a leader became quickly apparent: the Huns disintegrated, leaving in their wake a path of devastating destruction.

EMPIRES OF TIBET AND TANG 618–907

PARALLEL BEGINNINGS

AROUND THE YEAR 618, TWO EMPIRES WERE FOUNDED THAT WOULD CONTEND WITH ONE ANOTHER DURING THE SEVENTH CENTURY AS THEY BOTH EXPANDED INTO ONE ANOTHER'S TERRITORY: THE TIBETAN EMPIRE AND THE TANG DYNASTY OF CHINA.

ABOVE The Potala Palace in Lhasa, Tibet, is thought to stand atop earlier fortifications built during the reign of Songtsen Gampo.

In 618, Songtsen Gampo came to the throne in Tibet and continued the work of his father, Namri Songtsen, unifying and consolidating his power in Tibet. At the same time, the short-lived Sui Dynasty in China gave rise to the Tang, which would go on to become one of the most prosperous civilizations in history.

The armies of Tibet were large and powerful, quickly conquering its smaller neighbouring kingdoms. The Tibetan Empire soon encompassed Nepal, Kamarupa, Shang Shung, Tuyuhun and additional territories and tribes. As the Tibetans expanded and brought various tribal peoples under their dominion, the Tang were also expanding, until the two great empires found themselves bordering one another.

CLASH WITH TANG

Songtsen established his capital in Lhasa and initiated large building works throughout the country. Perhaps most importantly, however, he and his government worked vigorously to spread Buddhism throughout Tibet. In 635, Songsten demanded a Chinese bride – it was his custom to demand a bride from the royal families of those he had

RIGHT The Tang court takes a leisurely ride in springtime. Painting and poetry were widely celebrated in Tang Dynasty China.

ABOVE A Tang Dynasty ceramic statue of a horse. Note the detail in the mane and blankets beneath the sculpted leather saddle.

conquered. Emperor Taizong of the Tang, however, denied Songtsen his claim, and Songtsen struck quickly against the Tang.

Songtsen's large armies moved swiftly and conquered several of the borderlands between China and Tibet, though it is unclear who actually got the upper hand. Things remained relatively quiet after this foray, but in 649, both emperors died, and the two nations fell back into violent patterns. For the next century and beyond, the two nations would fight with one another; tensions mounted, as the Silk Road – and control thereof – became more important and more lucrative.

Taking advantage of the An-Shi Rebellion in China, Trisong Detsen of Tibet invaded China and took control of the Tang capital of Chang'an in 763. This height of Tibetan power, however, was not sustainable. The Tang slowly recovered from their rebellion and the Tibetans fell into disarray as they fought over the succession after Trisong's death in 797.

DISCORD WITHIN

The Tang Dynasty was an exceptionally strong and well-run society. It was home to artists and musicians from all over the world, and the great city of Chang'an was the largest city in the world at the time, with a population of more than a million. With a large force of probably more than 100,000, military commander An Lushan rebelled in 755, marching towards the Imperial Court. An Lushan's strength as a military commander and warrior were well known, and the court dared not oppose him, so people fled. An Lushan declared himself emperor, but his reign would be short-lived. The Tang eventually recovered from the rebellion, but it put an end to the great period of flourishing prosperity during the first half of the eighth century.

ABOVE A Ming Dynasty painting of the Tang Emperor fleeing Chang'an to escape the An-Shi Rebellion in the mid-8th century.

KHMER EMPIRE 802–15TH CENTURY

SPRINGS OF GLORY

THE KHMER EMPIRE WAS FOUNDED IN 802 WHEN JAYAVARMAN II DECLARED INDEPENDENCE FOR THE KHMER FROM THE SAILENDRA DYNASTY OF JAVA. THE KHMER WOULD BECOME A DOMINANT POWER IN SOUTHEAST ASIA FOR THE NEXT SIX CENTURIES.

The Sailendra Dynasty controlled the Medang and Srivijaya kingdoms, as well as much of the mainland of Southeast Asia in what is now Cambodia. When Jayavarman II declared independence from the Javan rulers, he established his base in the Kulen Hills near the holy waters of the Puok and Siem rivers. Jayavarman and his successors would build great cities and temples along the River Mekong, and wage many wars with the neighbouring kingdoms on the peninsula of Southeast Asia.

THE GREAT CITY

The most enduring remnants of the Khmer Empire are its many stone buildings and temples, particularly those in the capital of Angkor. In the late ninth century, many building projects were already under way, and the Khmer were able to expand their power greatly through trade and agriculture. They relied heavily on intricate irrigation systems to manage the seasonal rainfall and increase their production of rice. The profits from this well-planned agriculture allowed the kingdom to build large cities and fortresses, as well as pay for the expense of waging wars. The irrigation systems were necessary to support the large population of Angkor, which may have been more than 750,000.

RIGHT Bust of King Jayavarman VII, who was devoutly Buddhist and commissioned the famous temple of Ta Prom to be built in the late 12th century.

LEFT Ornate stonework characterizes Khmer architecture, as seen in this photo of Phanom Rung in what is now Thailand.

Yasovarman I (r. 890–910) founded the city of Angkor around 900, though it was initially called Yasodharapura. It was abandoned in its early years, and only came into heavy

ABOVE At its height, the Khmer Empire covered much of Southeast Asia.

TOP The great temple of Angkor Wat is one of the most iconic monuments of the Khmer Empire.

use later in the tenth century. The Khmer, though relatively stable in their government, often fought with their many neighbours, including Pagan and Chola, Dai Viet and Annam, and Champa in the east. The biggest rival of the Khmer, however, was the Cham people. The Khmer armies sacked Vijaya, the capital of Cham, in 1145 and 1190, and Cham forces sacked Angkor in 1177, 1430 and 1444. The last assault on Angkor contributed to the rapid decline of the Khmer Empire in the mid-fifteenth century.

TEMPLES AND ART

Among the most famous buildings from the Khmer Empire are the temples of Angkor Wat and Ta Prohm. Large and intricate stonework characterize the architecture of this time, and the walls are covered in detailed relief carvings that provide insights into all manner of life in the Khmer Empire. The reliefs give us glimpses of the military engagements of the day, depicting armies of warriors with spears and shields made of rhinoceros hide, as well as archers riding war elephants.

SONG DYNASTY 960–1279

A NEW UNIFICATION

AFTER THE COLLAPSE OF THE TANG DYNASTY AT THE BEGINNING OF THE TENTH CENTURY, CHINA ENTERED A PERIOD OF UPHEAVAL AND WAR, KNOWN AS THE FIVE DYNASTIES AND TEN KINGDOMS PERIOD. IN 960, HOWEVER, THE SONG WOULD UNITE CHINA ONCE MORE.

Through conquest, the first Song emperor, Taizu, was able to unite the lands that had fragmented after the collapse of the Tang. Taizu's capital was at Kaifeng, and the first portion of the Song Dynasty until 1127 is known as the Northern Song because of the capital's location. In 979, the Song began efforts to reclaim territories lost to the Liao, invading and attempting to reach the Liao capital of Yanjing in modern-day Beijing. They were largely unsuccessful, and when the Liao struck back in 999, the Song eventually had to pay tribute of silver and silk to Liao.

Shortly after the conflicts with Liao ended, the Song found another opponent in the Xia. The Song armies boasted hundreds of thousands of soldiers, but fared badly in the border wars with Xia between 1039 and 1044. The Xia likewise exacted tribute of silver and silk. A brief period of relative peace followed, but the Song went on the offensive in 1081 and fought a series of wars over the next four decades. The outcomes of these battles were largely unsuccessful.

In the early twelfth century, the Jurchen rebelled against their Liao emperor and established the Jin Dynasty. Despite initial support from the Song, the Jin entered Song territory in the winter of 1125 and toppled the Song government after taking Kaifeng and most of the imperial court captive.

ABOVE The Song Dynasty is split into two periods – the Northern Song and the Southern Song – based on the location of the capital. Here, we see the later Southern Song Dynasty, with the Jin Dynasty in the north and the Western Xia Dynasty in the west.

RIGHT Lu Xiufu, here shown carrying a young Emperor Huaizong, was one of the heroes of the late Song Dynasty.

OPPOSITE LEFT An 11th-century Song Dynasty painting on silk, showing the Emperor on a journey.

OPPOSITE RIGHT Emperor Taizu founded the Song Dynasty in 960 after reuniting China.

SOUTHERN SONG

Fleeing south, the emperor's brother Gaozong moved the Song capital to Hangzhou and took the title of emperor. During the following two years before the Jin were able to pursue, the Southern Song Dynasty prepared itself for war. In 1129, the Jin crossed the Yangtze and attacked, but the Song were able to repel the offensive. Over the next few decades, the Song and Jin fought in several wars. During this time, the Song established China's first permanent navy and began using paddle boats. Gunpowder also came into heavy use during this time, and the Song were in part able to defeat the larger armies of their northern opponents by launching gunpowder bombs with catapults. Relying heavily on their horses and cavalry, the Jin ran into serious difficulties against Song's navy.

Despite managing to hold the Jin at bay, a new enemy would soon defeat not only the Song, but also the Jin and Xia: the Mongols. Under Kublai Khan in 1279, the Mongols would destroy the last resistance of the Song.

TIMELINE OF THE SONG DYNASTY

907–979	Five Dynasties and Ten Kingdoms
960	Establishment of Northern Song Dynasty
981	Battle of Bach Dang
1004	Liao and Song wars
1005	Treaty signed between Song and Liao; Song send tribute
1038	Western Xia Dynasty founded
1041	First moveable type printing
1080	Successful campaigns of the Song against the Western Xia
1125	Jurchens and Song unite to defeat Liao
1125	Jurchens found Jin Dynasty
1127	Jin Dynasty defeats former ally, Song
1127	End of Northern Song, beginning of Southern Song
1132	Song establish first permanent navy at Dinghai
1141	Treaty of Shaoxing between Jin and Southern Song
1161	Song use paddle boats and explosives to defeat Jin invasion
1205	Mongols invade Jin Dynasty
1234	Mongols conquer Jin Dynasty with Song aid
1260	Yuan Dynasty founded
1279	Fall of the Song Dynasty

GEMPEI WAR 1180–1185

A CLASS OF WARRIORS

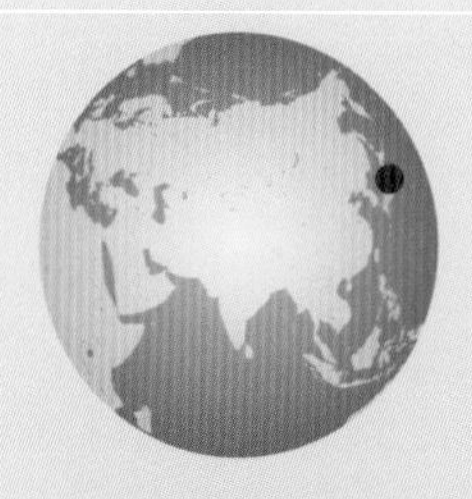

THE HEIAN PERIOD OF JAPANESE HISTORY (794–1185) ENDED WITH AN EPIC BATTLE THAT HELPED SOLIDIFY THE DEMARCATION OF A NEW CLASS OF WARRIORS THAT WOULD BECOME FAMOUS THE WORLD OVER – THE SAMURAI.

The Gempei War helped forge Japanese history and culture. The war was fought primarily between two warring clans: the Taira and the Minamoto. Even the flag of Japan today bears the colours of these two clans: the nation as we know it was formed out of the conflict between them.

The two tribes had feuded for decades, each trying to gain the upper hand in controlling the imperial court at Kyoto. When Taira no Kiyomori, who had taken control of the Imperial Court in 1160, named his grandson as emperor in 1180, he sparked a massive controversy over succession that led to a Minamoto revolt. Plans of the attack leaked out, however, and a force of some 20,000 Taira forces chased and caught Minamoto no Yorimasa and his small band of 300 at the Battle of Uji, fought on the banks of the River Uji on 20 June 1180. Despite their bravery, the Minamoto were slaughtered. Yorimasa, however, defying capture, committed *seppuku*, the ritual suicide that would become common among samurai as an alternative to shame. The Battle of Uji began the Gempei War, and the epic clash between the Taira and Minamoto clans.

LEFT Minamoto no Yoshinaka's grave in Shiga Prefecture near Kyoto.

WORTHY OF SONG

The Gempei War is best remembered through the famous *Heike Monogatari*, or *Tale of Heike*. The name *Heike* is formed from an alternate reading of the Chinese character that forms the name of the Taira clan.

ABOVE This 18th-century painting of a kabuki actor playing a samurai attests to the longevity and importance of the samurai class in Japan following the Gempei War in the late 12th century.

ABOVE Tomoe Gozen, the concubine of Minamoto no Yoshinaka, was a rare female warrior who fought in the Gempei War. Here, she has just decapitated Honda no Moroshige at the Battle of Awazu in 1184.

EMERGING RULER

Minamoto no Yoshinaka went on a furious round of assaults, fighting several battles with the Taira in 1182 and working his way to Kyoto in 1183. He attacked the Imperial city, forcing the Taira to flee along with the child emperor, Antoku. But Yoshinaka, with extreme hostility, had more to fear than his Taira opponents. His cousin, Minamoto no Yoritomo, felt that Yoshinaka had crossed a line and had grabbed too much power for himself. Yoritomo fought with Yoshinaka, defeating him and taking full leadership of the Minamoto.

Yoritomo turned once again to fight the Taira. The ultimate battle of the Minamoto and Taira was fought at sea in the Battle of Dan-no-ura. The Minamoto prevailed and the young Antoku drowned, apparently with his imperial sword, a great treasure of Japan. After the war, the Minamoto clan established the Kamakura Shogunate, which would rule Japan until 1333. Minamoto Yoritomo became Japan's first Shogun.

GENGHIS KHAN 1162–1227

LORD OF THE MONGOLS

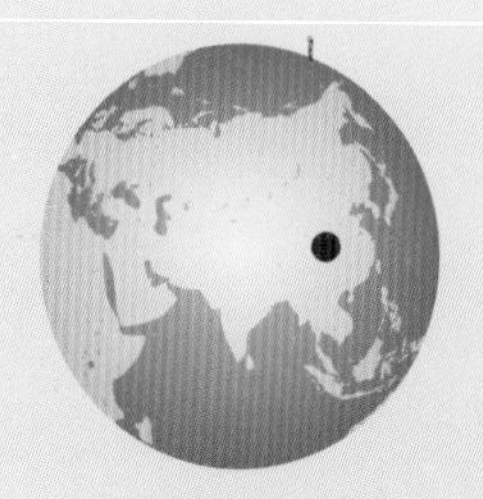

AFTER YEARS OF BATTLE, CONSOLIDATING THE VARIOUS TRIBES AND GROUPS OF THE MONGOLS, A MONGOL WARRIOR NAMED TEMUJIN RECEIVED THE NAME *GENGHIS KHAN* FROM THE CLAN LEADERS AT THE RIVER ONON IN 1206.

Genghis Khan means something along the lines of 'Universal King'. The appellation itself can be seen as a major victory, but uniting the Mongols under his leadership was really just the beginning for Temujin, who would lead one of the most powerful military forces of all time. The Mongols would eventually create the largest land empire the world has ever known. At its peak, the Mongol Empire stretched all the way from Korea in the east to Europe in the west, reaching south to Vietnam, India and across the Middle East.

THE FAMILY BUSINESS

For 20 years after his unification of the Mongol clans, Genghis would set out on massive campaigns to bring all lands adjoining the steppes under his control. Turning first to their nearest neighbour and historical competitor, the Mongols attacked the dynasties of China, beginning with the Xia in 1209 and progressing to the Jin in 1211. The Mongols took the Jin capital, located at modern-day Beijing, in 1215.

With the Jin Dynasty now under Mongol control, Genghis directed his efforts westwards, turning to Khwarezm. The Muslim kingdom of Khwarezm made a fatal mistake in its relations with the Mongols by capturing and killing Mongolian merchants who had been sent as ambassadors to the Khwarezmid ruler in 1218. The Shah believed them to be engaged in espionage. This provoked a long series of conflicts that would ultimately end in the demise of the Khwarezmian Empire. Genghis stormed through the land with his army of 200,000 warriors, bolstered by the use of siege engines he had learned from the Jin.

The Xia Dynasty fell in 1227. Genghis died in the same year, and control of the empire fell to his four sons, among whom the seeds of discord had already begun to sprout before Genghis's death.

ABOVE This statue of Genghis on horseback stands today in Ulan Bator, the capital of Mongolia.

ABOVE AND BELOW On horseback, the Mongols were unstoppable. On ships, they were often defeated.

THE HORDES

The Mongol Empire was passed to Genghis's son, Ögedei. To facilitate governance of the massive empire, it began to be divided into smaller khanates, of which Genghis's descendents took control. The Il Khanate of the Middle East went to Hulagu; the Chaghatai Khanate of Central Asia went to Chaghatai; the Kipchak Khanate, or 'Golden Horde' of the west, went to Batu. Later, the Yuan Dynasty of China, founded by Kublai Khan, would claim overlordship of the Mongol Empire. The Golden Horde would take control of the Kievan Rus' in the west, while Kublai Khan would take Goryeo (Korea) in the east after six invasions. The Mongols also invaded Japan twice, but were unable to conquer the nation.

BELOW The Japanese built walls to defend their country against the second invasion of the Mongols in 1281 under Kublai Khan.

MONGOL WARS IN JAVA 1289–1292

DEFIANCE OF JAVA

THE MONGOLS WERE A HORSE PEOPLE, AND WERE ESSENTIALLY UNSTOPPABLE WHEREVER HORSES COULD BE DEPLOYED EFFECTIVELY. THEIR EXPEDITIONS OVERSEAS, HOWEVER, WERE LARGELY UNSUCCESSFUL – NOT LEAST OF ALL IN JAVA, IN THE KINGDOM OF SINGOSARI.

In 1222, a commoner named Ken Angrok took control of Tumapel and proceeded to bring all of the kingdom of Kediri under his control, defeating its king in the Battle of Gantër later that same year. Thus began the Singosari Kingdom of Java.

Kertanagara (r. 1268–1292) was the last king of Singosari. He greatly expanded the kingdom, conquering many of the neighbouring kingdoms. He also formed an alliance with the Champa, a kingdom on the mainland of Southeast Asia. The alliance was designed to help protect both kingdoms from the impending threat of the Mongols under the Yuan Dynasty leadership of Kublai Khan. The Mongols had already invaded Dai Viet in 1257, and it seemed likely that they would return and redouble their efforts in Southeast Asia. In 1289, a Mongol envoy arrived and demanded tribute; but Kertanagara not only refused to grant tribute, he also branded the ambassador's face. Unsurprisingly, this sparked a Mongol invasion.

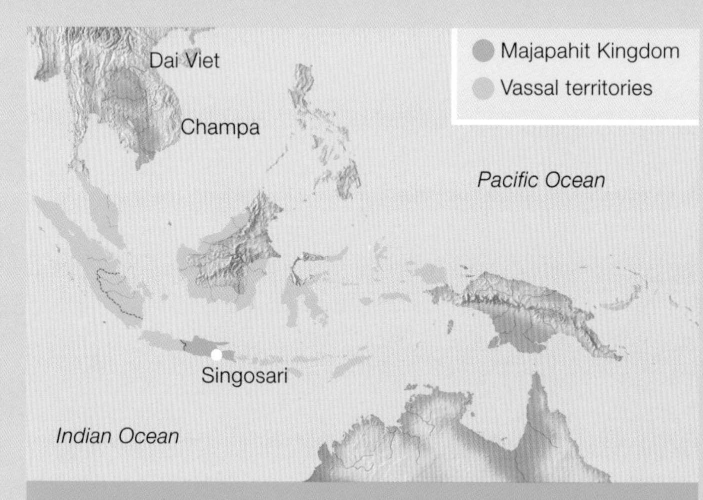

ABOVE The Majapahit Empire dominated the islands of Southeast Asia after Wijaya defeated the Mongols.

BELOW Relief carvings in Jakarta depict scenes from the Majapahit Empire that emerged in the wake of the Mongol invasions at the end of the 13th century.

THE MONGOLS INVADE

Kertanagara was assassinated in 1292, shortly before the Mongols invaded. The Mongol fleet arrived in spring 1293. They found Singosari in a state of civil war. Kertanagara's son-in-law, Raden Wijaya, was fighting against Jayakatwang of Kediri, Kertanagara's assassinator. Unable to defeat two opponents, Wijaya cleverly sent word to the Mongols that he would submit to their overlordship, and thereby gained a strong ally in the Mongol army, who marched on Kediri and soundly defeated Jayakatwang's forces. Wijaya, however, still held the principles of his late father, and quickly turned

ABOVE Kublai Khan demanded tribute from Kertanagara, who refused to pay, inciting the Mongol invasion.

on the Mongol force, ambushing them. Weakened by travel, disease, the unfamiliar tropical climate, and their recent battles, the Mongols could not withstand the assault, and eventually returned home.

After the Mongols departed, Wijaya established a new kingdom, called Majapahit, which would go on to become one of the most prosperous Hindu kingdoms in Indonesia.

HANDLING THE HEAT

Several factors slowed and prevented Mongol progress in Southeast Asia. Despite their remarkable adaptability to a number of terrains and circumstances, the Mongols were not particularly adept at naval expeditions. In 1288, for example, they were famously defeated by Annam and Dai Viet at the Battle of Bach Dang, where their fleet was sunk. But Southeast Asia provided many more challenges that would prove decisive. Perhaps most significant was the climate. The Mongols were not accustomed to the hot and humid weather. In addition to the severe discomfort this caused, it also made the Mongols more susceptible to new diseases, which spread quickly and weakened the armies' fighting capabilities. Combining the challenges of fighting on rivers or at sea, the confrontations with war elephants, and the climate and disease, the Mongols could not sustain the power they had used to dominate the rest of their empire.

RIGHT Statue of Wijaya deified as Harihara, a combination of Shiva and Vishnu.

SECOND BURMESE EMPIRE 1486–1752

TOUNGOO DYNASTY

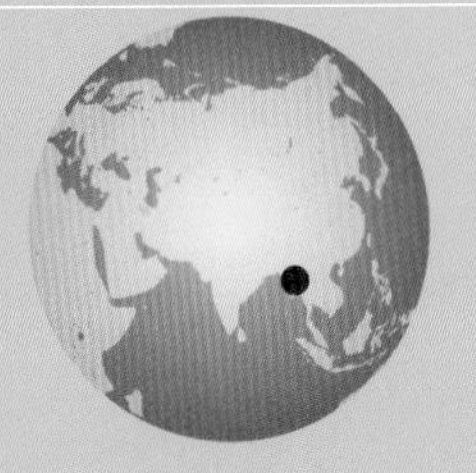

FOLLOWING THE MONGOL CAPTURE OF PAGAN IN 1287, THE KINGDOM OF BURMA BEGAN TO BREAK APART AND DISINTEGRATE INTO CIVIL WAR. THE VARIOUS FACTIONS WOULD CONTINUE TO STRUGGLE AGAINST ONE ANOTHER UNTIL THE SIXTEENTH CENTURY, WHEN THE TOUNGOO DYNASTY EMERGED.

The foundation of the Toungoo Dynasty lies with King Minkyinyo (r. 1486–1531). Minkyinyo declared Toungoo independent from the ruling state of Ava in 1510. Wars ensued over the next 17 years, but in 1527, Minkyinyo managed to conquer Ava entirely. This was the essential first step for Minkyinyo's son and heir to strengthen the position of the Toungoo Dynasty and establish a large and powerful kingdom.

One of the largest threats lay to the south among the Mon people. Minkyino's son, Tabinshwehti, ascended the throne at only 16 years of age, but quickly proved himself to be a capable ruler and powerful military commander. Soon after ascending the throne, he conquered Kyaukse and the Mohnyin Shan people. In 1535, with the aid of 700 mercenaries (many of them Portuguese), Tabinshwehti moved south against the Mon of Pegu. Bassein and Myaungmya fell before him. The capital of Pegu fell four years later in 1539. Tabinshwehti did not stop there, however, and by 1542 had also conquered the Irrawaddy Delta and Prome. Despite attacks by the Shan, Tabinshwehti was able to defend his conquest and fight back, eventually seizing Pagan in 1546. He had effectively reunited Burma after centuries of fragmentation and war.

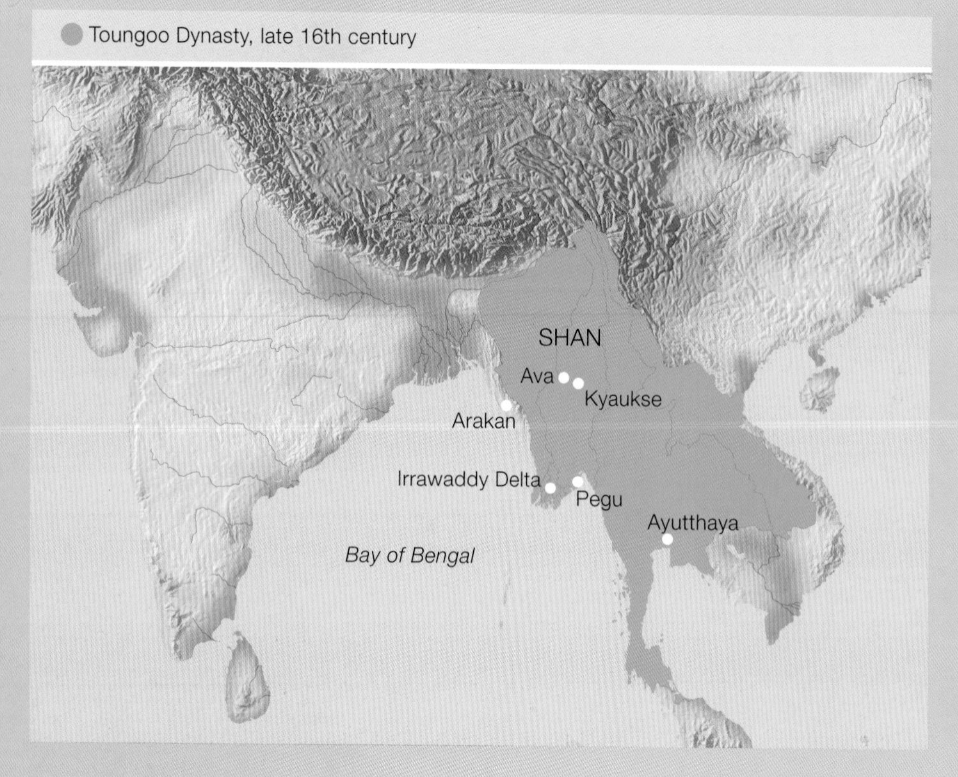

LEFT At its height, the Toungoo Empire stretched from Tibet in the north to what is now Malaysia in the south.

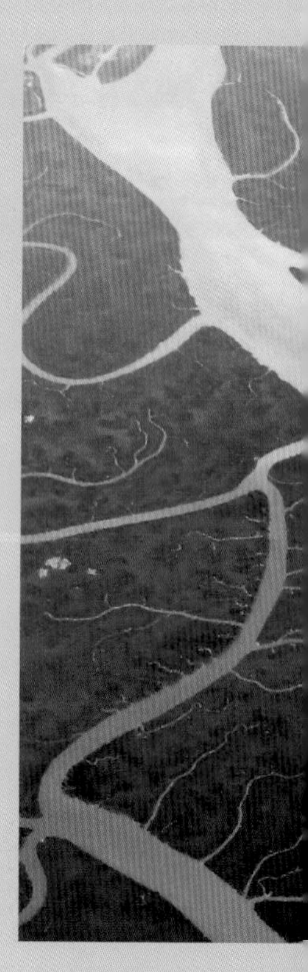

RIGHT The River Irrawaddy was an important part of the Toungoo Empire, as it was used for both trade and irrigation.

ABOVE A heavily armoured King Bayinnaung, who ruled the Toungoo Dynasty from 1551–81.

ABOVE The Toungoo conquered Ayutthaya in the 16th century. These three pagodas of Wat Phra Si Sanphet contain the remains of Ayutthaya kings.

PASSING THE TORCH

In 1551, Tabinshwehti was assassinated and his brother-in-law, Bayinnaung ascended the throne. Quickly putting down the Mon rebellion that had taken Tabinshwehti's life, Bayinnaung then turned his attention to defeating the Shans and the Ayutthaya, who had bested his predecessor. Bayinnaung managed to defeat the Shans in 1554 and the Thai kingdom of Ayutthaya in 1569. The last victory would have been to claim Arakan, a small kingdom protected by a difficult mountain range. Tabinshwehti had launched an expedition against Arakan, even besieging the capital, but had been forced to withdraw to deal with the threat of the Ayutthaya. Bayinnaung died in 1581 before the assault on Arakan could be launched, and the lack of sturdy leadership soon took its toll on the Toungoo Dynasty. While the dynasty lasted until 1752, it began to weaken after the reign of Bayinnaung. Under Bayinnaung, the Myanmar kingdom of the Toungoo Dynasty was the most powerful kingdom in all of Southeast Asia.

MUGHAL EMPIRE 1526–1857

BABUR OF THE CHAGHATAI

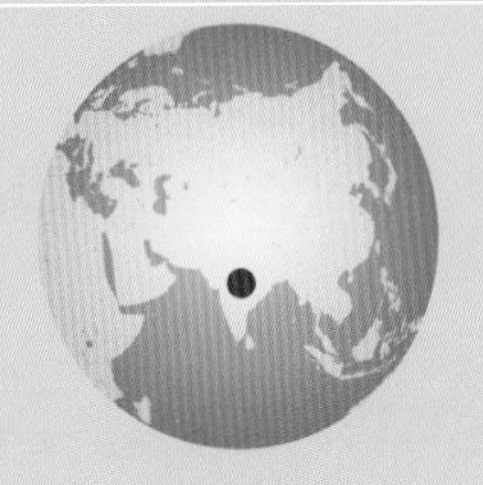

IN 1526, ZAHIR-UD-DIN-MUHAMMAD BABUR OF THE CHAGHATAI TURKS, A SUNNI MUSLIM RULER, STORMED INTO INDIA. THE RESULT WAS THE FOUNDATION OF THE MUGHAL EMPIRE, A PROSPEROUS KINGDOM THAT WOULD RULE OVER NORTHERN INDIA FOR THE NEXT THREE CENTURIES.

ABOVE Mughal Emperor Babur shown in high spirits at the conclusion of Ramadan in 1519.

Babur was descended from Timur on his father's side and Chaghatai, son of Genghis, on his mother's. Conquest flowed in his veins, and in 1526 he struck out from his base in Kabul, Afghanistan, to attack the Delhi Sultanate and the Rajput of India. In Panipat, home to a number of important conflicts in Indian history, Babur defeated the armies of Delhi in the First Battle of Panipat. The following year he went on to defeat an army almost eight times the size of his own forces at the Battle of Khanua in 1527. Babur combined clever strategy with the latest advances in weaponry and military technology to inflict heavy losses on his opponents. His reign, however, would come to an end in 1530, only four years after it had begun.

The momentum of Babur's conquests was lost when Babur's son, Humayun, failed to defeat armies from Afghanistan, including those of Sher Khan. Despite this serious setback, the Mughal Dynasty would find a new and highly capable ruler in the hands of Humayun's son, Akbar, now known as Akbar the Great. In 1556, an army of the Sur Dynasty marched on Delhi under the direction of General Hemu. Akbar rose to meet him with a small force at the Second Battle of Panipat. Though only 13 at the time, his

AKBAR'S ELEPHANTS

One of the decisive factors of Akbar's conquests was his use of war elephants, which he developed into an art form. With thousands of elephants under his control, he explored and exploited the beasts' various uses to great effect, covering them in armour to protect them, and even mounting firearms atop their backs. Akbar also reportedly used elephants to execute those who rebelled against his kingdom.

ABOVE Cavalry and war elephants were the most powerful forces on the battlefield under Akbar.

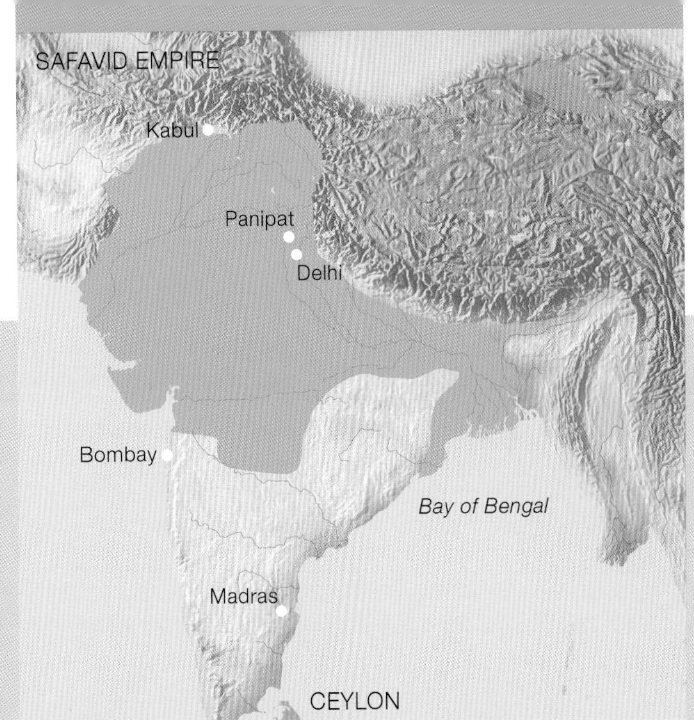

ABOVE The Mughal Empire began in northern India, Pakistan and Afghanistan, and grew to cover most of the Indian subcontinent.

ABOVE Aurangzeb sent Raja Jai Singh I to defeat Shivaji, leader of the rebellion against the Mughal Empire. Here, Jai Singh and Shivaji greet before agreeing to the Treaty of Purandar.

armies were led by General Bairam Khan. Hemu was shot in the eye by an arrow, and failed to lead his armies further. Akbar's armies were thus able to defeat Hemu's larger force and secure control of Delhi.

Akbar grew to become a wise military leader and strategist. For the first two years of his reign, he sought to regain control of territories lost under his father and to quell any remaining opposition from the Sur. He then set about expanding his territory, starting with Malwa in 1561, Mewar and Rajasthan in 1569, Gujarat in 1573 and Bengal in 1576. In the 1580s and 1590s, he established solid control in Afghanistan. Akbar died in 1605, having built the Mughal Empire into a large and powerful kingdom. Due to oppression by Aurangzeb, the Hindus would rebel under the leadership of Shivaji in the late seventeenth century, seriously weakening the Mughal Empire.

SENGOKU JIDAI 1467–1600

WARRING STATES OF JAPAN

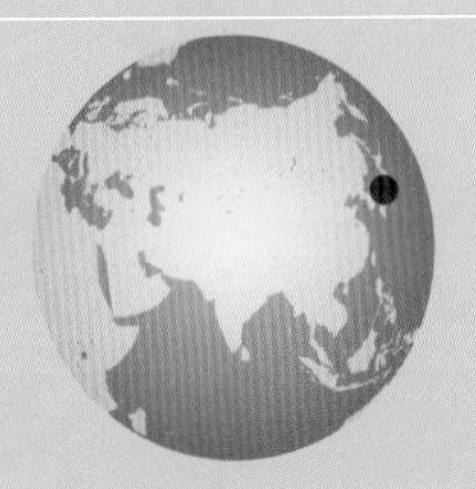

THE SENGOKU JIDAI, OR WARRING STATES PERIOD OF JAPANESE HISTORY, IS ONE OF THE BLOODIEST AND MOST VIOLENT, CHARACTERIZED BY CONSTANT WARFARE BETWEEN THE REGIONAL RULERS, OR *DAIMYO*. ONLY AT THE END OF THIS PERIOD WAS JAPAN FINALLY UNITED.

In 1467, war erupted in Japan between the Hosokawa in the east and the Yamana in the west. Both economic factors and disputes over succession to the Shogunate spawned the war, which would last a full decade and become known as the Onin War. This was the beginning of the Sengoku Jidai. While the stories that emerged from this time period often involve fierce fighting and bloodshed, betrayal and backstabbing, and the constancy of violence, several of Japan's most famous samurai and most famous treatises on strategy emerged from the Sengoku Jidai.

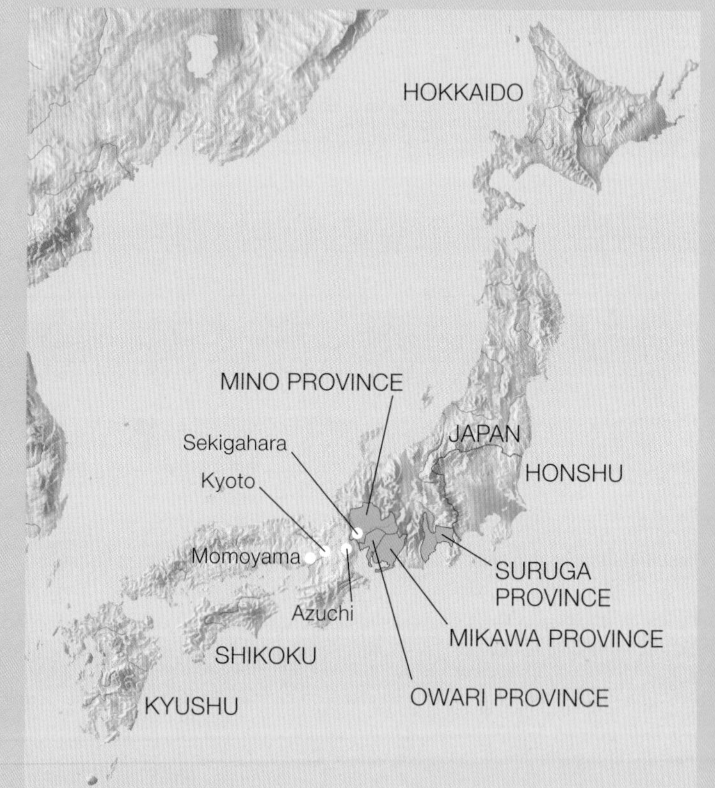

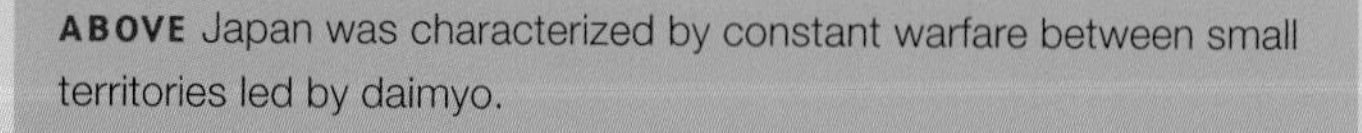
ABOVE Japan was characterized by constant warfare between small territories led by daimyo.

THE UNIFIERS

Three great leaders are typically cited as responsible for the unification of Japan: Oda Nobunaga, Toyotomi Hideyoshi and Tokugawa Ieyasu. Oda Nobunaga was the first of these. Nobunaga was known for strange and even reckless behaviour as a youth. He proved himself a capable leader through battle, however, defeating Imagawa Yoshimoto in 1560 and thereby taking control of Owari Province. The victory surprised many. Yoshimoto's defeat and death led in turn to the release of several hostages, including Tokugawa Ieyasu, with whom Nobunaga would later form an alliance. Ieyasu controlled Mikawa Province.

Nobunaga conquered Mino in 1567, defeating Saito Tatsuoki. Tatsuoki was the incompetent son of Saito Yoshitatsu, and his weakness as a ruler provided the necessary opportunity for Nobunaga. In 1570, Nobunaga turned his

RIGHT Samurai armour was both effective and intimidating. Depending on the variety, it had to be flexible enough to allow one to shoot a bow and arrow from horseback.

ABOVE Portrait of Oda Nobunaga by an Italian Jesuit.

LEFT One of Hideyoshi's retainers, Horio Yoshiharu, leads the way through the dark during the assault on Inabayama Castle in 1567.

attention to combating the warrior monks of Japan. Despite their religious status, these monks were highly trained warriors and exercised considerable political power. Then in 1573, Nobunaga overthrew the Ashikaga Shogunate in Kyoto.

HIDEYOSHI AND IEYASU

Unification of Japan was well under way by the time Nobunaga died in 1582. The process continued under Toyotomi Hideyoshi, a man of humble origins and a loyal retainer of Nobunaga. Through battle after battle, Hideyoshi unified the remainder of the country, ruling Japan until his death from bubonic plague in 1598. He even invaded Korea twice with the aim of conquering China's Ming Dynasty, but these expeditions were unsuccessful. After his death, the old rivalries were renewed, and Japan teetered on the verge of collapse back into a state of constant war. Tokugawa Ieyasu maintained unity, however, by defeating Ishida Mitsunari at the Battle of Sekigahara in 1600. One of the most famous battles in Japanese history, Sekigahara facilitated the establishment of the Tokugawa Shogunate, which would last for more than 250 years.

LEFT A woodblock print depicting Hideyoshi as a young man scaling a cliff by moonlight during the attack on Inabayama Castle.

THE BATTLE OF NAGASHINO 1575

RISE OF THE ARQUEBUSIERS

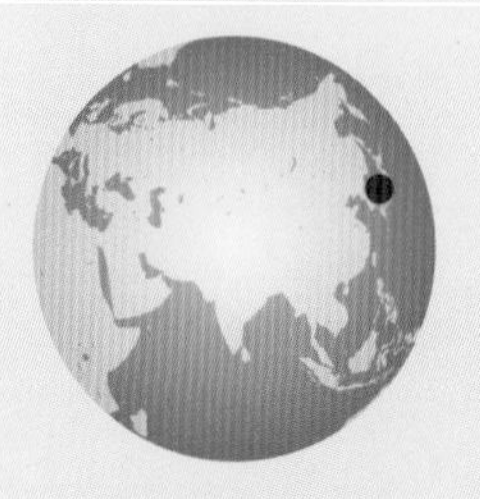

THE BATTLE OF NAGASHINO IN 1575 IS KNOWN FOR THE EFFECTIVE DEPLOYMENT OF FIREARMS AGAINST THE CAVALRY CHARGES OF TAKEDA KATSUYORI. SEEKING TO RELIEVE HIS MEN AT THE CASTLE OF NAGASHINO, TOKUGAWA IEYASU SENT HIS ALLY, ODA NOBUNAGA, TO THE RESCUE.

ABOVE Oda Nobunaga's Azuchi Castle in Ōmi Province.

In the spring of 1575, Takeda Katsuyori invaded Mikawa, a territory of Tokugawa Ieyasu. Katsuyori attacked and besieged the castle of Nagashino, which was defended by a small band of Ieyasu's men. Though they held the defences bravely, they were too small a force to repel the 15,000 or so troops besieging the castle's walls.

Ieyasu had forged an alliance with Oda Nobunaga in 1561. Calling on this alliance, Ieyasu sent forces to accompany Nobunaga to support the defenders of Nagashino. The combined force was reported to be approximately 38,000 strong, far larger than Katsuyori's forces at the castle. The battle took place on the fields in front of the castle, known as the Plain of Shitaragahara. Nobunaga positioned his troops behind the Rengogawa, a stream with steep banks. This decision was designed to help break the inevitable cavalry charge of Takeda's forces.

RIGHT A large folding screen portrays the Battle of Nagashino. Note the stockades and use of arquebusiers.

ABOVE Painted more than 300 years after the battle, this image romantically depicts a general deploying his men at Nagashino.

NEW DEFENCES

As in Europe, the use of firearms spurred the creation of new defences. In 1576, Oda Nobunaga began construction of a massive fortification known as Azuchi Castle. An impressive fortress made largely of drystacked granite blocks, Azuchi was designed to challenge even the heaviest of onslaughts. So influential was this castle that the last quarter of the sixteenth century is known as the Azuchi-Momoyama Period. Momoyama Castle was built by Toyotomi Hideyoshi in Kyoto.

ABOVE A powerful image of Nobunaga throwing an opponent into a raging fire. Brilliant in mind as a strategist, he was also strong in limb as a warrior.

BRINGING THE GUNS

The defeat of Katsuyori's forces at Nagashino was more the result of strategy than numbers. Among Nobunaga's forces were a few thousand arquebusiers, specialists in the use of firearms. The large-scale deployment of firearms was relatively new to Japan, and the Battle of Nagashino would prove to be one of the most influential.

Nobunaga knew the signature move of the Takeda Clan was its cavalry charge, pioneered by Katsuyori's father, Takeda Shingen. To guide and break the charge, Nobunaga set up several stockades in layers, protecting the arquebusiers and funnelling the cavalry into an area where they could be taken more easily by guns, arrows and swords. By rotating the volleys of shots from the arquebusiers, Nobunaga was able to maintain constant shooting, allowing the arquebusiers time to reload between volleys.

The new tactics worked brilliantly. Charge after charge was mown down by gunfire, and Nobunaga and his forces were eventually able to abandon the stockades and chase after the Takeda force. Nobunaga successfully broke the siege and relieved the soldiers at the castle of Nagashino. This battle is often considered Japan's first modern battle because of Nobunaga's brilliant use of firearms.

TEN GREAT CAMPAIGNS 1747–1793

EMPEROR QIANLONG

DURING THE COURSE OF HIS REIGN, THE FOURTH EMPEROR OF THE MANCHURIAN QING DYNASTY ENGAGED IN TEN LARGE CAMPAIGNS TO EXPAND THE EMPIRE CONSIDERABLY. DESPITE CLAIMS FROM QIANLONG HIMSELF, HOWEVER, NOT ALL OF HIS CAMPAIGNS WERE SUCCESSFUL.

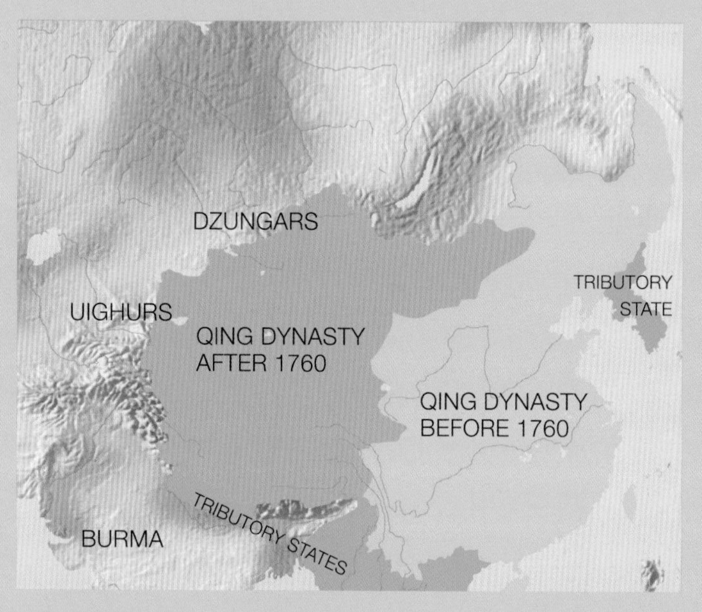

ABOVE Though not all his campaigns were successful, Emperor Qianlong expanded Qing territory considerably during his long reign.

In 1747, Qianlong began his campaigns against the Jinchuan hill peoples, a nomadic people related to the Tibetans. For two years, the Qing Dynasty poured resources into the battle, making this the most costly of the ten campaigns, despite the relatively small size of the Jinchuan armies. Unrest would require the Qing to return 22 years later, in 1771, for an additional five years of fighting.

In 1755, Qianlong continued his campaigns by fighting against the Dzungars of Dzungaria, the last nomadic empire of the Eurasian steppes. The Dzungars are often considered a western branch of the Mongols. Joining with other Turkish peoples, the Dzungars put up a solid effort, but eventually

BELOW LEFT A Qing general secures a victory against the Vietnamese, in 1788.

BELOW RIGHT The Jinchuan hill peoples benefited from a challenging terrain. Qianlong's campaigns against the Jinchuan were extremely expensive.

ABOVE Emperor Qianlong on horseback, wearing richly adorned clothing and carrying a bow and arrows.

THE TEN CAMPAIGNS OF QIANLONG

Year of Campaign	Campaign	Result
1747–49	First Jinchuan War	Stalemate
1755	Invasion of Zunghar Empire	Victory
1756–57	Conquering the Zunghars	Victory
1755–59	Campaign against the Uighurs	Victory
1765–69	Invasion of Burma (Konbaung Dynasty)	Loss
1771–76	Second Jinchuan War	Victory
1787–88	Repression of Taiwan rebellion	Victory
1788–89	Invasion of Vietnam	Loss
1788	Defence of Tibet against the Gurkhas	Stalemate
1791–93	Campaign against Gurkhas of Nepal	Victory

succumbed to the power of the Qing. This not only expanded the dominion of the Qing Empire considerably, it also protected the land from the threat of invasion.

In 1765, the Qing invaded Burma to the south, but were unsuccessful in their efforts. The Burmese were experienced warriors from their conflicts with Siam, and defeated the first two Qing invasions. The third invasion looked promising at the start, but suffered from some of the same plights as the Mongol invasions centuries earlier. The hot and humid weather and unfamiliar diseases weakened the invasion force. Eventually, the Qing were beaten back after four attempts at taking Burma between 1765 and 1769.

The Qing met a similar fate in its campaigns in Vietnam, where rulers had often acknowledged the overlordship of the Chinese. In 1788, the Qing sent a force to restore the Lê ruler to the throne of Annam. They enjoyed some success initially, but were soundly defeated when Annam rebels surprised the Qing armies during the Chinese New Year in 1789.

THE LAST CAMPAIGN

The final campaigns were against a rebellion in Taiwan in 1788 and against the Gurkhas, first in 1788, then again in 1791. When the emperor sent an army against the first invasion, the Gurkhas retreated before any engagement. Qianlong sent a force of 10,000 against the Gurkhas in 1791 and drove them back to Kathmandu, eventually exacting tribute in 1793.

Qianlong claimed to be victorious in all ten of his great campaigns, despite suffering a number of defeats, particularly in Burma and Annam. In total, however, the Qing Empire grew considerably during the long reign of Qianlong. The wars were not without their cost, however. They seriously depleted the national treasury.

LEFT Painting of a victory banquet hosted by Qianlong. Note the colourful uniforms and careful organization of people and tents.

OPIUM WARS 1839–1842

WEAPON OF ADDICTION

IN THE EARLY NINETEENTH CENTURY, GREAT BRITAIN IMPORTED MILLIONS OF POUNDS OF OPIUM, GROWN IN BRITAIN'S IMPERIAL HOLDINGS IN INDIA. BY CREATING A NATION OF ADDICTS, BRITAIN NOT ONLY ACHIEVED GREAT WEALTH, BUT ALSO WEAKENED THE QING EMPIRE.

ABOVE Carnage in Beijing as French and British forces fight against the Chinese during the Second Opium War.

Opium is the name for the drug extracted from the seed-pods of poppy plants, and contains significant amounts of morphine and codeine. The drug can be digested or smoked and causes a sense of euphoria. Refined opium is known today as heroin.

Seeking to increase its revenues from trade with China, Britain encouraged the sale of opium and imported more and more from its holdings in India. By 1833, more than 2.3 million kilograms of opium were being imported annually, creating roughly 12 million addicts in China. Non-drug users in China watched as increasingly more of those around them became addicted to the drug, ruining themselves financially to pay for opium, and at the same time becoming so lethargic and complacent as to be incapable of functioning properly. In 1839, official Lin Tze-hsu travelled to Guangzhou, confiscating and destroying 20,000 chests of opium. This sparked enmity not only from the local opium dealers, but more significantly from Great Britain.

RIGHT The British and French defeated the Chinese at the Battle of Palikao in 1860, allowing them to take Beijing.

LEFT French cavalry officer, Charles Cousin-Montauban, leads a charge in 1860.

BELOW Cannon blasts destroy Chinese junks in 1841 during the First Opium War.

BOTTOM The Treaty of Tientsin, signed in 1858 during the Second Opium War, legalized the importation of opium to China.

DRUG LORDS

With its highly lucrative drug trade threatened, Great Britain sailed against China. With their technologically superior ships and weapons, the British gunships easily took control of the coastal areas and penetrated the mainland via the rivers. The Chinese, weakened in part because of poor governance, but also in large part by the widespread use of opium, were unable to resist effectively. On 29 August 1842, they signed the Treaty of Nanking. The treaty represented a sad defeat, for the Chinese had to cede control of several coastal areas to Great Britain, including Hong Kong. They also had to the pay the British for all the opium that had been confiscated and destroyed.

A SECOND WAR

With such an unfair treaty, it was not long before China and Great Britain clashed again. In 1856, the Second Opium War began, this time with the French also opposing the Chinese. Using slight infractions as justification for war, the French and British captured Guangzhou in 1856 and Tianjin in 1858. War broke out again within the year, and more British and French troops stormed Tianjin and Beijing. The troops destroyed and burned the Summer Palace in Beijing, a huge and elaborate complex of impressive buildings and gardens, filled with valuable artworks and treasures. The Treaty of Tianjin was signed by the emperor's brother on 18 October 1860, but troubles were not over for China. At the same time as the Chinese resisted invasions from Western powers, they were also battling a rebellion within their own borders. The Taiping Rebellion from 1850–1864 was led by Hong Xiuquan, who claimed to be the younger brother of Jesus Christ. The rebellion claimed the lives of some 20 million people.

SEPOY MUTINY 1857–1858

FIRST WAR OF INDEPENDENCE

UNREST MOUNTED IN THE FIRST HALF OF THE NINETEENTH CENTURY IN INDIA AS BRITISH RULE CHALLENGED TRADITIONAL WAYS OF LIFE, THREATENING TO DESTROY INDIAN CULTURE AS IT HAD EXISTED. THE MATCH THAT TOUCHED THE POWDER KEG, HOWEVER, WAS A GUN.

In 1856, a new firearm was introduced to the Indian armies under British control: the Enfield rifle. In order to use the weapon, a soldier had to bite off the end of the ammunition cartridges, as well as revitalize the bullets' lubricant with saliva. A rumour quickly spread that the cartridges were greased with cow and pig fat. The cow is a sacred animal in Hinduism, and the pig a sacred animal in Islam; having to bite cartridges covered in these animals' grease greatly offended Hindu and Muslim soldiers alike, spawning the mutiny. In April 1857, Indian soldiers, or 'sepoys', at Meerut refused to use the cartridges, and were subsequently imprisoned. Their fellow soldiers, however, shot the British officers and freed their comrades, then marched to Delhi.

ABOVE The cow is a sacred animal in Hinduism, as shown at this temple in Chennai. The thought of licking bullets greased in cow fat was abhorrent to Hindu soldiers.

ABOVE Suttee, the practice of burning a widow on the funeral pyre of her dead husband, was one custom the British sought to abolish in India.

BIGGER ISSUES

The scandal over the ammunition for the Enfield rifle was really just the event that tipped the scales for the Indian sepoys who mutinied. Several other factors contributed to the uprising, including an apparent disregard by the British for the local customs and traditions in India. Britain was taking more and more control of India under the guise of the British East India Company. But their dominance extended far beyond the marketplace, and British officials in India sought to reform many aspects of the country they deemed to be barbaric, wrong or simply unnecessary. For example, they attempted to remove the practice of *suttee* (also spelled *sati*), whereby a widow burns herself to death on the funeral pyre of her husband. Even the caste system, a basic principle of Hindu society, appeared threatened, and the hundreds of Christian missionaries spreading throughout India only increased the unrest.

ABOVE An illustration of violent action during the Sepoy Mutiny near Delhi.

ABOVE Field Marshal Hugh Henry Rose led British troops against the Sepoy Mutiny.

MUTINY SPREADS

Although the initial mutiny was relatively small in scale, it quickly spread to neighbouring regions in India, confirming the widespread dissatisfaction with British rule throughout India. Organizing in Delhi, the sepoys named Bahadur Shah II of the Mughal Dynasty the ruler of all India, and grouped together under his name. The first major engagements were at Lucknow and Karnal two months after the initial mutiny. At Karnal the British were able to drive the rebels back to Delhi, where a siege ensued during the summer of 1857. By this point in history, the British had already reduced the number of British troops in India considerably, so it took a long time for reinforcements from Britain to arrive and organize into a meaningful force in India. Though the British besieged Delhi, they did not have enough men to do so effectively. However, when reinforcements arrived, the British were eventually able to defeat the sepoys at Delhi.

Fighting continued for much of the next year, and British retaliation against the mutineers was swift and brutal. In the end, both sides committed many atrocities; independence for India, however, would have to wait until Mohandas Ghandi in the 1940s.

ABOVE A mosque in Meerut where rebels took refuge.

THE BOXER REBELLION 1899–1901

THE RIGHTEOUS FISTS

BY THE END OF THE NINETEENTH CENTURY, CHINA HAD BEEN WEAKENED BY WARS WITH THE BRITISH AND FRENCH, BY THE MASSIVE TAIPING REBELLION AND BY WIDESPREAD USE OF OPIUM. IN REACTION TO FOREIGN POWERS, A SECT OF MARTIAL ARTISTS ROSE UP.

The 'Boxers' were a group of martial artists known in Chinese as the Yihetuan, or 'Righteous and Harmonious Fists'. The sect included a range of martial artists, but in its extreme form it became known for various rituals that were supposed to make the practitioner impervious to bullets. Unsurprisingly, they didn't.

As antiforeign members won more control in the Chinese government, they helped the Boxers attain more official status by organizing them into militias, the Yihetuan. In 1899, the Boxers went on the offensive, attacking foreigners in Beijing. The size of the uprising helped convince Empress Dowager Cixi to declare war on foreign powers, despite having initially sent the imperial army to quell the rebellion.

A ROCK AND A HARD PLACE

Wars with foreign powers had not gone well for China during the nineteenth century, and it was in part because of the unfair treaties China had been forced to sign that there was so much unrest in the country. When the Boxers rebelled in 1899, there was a kind of damned-if-you-do, damned-if-you-don't quality to the whole affair. The situation was deteriorating as foreign powers claimed more political, economic and even religious control in China; many feared they would even lose their lands. However, China lacked the organization and weapon technology to combat Britain, France, Russia, the United States, Germany, Japan and other powers that were taking over.

The Boxers, who began targeting Christian missionaries, quickly involved foreign nations after killing a few foreign railway engineers in June 1900. The Boxers marched on Peking (Beijing), and the foreigners grouped together in the Legation Quarter and in the cathedral, where a siege soon followed from 20 June to 14 August 1900. The siege ended when foreign armies of some 20,000 men were able to break through because of their advanced weaponry and training in battlefield tactics.

The rebellion was broken at this point, but officially ended in September 1901 with the Boxer Protocol. The treaty stated that China would have to pay reparations to the foreign powers over a period of 39 years.

OPPOSITE LEFT US Army soldiers during the siege of Beijing in 1900.

OPPOSITE RIGHT The Imperial Palace at Beijing being taken by British and Japanese soldiers.

ABOVE Many Chinese priests and Christians were killed during the Boxer Rebellion and have subsequently been considered martyrs.

RIGHT The Japanese and Western powers captured the Dagu Forts near Tianjin after hard fighting.

THE RUSSO-JAPANESE WAR 1904–1905

TWENTIETH-CENTURY WAR

THE RUSSO-JAPANESE WAR WAS REALLY THE FIRST MAJOR CONFLICT OF THE TWENTIETH CENTURY. BOTH RUSSIA AND JAPAN AIMED TO ESTABLISH CONTROL OF MANCHURIA. THE WAR ALLOWED JAPAN TO SHOW THE EXTENT OF ITS NEWFOUND POWER.

Following the Meiji Restoration of 1868, Japan sought to modernize its society, aggressively adopting Western practices and customs. Japan also adopted Western technology and weaponry. Rather than combating the Western powers, Japan sent its generals and leaders to learn from them, eventually enabling the island nation to strike out with tremendous power and the most advanced technology and tactics of the day.

THE POWERS CONVERGE

Japan had long harboured ambitions of conquering China. In 1894, the Japanese fought against the Chinese in the first Sino-Japanese War, taking control of several territories, including Taiwan and the Liaodong Peninsula. China also gave up its control of Korea, a massive victory for Japan, which viewed Korea as a buffer state between itself and China. Korea was also rich in natural resources – resources Japan lacked and desperately needed.

ABOVE The Japanese won an important victory at Tsushima in 1905. Here, Admiral Togo stands onboard the battleship *Mikasa*.

BELOW LEFT Russian soldiers retreat to the Chinese border with their horses and equipment following their defeat at the Battle of Mukden.

BELOW RIGHT View from a cliff looking down towards Port Arthur.

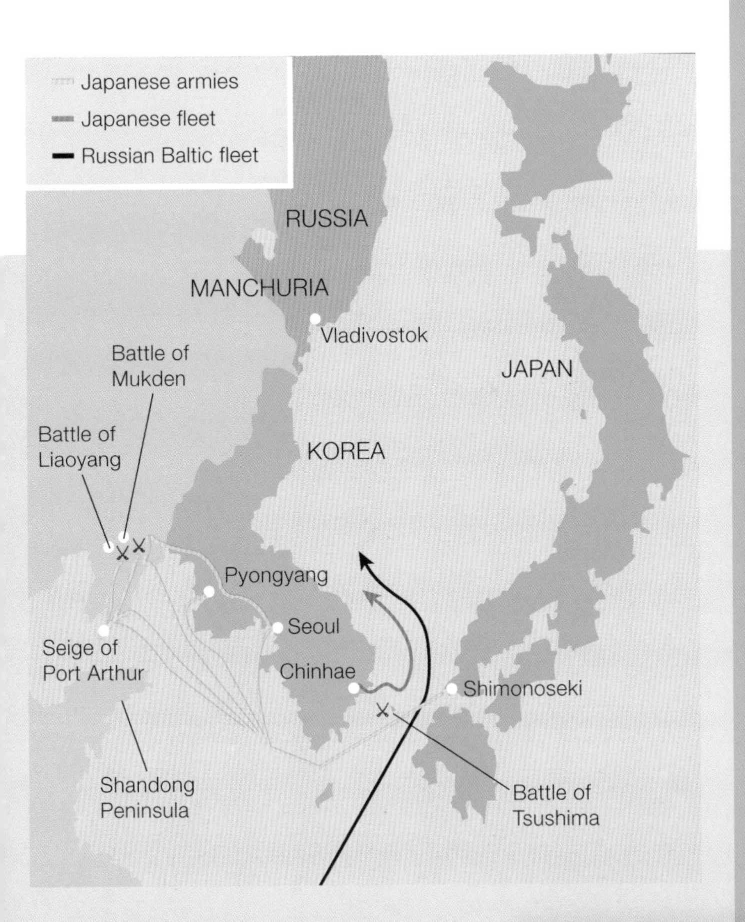

ABOVE Russian soldiers enter the gates of Mukden. Russian forces at the Battle of Mukden totalled more than 300,000.

LEFT Japan shocked the world when it defeated enormous Russia.

Only three years after the Treaty of Shimonoseki, the Russians started to move in. Russia negotiated with China for use of Port Arthur in 1898. They quickly fortified their position there, as it was a vitally strategic port for them. While they had another port on the Pacific coast at Vladivostok, Port Arthur differed in that it could be used all year instead of just during the summer. At the same time, Russia began building a railway across Siberia to Port Arthur, and also started moving into Korea. All of these actions put Japan on edge.

Both Japan and Russia were part of an eight-nation force that entered Beijing in 1900 to quell the Boxer Rebellion. The rebellion gave Russia justification for sending more troops to Manchuria. Despite Russia's claims that it would withdraw the troops later, this did not seem their true intention. In 1902, Japan formed a strategic alliance with Britain. A year later, in 1903, Japan entered negotiations with Russia over control of Manchuria and Korea. Japan proposed Russia

ABOVE The Battle of Port Arthur in 1904 was the first battle of the Russo-Japanese War.

taking control of Manchuria, while Japan would take Korea. Despite appearing willing to negotiate, Russia eventually did not respond further to these negotiations. Japan severed ties on 4 February; four days later, on 8 February 1904, the Japanese fleet attacked the Russians at the Battle of Port Arthur.

CONSEQUENCES

The Japanese and Russians fought several battles, both at sea and on land. British intelligence officers aided Japan throughout the war on account of the alliance between Japan and Britain. Japan managed to get the upper hand at the final clash on land, the Battle of Mukden, where some 270,000 Japanese soldiers fought against approximately 330,000 Russians. Japan then delivered a crushing blow at the Battle of Tsushima in May 1905, sinking the Russian's Baltic fleet. Russia was now ready to negotiate. US President Theodore Roosevelt served as the mediator in the peace discussions and the signing of the Treaty of Portsmouth. Japan won control of all of Korea, the Liaotung Peninsula, including Port Arthur, and half of Sakhalin Island. It was an important victory for Japan, which had shocked not only Russia, but the entire world with its strength both on the battlefield and at sea.

ABOVE Despite being outnumbered, the Japanese defeated Russia at the last major land battle of the war, the Battle of Mukden.

FAR LEFT Cold and weary Russian soldiers rest by a pile of Japanese corpses at Port Arthur.

LEFT Japanese soldiers march across the River Yalu separating Korea and Manchuria.

BATTLE OF TSUSHIMA

The decisive final victory of the Russo-Japanese war was won at the Battle of Tsushima, fought in the Tsushima Strait on 27-28 May 1905. The Japanese fought against the Russian fleet that had sailed all the way from the Baltic Sea. As the Russian fleet in the Far East met its demise at the hands of the Japanese, the Tsar decided to send part of the Baltic fleet all the way to Vladivostok. The Japanese, under the direction of Tōgō Heihachirō, benefited from more advanced communication systems developed by the Japanese. They used, for one of the first times in history, wireless telegraphy to help manage the tactical manoeuvres and adjustments at sea. The Russians also used wireless telegraphy, but had inferior German-built machines, and suffered as a result. Using their more advanced communications systems and naval intelligence, the Japanese destroyed two-thirds of the Russian fleet.

ABOVE A bird's-eye-view of some of the major battlefields of the Russo-Japanese War. Port Arthur can be seen at the tip of the Liaodong Peninsula.

BELOW The Japanese won an important early victory at the Battle of River Yalu in 1904, the first major land battle of the Russo-Japanese War.

IWO JIMA 1945

TAKING THE HILL

ONE OF THE FIERCEST ENGAGEMENTS OF WORLD WAR II, THE BATTLE OF IWO JIMA WOULD COST THE LIVES OF THOUSANDS. THE AMERICAN CAPTURE OF MOUNT SURIBACHI WOULD ALSO BECOME ONE OF THE MOST ICONIC IMAGES OF THE WAR.

The Battle of Iwo Jima was fought in order to gain three airbases on the volcanic island. These would prove strategically important in launching any kind of invasion of the main islands of Japan. By this point in the war, the US and Japan had already engaged each other in numerous battles throughout the Pacific. This invasion brought the war to Japan's home soil, and they defended it to the death. Iwo Jima provided a critical first step for American and Allied forces to take Okinawa only a few months later.

OPERATION DETACHMENT

For months prior to the landing, US Navy and Air Forces had been bombarding the island, testing the strength of the resistance and attempting to weaken the Japanese forces resisting capture. Then, on 19 February 1945, the US launched a massive amphibious landing, sending in about 30,000 Marines onto the beaches. The volcanic black sand made the going tough. Soldiers could not dig effective foxholes in the sand, and tanks struggled to advance. When they came onto the beach, the Japanese were nowhere to be seen.

The Japanese forces who defended Iwo Jima had hunkered down inside the caves on the island, and were prepared for the invasion. As the US Marines advanced with trepidation, the hidden Japanese at last revealed themselves by mowing down American troops with machine-gun fire. Fierce fighting ensued as the Americans struggled to get near the caves and hideouts of the Japanese. The Americans soon began using grenades and flamethrowers to blast and burn their opponents out of their defences. Thousands of litres of oil were used every day in the flamethrowers. Meanwhile, the Navy continued to assist from the sea. On 23 February, the Marines took Mount Suribachi, a stronghold of the Japanese

ABOVE The USS *New York* blasts the island of Iwo Jima in February 1945.

BELOW Volcanic black sand made vehicular transport on the island extremely difficult.

defence. A group of American soldiers famously raised the American flag on top of the volcano in what has become – in America at least – perhaps the most iconic image of World War II.

TO THE MAN

Surrender was not an option for the Japanese. Fewer than 300 Japanese soldiers surrendered, and out of more than 20,000 Japanese soldiers who initially defended the island, only about 1,200 survived the battle by its conclusion on 26 March. Casualties on the American side were likewise high, with roughly 6,000 killed and an additional 20,000 wounded. Such valour was displayed by American servicemen during this 36-day battle that an astounding 27 Medals of Honor were awarded to American soldiers for their contributions at Iwo Jima.

ABOVE The USS *Bunker Hill* in flames after kamikaze attacks while supporting the Battle of Okinawa, just weeks after Iwo Jima.

BELOW Map showing the advance of American soldiers onto Iwo Jima.

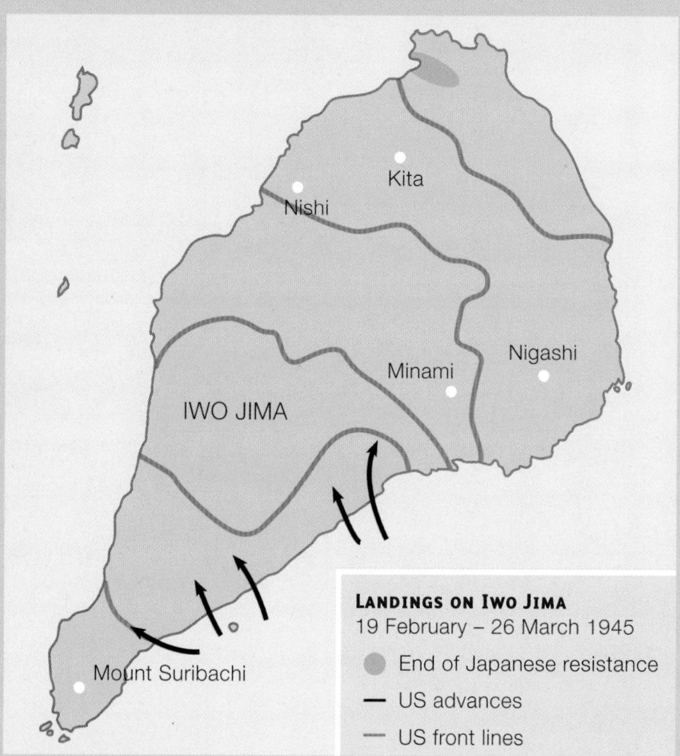

BELOW The American flag flies on top of Mount Suribachi on Iwo Jima.

NUCLEAR WEAPONS

THREAT OF ANNIHILATION

The development of nuclear weapons during World War II completely changed the nature of combat and warfare. Though only two nuclear bombs have been deployed on human opponents so far, the sheer devastation they caused has changed how we conceptualize and even how we regulate warfare.

Two atomic bombs, or A-bombs, were dropped on Japan by US forces at the end of World War II: one on Hiroshima on 6 August, and the other on Nagasaki three days later on 9 August 1945. Although tests of these weapons had been carried out prior, no one could have known for sure how devastating they would be when

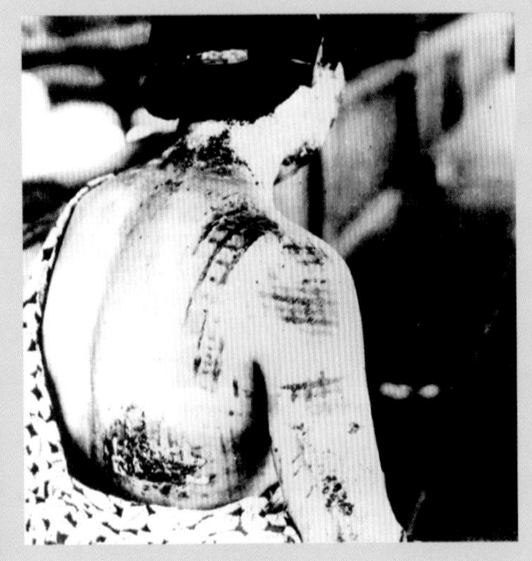

TOP **Skin burns reveal the pattern of cloth worn by this Japanese victim of an atomic bomb.**

ABOVE **These ruins would later be turned into the Hiroshima Peace Memorial.**

LEFT **The famous mushroom cloud towers about Nagasaki.**

FISSION AND FUSION

There are two types of nuclear weapons: fission and fusion. In fission weapons, atoms are split, releasing a huge amount of energy. In fusion reactions, atoms are fused together, creating an even greater release of energy. Fusion bombs, often referred to as hydrogen bombs, use a fission reaction to power the fusion, and are several times more powerful. The bombs dropped in Japan created fission reactions.

ABOVE The *Enola Gay* was the plane used to drop the atomic bomb on Hiroshima.

used on an actual city. Sadly, the bombs were in fact dropped on these two cities, and most of the casualties were civilians. It is estimated that around 70,000 people were killed in the single blast at Hiroshima; thousands more would die from burns and radiation. Some estimates put the total number of deaths from these two bombs at over 200,000.

NEVER BEFORE IN HISTORY HAS A WEAPON BEEN SO POWERFUL AS TO COMPLETELY ANNIHILATE THE OPPOSITION AND CREATE A DESTRUCTIVE FORCE WHOSE EFFECTS WOULD BE FELT FOR GENERATIONS.

YOU WOULD BE MAD

The shocking destruction by the atomic bombs in Japan raised many moral and ethical questions in the years to come. Other world powers quickly sought to obtain nuclear weapons, and before long the capability of mass destruction appeared to actually prevent it. A strategy emerged, known as Mutually Assured Destruction (MAD). When two nations, both possessing nuclear weapons, use a nuclear weapon on the other, then they have ensured their own destruction through the inevitable nuclear retaliation. This strategy gave rise to the arms race of the Cold War between the United States and the Soviet Union. What is frightening to consider is that the nuclear weapons developed since World War II are far more powerful than the ones dropped on Hiroshima and Nagasaki.

BELOW Catholic cathedral in ruins at Nagasaki.

INDO-PAKISTANI WARS 1947–PRESENT

INITIAL SPLIT

IN 1947, INHABITANTS OF NORTHERN INDIA WANTED TO SPLIT BRITISH INDIA INTO TWO DISTINCT STATES ALONG RELIGIOUS LINES, SEPARATING MUSLIM PAKISTAN FROM HINDU HINDUSTAN. THE SPLIT CAUSED DISPUTES OVER CERTAIN TERRITORIES, HOWEVER, AND WAR ERUPTED.

The initial division left large groups of Muslims still in Hindu India, as well as Hindus in Muslim Pakistan. As people scrambled to move to their respective sides, tensions between Muslims, Sikhs and Hindus mounted, quickly turning violent. The first war in 1947 centred around the territory of Jammu and Kashmir, where the Maharaja was given control of the decision of which side to join: India or Pakistan. Fearing he would choose the former, Pakistani Muslims invaded Kashmir, ironically prompting the Maharaja to choose to join India – exactly the outcome they sought to avoid.

The violence of this first war was widespread, resulting in the deaths of approximately half a million people. Eventually, the United Nations intervened, establishing a division of Kashmir on 21 April 1948. The northwest of the territory went to Pakistan, while the south and east went to India, divided by a Line of Control.

WAR NOT OVER

In 1965, Pakistan sent forces covertly into Jammu and Kashmir as part of Operation Gibraltar, designed to spark an insurgency against Indian rule in Kashmir. India fought back, however, and the two nations clashed heavily on the battlefield, resulting in thousands of casualties over a period of just five weeks. The war is known for the extensive deployment of tanks. At the end of the war, little had changed in terms of territorial holdings. Animosity continued to brew between India and Pakistan.

In 1971, war broke out again, this time in modern-day Bangladesh. At the time, the territory was known as East Pakistan. The Pakistani army targeted Hindu civilians in Bangladesh in what are now known as the Bangladesh Atrocities of 1971. The atrocities were committed during

ABOVE Pakistani fighter planes in tight formation.

LEFT In 1965, Pakistani troops capture Khem Karn in India.

LEFT The Indo-Pakistani Wars saw extensive use of tanks.

ABOVE Pervez Musharraf, President of Pakistan, in 2002.

BELOW Indian soldiers fighting for Kashmir in the first Indo-Pakistani War of 1947–48.

the Bangladesh Liberation War, waged between East Pakistan and Pakistan. Refugees poured into India from East Pakistan; Indian joined the conflict on 3 December, claiming victory within two weeks. The result was the creation of Bangladesh as an independent nation.

ARMS RACE

In 1974, India detonated its first test nuclear weapon, causing a stir internationally and provoking an arms race with neighbouring Pakistan. Over the next 25 years, both nations would acquire and test nuclear weapons in a kind of cold war. In 1999, however, Pakistan invaded the Kashmiri region of Kargil, perhaps hoping the possession of nuclear weapons would deter a military response. But India responded, sending troops into the region and driving the Pakistanis out. Tensions between the two nations continue to this day. India claims that Pakistan has supported terrorist violence against India, including the 2008 bombing in Mumbai that claimed the lives of more than 170 people.

KOREAN WAR 1950–1953

CLASH OF IDEOLOGIES

FOLLOWING THE COLLAPSE OF THE JAPANESE EMPIRE AT THE END OF WORLD WAR II, KOREA HAD NO FORM OF GOVERNMENT TO LEAD THE NATION. BEFORE LONG, THE STRUGGLE FOR CONTROL OVER KOREA BECAME A CLASH OF IDEOLOGIES.

Japan annexed Korea in 1910 and controlled the territory until the collapse of the Japanese Empire in 1945, at which point Russian troops entered from the north. Initially greeted as liberators, the Russian advance south would stop at the 38th parallel, because of an agreement with the United States designed to facilitate establishing a new government. However, by the time elections were held in 1948, the friendly relations between the Soviet Union and the United States had ended and the Cold War was under way. It became impossible to foster the establishment of a new government because of extreme ideological differences between the Soviet Union and the United States.

ABOVE RIGHT An American airstrike on railway bridges with B-29 bombers in 1950.

RIGHT A young Korean girl carries her brother on her back. Millions were displaced by the war.

ABOVE An executed American POW lies face down in a pile of stones.

ABOVE Korea was arbitrarily divided along the 38th parallel for administrative purposes. This division subsequently became political and military.

DEEP DIVISIONS

North Korea fell under the influence of the Soviet Union and the People's Republic of China, which pushed the Kuomintang south to Taiwan in 1949. Communism ruled the north, while the south held democratic elections in 1948, electing anti-communist leader Syngman Rhee. On 25 June 1950, North Korea under the leadership of Kim Il-sung invaded South Korea, beginning the Korean War.

The conflict quickly escalated into an international war, with the Soviet Union and the People's Republic of China assisting the North, and the United Nations force comprised mostly of American and British troops assisting the South. Almost 350,000 international soldiers were sent to assist South Korea in repelling the invasion, most of them American. General Douglas Macarthur was stationed in Japan with a large force, so he and his men were the first to be deployed.

LEFT Billowing flames erupt after an American plane drops napalm in North Korea in 1951.

BACK AND FORTH

The Korean People's Army (KPA) of North Korea forced the Republic of Korea (ROK) south, quickly seizing control of much of South Korea. The UN forces were pushed back to an area around the port of Pusan, known as the Pusan Perimeter. The North Koreans exhausted themselves and their supplies trying to defeat the UN troops, but were unable to do so. Then, in September, General Macarthur launched an assault, landing at Inchon and driving the KPA north, eventually all the way across North Korea to China. But China and the Soviet Union sent reinforcements to the KPA, and the ROK and UN forces were driven south again. War continued to drag on in a horrible seesaw. American forces dropped thousands of pounds of explosives and napalm on North Korea, destroying many of its cities. The KPA killed thousands of civilians.

It is difficult to know the total number of casualties from the war, but most estimates put the death count at around three million, most of which were civilians. Both sides committed horrors, and the US even considered using nuclear weapons. North Korean mistreatment and killing of POWs also became an issue of international controversy. The war eventually came to an end on 27 July 1953, with Kim Il-sung controlling the north, and Syngman Rhee controlling the south. The deep division between North and South Korea can still be seen today. A demilitarized zone continues to separate the two countries.

THE VIETNAM WAR 1955–1975

THE TIDE OF COMMUNISM

THE VIETNAM WAR, WHICH ERUPTED SHORTLY AFTER THE END OF THE KOREAN WAR, GREW FROM THE SAME ROOTS: AN INTERNATIONAL – PARTICULARLY AMERICAN – DESIRE TO STEM THE TIDE OF COMMUNISM AS IT SPREAD ACROSS ASIA.

Even before gaining independence from French colonial rule, Vietnam was split in two: the south, which gained independence in 1949, and the north, which gained independence in 1954 after protracted fighting with the French and other international forces. The split of the country was more than geographic, for the south was anti-communist while the north was communist. The United States supported France in its efforts to maintain possession of its colony.

War broke out between north and south as the communist government of North Vietnam, under Ho Chi Minh, sought to unite the country and throw off the remnants of colonial rule. When John F Kennedy was elected President in 1960, he committed to stemming the global tide of communism. American anti-communism, however, did not deter the actions of the Soviet Union or succeed in stopping communism in Cuba. Determined, Kennedy entered the Vietnam War, sending thousands of American troops to support South Vietnam.

BELOW LEFT An American soldier walks before the burning ruins of a Viet Cong camp.

BELOW RIGHT Ho Chi Minh's communist North defeated the South.

ABOVE The Tet Offensive left tremendous destruction in its wake, as seen here in this image from Saigon.

ABOVE Negotiating the jungles posed many difficulties for American soldiers.

AN UPHILL BATTLE

Several factors made the Vietnam War difficult for American and South Vietnamese forces. First, Ho Chi Minh was far more popular than his southern counterpart, Ngo Dinh Diem, who was seen as a dictatorial elitist in support of colonial rule. Diem sought to control the people of the south through harsh policies, imprisoning and even killing thousands who opposed his anti-communist rule. Not surprisingly, this only made him even less popular.

Though the south had its own forces, many view the war in Vietnam as a war between North Vietnam and the United States. Once America committed troops to combat the North Vietnamese, it was impossible to withdraw without admitting some form of defeat. The Americans therefore sent thousands more troops under Pres Lyndon B Johnson, but seemed unable to defeat the combination of guerrilla war waged by the National Liberation Front (NLF – more commonly, Viet Cong) in the south and the more traditional war waged by the Vietnam People's Army of the north.

AN INCREDIBLE SHOT

Of the many tales of heroism and daring that came out of the Vietnam War, one of the most incredible is that of Carlos Hathcock, one of the greatest US Marine snipers of all time. Seeing the glint of an enemy sniper's scope in the bushes, Hathcock quickly took aim and fired. The body of the enemy sniper was found with his broken scope lying next to him. Hathcock had shot the sniper in the eye through the sniper's own scope.

TET OFFENSIVE

In 1968, the communists launched a massive attack, taking the south by surprise by striking during the Vietnamese lunar New Year. Despite storming cities across the country, the North Vietnamese were unable to sustain the attack or maintain possession of their conquests, and were quickly repulsed. More importantly, however, the offensive did not trigger a people's uprising in the south as was hoped. The communists suffered heavy casualties, and the failure of the Tet Offensive presented an opportunity for the south and the Americans to finally gain a foothold in the war. But American casualties mounted in a war far from home that seemed increasingly pointless. With support for the war at an all-time low, it was impossible to commit more American troops to the effort.

President Nixon began slowly withdrawing troops. American involvement would last until 1973, however, after the Paris Peace Accords were signed. Without American military support, the Republic of Vietnam in the south could not hold out against Ho Chi Minh's forces. Saigon was captured in 1975, and Ho Chi Minh managed to unite Vietnam under communist rule.

LEFT A US Marine escorts a suspected NLF member near Da Nang.

THE SRI LANKAN CIVIL WAR 1983–2009

THE TAMIL TIGERS

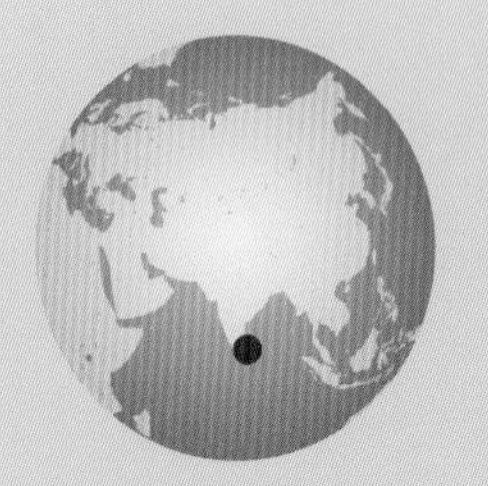

IN 1983, A GROUP KNOWN AS THE TAMIL TIGERS ROSE UP AGAINST THE SRI LANKAN GOVERNMENT WITH THE AIM OF FOUNDING A TAMIL NATION IN THE NORTH AND EAST OF SRI LANKA.

Sri Lanka is inhabited by two major ethnic groups: the Sinhala and the Tamil. After British colonial rule, there were early efforts to replace English with Sinhalese and Tamil as official languages. But when certain officials started promoting the use of only Sinhalese, tensions between the ethnic groups began to mount, leading to the formation of the Liberation Tigers of Tamil Eelam (LTTE), also known as the Tamil Tigers. Their goal was to create their own Tamil state, known as Eelam.

VIOLENCE ESCALATES

Violence and assassinations started long before the outbreak of civil war in 1983. But when the LTTE attacked an army post and killed 13 soldiers in July 1983, it prompted a large and violent reaction from the Sinhalese, spawning pogroms that resulted in the deaths of up to 3,000 Tamils. The month is known as Black July and is regarded as the start of the civil war.

The tactics of the Tigers led several nations around the world to regard them as terrorists. Funding their activities through drug trafficking and using suicide bombings as a prominent tool in their campaigns, the Tamil Tigers killed many civilians in addition to their political targets. Despite initially showing support for the Tamils, India attempted to intervene in 1987 with the aim of bringing the war to an end and establishing peace. The Indian army ended up fighting the Tamil Tigers, resulting in more than 1,000 Indian deaths, and perhaps eight times that number for the Tigers.

BELOW LEFT A platoon of LTTE infantry on bicycles.

BELOW RIGHT Armed Tamil Tigers piled into the back of a camouflaged truck in Killinochi in 2004.

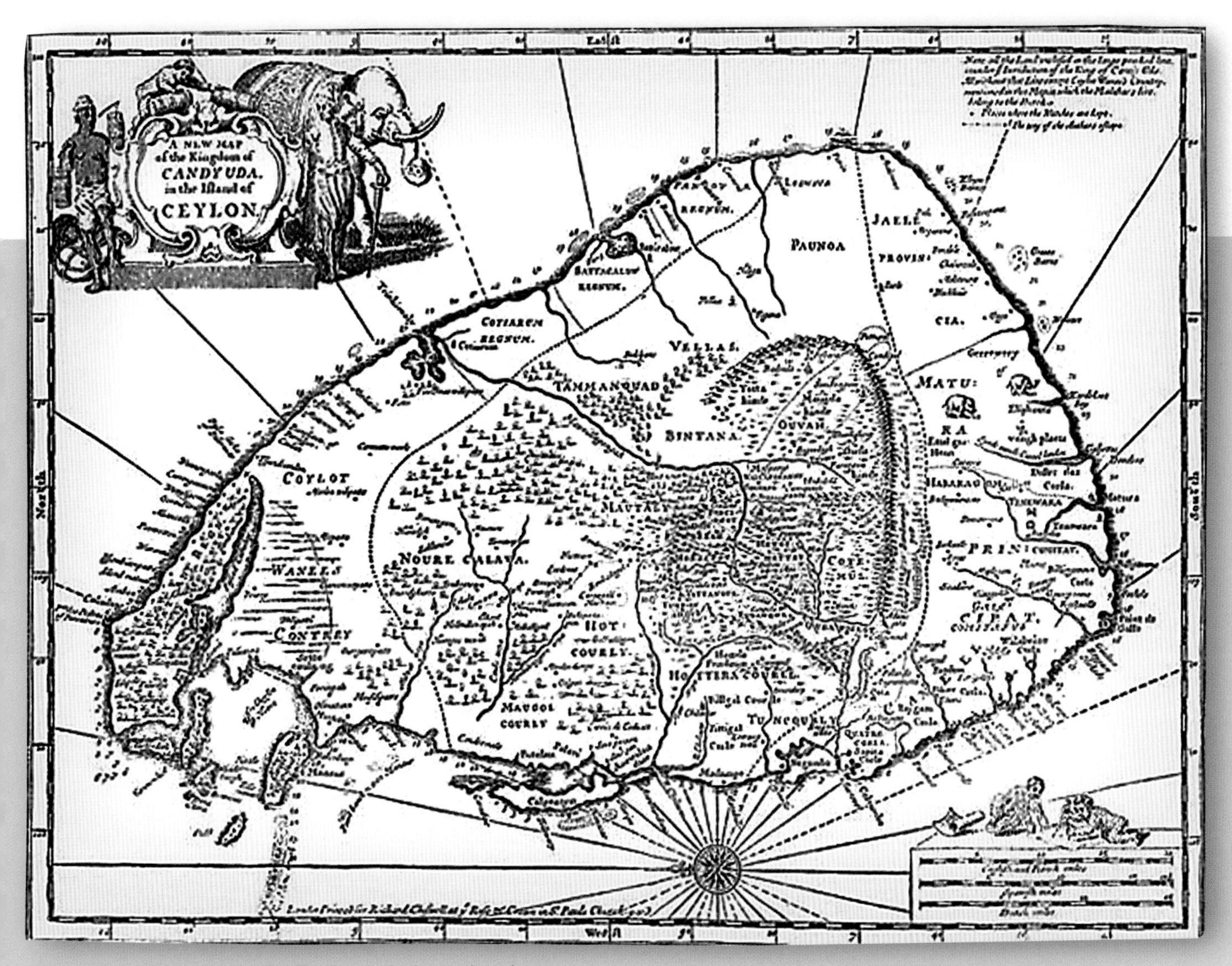

ABOVE Map of Sri Lanka showing Tamil areas in the north and east.

Several attempts at peace were made throughout the course of the civil war, including promising talks in 2001, resulting in a ceasefire in 2002. In 2004, the devastating tsunami in the Indian Ocean struck Sri Lanka hard, killing more than 35,000 people on the island. Rather than serving as an opportunity to unite the country, disputes broke out over the distribution of foreign aid to territories claimed by the LTTE. Violence erupted again in 2006, and the Sri Lankan government decided to go on the offensive in 2007. By this point, the international community was decidedly against the LTTE, especially following the assassination of the former Sri Lankan Minister of Foreign Affairs in 2005. The Sri Lankan government began by taking Tamil territories in the east in 2007, then moved north, officially breaking the ceasefire in 2008 and taking the Tamil capital of Killinochi early in 2009. They continued to wipe out Tamil resistance within the next few months during 2009, finally bringing the war to an end. Roughly 80,000 people were killed during the course of the war.

ABOVE Female Tamil Tigers parade in Killinochi.

Iapan ins. nuper ad Fidem Christianam conversa
Foquiem
Cequi
Circulus Cancri.
Islas de Lucois.
Philippinas.
Los Bolcanes
Timor
Baixos
Nova Guinea, quibusdam Terra de Piccinacoli.
Insulæ Salomonis.
Circulus Capricorni.
SPE ET METV.
GENIO ET INGENIO NOBILI DN. NICOLAO ROCCOXIO, PATRICIO ANTVERPIENSI, EIVSDEMQVE VRBIS SENATORI,
Abrahamus Ortelius Regiæ Mtis geographus lub. merito dedicabat.
1589.

MARIS PACIFICI,
(quod vulgò Mar del Zur)
cum regionibus circumiacentibus, insulisque in eodem
passim sparsis, novissima descriptio.
Noua Hispania
MARIS ATLANTICI
SIVE MAR DEL NORT
Cuba
Jamaica

OCEANIA

Circulus Aequinoctialis.
Y. de Cocos
Y. de Galopagos
La Trinidad
Isolas de lobos
Chili
Prima ego velivolis ambivi cursibus Orbem,
Magellane novo te duce ducta freto.
Ambivi, meritoq; vocor VICTORIA: sunt mi
Vela, alæ; precium, gloria; pugna, mare.

PREHISTORIC POLYNESIA

THE SEAFARERS

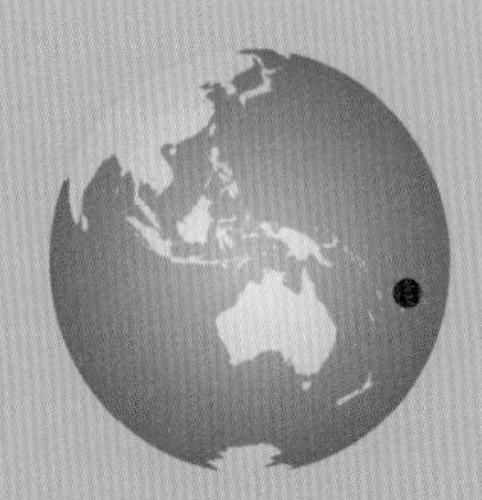

POLYNESIA IS A SUBSET OF ISLANDS IN OCEANIA IN THE SOUTH PACIFIC. ALMOST ALL THE PEOPLES OF POLYNESIA STEM FROM AN ORIGINAL AUSTRONESIAN SOURCE AND, FROM THE THE SECOND MILLENNIUM BCE, THEY SPREAD THROUGH THE SOUTH PACIFIC FROM TAIWAN, EAST TO HAWAII AND SOUTH TO NEW ZEALAND.

ABOVE Megalithic ruins from the prehistoric town of Nan Madol on the island of Pohnpei in Micronesia.

Oceania includes the groupings of islands known as Polynesia, Micronesia and Melanesia. The peoples of Polynesia originally came from Taiwan and were powerful seafarers, gradually spreading through the South Pacific by island-hopping. Linguistically, genetically and culturally, the Polynesians belong to the Austronesian family. Austronesian languages are widespread and are spoken as Malagasy in Madagascar, Taiwanese in Taiwan and Hawaiian in Hawaii. The significant prehistoric dispersion of Austronesian languages attests to the incredible skill the Polynesians had in navigation. The most vigorous expansionary expeditions probably began around 1000 CE, when Polynesians sailed east to Hawaii and south to New Zealand.

WARFARE OF POLYNESIA

Warfare in Polynesia was relatively small scale for the most part, especially early on. In New Zealand, later settlements would become quite large in size and be dominated by elaborate hillforts or 'pa'. With a few exceptions, the weaponry consisted of spears, clubs and daggers. The Polynesians were essentially a Stone-Age people, so their weapons were tipped with stone or bone points. Some clubs, like those used in Hawaii, were studded with sharks' teeth, making them gruesome weapons of war. Polished stone clubs, called *patu*, were common among the Maori in New Zealand.

LEFT A polished jade axe from New Zealand.

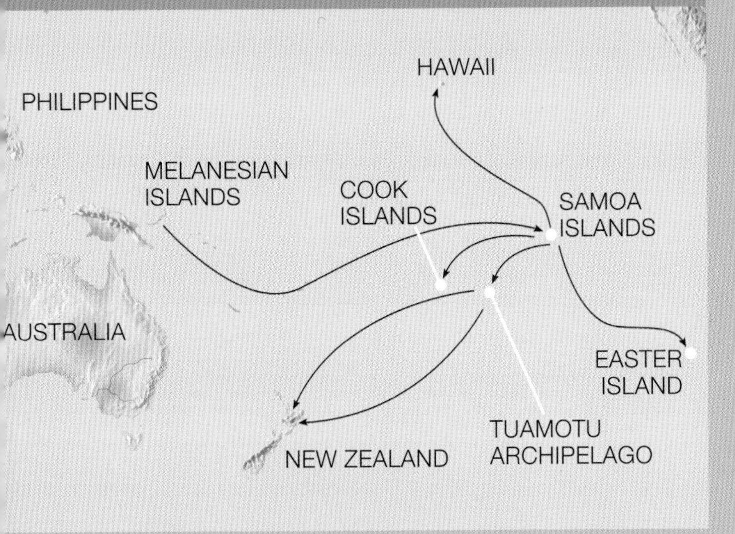

ABOVE This map shows the impressive migrations of the prehistoric Polynesians across the South Pacific.

ABOVE Wooden swordlike club. With no metal, prehistoric Polynesians relied on stone, bone and wood to make their weapons.

TOP Cannibalism was practised throughout much of Polynesia.

War was often waged for revenge and for taking captives. Captives could become warrior's wives, they could become slaves or they could be sacrificed. Warriors taken captive were often cannibalized owing to the belief that one would take the strength of his enemy by eating his flesh. When European explorers reached the islands of Polynesia, they sometimes found the inhabitants curious and ready to trade; but, equally, Europeans quickly learned the warlike nature of the Polynesians – even the famous Captain Cook met his fate at the hands of Hawaiians armed with clubs and knives in 1779. Sadly, we have to rely on archaeological evidence – as well as legendary tales – for any knowledge of warfare in Polynesia before the arrival of the Europeans.

KAMEHAMEHA THE GREAT 1782–1810

UNIFICATION OF HAWAII

IN THE MID-EIGHTEENTH CENTURY, A STAR APPEARED IN THE NIGHT SKY, PROMPTING THE *KAHUNA* OF HAWAII TO PROPHESY THE BIRTH OF A NEW KING WHO WOULD UNITE THE HAWAIIAN ISLANDS. THAT KING WOULD BE KAMEHAMEHA I.

ABOVE Hawaii is home to landscapes of exquisite beauty, as seen here in this photo of volcanic cliffs of the Ko'olau Range.

The star was named Kokoiki, and was probably Halley's Comet, which appeared in 1758. While no one knows for sure when Kamehameha was born, it was likely shortly after the comet appeared. Originally named Paiea, the 'hard-shelled crab', the future leader would later earn the name Kamehameha, 'The Very Lonely One'. He would be a king set apart from other chiefs and rulers.

RISE TO POWER

The story goes that Kamehameha was sentenced to be put to death upon his birth, owing to the prophecy, but he was raised in secret. The story is not dissimilar to that of many kings throughout world history who have achieved legendary status, such as Cyrus the Great. In 1782, Kamehameha's uncle, King Kalaniopuu of the island of Hawaii, died and left the kingdom to both his son, Kiwalao, and his nephew, Kamehameha. Kamehameha was entrusted with the 'war god' of the kingdom. Despite Kamehameha's tenuous claim to his cousin's kingship, bitter rivalry would soon spring up and turn to war. Within six months, the two were at war with one another, and Kamehameha had won the support of many of the local chieftains. Kiwalao was killed at the Battle of Mokuohai in 1782, and Kamehameha took control of the kingdom.

Kamehameha then set about conquering the neighbouring islands. By 1795, he had conquered all the islands but two: Kauai and Niihau. These would be ceded to Kamehameha in 1810 without bloodshed. Kamehameha thereby became sole ruler of all the Hawaiian Islands in 1810, unifying them. Kamehameha is known for establishing the 'Splintered Paddle' law, which was designed to protect civilians from harsh rulers and war. He is also known for building up the wealth of his kingdom through trade.

RIGHT Portrait of Kamehameha I, who united the Hawaiian Islands by 1810.

CAPTAIN COOK

The Hawaiian Islands became widely know in the English-speaking world after the expeditions of Captain James Cook. Cook came to Hawaii in 1776 on his third voyage and was received well by the native population. He was able to communicate by using some of the Polynesian language he had learned from the Maori and the Tahitians. Despite the relatively friendly relations with the natives, Cook would ultimately meet his demise in the islands. After one of his ships was stolen, he took some men to intervene, and some of the natives attacked them, striking Cook in the head and then stabbing him to death on 14 February 1779. Kamehameha had met Cook and been aboard his ship, HMS *Resolution.*

TOP This painting shows King Kalaniopuu sailing to meet Captain Cook.

TOP RIGHT A coin commemorating Captain James Cook.

CENTRE RIGHT Plaque commemorating the Battle of Kepaniwai in 1790. In one of Hawaii's bloodiest battles, Kamehameha fought against the forces of Maui. It would be another three years before he would gain control of the island.

RIGHT There are hundreds of islands in the Hawaiian Island chain, but only eight main islands.

MAORI CONQUESTS 1300–1843
FROM ACROSS THE SEA

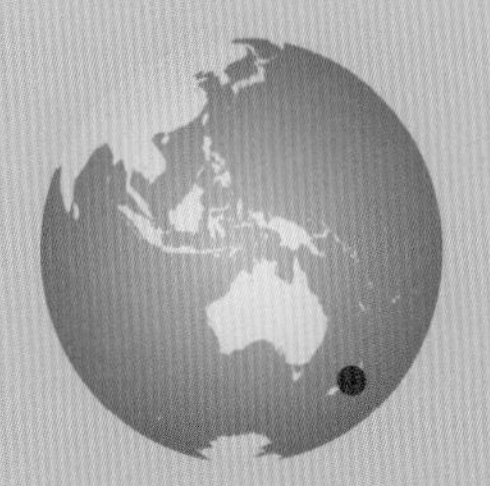

AROUND 1300 CE, AN AUSTRONESIAN PEOPLE CAME TO NEW ZEALAND FROM EASTERN POLYNESIA AND SETTLED THE ISLANDS. THEY WERE THE MAORI, A STRONG AND WARLIKE PEOPLE, WHOSE CULTURE AND LANGUAGE WOULD LAST UNTIL TODAY.

When the Maori settled New Zealand in the fourteenth century, they brought with them an advanced seafaring culture with a strong warrior tradition. Several different tribes developed across the islands, and the wars between them were often fierce and bloody. Indeed, when Europeans began coming to the islands after the voyages of Captain James Cook, the introduction of muskets and firearms would be used initially in fighting other Maori tribes, rather than the Europeans who eventually took control of the islands.

BELOW Hongi Hika befriended English missionary, Thomas Kendall, but never converted to Christianity himself, as he considered it to be a religion for the weak.

A MYTHICAL PAST

By the time Cook arrived in 1769, New Zealand had only been settled for a few centuries, so the settlement of the islands lived on in the legendary tales of the local populations. Some of these have been shown to have a basis in historical fact. For example, the Maori claim their people came from across the sea in oceangoing *waka*, the large canoes of the Maori; archaeological and linguistic evidence suggests that they arrived around 1300 from east Polynesia. There are also legends that when they arrived, there were large birds capable of killing human beings. In fact, by the time Cook arrived two types of birds had become extinct in New Zealand from overhunting and destruction of their

ABOVE Maori leader, Hongi Hika, quickly saw the value of European firearms and sought to procure as many as possible.

BELOW Illustrations from a 17th-century manual illustrating the safe handling of a musket.

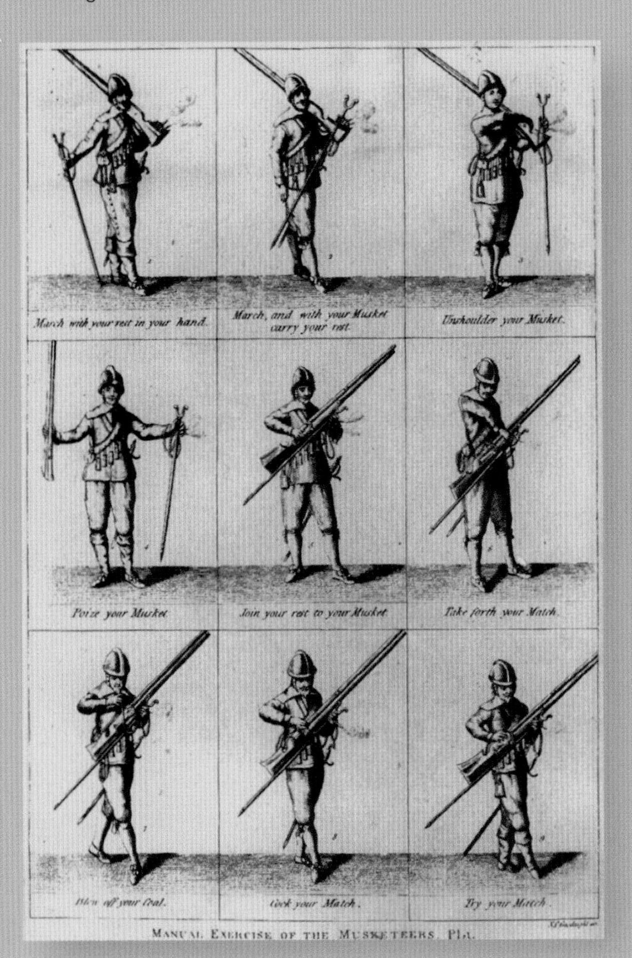

ABOVE Although not the first European to travel to New Zealand, Captain Cook was the first to circumnavigate the islands. Cook was brutally killed in Hawaii, as shown here.

habitat. The first was the moa, a large, flightless bird, some varieties of which stood as high as 3.7 m (12 feet). The second was the Haast's eagle – an eagle larger than any on earth today, which lived in the forests and hunted moa.

As muskets and firearms were gradually introduced to the Stone-Age societies of the Maori in the late eighteenth century, Maori warriors soon discovered their effectiveness at settling scores on the battlefield. In 1807 or 1808, the first major musket battle between the Maori took place at Moremonui between the Ngati Whatua and the Nga Puhi. The Nga Puhi possessed the muskets, but were defeated by a counter-attack while reloading. Hongi Hika, the chief of the defeated Nga Puhi, was unfazed, for he realized the effectiveness of the new firearms and quickly worked to obtain more.

MORE GUNS

For the next 15 years, he would continue his efforts to obtain more muskets – he even travelled to England. He used the muskets to conquer neighbouring tribes and take captives who worked as slaves to fund the purchase of yet more muskets. Nearly 20,000 people were killed in the Musket Wars that lasted until the early 1840s. Considering that the Maori population was only about 100,000 at the time, this is a significant portion of the population. The Maori soon found themselves facing an outside opponent, however, as they began opposing the sale of their land to British settlers. This sparked the New Zealand Wars, beginning in 1845. The Europeans found the Maori hill forts very difficult to take, even with superior firepower. Nonetheless, the Maori eventually succumbed to the superior military power of the British.

BLACK WAR 1804–1835

FALL OF TASMANIAN ABORIGINES

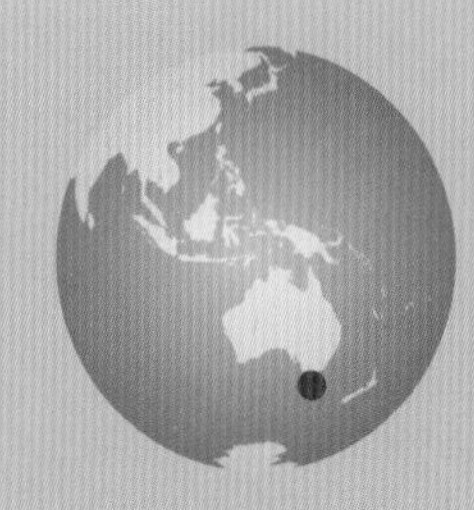

IN THE EIGHTEENTH CENTURY, BRITISH COLONISTS FOUND LARGE, UNTOUCHED TRACTS OF LAND ON THE ISLAND OF TASMANIA. THE ONLY THING IN THE WAY OF TAKING THIS VALUABLE REAL ESTATE WAS THE POPULATION OF TASMANIAN ABORIGINES.

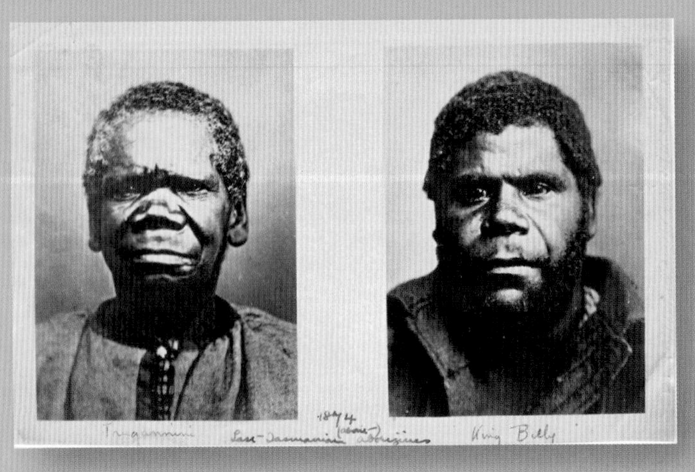

An existing population was not something that deterred the British elsewhere in establishing new settlements and exploiting foreign lands for their natural resources. The population of Aborigines in Tasmania was only about 5,000 when Europeans first arrived at the end of the nineteenth century. This number fell quickly after European settlement began, and only 200 had survived by 1830. Many dispute the use of the word 'war' to describe the violence between

ABOVE A 19th-century painting of Tasmanian Aborigines.

LEFT Truganini (left) is often considered the last full-blood Tasmanian Aborigine woman, and King Billy (right) the last Aborigine man.

ABOVE Governor Davey's Proclamation Board, showing through pictures the equal legal status of European settlers and Aborigines.

the Europeans and the Aborigines, as there was little in the way of organized aggression, and the death toll was heavily lopsided.

AN UNFAIR CONFLICT

Europeans first arrived in Tasmania in the seventeenth century, but did not begin settling the island until the late eighteenth century. The island was inhabited by Aborigines who had been cut off and isolated from other cultures for 10,000 years. They had come to the island when it was still connected to the Australian mainland by a land bridge. Subsequently it became submerged, cutting off the island from the rest of Australia and isolating its inhabitants. Enough time passed that the languages between the Aborigines of Tasmania and those on the mainland were in no way mutually intelligible.

As British settlers carved up the land of Tasmania, they quickly took the best hunting grounds from the Aborigines,

ABOVE Truganini, with the last of her people.

and also depleted the populations of kangaroo and other game that were staple food sources for the Tasmanians. With their land and way of life threatened, a group of Aborigines attacked a European settlement on 3 May 1804. As a Stone-Age people, the Aborigines had only wooden spears and clubs. This started a series of violent attacks between the two peoples. With food growing scarcer, territory diminishing and far inferior weaponry, the Aborigines did not stand a chance. Add to this the effects of European diseases, and the result was that the population plummeted during the 25 years following the initial incident.

Settlers often mistreated the Aborigines, sometimes murdering them or raping the women. The Aborigines could only fight back against isolated individuals. Violence escalated to the point where the lieutenant governor, Sir George Arthur, declared martial law in 1828. Two years later in 1830, Arthur created the 'Black Line', a human line of white settlers designed to walk across the island and flush the Aborigines out of the bush. His plan failed, but four years later, in 1834, the few remaining Aborigines were transported to Flinders Island in the Bass Strait.

A VANISHING PEOPLE

The Aborigines of Tasmania were hunter-gatherers, and relied on their skills to succeed in obtaining food. They were amazing trackers and could blend into the landscape of the island with astonishing ease, seeming to disappear completely. The Aborigines likewise seemed to vanish from the consciousness of the European colonists. While pure-blood Aborigines died out, their descendents live on, as their heritage was passed on through intermarriage – and they have not disappeared.

PHILIPPINE WARS OF INDEPENDENCE 1892–1902

DEFYING COLONIAL POWERS

IN THE 1890S, THE PEOPLE OF THE PHILIPPINES ROSE UP AGAINST THE SPANISH COLONIAL POWER THAT CONTROLLED THE ISLANDS. THEY RECEIVED AID FROM THE UNITED STATES, BUT IN THROWING OFF ONE COUNTRY'S RULE, THEY TOOK ON ANOTHER.

Efforts to gain independence were already under way in the Philippines during the mid to late nineteenth century. The Spaniards quelled these quickly, executing their leaders. In 1892, Andrés Bonifacio established the Katipunan, a secret society aimed at gaining independence from Spain, primarily through armed revolt. By this point, both native Filipinos (*indios*) and those born in the Philippines of Spanish descent (*insulare*) were eager for independence. Bonifacio launched his first assault in 1896, after the execution of José Rizal, a man who had campaigned for independence.

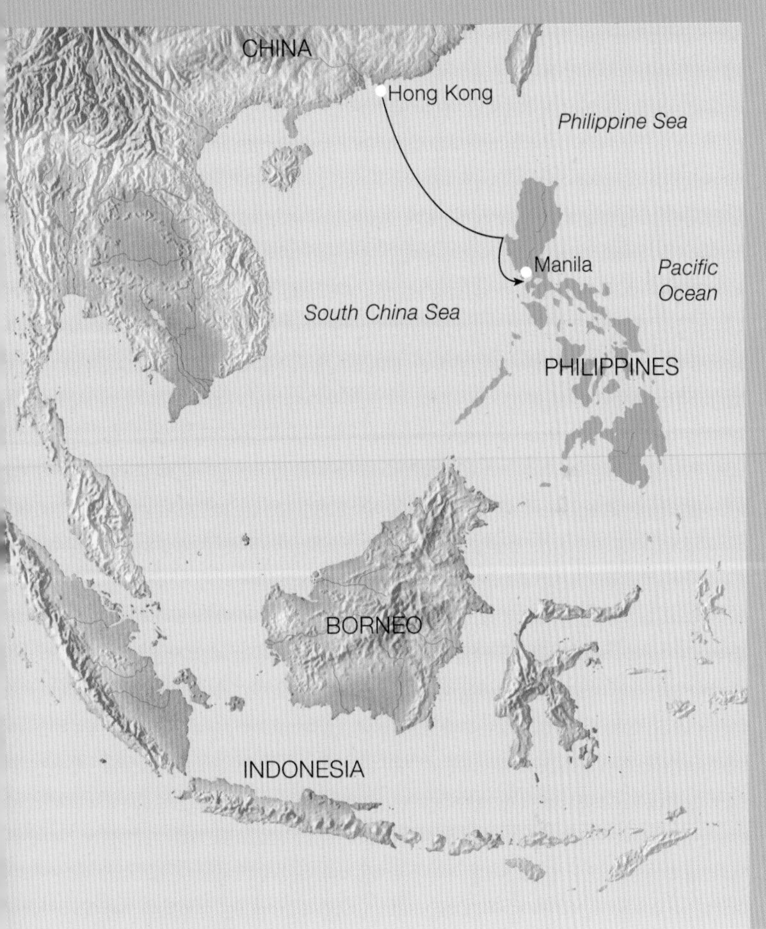

DECLARATION OF INDEPENDENCE

Bonifacio led an attack on Manila in 1896, which failed, but his call to arms was taken up in the neighbouring cities and towns. One of the more successful leaders was Emilio Aguinaldo from Cavite. Bonifacio was eventually ousted by Aguinaldo and executed in 1897. Aguinaldo would then lead the Philippine Revolution. After Aguinaldo put Bonifacio to death, he signed the Pact of Biak-na-Bato in December 1897, designed by the Spanish to put an end to the revolution. Aguinaldo was then sent into exile in Hong Kong.

Within a few months, however, the Spanish-American War broke out in Cuba, providing what seemed like the perfect opportunity to rise up against the Spanish once more. Aguinaldo sided with the United States, and, on 12 June 1898, he declared independence from Spain for the First Philippine Republic. The declaration was not recognized by either Spain or the United States.

ABOVE José Rizal was executed in 1896, precipitating the armed revolutions of the Philippines. Rizal's execution in Bagumbayan is shown here.

LEFT American forces – and later Aguinaldo himself – came to the Philippines from Hong Kong to fight the Spanish in 1898.

ALLIANCE WITH THE UNITED STATES

After the Spanish-American War broke out in Cuba, it quickly spread to the Pacific. Admiral George Dewey sailed from Hong Kong to the Philippines, engaging the Spanish in the Battle of Manila Bay on 1 May 1898, destroying the Spanish fleet. Aguinaldo, meanwhile, had entered into discussions with the Americans. Under the belief that the United States would honor Philippine independence, Aguinaldo returned to lead the revolution. The Americans brought Aguinaldo back to the Philippines, where he was greeted as a hero. When American reinforcements arrived a few months later, the US took Manila from the Spanish. Instead of handing control of the archipelago back to Aguinaldo and the Filipinos, however, the United States ended up taking possession of the islands through the Treaty of Paris on 10 December 1898. The outrage at this led to another war, this time between the peoples of the Philippines and the United States. US troops pushed across the Luzon Plain, inflicting heavy casualties. Some reports estimate as many as 200,000 Filipinos were killed before the war's end in 1902. Guerrilla fighting continued for some years, but the US maintained possession of the Philippines until 1946, during which time US soldiers committed a number of atrocities against the local population. In ousting one colonial power, the Filipinos soon found themselves shackled by another.

RIGHT A calendar cover depicting Admiral George Dewey. Dewey was exceptionally distinguished in the US Navy, and was entered on the democratic ticket in 1900 as a presidential candidate, though he withdrew from the race.

TOP LEFT This painting depicts the USS *Olympia* wreaking havoc at the Battle of Manila Bay.

TOP Despite promises to recognize Philippine independence, the US raised its own flag at Manila in 1898.

LEFT Photo of American troops at Fort San Antonio Abad beneath the American flag, in 1899.

THE PACIFIC THEATRE 1941–1945

THE FURY OF JAPAN

WAR IN THE FAR EAST HAD STARTED LONG BEFORE WORLD WAR II BROKE OUT IN EUROPE: JAPAN INVADED MANCHURIA IN 1931. BUT AS JAPAN SPREAD ITS DOMINANCE ACROSS THE SOUTH PACIFIC, THIS ISLAND NATION PROVOKED THE WRATH OF MANY ENEMIES.

Japan had its sights set on building an empire. Desire to conquer China was not new, but with China in a state of weakness and Japan having advanced tremendously in the technology of its military, the 1930s seemed like the best time to make that dream come true. In 1937, Japan invaded China, quickly seizing control of huge coastal areas. But as the tide of their expansion stemmed in China, the Japanese soon turned their attention to other parts of Asia, notably the islands of the Pacific.

MAKING ENEMIES

Japan spread its military might through Southeast Asia and the Pacific with shocking efficiency, quickly conquering Guam, Wake Island, Thailand, Burma, the Dutch East Indies, the Solomon Islands, Singapore and part of the Philippines.

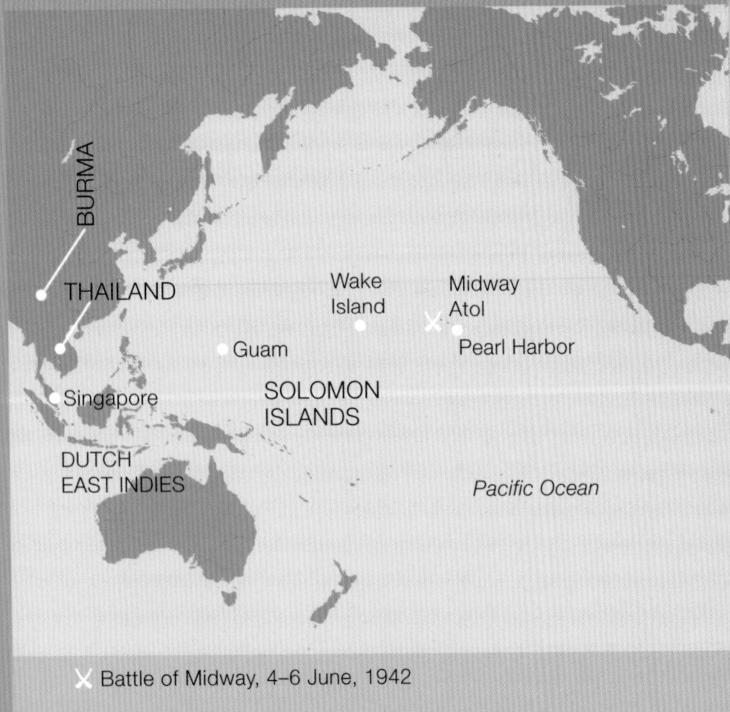

ABOVE LEFT Photo taken from a Japanese plane during the attack on Pearl Harbor, 1941.

FAR LEFT The Midway Atol was a key strategic target for the Japanese in World War II.

LEFT Uncle Sam rolls up his sleeves to take on Japan in an American Army propaganda poster.

ABOVE The USS *Bunker Hill* in flames after being struck by a *kamikaze* attack, 11 May 1945, not far from Okinawa.

To support its efforts in China, Japan needed oil, and that was something it could get in the Dutch East Indies.

In the midst of these conquests, Japan also attacked Pearl Harbor in Hawaii, on 7 December 1941. This immediately brought the United States into the fighting in the Pacific Theatre. Allied resistance had been quite weak, with Allied forces concentrating their attention and resources on the battles in Europe and North Africa. Despite the momentum of the Japanese forces at the end of 1941 into 1942, the American forces were able to start making headway in the Coral Sea in May, preventing the Japanese from landing on New Guinea. In June 1942, the Americans won an important victory at the Battle of Midway. After breaking the Japanese code, the Americans discovered the Japanese intended to take the Midway Atoll – located in the Pacific midway between Asia and the Americas – and use it as a base to then take territories in Alaska. With this intelligence, US forces were able to intercept the Japanese fleet and prevent them from taking Midway.

Stretched thin, Japan could not maintain its position against the Allies after the US bolstered their strength in the Pacific. Slowly, Japan started losing control of territories in the Pacific, and by 1945, the Allies were preparing to take the war to Japan's home soil.

WAR IN THE AIR

The Pacific Theatre saw some impressive developments in the use of fighter planes. The Allies had to combat *kamikaze* attacks by the Japanese, and also had to combat their faster, nimbler planes. Among the more famous innovations was the so-called 'Thach Weave', an aerial manoeuvre designed by U.S. fighter pilot John S Thach to combat the Japanese Mitsubishi Zero fighter planes. By weaving paths, pairs of fighter pilots could use the wingman to take out trailing Japanese planes. This was the most effective tactic against the quicker planes of the Japanese.

ABOVE Smoke trails from a Japanese plane shot down while on its way to attack the USS *Kitkun Bay* in June 1944.

ABOVE One of the Japanese Mitsubishi Zero fighter planes, crashed at Fort Kamehameha during the attack on Pearl Harbor.

THE BATTLE OF GUADALCANAL 1942–1943

FIGHT ON STARVATION ISLAND

IN JUNE 1942, JAPAN LANDED ON GUADALCANAL – A SOUTHERLY ISLAND IN THE SOLOMONS – AND BEGAN BUILDING AN AIRFIELD. TWO MONTHS LATER, THE US MARINES LANDED ON THE ISLAND, LAUNCHING THEIR FIRST OFFENSIVE OF WORLD WAR II.

Battle of Guadalcanal 7 August 1942–9 February 1943

ABOVE The airfield Allied forces captured and defended at Lunga Point on Guadalcanal. The airfield would later be renamed Henderson Field.

TOP The Battle of Guadalcanal against the Japanese troops in the Solomon Islands played a pivotal military role in World War II.

When the Americans landed at Guadalcanal on 6 August 1942, they outnumbered and caught the Japanese unawares; they quickly seized control of the Japanese airfield that was under construction. The United States and Australia saw the airfield as an important strategic base. Naval defeat at the Battle of Savo Island on 9 August, however, left the Marines stranded on the island without supplies or reinforcements. So began six months of hard fighting at Guadalcanal.

DIGGING IN THE HEELS

The Japanese did not waste much time in striking back and attempting to regain control of the airstrip. By the end of August the battle was well under way and became characterized by the hard-hitting frontal assaults of the Japanese. Digging in, however, the US Marines were able to repulse the attacks, inflicting heavy casualties against the Japanese. Aerial attacks occurred on a day-to-day basis, and the Japanese and Allied forces engaged in a number of land and naval battles over the coming months. The Japanese,

expecting to gain a quick victory over the Americans on the island, did not send enough supplies for their troops. They brought troops to the island under cover of night on destroyers, making quick trips without heavy equipment. These became known as the 'Tokyo Express'. Likewise, Americans had to wait for reinforcements and food. Guadalcanal came to be known as 'Starvation Island'.

The Japanese death toll on Guadalcanal itself was over 20,000; the US Marines lost 2,500 (these figures don't include the naval battles). The staggering difference attests to the reckless abandon with which the Japanese were accustomed to attacking. Large numbers of casualties were not treated as evidence of a failing strategy. The Allies were able to get reinforcements to the island in November, bolstering the initial force of roughly 10,000 Marines. Allied forces on the island would peak in January at 44,000. The Japanese force reached a maximum of about 36,000. Outnumbered and suffering heavy losses, the Japanese were finally forced to withdraw by 7 February 1943.

TOP Brigadier General Alexander Vandegrift and Rear Admiral Richmond K Turner review plans on their way to Guadalcanal.

ABOVE US Marine Corps Brigadier General, Alexander Vandegrift, stands with his men. Vandegrift commanded the victorious 1st Marine Division at Guadalcanal.

ABOVE RIGHT The number of US Marines at Guadalcanal reached a total of 44,000.

CODE MAKING AND BREAKING

The Allied forces were able to gain important early successes in the Pacific in part due to intelligence efforts to break the Japanese codes and create codes of their own. Cracking Japanese codes facilitated Allied victories at Midway and Guadalcanal, and the codes created by a division of Navajo Indians in the US military helped facilitate secure communications during the remainder of the war.

ABOVE Taken in September 1942, this picture shows US Marines patrolling along the River Matanikau on Guadalcanal.

AMERICA
AMERICA SEPTENTRIONALIS
NOVA GRANADA
TROPICUS CANCRI
MAR DEL ZUR Hispanis
AEQUINOCTIALIS LINEA
SALOMONIS INSULÆ
MARE PACIFICUM
TROPICUS CAPRICORNI

THE AMERICAS

THE OLMEC 1200–500 BCE

EARLY MESOAMERICAN CIVILIZATION

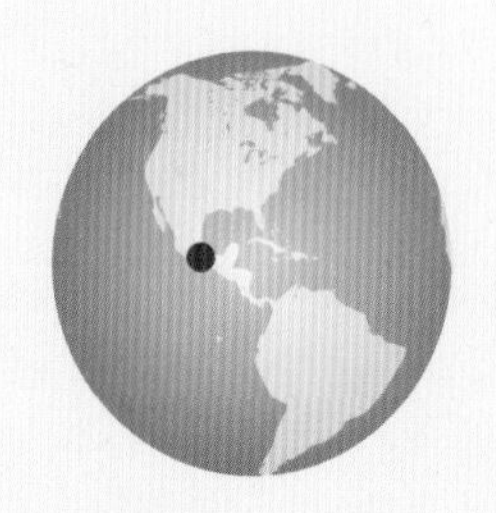

THE OLMEC WERE A PEOPLE WHO DEVELOPED A CIVILIZATION IN WHAT IS NOW SOUTHERN MEXICO. WHILE WE KNOW RELATIVELY LITTLE ABOUT THE OLMEC, THE IMPRESSIVE QUANTITY AND QUALITY OF THE ART AND ARCHITECTURE THEY LEFT BEHIND BESPEAKS AN ADVANCED CULTURE.

The Olmec are often credited with being the first civilization of Mesoamerica. Initially developing in San Lorenzo (what is now Veracruz), the Olmec heartland also included La Venta and Tres Zapotes. The Olmec were master stonemasons, and left behind massive stone statues of heads. Believed to represent the heads of rulers, these statues stand up to 3.4 m (11 feet) high and are made from stones weighing more than 30 tons, which were transported distances of nearly 160 km (100 miles). No one knows how the Olmec achieved this. The carved heads depict some form of headgear, perhaps helmets. The Olmec also built one of the oldest pyramids in Mesoamerica at La Venta.

ABOVE Olmec heads show flat faces with thick lips and wide noses. This one was found in Veracruz.

AN ADVANCED CULTURE

The statues and carvings of the Olmec are remarkably detailed and polished, making this civilization feel immediate and tangible, yet we have to rely almost entirely on archaeological evidence for our knowledge of the civilization. Although the Olmec appear to be the first culture in the western hemisphere to have developed writing, little of it remains. Scenes of violence depicted in Olmec artwork could be interpreted in several ways, and may represent images of warfare, or perhaps religious sacrifice. One of the scenes depicted in a relief carving on Altar 4 at La Venta provides one such example: the carving shows a man with a rope around his neck.

LEFT In addition to their colossal head sculptures, the Olmec also produced many masks in a similar style.

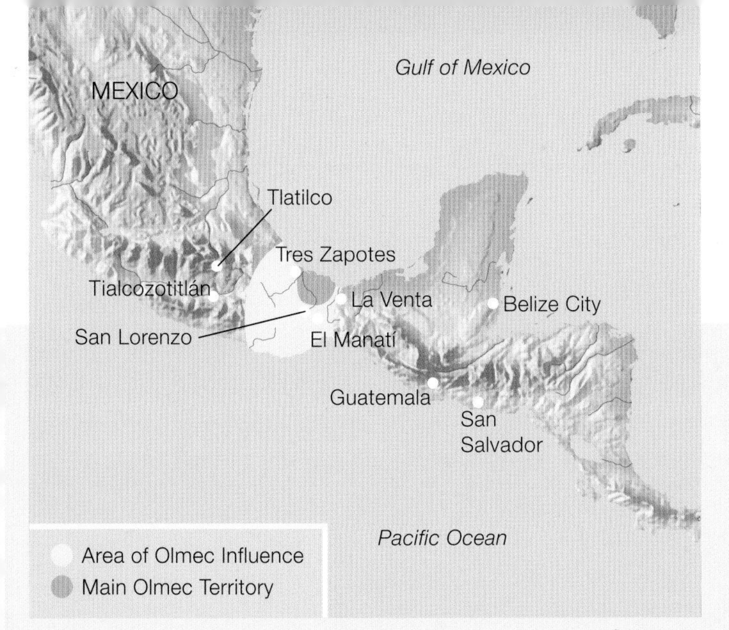

ABOVE The Olmec inhabited the region of Central America that is now southern Mexico.

The Olmec appear to have developed a large trading network. Archaeological finds of Olmec artefacts provide a trail map of Olmec trade routes. While we know virtually nothing of Olmec military organization, Olmec artwork depicts objects that could be knives, daggers and clubs. Olmec warriors almost certainly defended king and country, and protected the vast wealth amassed through trade. If later practices can be seen as continuations of Olmec traditions, then we can speculate that the Olmec exacted tribute from neighbouring peoples, and likely organized in small warrior bands.

LEFT Basalt stone for the Olmec's colossal heads was taken from the Tuxtlas Mountains.

RIGHT Some carvings depict what appear to be a mix between human and jaguar forms, and are often referred to as the *were-jaguars*. This monument from the San Martin Pajapan volcano shows a man wearing a were-jaguar headdress.

BELOW Stone Altar 4 from La Venta. The altar includes a statue of a ruler. Note the clean and clear relief carvings decorating the altar.

MAYAN CIVILIZATION C.1500 BCE–900 CE

MYSTERIES IN THE ROCK

THE MAYA WERE ONE OF THE GREATEST PRE-COLUMBIAN CIVILIZATIONS OF THE AMERICAS, POSSESSING AN ADVANCED CULTURE BASED AROUND AGRICULTURE AND BUILDING IMPRESSIVE MONUMENTS OF STONE THAT CONTINUE TO BAFFLE SCHOLARS TODAY.

The Maya first developed in the south of Mesoamerica probably around 2000–1500 BCE. The Classic Period of Mayan civilization, however, began around 250 CE when the Maya started building large city-states throughout the Yucatán Peninsula, Guatemala and southern Mexico. While many scholars originally believed these city-states coexisted more or less peacefully, that view has changed considerably in recent years. Mayan rulers often clashed with one another, though no ruler ever seems to have been able to unite the Mayan states into a single empire.

BELOW Detailed sculpture from the period of the so-called 18 Rabbit, the 13th ruler of the Mayan city-state Copán.

STORIES IN STONE

The Maya developed an advanced writing system and left many records, several of them carved in the stone walls of their monuments. They also developed a kind of paper from bark and actually compiled sheets of this paper into codices. From these texts and archaeological evidence we learn about the struggles for dominance during the eighth century CE between the powerful city-states of Tikal, Palenque and Calakmul. These individual kingdoms could control hundreds of square kilometres of territory and had populations in the tens of thousands. Extensive manpower was necessary to build the impressive monuments, palaces and step pyramids characteristic of Mayan architecture. Tikal was the most powerful city-state in the Early Classic Period and is home to the step pyramid known as Tikal Temple I, built during the eighth century. The temple stands more than 46 m (150 feet) tall and is made of limestone.

Despite the creation of huge monuments and the apparently intricate political organization of the Maya, the civilization somehow could not sustain itself. Perhaps the violent struggles between city-states eventually weakened the civilization as a whole. The Maya gradually began to decline, abandoning their cities and leaving them to be reclaimed by the jungle.

Gulf of Mexico
MEXICO
Uxmal
Sayil
Tulum
Palenque
Uaxactún
Yaxchilán
Quiriguá
Bonampak
Copán
Pacific Ocean

Mayan Civilization, c. 1500 BCE – 900 CE

ABOVE The Maya covered a large area in the Yucatán, but their influence spread even wider.

PERIODS OF MAYAN CIVILIZATION

Early Preclassic	1200–1000 BCE
Middle Preclassic	1000–300 BCE
Late Preclassic	300 BCE–250 CE
Early Classic	250–600 CE
Late Classic	600–900 CE
Terminal Classic	800–1000 CE
Early Postclassic	900–1200 CE
Late Postclassic	1200–1524 CE

ABOVE A Mayan stucco head from the Classic Period.

RIGHT Bust of K'inich Janaab' Pakal, a seventh-century Mayan ruler of Palenque, buried at the Temple of Inscriptions.

STONE WEAPONS

It is astonishing to look upon the pyramids and other stone structures and carvings of the Maya and know that only stone tools were used to create them. All tools and weapons used by the Maya were made of stone, bone, and wood. The weaponry of the Maya likely consisted of clubs, daggers, spears and atlatls. Blades and weapon points were made of obsidian or chert. We can only speculate as to the actual tactics employed during military engagements, though it seems likely that captives were taken during battles to serve as blood sacrifices to the Mayan deities.

THE MOCHE C.100–750

MASTERS OF THE STREAM

AROUND 100 CE, AN ADVANCED CIVILIZATION SPRUNG UP IN WHAT IS NOW NORTHERN PERU. THE MOCHE DEVELOPED INTRICATE IRRIGATION SYSTEMS TO CHANNEL THE WATERS COMING DOWN TO THE SEA FROM THE ANDES.

These waters supported the agriculture that allowed the Moche to build large cities. Growing corn (maize), beans and other crops, the Moche could support large populations and quickly developed urban centres around their agricultural bases. Despite a consistency of culture, language and artwork across the region inhabited by the Moche, each river valley was likely controlled by a different ruler and warrior band. War between the polities of the Moche was common.

FACES OF THE PAST

Today, the Moche are known for producing some of the most exquisite artwork of the pre-Columbian Americas. In particular, Moche pottery and ceramics are often adorned with amazingly detailed and lifelike faces. Their artwork provides a glimpse of the types of warriors who dominated Moche civilization and the types of conflicts in which they engaged. It appears that battles were fought in the open desert between polities, and that fortifications were unnecessary, though the Moche built large and impressive stone temples and pyramids. The individuality expressed in the faces of Moche artwork seems to have been mirrored in the heavily individual nature of the combat. Though groups of warriors would have engaged each other in battle, the larger conflicts would have been settled through a collection of smaller individual contests.

LEFT A Moche vessel depicting a prisoner.

RIGHT This Moche vessel is made in the shape of a warrior holding a shield above his head for protection. Note the decoration of his fine tunic.

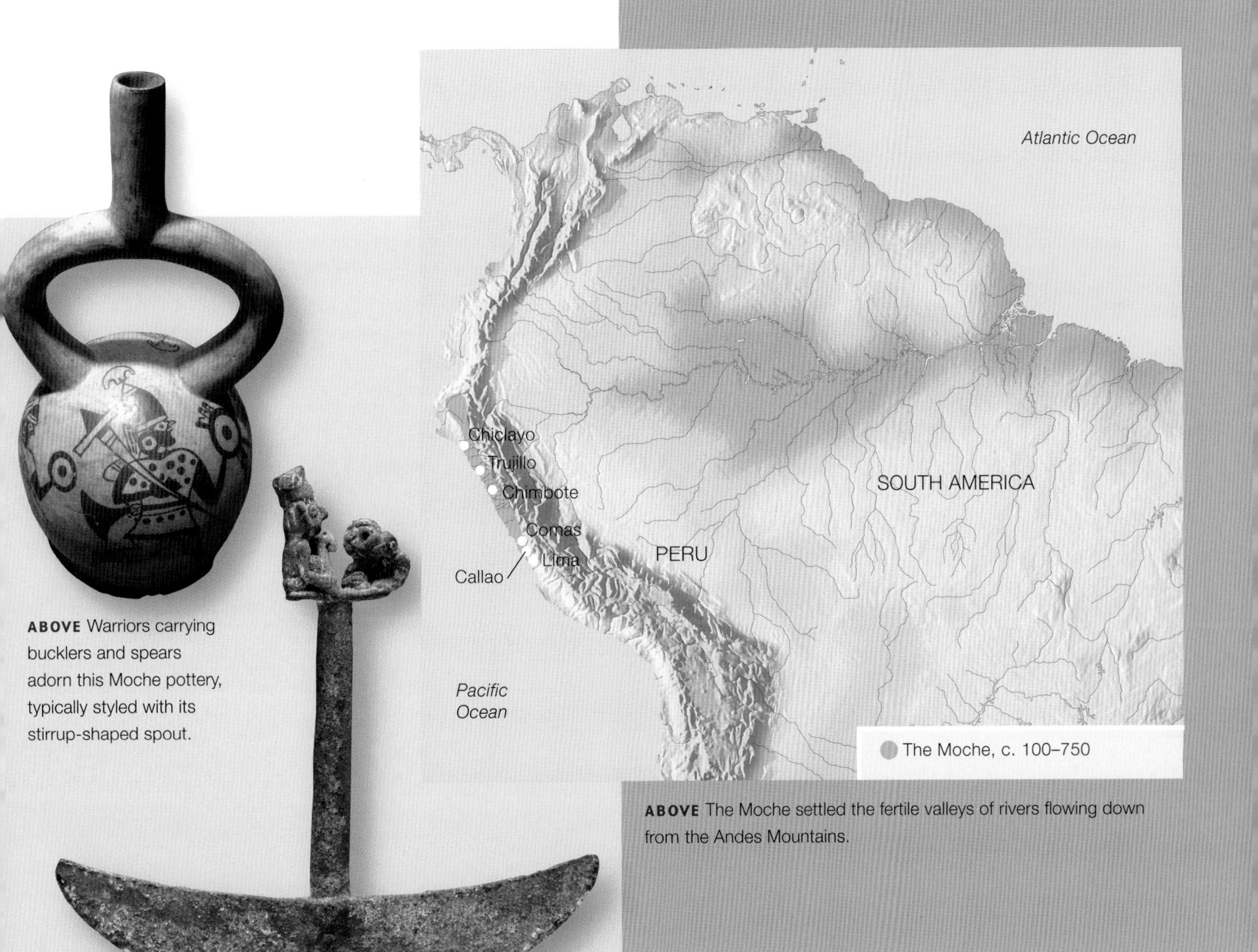

ABOVE Warriors carrying bucklers and spears adorn this Moche pottery, typically styled with its stirrup-shaped spout.

ABOVE The Moche settled the fertile valleys of rivers flowing down from the Andes Mountains.

ABOVE The round blade of a Moche copper *tumi*, a ritualistic knife or axe.

BELOW A Moche mask made of copper with shells inserted for the eyes.

Moche warriors wore ornate armour and had conical helmets and small bucklers shields to parry blows from opponents' weapons. They used clubs and spears, slings for hurling stones, atlatls and axes. The Moche did know metalwork, and carried copper or even bronze axes. We know little of the actual tactics employed on the battlefield, but we do know that battles often resulted in the taking of captives who would serve as human sacrifices. The iconography of blood is common in Moche artwork.

We cannot know for certain why the Moche civilization declined in the eighth century, but climate change, drought or famine may have contributed. Eventually, the civilization disappeared, leaving behind only their monuments, artwork, tools and weapons.

THE INCA C.1250–1532

RISE AND FALL IN THE ANDES

WHEN THE SPANISH CONQUISTADORS LED BY FRANCISCO PIZARRO ARRIVED IN THE ANDES, THEY FOUND A LARGE EMPIRE TORN APART BY CIVIL STRIFE. THE INCA REACHED THE PINNACLE OF STONE-AGE TECHNOLOGY, BUT THEY WERE UNABLE TO WITHSTAND THE STEEL OF THE CONQUISTADORS.

The Inca originated around Cuzco in modern Peru during the thirteenth century. A century later, the leaders of the Inca began consolidating the power of the many small tribes and peoples, conquering neighbouring lands and building an empire that stretched throughout the Andes of South America, from modern-day Colombia in the north to Chile in the south. The Inca had vast amounts of gold and silver, and did possess some bronze tools and weapons. For the most part, however, they were still a Stone-Age people, using mostly stone tools and blades. Even with this limited technology, however, they built large cities of stone in the mountains with complex irrigation systems to water the crops that sustained their people. At its peak, the population of the Inca Empire may have reached as many as 12 million.

The population, however, began to fall drastically during the first half of the fifteenth century. The greatest enemy of the Inca – as for many of the peoples of the Americas – was an unintended weapon: smallpox. The Spanish conquests in Mexico had introduced the disease into South America. With the complex trade routes that existed throughout the Americas at the time, the disease spread quickly. With no immunity, the Inca were devastated by smallpox. Whole populations were decimated by the disease, and the Inca himself (the ruler) was killed by smallpox, sending the country into chaos as a struggle for power ensued. Amidst this chaos, Francisco Pizarro arrived with his band of roughly 170 foot soldiers and mounted warriors.

Despite being vastly outnumbered, the conquistadors were able to conquer the Inca Empire, taking Cuzco in 1533 and continuing from there until they had complete control by 1535. Pizarro captured Atahualpa, the last ruler of the Inca Empire, and eventually put him to death. Despite continued resistance, the empire quickly began to disintegrate after the death of their ruler.

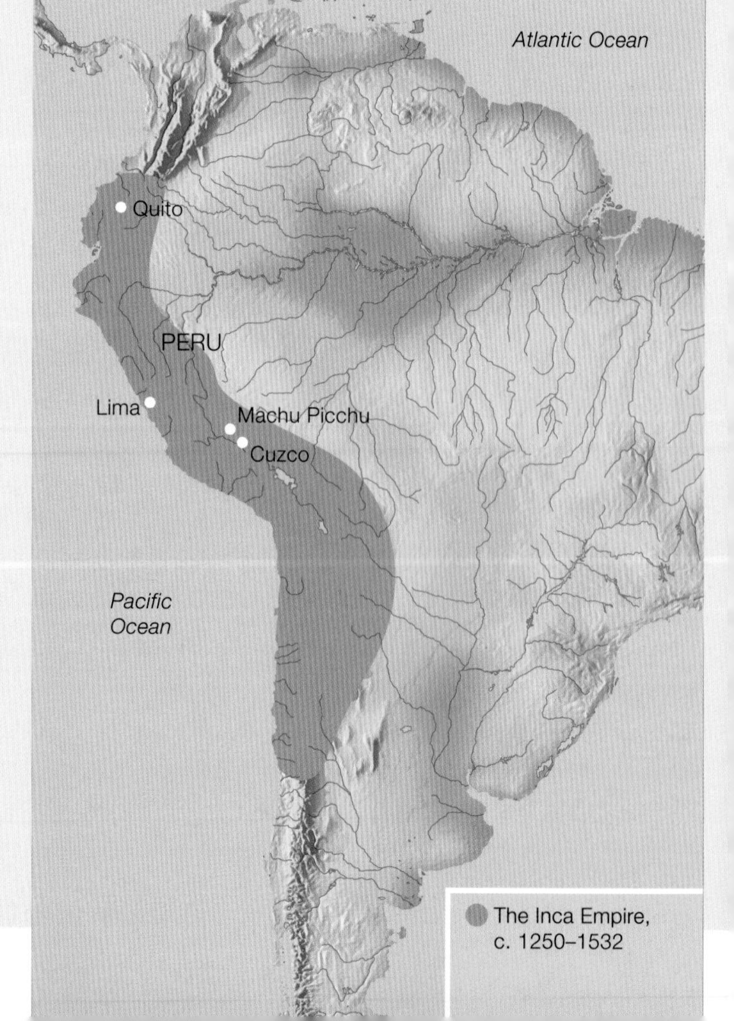

RIGHT The Inca Empire extended throughout the Andes mountain range and along much of the western coast of South America.

LEFT Atahualpa converted to Christianity before his execution, in order to be strangled rather than burned to death.

TECHNOLOGICAL ADVANTAGE

With the exception of their firearms, the type of weaponry used by the Spanish did not differ tremendously from that used by the Inca. The Spaniards benefited from a few key technological advantages, however, that made their astonishing victory over the thousands of Inca possible.

First, was their use of steel for both blades and armour. Their steel swords and lance tips easily broke and cut through the weapons and armour of their opponents. Their plate armour similarly could not be pierced by the stone points of the Inca weapons. The conquistadors also had horses, which were unknown to the Inca, and gave the Spaniards an advantage of speed, power and fearsomeness.

The conquistadors had some muskets and artillery, but it is easy to overestimate the importance of these weapons in the conquest of the Inca. The Inca, meanwhile, used spears, slings and clubs.

ABOVE RIGHT Before his death, Atahualpa offered to fill a large room with gold and silver as ransom. His subjects brought 24 tons of gold and silver from throughout the empire, but he was executed all the same.

BELOW Ollantaytambo near Cuzco. The cities of the Inca were so magnificent that Pizarro remarked that they would be considered grand even back in Spain.

THE AZTEC EMPIRE 1427–1521

THE WHITE LAND

THE AZTEC CAPITAL OF TENOCHTITLÁN HAD A POPULATION OF ALMOST A QUARTER OF A MILLION IN THE EARLY SIXTEENTH CENTURY WHEN THE CONQUISTADORS ARRIVED, MAKING IT LARGER THAN MOST EUROPEAN CITIES AT THE TIME, INCLUDING LONDON AND ROME.

The Aztecs rose to prominence during the early fifteenth century, though they had, of course, been around for much longer than that. Their great city, Tenochtitlán, was founded around 1325 in Texcoco Lake in southern Mexico. The Aztec people were also known as the 'Mexica'. from which the country of Mexico takes its name. They used a system called *chinampa* to solidify and expand the land on the island where they built Tenochtitlán. The choice of location was supposedly dictated by a vision that had been foretold in prophecy: an eagle eating a snake atop a cactus. Chinampa was a system of walling in squares of land in the marshes, then using this land for agriculture. Over time, they added more and more of these squares around Tenochtitlán, effectively expanding the island out into the lake.

A MARVEL OF THE NEW WORLD

When Spanish conquistador Hernán Cortés arrived at Tenochtitlán, he and his companions were so amazed by the city that they wondered whether they had entered into a dream. All the buildings were built of stone, the streets were clean and tidy, and the city was planned out with exceptional regularity and care. It was unlike anything they had ever seen. The magnificence of the city clashed strongly with the brutality of human sacrifice that they witnessed within its temples. Men were dragged up the steps of the temples and their hearts were removed with knives and offered to the gods by the priests.

LEFT Steep steps and intricate stonework at Teopanzolco.

RIGHT Acatitlan was another important Aztec centre. This pyramid was built by the Aztecs.

ABOVE Owing to a prophecy about a bearded god, Cortés was greeted like a deity when he arrived.

ABOVE Conquistadors considered themselves deeply religious, bringing Catholicism to the Americas.

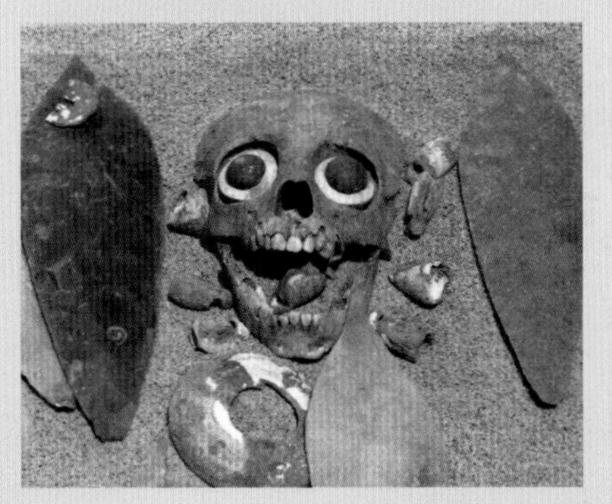

LEFT This Aztec skull is flanked by impressive blades made of chert.

POWER AND WEAKNESS

The Aztecs possessed indisputable power, but they had built their magnificent civilization largely with stone tools. Likewise they dominated their vast territory with primitive weapons. The skill and bravery of the warriors were irrelevant when stone and copper points failed to bite the iron armour of the conquistadors. The firearms of the Spaniards terrified the defenceless Aztecs. Furthermore, outbreaks of smallpox among the Aztecs weakened the empire considerably, allowing the conquistadors to take Tenochtitlán in 1521. With Montezuma II, the ruler of the Aztecs, dead in 1520, little stood in the way of the Spanish conquistadors. Allying with other native forces, Cortés bolstered his small band of Spanish warriors to lay siege to this great city.

FRENCH AND INDIAN WAR 1754–1763

BATTLE FOR THE COLONIES

IN THE MID-EIGHTEENTH CENTURY, FRANCE AND GREAT BRITAIN WERE BOTH JOCKEYING FOR POSITION IN THE NORTH AMERICAN COLONIES. WAR SOON BROKE OUT TO DETERMINE WHICH EUROPEAN POWER WOULD DOMINATE NORTH AMERICA.

TOP French soldiers celebrate Montcalm's victory at Carillon.

ABOVE Fighting in the wilderness of North America posed many challenges for British soldiers in the early years of the war.

While the British had a firm base on the eastern coast, the French had explored much of the interior of the future United States and Canada, actively pushing out British settlers in an effort to control as much territory as possible. In the 1750s, a dispute arose between France and Great Britain over who had legitimate claim to the upper Ohio River valley. This dispute sparked the beginning of the French and Indian War.

NECESSITY BEGINS

In the spring of 1754, the French pushed a force of Virginians out of the Ohio River valley. This led to an engagement between the French forces and British troops under the direction of Colonel George Washington, future president of the United States. Washington surprised the French, winning a quick victory at the Battle of Jumonville Glen, where the French commander, Joseph Coulon de Jumonville, was killed. Washington then withdrew to Fort Necessity, where he and his men were subsequently surrounded by a counter-attack and forced to surrender.

The French were historically better than their British and Spanish counterparts at earning the favour of the native populations in the Americas. French forces were significantly bolstered by large numbers of Algonquin, Ojibwe and other Native Americans, though the Iroquois and Cherokee would join on the side of the British.

FRENCH FAILINGS

The early years of the war saw French victory after victory. The British and American forces were put against the ropes, but in 1757 British Prime Minister William Pitt started directing more of his attention (and more of Britain's resources) towards defeating the French. Beating the French had significant implications not only in the colonies, but also back in Europe. With better equipment and more supplies, the British began to turn the tides of battle. The war gradually came to an end after the British victory at the Plains of Abraham in Quebec City, in 1759. Both British commander James Wolfe and French commander Louis-Joseph de Montcalm were fatally wounded at the battle, but the British carried the day. France handed over its territories in North America to Britain in the Treaty of Paris, signed on 10 February 1763.

ABOVE A battle between the French and British in Newfoundland.

BELOW Commander James Wolfe was shot and killed at the Plains of Abraham. His death is immortalized here in a dramatic painting.

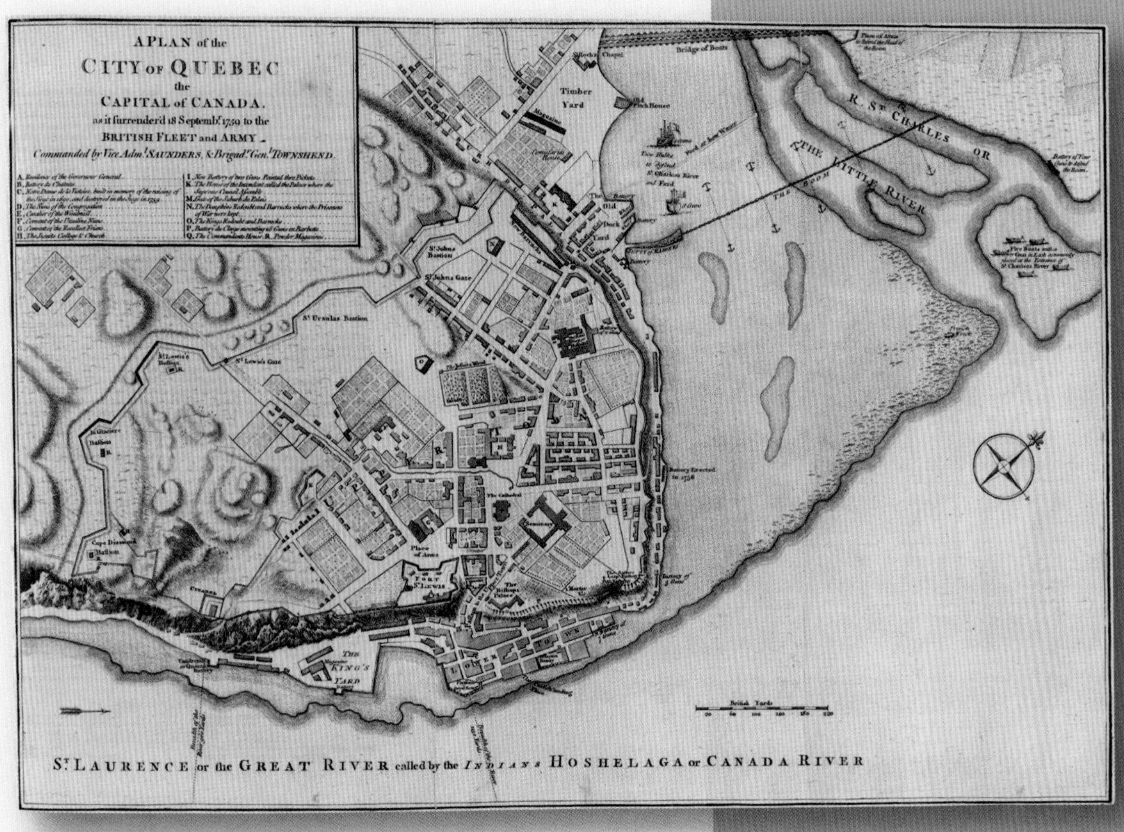

LEFT Quebec surrendered to the British in 1759, but only after both Wolfe and Montcalm had been killed.

THE AMERICAN REVOLUTION 1775–1783

BIRTH OF A NATION

BY THE SPRING OF 1775, THE AMERICAN COLONISTS HAD LOST PATIENCE WITH THE REPRESSIVE POLICIES OF THE BRITISH GOVERNMENT, WHICH CONTROLLED THE COLONIES FROM AFAR. COMMITTING TREASON, THE COLONISTS BOLDLY FOUGHT FOR FREEDOM.

The British government imposed increasingly intolerable laws on its American colonies without an understanding of life in the colonies themselves. Tensions boiled as Britain exacted tax from the colonists without providing political representation. Fighting kicked off when British General Thomas Gage sent his men to destroy the militia stores in and around Concord, Massachussets. The colonists learned of these plans well in advance and moved their stores. Word the night before the attack was the impetus for Paul Revere's famous ride from Boston to Concord. Resisting the British, the American militiamen rose up to fight the Battles of Lexington and Concord on 19 April 1775. At Lexington, the colonists were forced back, but the British found no weapons so continued on to Concord where they were defeated in a pitched battle by the minutemen of the local militia.

LEFT A painting depicting George Washington's appointment as commander-in-chief.

LEFT British General John Burgoyne surrenders after the Battle of Saratoga in October 1777, a turning point in the war.

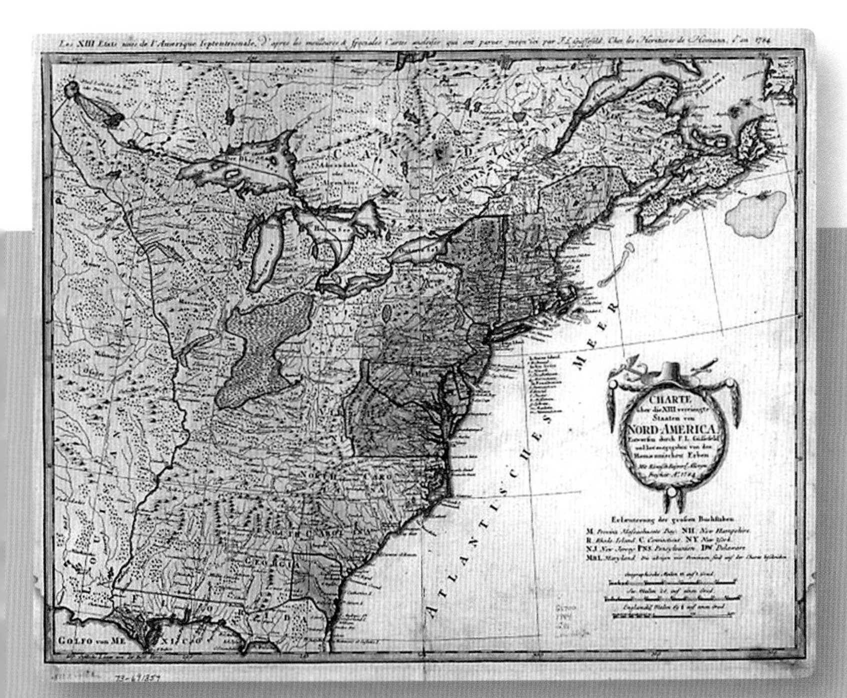

LEFT This map from 1778 shows the original Thirteen Colonies.

LEFT Though the Americans lost the Battle of Guilford Court House, the battle saw the rise of an important American military leader: Nathanael Greene.

BELOW A portrait of George Washingtin in 1776.

UNLIKELY VICTORIES

The rebels in America achieved a very unlikely victory against Britain, which was far more powerful. A confluence of factors contributed to the success of the Patriots.

Ill-trained, outmanned and outgunned, the revolutionary forces had little chance of defeating the British in conventional warfare. Benjamin Franklin even considered returning to bows and arrows to increase the number of weapons and fighting power of the colonists. But the colonists had the home-field advantage and were able to use it to grind down the opposition of the British. Not conforming to British military practice of wearing bright red and marching in straight lines, the minutemen of the colonies were able to use the cover of wilderness terrain to harry British troops through guerrilla warfare, conserving energy and supplies and avoiding pitched battles. Despite Washington's victories at Trenton and Princeton in the winter spanning 1776–1777, the Patriots did not meet much success in open battle.

As the colonists held onto their resistance tenaciously, factors outside their control lent unlooked for, but very welcome, aid. Britain was stretched thin in the creation of its vast empire. The nation poured resources and money out across the seas to places such as India, the East and West Indies and beyond. Unable to concentrate the military power necessary to put down the rebellion in the colonies, the Patriots were able to take advantage of this situation. In 1777, France joined the war on the side of the colonists, marking a turning point in the war. Thousands of French troops supported the Americans at the Battle of Yorktown on 19 October 1781 – a decisive and important victory for the Patriots, and the leadership of French General Lafayette helped turn the tide of battle in favour of the Americans. The war was effectively over, but it would not be entirely until 1783, when the Treaty of Paris was signed, recognizing American independence.

HAITIAN WAR OF INDEPENDENCE 1791–1804

REVOLUTION IN THE CARIBBEAN

THE FRENCH COLONY OF HAITI WAS GOVERNED IN THE LATE EIGHTEENTH CENTURY BY A SMALL POPULATION OF FRANCOPHONE WHITES. MOST OF THE POPULATION, HOWEVER, WAS COMPRISED OF BLACK SLAVES BROUGHT FROM AFRICA. TENSIONS MOUNTED UNTIL WAR BROKE OUT.

The extreme imbalance between the slavery of hundreds of thousands of black slaves compared to the tens of thousands of wealthy white colonists was simply unsustainable. Only about ten per cent of the population was white, yet this small portion exercised control over the territory and its inhabitants, often brutally mistreating the slave populations that brought them wealth. The deep divisions between master and slave happened to fall along colour lines, creating deep-running racial hatreds. The presence of mulattoes and *affranchis* (former slaves who had become free) only further complicated the racial and social tensions on the island.

THE STRING SNAPS

When a string is wound too tightly it will snap, and that's essentially what happened in Haiti during the final years of the eighteenth century. The injustices and mistreatment of the slave population were too great for any human to withstand without rising up in revolt. With the French Revolution erupting in 1789, the population of Haiti took inspiration and saw a chance to gain freedom by rising up against the French colonial powers that imprisoned and enslaved them. Violence broke out in 1790 with an uprising led by Vincent Ogé, but this mulatto leader was captured and killed, and his uprising was put down.

ABOVE RIGHT Saint-Domingue is the western portion of the Caribbean island. The east was controlled by the Spanish and is now the Dominican Republic.

RIGHT French-led troops battle rebel forces on Santo Domingo.

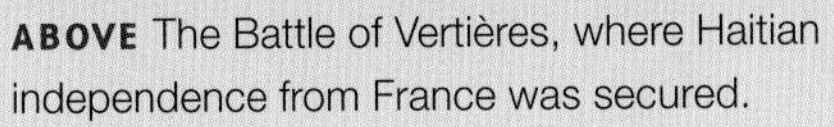

ABOVE The Battle of Vertières, where Haitian independence from France was secured.

ABOVE RIGHT Toussaint Louverture raises his sword in an idealist painting of the Haitian leader.

RIGHT Toussaint Louverture successfully led his forces in many campaigns, but was eventually defeated. His efforts contributed significantly to eventual Haitian independence.

The new government in France granted citizenship to certain affranchis in 1791, but local colonists didn't recognize their new legal status. Citizenship was granted to all affranchis in 1792, but this was not enough to stop the deep dissatisfaction in the country. Whites, black slaves, affranchis and mulattoes all opposed one another; the Spanish supported the slave populations and the British supported the French rulers. Slavery was abolished on 4 February 1794, by the French politician Maximilien de Robespierre, but even this decision did not address or redress several of the underlying motives for revolt. Instead, it gave slaves the freedom necessary to then take control of the land.

NEW COMMAND

In the late 1790s, former slave turned soldier, Toussaint Louverture, began seizing control through his position as military commander. After defeating other rivals for power, Louverture led a force east into Santo Domingo in 1800, where he freed the slaves. Louverture was self-educated, and in 1801 he declared the sovereignty of Saint-Domingue and himself as governor for life. But his life would not last long: he was deceived into conceding to a French force of Napoleon Bonaparte and was subsequently imprisoned. He died in 1803. The French forces then took over, creating such animosity among the local populations that another uprising broke out in 1803, finally destroying French rule for good at the Battle of Vertières on 18 November. The land was proclaimed independent on 1 January 1804, and renamed Haiti, which was the Arawak name for the island.

MEXICAN WAR OF INDEPENDENCE 1810–1821

DEFYING SPAIN

THE LATE EIGHTEENTH AND EARLY NINETEENTH CENTURIES SAW REVOLUTION SPREAD LIKE WILDFIRE THROUGHOUT THE EUROPEAN COLONIES IN THE AMERICAS. IN 1810, INDIANS AND MESTIZOS ROSE UP TO OPPOSE SPANISH RULE IN MEXICO.

ABOVE When Mexico achieved its independence, the country's territory included what is now Texas and parts of the southwestern United States.

Despite the size of the initial uprising, which included thousands from the poor population of Mexico, it would be eleven years of struggle between the initial declaration of independence in 1810 and actual independence in 1821.

WAR OF THE PEOPLE

Mexico in the early nineteenth century was controlled by a small group of Spaniards and the so-called *Criollos*, or Creoles – Mexican-born Spanish. Most of the population, however, was pure-blood Indian, or *Mestizo*, people of mixed Spanish and Indian blood. Following the French Revolution, the government in Spain began to weaken. When France invaded Spain in 1808 under the command of Napoleon Bonaparte, the Bourbon king was deposed. This provided an opportunity for the people of Mexico to rise up and take control of the land.

The revolution began on 16 September 1810, when a priest, Miguel Hidalgo y Costilla, gave a speech known as the 'Cry of Dolores' and led the poor in revolt. Thousands of impoverished Mexicans flocked to his command; he led his force successfully against the Spanish in the initial encounters. But his men were untrained and often unarmed, so when they came up against 6,000 highly trained and well-armed Spanish soldiers, their rebellion was smashed. Hidalgo was executed in 1811.

BELOW Sabres like this one would have been common during the Mexican War of Independence.

ABOVE Vincente Guerrero was instrumental in the successes of the final years of the revolution.

PICKING UP THE STANDARD

Despite the failure of Hidalgo's revolution, others in Mexico took up his banner and continued the struggle for independence. Fighting continued for the next several years in a guerrilla fashion. The Mexican resistance did not have the skill or resources to fight the Spanish in open warfare.

José María Morelos took control of the revolutionary forces after the death of Hidalgo. Morelos was captured and killed in 1815. Vincente Guerrero, Guadalupe Victoria and Francisco Javier Mina – among others – led forces in revolt.

The war for independence seemed doomed. In 1820 in Spain, however, a coup led to governmental changes that upset loyalists in Mexico. Agustín de Iturbide, the man sent to quell the rebellion, turned against the Spanish government and joined with the revolutionaries, securing Mexican independence in 1821.

ABOVE Iturbide became Augustine I of Mexico after ending the war and gaining independence for Mexico. His tenure as emperor would be short-lived.

LEFT Miguel Hidalgo was the person who initiated the revolutionary fervour in Mexico, despite not living to see much of the war itself.

BELOW Iturbide rides into Mexico city in September 1821.

WARS OF INDEPENDENCE 1809–1825

LATIN AMERICAN REVOLTS

WHEN NAPOLEON BONAPARTE INVADED SPAIN IN 1808 AND OPPOSED ITS RULER, HE UNWITTINGLY PROVIDED A MUCH DESIRED OPPORTUNITY IN SPAIN'S SOUTH AMERICAN COLONIES TO RISE UP AND FIGHT FOR INDEPENDENCE. WAR BEGAN IN 1809.

In 1809, inhabitants of Spanish colonies in Latin America rose up against the local arms of Spanish government and established Juntas in their place. Important early rebellions included the rebellion in Sucre, known as the Chuquisaca Rebellion, and the uprising in La Paz, known as the La Paz Rebellion. Although royalists were able to defeat these Juntas quickly and with relative ease, the revolutionary process was under way, and would ultimately lead to Bolivian independence in 1825.

BUENOS AIRES HOLDS FAST

In the spring of 1810, another wave of revolution overthrew the viceroy in Buenos Aires and established a Junta there. Buenos Aires was not so easily defeated. For the next few years, the Creoles began exercising more and more control. Worried by the prospect of losing their colonies, however, the Spanish government began sending forces to combat the Juntas, in 1814. In Bolivia, revolutionaries were forced underground, but continued to pester the Spanish forces through guerrilla warfare. They wore down the Spanish opposition, not allowing the dream of independence to fade away.

BELOW The so-called Cry of Asencio in 1811 marked the beginning of the revolution that would gain Uruguay its independence.

BELOW Argentinian revolutionary leader, José de San Martín.

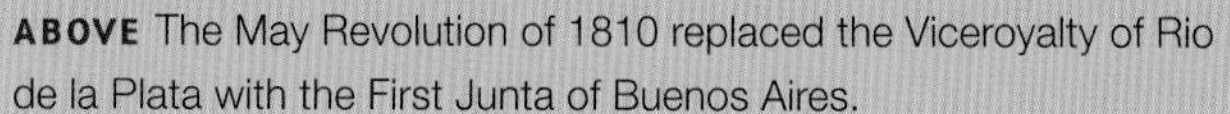

ABOVE The May Revolution of 1810 replaced the Viceroyalty of Rio de la Plata with the First Junta of Buenos Aires.

BELOW The viceroyalties of Spain in South America do not correspond to national boundaries today, but rather encompassed large territories along the Pacific that later fragmented into the countries of present-day South America.

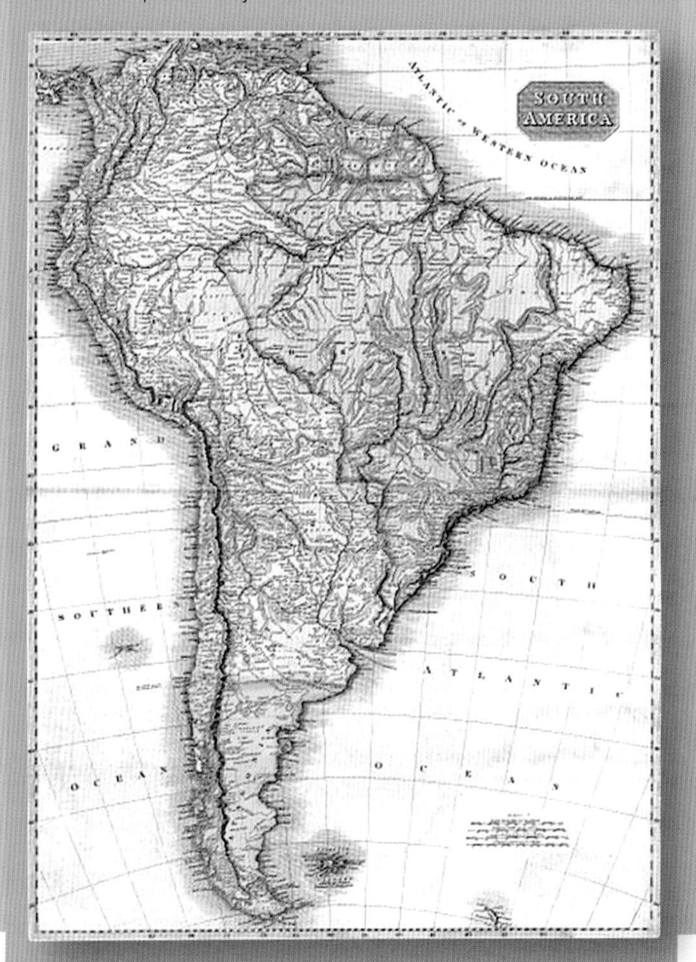

REVOLUTION ACROSS LATIN AMERICA

At the same time that rebels rose up against the Spanish colonial power in Buenos Aires and Bolivia, similar revolutions sprung up across Latin America in Spain's colonies. Tens of thousands of Mexicans fought for an independent state of Mexico; Criollos and Mestizos in what is now Peru, Venezuela, Argentina, Chile, Colombia and Nicaragua, all began clambering for independence, most rising up in armed revolt. Spain began to regain some of its control and composure back in Europe, and turned its attention to addressing the rebellions in its colonies in Latin America, sending troops to put down the rebellions.

The revolutionaries found a hero in Argentine leader, José de San Martín (1778–1850). San Martín had been a professional soldier in the Spanish army, and used his training and a sound sense of military strategy to gradually beat back the royalist opposition to the revolutionary's calls for independence. Crossing the Andes in 1817, to avoid Spanish forces who had reconquered Chile, San Martín managed to defeat the royalists in Chile, and then move on from there to Lima, Peru.

WARS OF INDEPENDENCE 1809–1825

ABOVE Colombians fight for independence at the Battle of Boyacá in 1819.

SAN MARTÍN AND BOLÍVAR

As San Martín worked his magic across the southern territories, another revolutionary fought for independence in the north. Simón Bolívar (1783–1830) was inspired by the American Revolution and the revolutions he was witnessing around him in Latin America. Though born of Spanish descent in Latin America, Bolívar was educated in Europe and was not afraid to dream big about the possibilities for creating an independent state in South America. He began leading armed forces in 1813, freeing Caracas from royalist control on 6 August of that year. This feat earned him the title of 'The Liberator', but he was soon to meet a number of defeats from which he would be forced to flee to Jamaica.

A few years later Bolívar returned to Venezuela, where he commenced revolutionary activities once again. Assembling a small force of roughly 2,500, Bolívar and his men travelled across treacherous terrain to combat the royalists in Colombia. Arriving out of the seemingly impossible wilderness, he took the Spanish by surprise and defeated

ABOVE Portrait of Simón Bolívar.

RIGHT Conflicts in Spain, like the Battle of Bailén in 1808 shown here, provided an opportunity for uprisings in Latin America against Spanish rule. José de San Martín fought at Bailén.

RIGHT José de San Martín and the Chilean independence leader Bernardo O'Higgins embrace after defeating the Spanish at the Battle of Maipú near Santiago, Chile, in 1818.

them at the Battle of Boyacá on 7 August 1819. Bolívar received much needed aid in the battle from the British Legion. On the basis of this victory, Colombia gained its independence from Spain. He went on to free Venezuela and all of Gran Colombia by 1821.

FORMATION OF BOLIVIA

Turning his attention south, Bolívar joined forces with other revolutionaries, including San Martín and Antonio José de Sucre to liberate Peru from Spanish rule. Together with de Sucre, Bolívar launched a series of military campaigns, defeating the Spanish at the Battle of Junín in August 1824. A few months later, de Sucre finished off the Spanish at Ayucucho. Spanish and royalist resistance could not last, and Peru gained its independence. In August 1825, the Republic of Bolivia was established, named after the man who had set the country free – Simón Bolívar.

LEFT Bolívar, celebrated as the liberator of his country.

THE WAR OF 1812 1812–1815

AMERICA TAKES ON BRITAIN AGAIN

BY THE TURN OF THE NINETEENTH CENTURY, AMERICA WAS DEVELOPING INTO A STRONGER AND STRONGER NATION, BOLSTERED BY THE WEALTH IT EARNED THROUGH TRADE. CONFLICTS BETWEEN FRANCE AND BRITAIN, AS WELL AS THE THREAT OF NATIVE AMERICANS, LED TO THE WAR OF 1812.

ABOVE Commodore Perry of the United States defeated the British Royal Navy at the Battle of Lake Erie, despite losing his ship, the USS *Lawrence*.

LEFT Tecumseh led the Shawnee against the United States. This painting depicts his death in battle in 1813.

As Britain and France fought one another, each vying for power at the end of the eighteenth and beginning of the nineteenth centuries, each sought to hinder the other in any possible war. America was caught in the middle, for it prospered from trade with both nations. Two factors threatened the maritime security of the Americas, however: restrictions on trade with Britain and France, and the British practice of 'impressment'.

WAR FROM THE SEA

America largely became a casualty of French and British rivalry. Seeking to hold a monopoly of the seas, each power began outlawing ships that traded with the other. American ships that traded with the British could therefore be seen as enemy vessels by the French. The British likewise sought to restrict commerce between America and France. As the fledgling nation prospered, largely from its trade with France, Britain and Spain, these new measures hit hard. They led President Jefferson to pass the Embargo Act, which aimed to stop all exports from the United States, but this was detrimental to the American economy.

Another factor affecting American discontent with the British naval power was the practice of impressment. Impressment was the British practice of seizing American vessels and taking captive American citizens, forcing them to serve in the British Navy. By the end of the first decade of the nineteenth century, tensions between the United States and Britain were high.

ABOVE Heated discussions between Tecumseh and Harrison over Native American land.

LEFT Future president Andrew Jackson led the Americans to victory against the British at the Battle of New Orleans in January 1815. The Americans did not know it at the time, but peace had already been signed a couple of weeks prior in Ghent, Belgium. The ships bearing the news had not yet arrived.

TROUBLE ON THE FRONTIER

As frictions increased at sea, the Native Americans in the interior of North America grew increasingly concerned by American expansion and began banding together under the leadership of Tecumseh of the Shawnee. The Native Americans saw their hopes of fighting off the Americans in forming alliances with Britain. In 1811, future president William Henry Harrison defeated Tecumseh at the Battle of Tippecanoe, but this only led to further Native American and British alliances. With the urgings of the 'War Hawks', such as House of Representatives speaker Henry Clay, America declared war against Britain on 18 June 1812.

With a number of battles fought on land and at sea, the Americans met with failure during the early years of the war. Invading Canada multiple times, to try to oust the British there, the Americans were unable to secure many military victories. In 1814, the British defeated the Americans at the Battle of Bladensburg and burned Washington, DC. American success in defending Fort McHenry just weeks later at the Battle of Baltimore became the impetus for Francis Scott Key's 'Star Spangled Banner'. The tide turned against the British.

ABOVE This illustration shows Native Americans presenting a British officer with the scalps of Americans.

RIGHT The old White House of the nation's capital was burned down by the British during the War of 1812.

THE AMERICAN CIVIL WAR 1861–1865

A LAND DIVIDED

WITH ECONOMIES DEVELOPING DIFFERENTLY IN THE NORTH AND SOUTH OF THE UNITED STATES DURING THE MIDDLE OF THE NINETEENTH CENTURY, THE COUNTRY BECAME MORE AND MORE DIVIDED, PARTICULARLY OVER THE ISSUE OF SLAVERY. WHEN THE SOUTH SECEDED IN 1861, WAR BROKE OUT.

The movement to abolish slavery in the South, and spread its introduction into the states developing in the West, was a serious threat to the agrarian economy of the southern states. The North, which had shifted its economic base to one more centred around manufacturing, became increasingly opposed to the 'peculiar institution' of slavery during the middle of the nineteenth century. In addition to the slavery issue, there were disputes over how much power should rest in the individual state, and how much should rest in the federal government. When the antislavery Republican candidate, Abraham Lincoln, was elected president in 1860, the South decided to take action. Early in 1861, the South seceded from the United States, creating the Confederate States of America.

BELOW Though he had little military experience, President Abraham Lincoln was commander-in-chief of the Union forces.

BELOW Stonewall Jackson earned his name by entrenching his soldiers so they could not be moved, as seen here in the Battle of Bull Run.

BROTHERS FIGHTING

The first shots of the Civil War were fired on 12 April 1861. Confederate troops shot at the US military at Fort Sumter in South Carolina. This was the beginning of a long and bloody war, which many consider to be the first modern war. The basis of hostilities was primarily ideological and economic, which meant that the divisions between the Confederacy of the South and the Union of the North did not always fall along clean boundaries – many families themselves were split between the two sides of the war, even brothers facing each other on the battlefield.

THE EARLY WAR

Union forces quickly ran into trouble, as they were not well-trained and many of them did not have the experience with firearms that was common among the soldiers of the South. In the early days of the war, the Union also suffered from a lack of leadership that could combat the mastermind of the Confederacy, Robert E Lee. Lincoln's Union soldiers lost badly at the First Battle of Bull

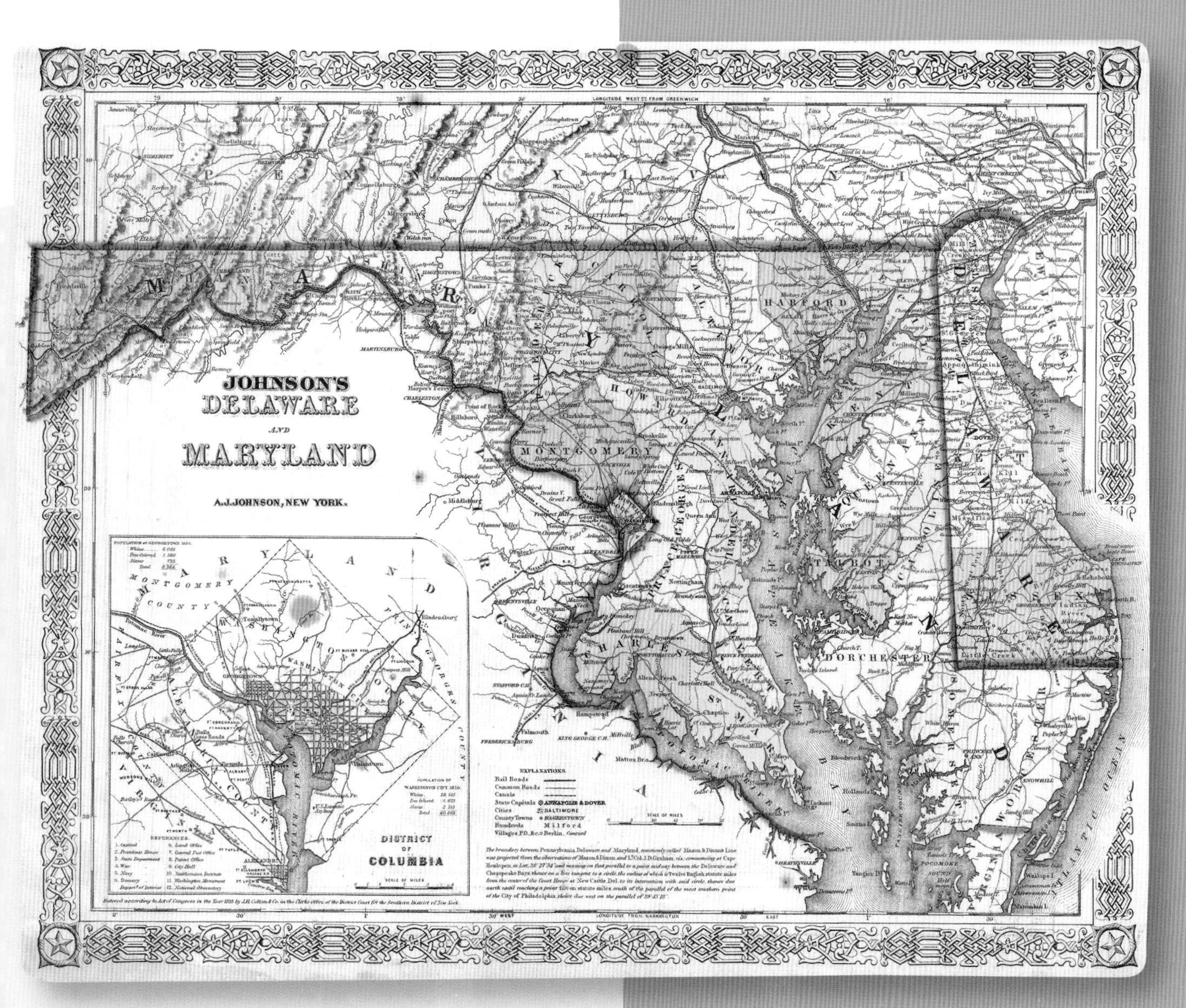

ABOVE The South and North were divided along the Mason-Dixon Line. Although Maryland was technically below the Mason-Dixon Line, it became a part of the Union because of the location of Washington, DC, where Abraham Lincoln and the federal government were based.

BELOW General Robert E Lee on his horse, named Traveller.

Run on 21 July 1861. The first year of fighting did not go well for the Union, and the Union under John Pope still lost badly at the Second Battle of Bull Run in August 1862. Robert E Lee and Thomas Jackson ('Stonewall Jackson') employed intelligent tactics outwitting their opponents. A draw between Union forces under George McClellan and Confederate forces under Robert E Lee at the Battle of Antietam on 17 September 1862, was the closest McClellan could come to an actual victory against Lee. But it is hard to call Antietam a victory of any kind, for nearly 25,000 men died at the battle in a single day.

THE AMERICAN CIVIL WAR 1861–1865

RIGHT Union soldiers won an important victory in Atlanta, Georgia, in 1864.

ULYSSES S GRANT

The military leadership of the Union was faltering by 1862. Relief was to come from an unexpected source: a brigadier general named Ulysses S Grant. Grant was a somewhat shabby commander of a ragtag regiment that came to be known as the 21st Illinois Volunteers. Grant himself had not initially been interested in a military career, but attended West Point after his father secured a place for him there. Upon graduating, however, Grant discovered an eagerness for action.

Grant defeated the Confederate forces at Shiloh in April 1862, and secured an important victory at Vicksburg, Mississippi, in 1863. Despite heavy losses at Shiloh, and Grant's unconventional tactics, he was promoted to major general. At the end of the day, he won his battles. In March 1864, Grant was given command of the US forces. He immediately set about executing a strategy to defeat Robert E Lee by attacking Richmond, the Confederate capital, while simultaneously sending William Tecumseh Sherman through Georgia. Sherman's March through Georgia is known as one of the most brutal parts of the American Civil War. Sherman left Atlanta, Georgia, in mid-November 1864 and marched with his men to Savannah on the coast. On their way, they left an incredible path of destruction. The aim was to destroy both the infrastructure of the South, and the Confederacy's will to continue resistance. Scars of that march are still visible in the landscape of Georgia today, as many question how necessary such destruction actually was.

BELOW President Lincoln confers with Generals Sherman and Grant, as well as Admiral Porter.

ABOLITION OF SLAVERY

On 1 January 1863, President Lincoln signed the Emancipation Proclamation, formally abolishing slavery in the United States. Much of the fighting, however, was still to come. Grant and Lee squared off against one another in an elaborate dance of strategy. Grant seemed unable to defeat the southern general, and sustained heavy losses at every encounter. But Grant continued to press against Lee's forces, eventually winning an important victory at the Battle of Five Forks on 1 April 1865. Lee finally surrendered on 9 April 1865. The war saw more than a million casualties, with more than half a million soldiers dead. The cost of the war was tremendous, but by the end slavery had been abolished, and the United States were once again United.

LEFT During the American Civil War was the first time in history that two ironclads battled each other. Here, the USS *Monitor* and CSS *Virginia* battle it out on 9 March 1862.

RIGHT Ulysses S Grant was instrumental to the victory of the North over the South.

ABOVE General Sherman and his men.

LEFT Casualties at the Battle of Gettysburg were higher than in any other Civil War battle.

SPANISH-AMERICAN WAR 1898

BECOMING THE ENEMY

IN 1898, THE UNITED STATES DECLARED WAR ON SPAIN TO AID CUBA IN ITS REVOLUTION AGAINST THE EUROPEAN COUNTRY AND GAIN INDEPENDENCE. IN HELPING ANOTHER COLONIAL COUNTRY GAIN INDEPENDENCE, HOWEVER, AMERICAN BECAME A COLONIAL POWER ITSELF.

Atrocities committed in Cuba against the Cuban population incensed the American public, which was whipped into a fury by the wild news stories being sold by journalists as the major newspapers vied for dominance of the American news scene. Though the stories fed to the American public were likely exaggerated, Cuba was being repressed by Spain, and the island's inhabitants wanted independence.

When the USS *Maine*, an American battleship sent to protect Americans in Havana, was sunk mysteriously on 15 February 1898, Spain's fate was sealed. While the cause of the blast that sunk the ship was unknown and could not be proven, popular opinion in America pointed the finger of blame unanimously at Spain.

LEFT Wreckage of the USS *Maine*, whose destruction catalysed American involvement in the Cuban Revolution through the Spanish-American War.

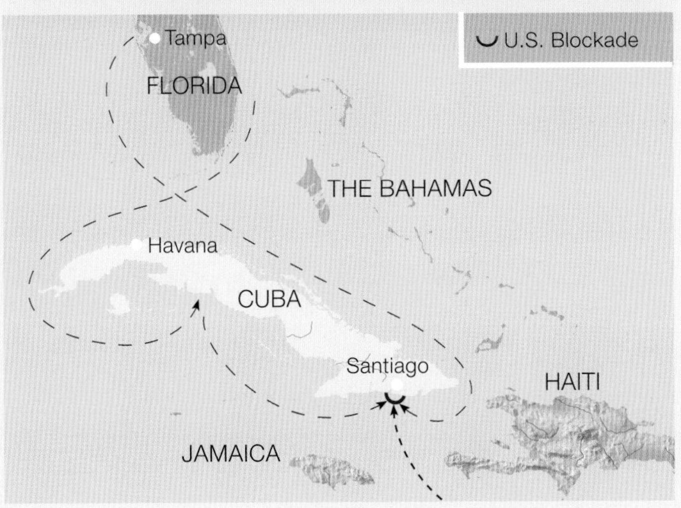

ABOVE Political cartoon from the popular American magazine *Puck* in 1901. It toys with America's newfound position as a world power.

ABOVE LEFT The Battle of Santiago as seen from the deck of the USS *Iowa*.

LEFT The Spanish-American War centred around Cuba, but was also fought in Manila Bay in the Philippines.

AMERICA'S NAVAL POWER

Spain declared war on the United States on 24 April, and the US followed suit the next day by declaring war on Spain. The war itself was surprisingly lopsided. Commodore George Dewey brought a force of Americans from Hong Kong to Manila and attacked the Spanish fleet in Manila Bay on 1 May. The Spanish crumbled. Dewey defeated the Spanish in the Philippines within hours without losing any men; only seven American soldiers were wounded.

Back in Cuba, the Spanish sought to avoid the more powerful US Navy. In early July, the US forces pinned the Spanish down at Santiago Harbor, where the Americans under General William Shafter completely destroyed the Spanish fleet. Among those who participated in the assault was future president, Theodore Roosevelt and his 'Rough Riders'. Santiago surrendered on 17 July. The Treaty of Paris that formally brought the war to a close was not signed until 10 December, but the war was effectively over at this point in July. Cuba was granted independence, but other Spanish territories were ceded to the United States, including Guam and Puerto Rico. The Philippines were sold for a price of $20 million, despite the United States having claimed to assist the Philippines in their own efforts for independence.

CIVIL WAR IN NICARAGUA 1912–1933

AMERICAN INTERVENTION

THE POLITICAL INSTABILITY IN NICARAGUA, FOLLOWING ITS INDEPENDENCE IN 1838, GAVE THE UNITED STATES JUSTIFICATION FOR SENDING MILITARY AID TO THE COUNTRY. IT WAS CLEAR, HOWEVER, THAT THE UNITED STATES HAD ULTERIOR MOTIVES.

US presidents began sending troops to Nicaragua in the mid-nineteenth century. Despite their apparently altruistic motives, the United States had a vested interest in controlling Nicaragua and its resources. In fact, following the Spanish-American War in 1898, the United States took greater and greater interest in Latin America and the Caribbean, sending the US Marines to several countries for the purpose of supporting political stability. The American military presence and its engagements throughout Latin America are referred to as the 'Banana Wars' because of the importance Latin America and its resources – including its produce – had to the US economy. This somewhat bent the rules of the earlier Monroe Doctrine. Armed resistance wore down the US forces, and the Great Depression of the 1930s eventually contributed to the United States' withdrawal from across Latin America in 1934.

LEFT Adolfo Díaz, President of Nicaragua from 1911–1917 and again from 1926–1929.

BELOW LEFT The US Frigate *Saranac* in Nicaragua.

BELOW RIGHT President José María Moncada and General Anastasio Somoza García conduct a review of the US Marines in Nicaragua in 1930.

HERO AND BANDIT

In Nicaragua, tensions between the Conservatives and Liberals in the government threw the country into turmoil in the mid-1920s, spawning US intervention. A leader emerged among the revolutionary forces of Nicaragua. His name was Augusto César Sandino and he would lead a guerrilla war against the US Marines between 1927 and 1933 when the Marines finally left Nicaragua. Sandino was not often successful in his military engagements, often driven back by the superior firepower of the US military. Despite being outnumbered and outgunned, Sandino evaded capture completely, and he and his loyal men continued to harry the US forces in Nicaragua. In 1933, the United States finally withdrew, and Juan Bautista Sacasa became president of Nicaragua. Sandino submitted to Sacasa and pledged loyalty. In 1934, however, Sandino and his men were captured and killed by the National Guard, whom Sandino saw as loyal to the United States. While US Marines considered Sandino a criminal, he was and still is considered a hero in Nicaragua.

ABOVE The 200,000 córdobas note bears the picture of Sandino.

RIGHT A political cartoon showing Hermes (right) extending his hand across the Nicaraguan channel to Peace (left) with Uncle Sam below.

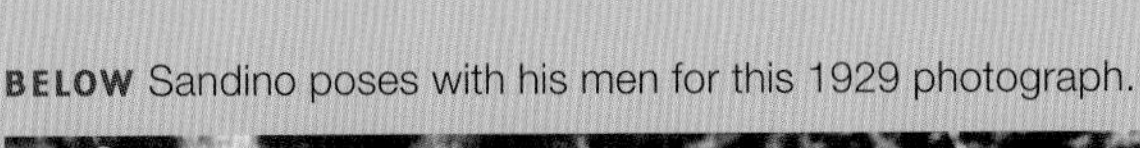

BELOW Sandino poses with his men for this 1929 photograph.

BELOW RIGHT Sandino led a guerrilla war against the US Marines.

THE CUBAN REVOLUTION 1953–1959

THE RISE OF CASTRO

ON 26 JULY, 1953, FIDEL CASTRO LED AN ATTACK ON MONCADA BARRACKS IN SANTIAGO. AS HE EXPECTED, THE ATTACK WAS A FAILURE; ITS WIDER PURPOSE – TO INSPIRE THE PEOPLE OF CUBA TO REVOLT AGAINST THE REPRESSIVE REGIME OF FULGENCIO BATISTA – ALSO FAILED.

By 1953, Batista had controlled Cuba for 19 years. A kind of underworld economy flourished during his rule, and urban centres were rife with gambling, prostitution and organized crime. The rural areas of the country, however, suffered great poverty. Castro's revolt of 26 July 1953, did not produce the results he hoped for initially. He was imprisoned without inspiring an uprising. But at his trial he gave a speech that became a political manifesto, published under the title of *History Will Absolve Me*. This speech started to create stirrings among the people he aimed to influence. Castro was released from prison in 1955 and went to Mexico, where he planed the next stages of his rebellion against Batista.

ABOVE President Fulgencio Batista was overthrown by the Cuban Revolution.

RIGHT The construction of missile launchpads in Cuba led to the Cuban Missile Crisis of 1962.

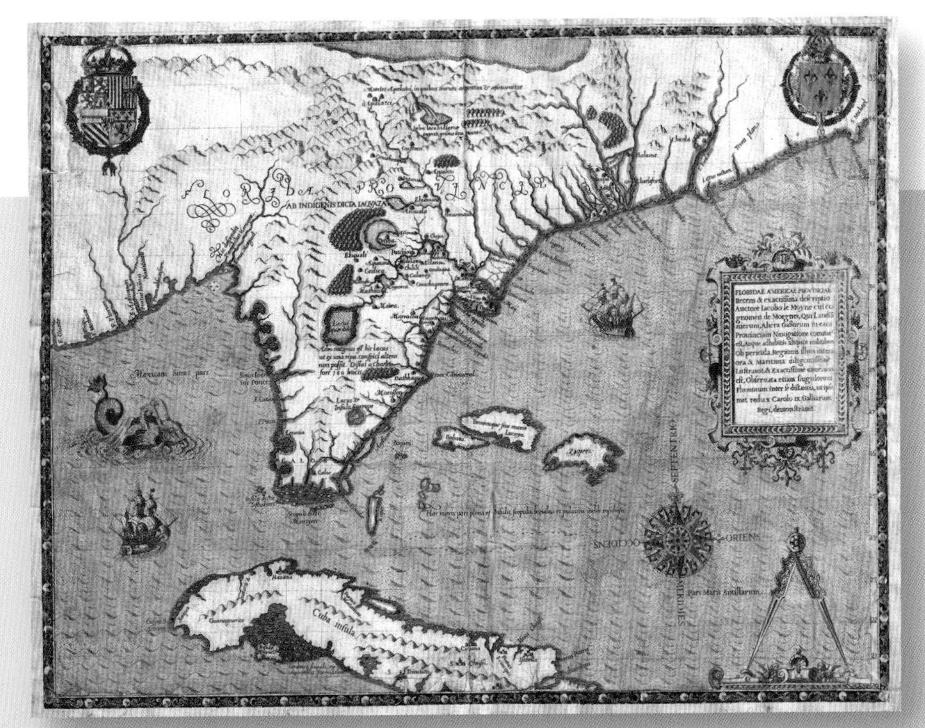

LEFT A 16th-century map of Florida and Cuba.

BELOW LEFT Raúl Castro and Che Guevara, Cuba, 1958.

BELOW Cartoon from *Puck* depicting Uncle Sam instructing Puerto Rico, Hawaii, the Philippines and Cuba.

CASTRO RETURNS

In December 1956, Castro returned to Cuba with a small force aboard a yacht called the *Granma*. Roughly 80 – including Castro's brother Raúl and Che Guevara – landed at Playa Las Coloradas and began marching into the Sierra Maestra. They were ambushed by Batista's forces, however, and severely weakened. Nonetheless, they regrouped and began a campaign of guerrilla warfare for the next two years. Their revolutionary movement was called the 26th of July Movement after the date of Castro's initial attack on Batista. Gradually, more and more people joined Castro's movement, as he and his men launched guerrilla attacks and constantly moved about the country to escape capture. Through avoiding direct confrontation, Castro and his men were able to deal heavy blows to Batista's forces without sustaining many losses themselves. After two years of fighting, Castro's rebel forces took Santa Clara, Havana and Santiago. Castro's revolution, which had begun in failure, ended in success.

SOVIET INVOLVEMENT

Radically reforming Cuban society and the Cuban economy, Castro began turning Cuba more and more into a communist nation along the lines of the Soviet Union. Connections between Cuba and the Soviet Union caused significant fear in the United States. In 1961, President John F Kennedy sent 1,500 Cuban exiles on an invasion mission of Cuba at the Bay of Pigs, intending to overthrow Castro's government. The invasion was a complete failure, and an international embarrassment to the United States. In order to prevent future invasions the Soviet Union began building a missile launch pad on Cuba. This became the Cuban Missile Crisis of 1962, a brief and very tense period during which nuclear war between the United States and the Soviet Union was a real possibility.

SEPTEMBER 11 ATTACKS 2001

GLOBAL TERRORISM

ON 11 SEPTEMBER 2001, MEMBERS OF THE ISLAMIC EXTREMIST GROUP AL-QAEDA HIJACKED FOUR SEPARATE PLANES WITH THE INTENTION OF CRASHING THEM INTO TARGETS THEY VIEWED AS SYMBOLIC OF AMERICA'S TYRANNY OVER THE REST OF THE WORLD. THIS WAS THE LARGEST ATTACK ON US SOIL SINCE PEARL HARBOR IN 1941.

The attacks of 9/11 were among the most successful terrorist attacks in history. They took tremendous amounts of planning and preparation, and were the work of al-Qaeda mastermind, Osama bin Laden. Nearly 3,000 people died that morning in an event that affected the entire world, and changed forever how we think of war itself.

ABOVE President George Bush was visiting an elementary school when he received word of the attacks.

THE WEAPON OF FEAR

Rather than attacking the United States military, the terrorists of 9/11 attacked symbols of American power. The Twin Towers were symbols of America's economic dominance, located in the financial capital of the United States, New York City. The Pentagon and the White House (or perhaps the Capitol building) represented the political and military power of the United States. By attacking symbols, rather than the Armed Forces themselves, al-Qaeda created a wave of fear that spread not only across the entire United States, but across the whole world as well. No one was safe. An attack could come anywhere and at any time because terrorists do not abide by the rules of engagement for warfare.

RIGHT The Twin Towers aflame after being struck by the planes. Both towers would later collapse entirely.

LEFT The Taliban in Afghanistan harboured members of the terrorist organization al-Qaeda responsible for the September 11 attacks.

RIGHT The crash at the Pentagon tore a huge hole in the side of the building and caused a massive fire.

THE FOURTH PLANE

Four planes were hijacked and used as missiles, redirected at al-Qaeda 's targets. Three of them found their mark: the two at the Twin Towers first, and then the plane that struck the Pentagon. But the fourth plane, United Airlines Flight 93, did not reach its target, but was instead brought down in Pennsylvania. Having been alerted by mobile phone to the attacks in New York, the brave passengers of Flight 93 chose to give up their own lives in order to prevent a greater catastrophe. They rose up against the hijackers and brought the plane down. We do not know for certain what the intended target of this fourth plane was, but it is suspected it was either the White House or the Capitol building in Washington, DC.

BELOW This map shows the flight paths of the four hijacked planes.

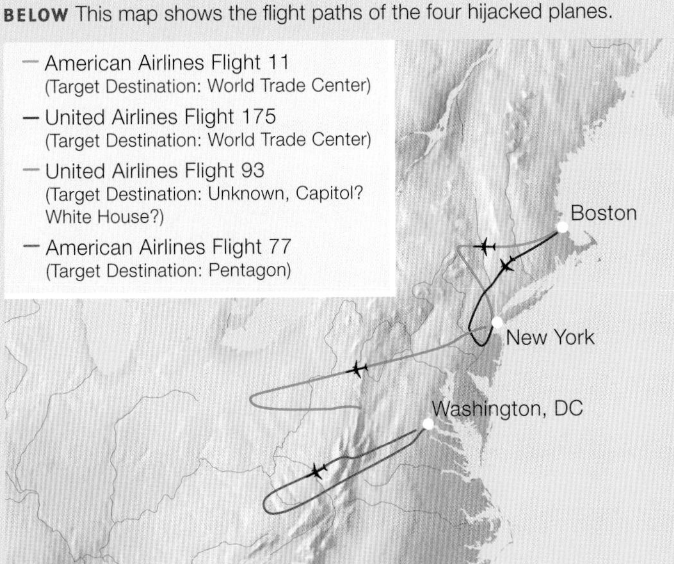

RIGHT US Special Forces members work with Northern Alliance fighters in Afghanistan in November 2001.

AFTERMATH

Osama bin Laden had proclaimed a *fatwa*, a declaration of war, against Western powers; with the aid of the Taliban in Afghanistan, bin Laden's al-Qaeda team of 19 were able to carry out the coordinated attacks of 9/11. In the wake of the shock and grief caused by the 9/11 attacks, the United States invaded Afghanistan in what it called the 'War on Terror'. It would take ten years, however, before Navy SEAL Team Six would locate and take out Osama bin Laden. Bin Laden was shot on 2 May 2011, at his compound in Abbottabad, Pakistan. Drone warfare – the use of computerized drones to strike targets – continues in Afghanistan today. With no pilots operating these machines, drone warfare raises serious issues regarding the ethics and responsibility for casualties it causes.

OCEANVS
DEVCALEDONIVS
OCEANVS
OCCIDENTALIS
MARE
LANTICVM
BARBARIA
FESSA
MAR

EUROPE

ANCIENT GREECE 1200–30 BCE

WESTERN INSPIRATION

ANCIENT GREECE IS OFTEN CONSIDERED THE FOUNDATION OF WESTERN CIVILIZATION. WITH THE REDISCOVERY OF CLASSICAL LITERATURE DURING THE MIDDLE AGES, THE TALES OF ACHILLES, HECTOR, AGAMEMNON AND ODYSSEUS BECAME REQUIRED READING FOR ANY EDUCATED PERSON.

ABOVE Ancient Greece was comprised of a number of independent city-states, each with its own king and army.

Very little was known in Europe about Ancient Greece until the High Middle Ages, when translations of Ancient Greek texts entered Europe via Arabic scholars. The writings of Aristotle, the mentor of Alexander the Great, quickly became widely influential. And the poetry of Homer, including his *Iliad* and *Odyssey*, would become the paragon of epic literature in Europe. Tales of great warriors from Ancient Greece – historic, legendary and mythical – would inspire the leaders of Europe and the West for centuries.

ORGANIZATION IN WARFARE

The Greeks rose to prominence in large part because of their military might. Disciplined and organized, they were able to overcome larger forces of warriors who lacked the same level of cohesion in military units. Over the years, the great individual heroes of Homer's epics were gradually replaced by the orderly ranks of hoplite soldiers, who wielded devastating power while acting as one unit. The phalanx became the most important component of Greek warfare. Arranged in ranks and files several men deep, soldiers stood shoulder to shoulder and locked shields in a tight defensive wall from behind which they could attack with long spears. The spear was the most important weapon. The depth of the phalanx meant that when the first row faltered or fell, another soldier was standing immediately behind to fill the gap. Organization into ranks and files gave warriors mobility on the battlefield, but allowed for multiple phalanxes to combine into larger, more powerful forces. The principal of the phalanx and its effectiveness in Ancient Greece continues to inspire military tacticians even today.

ABOVE A 16th-century Italian dish depicting part of the Trojan War. The tale of Troy dominated European literature for centuries.

LEFT According to legend, Polyxena's sacrifice was ordered by the ghost of Achilles. Achilles had told Polyxena of his one weakness, and she passed this on to her Trojan brothers.

BELOW This Renaissance painting shows the abduction of Helen of Troy amidst a sweeping scene of Ancient Greece.

THE HEROES OF ANCIENT GREECE

The wealth of written literature and contemporary documentation from Ancient Greece gives us a window into the culture and military traditions that we do not have for many other ancient civilizations. The exquisite and incredibly lifelike artwork from the classical period further brings to life the heroes of the past. From mythological figures, such as Zeus, Athena and Apollo, to legendary warriors, such as Theseus and his battle against the Minotaur, the martial traditions of Greece developed into the pinnacle of Bronze Age capability. We still marvel today at the feats of heroism performed by such warriors as the 300 men who defended Thermopylae to the death, preventing the Persians from taking Greece, or Alexander the Great, who established an enormous empire with seemingly supernatural speed.

Perhaps most enduring in its fame, however, is the legendary Trojan War, as described in Homer's *Iliad.* Homer describes the war as lasting nine years and being fought between massive armies. Nonetheless, much of the fighting described in Homer is of an individual nature, with the greatest warriors of both Greek and Trojan armies pitting their strength against one another. While Homer's account is likely to be largely fictional, the war itself has its basis in real history and archaeology.

SCYTHIANS C. 700 BCE–600 CE

PUNCHING A CLOUD

THE STEPPES OF CENTRAL ASIA HAVE BEEN HOME TO VARIOUS NOMADIC PEOPLES THROUGHOUT THE CENTURIES. AMONG THE MOST FEARED OF THE ANCIENT WORLD, HOWEVER, WERE THE SCYTHIANS, AN IRANIAN HORSE PEOPLE WHO CONTROLLED A VAST EMPIRE, AND WERE NEARLY IMPOSSIBLE TO DEFEAT.

The Scythians came from what is now Iran around 700 BCE, and overthrew the Cimmerians in the region around the Black Sea. They never employed any written records, so much of their past is shrouded in mystery; what we do know about them comes from outside sources, such as the Greek historian, Herodotus, who visited the lands of the Scythians in the fifth century BCE. Herodotus provides detailed accounts of the folkloric histories and contemporary practices of the Scythian peoples. We also know about the Scythians from the numerous attempts of other powers, such as the Persian Empire, to conquer or defeat them. These attempts usually did not go well.

HORSE, BOW AND ARROW

A warlike people, the Scythians were particularly known for their equestrian skills, and their early use of composite bows shot from horseback. With great mobility, the Scythians could absorb the attacks of more cumbersome foot soldiers and cavalry, just retreating into the steppes. Such tactics wore down their enemies, making them easier to defeat. Herodotus describes several brutalities practised by the

ABOVE Eugène Delacroix's painting of the Roman poet, Ovid, in exile among the Scythians.

LEFT A Pazyryk horseman in a felt painting from a burial around 300 BCE. The Pazyryks appear to be closely related to the Scythians.

Scythians, including the taking of enemy scalps as trophies of war, and even drinking the blood of their enemies. Herodotus's view as an outsider is undoubtedly biased, but even he must praise their bravery in battle, and the luxury of their courts. With no written records from the Scythians themselves, we know from archaeological evidence that they possessed advanced skills as artisans and craftsmen, leaving behind many beautiful treasures made of gold. The warriors of the Scythians were free men whose reward for fighting was a share in the spoils.

ABOVE This archaic map shows the land of the Sarmatians and the Scythians. The Caspian Sea can be seen on the right, and the Pontus Euxinus is the Black Sea.

SARMATIANS TAKE OVER

The Sarmatians were culturally, ethnically and linguistically related to the Scythians, and inhabited the lands east of the Black Sea. Though originally part of the same stock, the Sarmatians attacked the Scythians in the third century BCE. Also a horse people, the Sarmatians would gradually take the place of the Scythians after the defeat of King Atheas of Scythia in 339 BCE by the Macedonians under Philip II, the father of Alexander the Great. The Scythians and Sarmatians would continue to control parts of the steppes of Central Asia for centuries to come.

THE GRECO-PERSIAN WARS 490–480 BCE

THE GREEK UNDERDOGS

BY AROUND 500 BCE, THE PERSIAN EMPIRE UNDER DARIUS THE GREAT WAS EXPANDING FURIOUSLY, AND IT SEEMS NONE COULD WITHSTAND THE MILITARY MIGHT OF THE PERSIAN WARRIORS. BUT WHEN DARIUS INVADED GREECE IN 490, ATHENS ROSE UP AND WON A MAJOR VICTORY.

When Greek city-states on the border of the Persian Empire rose up against the power of Darius, Athens and Eritrea sent aid. The rebellions were put down, but Darius viewed Greek involvement in the rebellions as justification for invading Greece itself. With a relatively small force of 25,000, Darius launched an invasion directed at Athens.

THE CLASH AT MARATHON

Word of the Persian advance reached Athens, which was ill-equipped to deal with the threat. Sending a runner named Pheidippides to run the 240 km (150 miles) to Sparta in a single day, the Athenians requested aid from their warlike neighbours. The Spartans, however, were unable to respond in time, despite their appreciation of the threat from Persia.

ABOVE Much of what we know about Marathon – and ancient Greek history in general – comes from the writings of Herodotus.

OPPOSITE LEFT The Persian Empire extended through Anatolia, threatening the lands across the Aegean Sea.

ABOVE Alexander the Great defeated the Persians under Darius III, as depicted here.

The Athenians were effectively on their own in their defence of Greece against the mighty power of Darius the Great.

With little more than 10,000 men, the ten Greek commanders in charge of the armies were divided over whether to take a defensive or offensive position against Darius. In the end, they chose to attack, and uniting under the leadership of Miltiades, the Greeks launched their assault on the Persian camp after learning that the cavalry had temporarily left. Catching the Persians off guard, the Greek forces deliberately weakened their own centre and strengthened their wings. When the central Greek forces were pushed back, the two wings closed in around the Persians violently, effectively surrounding them. Greek sources state that only 192 Greek soldiers were killed compared to 6,400 Persians. While it is hard to determine the veracity of these figures, the overwhelming Greek victory at Marathon is indisputable. The strong formations and use of long spears proved invaluably effective against the Persian foot soldiers.

THE LEGEND OF MARATHON

It is said that after the Battle of Marathon, a runner ran the 40 km (25 miles) or so to Athens, announced the victory and died on the spot from exhaustion. There is confusion in the ancient sources, however, between this journey and the journey of Pheidippides to Sparta. Herodotus reports that the Athenian army itself marched from Marathon to Athens in order to head off the Persian forces.

THE GRECO-PERSIAN WARS 490–480 BCE

ABOVE The narrow strip of land between the mountains and the sea at Thermopylae.

TOP An inscription in three languages by Xerxes from Van, Turkey.

OPPOSITE BOTTOM Statue of King Leonidas at the top of the Spartan monument at Thermopylae.

OPPOSITE TOP The Battle of Salamis in 480 BCE.

THE PERSIANS RETURN

The victory at Marathon changed the course of Western civilization. But the threat of the Persians was not gone entirely. A decade after the invasion launched by Darius the Great, another far more powerful invasion would be led by his son and successor, Xerxes. Despite the overwhelming size and power of his forces, Xerxes I would be beaten by the alliance of Greek city-states that rose to meet him.

LEONIDAS'S LAST STAND

As the Persians advanced towards Greece, an alliance of city-states blocked their approach at the narrow pass of Thermopylae. While contemporary sources state outrageous figures of more than a million for the Persian forces, it is likely that Xerxes commanded at least 100,000 soldiers. Only about 7,000 Greeks blocked the pass. Realizing the futility of the defence, the Spartan king, Leonidas, sent the Athenian and other forces away, yet remained himself with 300 Spartans to cover their retreat. Bolstering the Spartan forces were a few hundred Thespians and Thebans – all told, a scant force as compared to the massive army of Xerxes.

For three days, the Spartans held the Persians at bay, blocking the narrowest part of the pass. Maintaining strict formations, the Spartans endured showers of arrows and frontal assault after frontal assault. The discipline and training of the Spartan warriors allowed them to hold their ground, using their long spears to take down the approaching enemies. But they were betrayed by a Greek, named Ephialtes, who showed the Persians a hidden path that led behind the Spartan lines. The Spartans continued to fight until virtually all of them had been slain.

SALAMIS

With the way now cleared at Thermopylae, Xerxes continued his march, still commanding an incredible force both on land and at sea. The Greeks, under the command of Themistocles, decided to engage the Persian fleet at Salamis.

Luring the Persians into the narrow strait, the massive fleet of Xerxes soon became immobile, allowing the Greeks to pen them in with their small and lightweight craft. Roughly 300 Persian ships were sunk, while the Greeks lost only about 40. This was a massive victory for the Greeks, but the wars with Persia were not yet over.

PLATAEA: THE FINAL BATTLE

In 479 BCE, the Greeks assembled a large army from the alliances of city-states and marched out to meet the Persians at Plataea. Not wanting to engage the Persians on unfavourable ground, however, the Greeks waited near the fortified camp of the Persians. After several days, the Persian commander, Mardonius, managed to disrupt the supply lines of the Greeks. Falling back to regroup, the Greeks broke from their positions, giving Mardonius the impression of retreat. Mardonius launched an assault. Rather than retreating, the Greeks turned and fought Mardonius, soundly defeating the Persian army. This was the last Persian attempt at invading the mainland of Greece. Xerxes, despite the size of his army, was finally defeated.

HOPLITES

The term 'hoplite' refers to a particular kind of ancient Greek warrior. The term itself comes from a Greek word for the equipment of the soldier. The primary weaponry of the hoplite – which would be supplied by the warrior himself at his own expense – was a large, round shield and a long spear. Helmets were also common and wealthier soldiers wore breastplates.

THE PELOPONNESIAN WAR 431–404 BCE

THE BATTLE FOR GREECE

OUT OF THE GRECO-PERSIAN WARS OF THE EARLY FIFTH CENTURY BCE, TWO CITY-STATES EMERGED AS DOMINANT: ATHENS AND SPARTA. LESS THAN 50 YEARS AFTER FIGHTING SIDE-BY-SIDE TO DEFEAT THE PERSIANS, ATHENS AND SPARTA WERE AT ODDS FOR CONTROL OF GREECE.

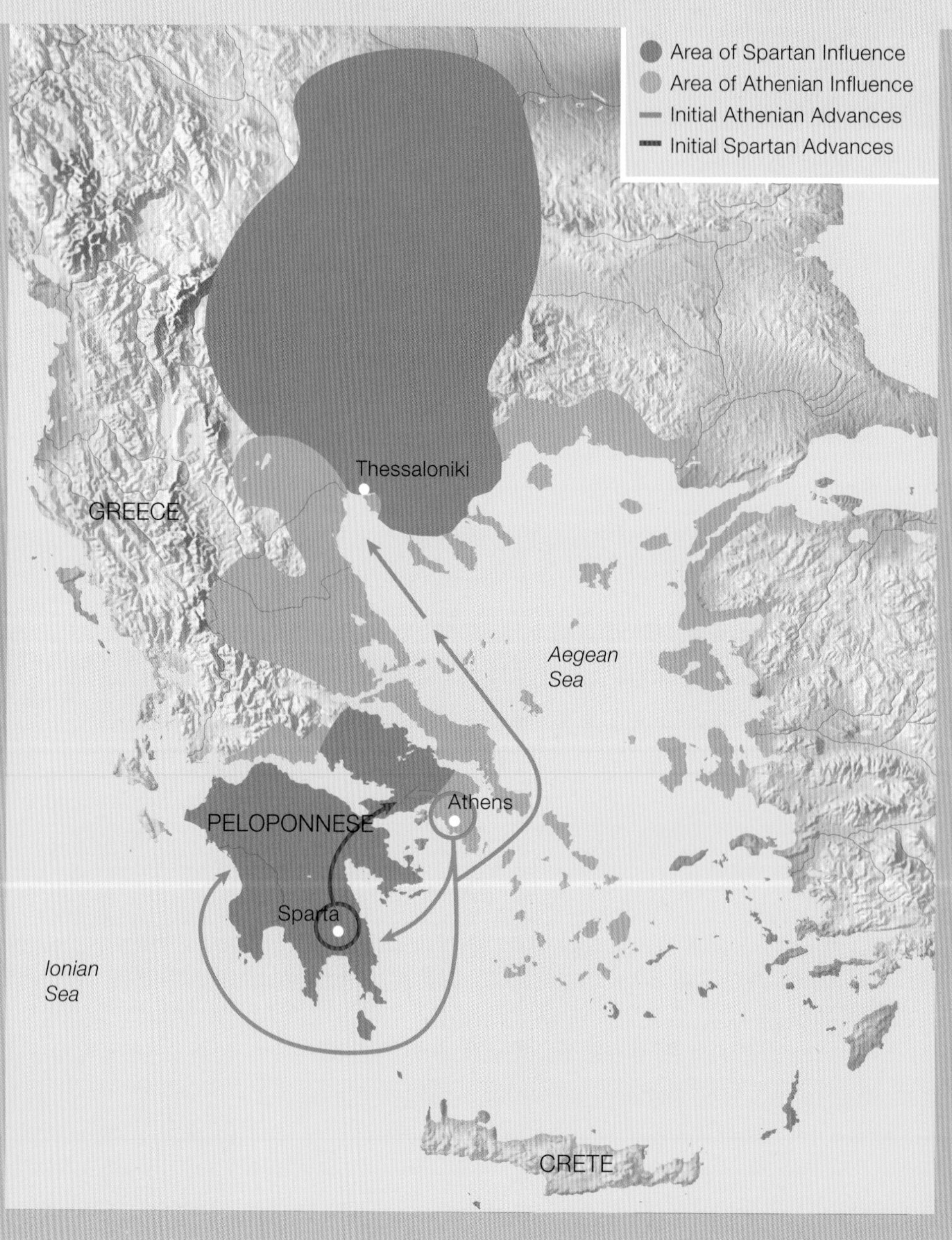

ABOVE Bust of Pericles of Athens. By avoiding direct engagement with Sparta on land, Pericles was able to conserve Athens's resources and gain victory over Sparta.

RIGHT Map showing the range of control and influence of the Spartan and Athenian city-states.

OPPOSITE The Athenian harbour housed the powerful navy of Athens and was an important centre for trade.

This was actually the second time Athens and Sparta had butted heads during the fifth century BCE, though the former quarrel had ended in a truce. This second Peloponnesian War was of a far greater scale and importance. The struggle was not just between the two city-states alone, but between all the territories they commanded as well. Both Athens and Sparta had established alliances with other Greek city-states, and Athens controlled most of the islands of the Aegean. Athens had the superior navy, while Sparta had the superior force on land.

THE FIRST PHASE

The early years were difficult for Athens, but saw the Athenians gaining the upper hand. When allies of Athens and Sparta attacked each other, the war officially began, and Sparta invaded Attica, the territory around Athens. Rather than meet them directly on land, Athenian leader Pericles withdrew to the city of Athens, and instead focused on using the city's naval power. Plague broke out in Athens, however, killing many of its inhabitants and weakening the Athenian position against Sparta. Nonetheless, the Spartans were unable to gain a victory over the Athenians, and the war continued until a truce was signed in 421 – the Peace of Nicias. The peace would last only six years. This first phase of the war is known as the Archidamian War after King Archidamus II of Sparta.

WAR RETURNS

Both Athens and Sparta continued to jockey for position, even after the peace treaty had been signed. Over the coming years, matters escalated to the point of armed conflict once again. In 415 BCE, Athens launched an attack on Syracuse in Sicily. Syracuse was a Spartan ally, and this brought the war back into full throttle. This time, however, things did not go well for Athens. Syracuse, with Sparta's aid, was able to repulse the attack. Despite protracted efforts, Athens was soundly beaten, and could not take Syracuse. Athens itself fell into political chaos, and tensions with Sparta continued until the Spartan commander, Lysander, was able to destroy the Athenian fleet in 405. The breaking of Athens made Philip II of Macedon's conquest of Greece possible during the fourth century BCE.

THE SELEUCID EMPIRE 312–64 BCE

THE LEGACY OF ALEXANDER

AFTER THE DEATH OF ALEXANDER THE GREAT IN 333 BCE, A POWER STRUGGLE AROSE BETWEEN HIS GENERALS ABOUT WHO WOULD TAKE CONTROL OF THE VAST EMPIRE THE YOUNG LEADER HAD CONQUERED. SELEUCUS, ONE OF ALEXANDER'S MAIN GENERALS, WOULD FILL THAT ROLE.

Kingdom of Pergamum
Seleucid Empire

MACEDONIA
THRACE
Pergamum
Mediterranean Sea
Alexandria
Memphis

ABOVE Bust of Seleucid king, Antiochus III, who led a brief revival.

LEFT The Seleucid Empire covered a vast area, but struggled to hold onto its territory. Pergamum declared its independence from the Seleucids in 263 BCE.

First becoming satrap of Babylonia in 321, Seleucus I Nicator would aggressively expand his dominion to control the eastern half of Alexander's empire. He fought tough wars in India, where he was defeated; however, he agreed peace with Chandragupta Maurya and received a herd of 500 war elephants, which he then used to establish greater dominance elsewhere. In 301, he won a major victory at the Battle of Ipsus, defeating Antigonus I Monophthalmus and taking control of territories all the way west through the Anatolian Peninsula.

Despite the size of the dominion, it still did not match the size of the empire under Alexander. Ptolemy's Egypt eluded him, as did Macedonia. After defeating Lysimachus at the Battle of Corupedium in 281 BCE, Seleucus planned to take control of Macedonia and Thrace, but was killed by Ptolemy's son. The empire was already beginning to decline when Antiochus I Soter succeeded his father to the throne of the empire.

PERGAMUM

Caught between the territories of the former Diadochi (generals) of Alexander were a few small city-states, such as Pergamum. Under King Eumenes I, Pergamum declared independence from Antiochus I in 263 BCE. Pergamum became an important Hellenistic kingdom in Anatolia and the home of the Attalid Dynasty (named after Eumenes's son, Attalus I). Pergamum had one of the greatest libraries of the ancient world. With the larger portions of what had been Alexander's empire contending against one another, Pergamum eventually submitted to the power of Rome in 133.

SELEUCID LEGACY

The Seleucid Empire fell into decline during the third century BCE. In 250 BCE, Diodotus I seceded from the Seleucid Empire, forming the Greco-Bactrian Kingdom. While the Seleucid Empire enjoyed a brief revival under the reign of Antiochus III the Great, it would eventually disintegrate under the pressure of a number of foreign powers. Nonetheless, the legacy of the empire would live on in the Hellenistic art, architecture, language and practices throughout the region of what is now known as the Middle East.

ABOVE Bust of King Attalus I of Pergamum.

TOP Ruins standing at Pergamum reflect the kingdom's earlier greatness.

EXPANSION OF THE CELTS 600–1 BCE

NAKED, SCREAMING BARBARIANS

THE CELTS SPREAD ACROSS EUROPE IN THE CENTURIES BEFORE THE COMMON ERA, COVERING HUGE TERRITORIES. THEIR LACK OF WRITTEN RECORDS, HOWEVER, FORCES US TO RELY LARGELY ON SOURCES FROM THE ROMANS, WHO VIEWED THE CELTS AS NAKED, SCREAMING BARBARIANS.

ABOVE An archaic exaggeration of the expansion of the Celts.

The obvious Roman bias contrasts with the exquisite artworks found in Celtic settlements. Nonetheless, we know very little about the early days of the Celts and must rely heavily on Roman and other contemporary writings, as well as archaeological and linguistic evidence. From the writings of the Celts' enemies, we know they were fierce warriors. The later legends of the Celts themselves, who adopted writing along with Christianity, bespeak a strong warrior tradition, but one that would falter against the force of Roman and Germanic threats.

COVERING EUROPE

Today, most people associate the word 'Celtic' with parts of Great Britain and Ireland (as well as Brittany) because these are the areas where Celtic languages and traditions have long endured. By the twelfth century BCE, however, the Celts occupied territories across Central and Western Europe. Over the coming centuries, they would expand throughout Europe, extending into the British Isles probably around the sixth century BCE. At the height of their expansion, the Celts settled areas as distant as Iberia in the west and Anatolia in the east. The Galatians, to whom Paul writes in the New Testament, were Celts who settled and ruled in Anatolia from the third century BCE, shortly after their sack of Rome in 390 BCE. Their expansion into Anatolia was stopped by Attalus I of Pergamum.

ABOVE Celtic king, Vercingetorix, surrenders to Julius Caesar.

ABOVE RIGHT Queen Boudicca led the Celts in revolt against the Romans in Britain.

Despite culturally and linguistically covering a vast territory at the height of their expansion, the Celts did not have any form of unified government to unite them. Politically, they organized into smaller kingdoms that could ally and unite in times of war. Within Celtic society, the warriors maintained an elite status. The lack of political unity, however, crippled the Celts' ability to withstand the organized and centralized power of Rome, or pressure from the Germanic tribes pushing in from the east and north.

ON THE BATTLEFIELD

Early Celts used chariots, a practice maintained in the British Isles up to Caesar's invasion in 55 BCE. Described as running naked into battle, the Celts had bronze and, later, iron weaponry consisting of spears, swords and ornate shields. Among the most famous Celtic warriors was Queen Boudicca of the Iceni tribe, who united forces in Britain to defend the land against the invading Romans around 60 CE. Boudicca led a successful campaign, even burning the fledgling city of London to the ground, but was eventually beaten by the Roman governor, Suetonius.

JULIUS CAESAR 100–44 BCE

RISE OF THE ROMAN EMPIRE

THE ROMAN REPUBLIC HAD EXISTED SINCE AROUND 509 BCE, BUT THE WORK OF ROMAN GENERAL JULIUS CAESAR WOULD HELP TRANSFORM THE REPUBLIC INTO ONE OF THE GREATEST EMPIRES IN HISTORY. THE ROMAN EMPIRE WOULD LAST FROM 27 BCE TO 476 CE.

ABOVE Julius Caesar was instrumental in the transformation of the Roman Republic into the Roman Empire.

OPPOSITE TOP The Roman Empire was born out of the Roman Republic and would continue to expand the territories of its domain and influence for more than a century to come.

OPPOSITE BOTTOM Caesar leads Cleopatra to the throne of Egypt after helping her in an Egyptian civil war.

In 60 BCE, Julius Caesar, Pompey and Marcus Licinius Crassus formed an alliance known as the First Triumvirate. This was the first major step towards the creation of the Roman Empire. As these three great military leaders rubbed elbows, each contending for greater power, the frictions between them escalated. Caesar would ultimately be betrayed, but not until he had become dictator of Rome.

GALLIC WARS

In 60 BCE, Caesar took control of Cisalpine Gaul and Illyricum. Deeply in debt, Caesar began waging wars throughout Gaul (mostly modern-day France) in an attempt to expand the dominion under his control. Politically, this was justified by attacks of Germanic and Celtic tribes, which seemed to pose a threat to the southern territories under Roman control. From 58–50 BCE, Caesar battled against the Celts and Germanic tribes, invading Britain in 55 BCE. Celtic ruler Vercingetorix managed to unite several Gallic tribes to put forward a staunch resistance to the Romans, defeating Caesar at the Siege of Gergovia. Caesar finally managed to subdue Gaul in 52 BCE at the Battle of Alesia, where he defeated Vercingetorix. For the next two years, Caesar put down rebellions and solidified control of Gaul.

In the same year as Caesar concluded his expeditions in Gaul, Pompey called the general back to Rome. Caesar's term as governor was over, yet he continued to wield power and to control several legions of trained and experienced warriors. In 49 BCE, Caesar crossed into Italy over the River Rubicon. Pompey and his men retreated south as civil war broke out in Rome.

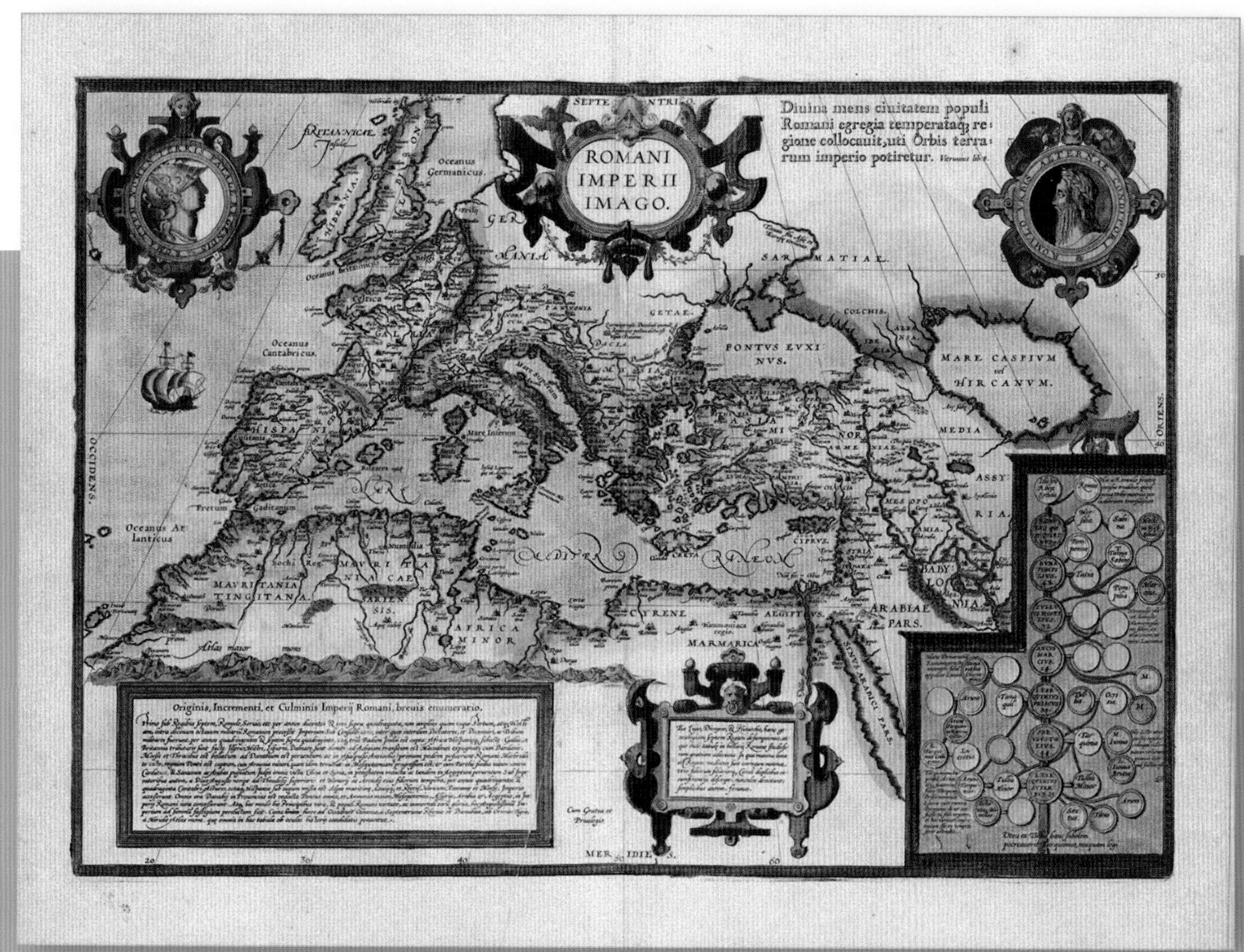

RISE OF CAESAR

Caesar and Pompey contended over the coming months and years. Caesar took control of Italy, then attacked Pompey's men in Spain, double-backed and engaged his enemy in Greece. He defeated Pompey at the Battle of Pharsalus in 48 BCE, despite being outnumbered more than two to one. Soon after, Pompey was assassinated in Egypt. Caesar became dictator of Rome and continued to wage wars to expand its dominion. He became the lover of Egyptian queen, Cleopatra, in 47 BCE, supporting her in an Egyptian civil war. Caesar defeated the Egyptian Pharaoh at the Battle of the Nile.

Caesar was eventually betrayed and murdered by a group of conspirators, among whom were Marcus Junius Brutus and Gaius Cassius Longinus. Caesar's second in command, Mark Antony, supported Caesar's adopted son and heir, Octavian, in a series of civil wars. Octavian became Augustus Caesar, first Emperor of Rome in 27 BCE.

EMPEROR TRAJAN 98–117

GREATEST EXTENT OF ROME

THE ROMAN EMPIRE IS KNOWN FOR ITS TREMENDOUS POWER THAT LASTED OVER THE COURSE OF SEVERAL CENTURIES; BUT THE EMPIRE REACHED THE HEIGHT OF ITS EXPANSION UNDER EMPEROR TRAJAN. DURING HIS REIGN, THE EMPIRE INCLUDED MUCH OF EUROPE, NORTH AFRICA AND THE MIDDLE EAST.

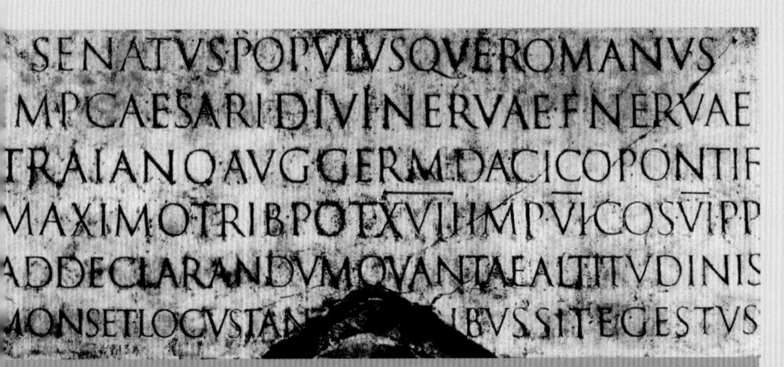

Trajan became emperor after the death of Nerva in 98 CE. By that point, Trajan had worked his way up through a number of positions, and distinguished himself as a political and military leader. As emperor, he was known for his benevolence and sound governance, building a reputation that would endure for centuries as one of the greatest Roman emperors. Before his death from a stroke in 117, Trajan had conquered Dacia in the northern Balkans, and all of Mesopotamia. Trajan was succeeded by his adopted son, Hadrian. Hadrian's Wall, built to defend Roman Britain from the Scots and Picts, still stretches across northern England today.

CONQUEST OF DACIA

Trajan launched an invasion of Dacia in 101, bringing an army roughly 100,000 strong. In a series of hard-fought campaigns, Trajan's Romans fought the Dacian army of Decebalus. Decebalus managed to prevent the Romans from encamping in the mountains before the onset of winter. However, as soon as spring brought warmer weather, Trajan continued his invasion, defeating Decebalus at the Second Battle of Tapae in 102. Trajan granted Decebalus the right to continue governing the region as a tributary, but Decebalus revolted in 105, and Trajan invaded again, swiftly destroying the revolt. Dacia occupied a strategically important area between the Germanic tribes around the Danube and the Sarmatians in the east. It was also a land rich in gold mines.

TOP An inscription from the base of Trajan's Column in Rome with the dedication to Trajan.

LEFT A bronze bust of Emperor Trajan.

MESOPOTAMIA

After defeating Dacia, Trajan turned his attention east, annexing Nabataea in the north of the Arabian Peninsula in 106 and engaging the Parthian Empire. In 113, Trajan waged a war against Parthia, eventually besieging and conquering the Parthian capital of Ctesiphon. With the conquest of Parthia, the Roman Empire now extended from Britain in the north, to Iberia in the west, to the Persian Gulf in the east, stretching across North Africa in the south.

ABOVE Emperor Trajan on horseback, fighting against the Dacians.

BELOW The Roman Empire reached its greatest extent under Trajan.

THE ROMAN LEGION

REFINING MILITARY ORGANIZATION

The Romans were able to build a large empire because of the strength of their military. Their military, in turn, derived strength from its precise organization and discipline. The military technology of the Romans did not differ tremendously from that of many of Rome's enemies. The Romans differentiated themselves from their opponents through the many levels of organization within their armed forces. The primary force in the Roman army was the legion.

RIGHT The standardization of equipment gave the Roman legions an impressively uniform look to match the uniformity of their movements on the battlefield.

ALL TOLD, THE LEGIONARIES LITERALLY CARRIED A HEAVY BURDEN OF ARMS, ARMOUR AND EQUIPMENT. FIGURATIVELY, THEY CARRIED THE BURDEN OF BUILDING AND PROTECTING AN EMPIRE.

LEGION BREAKDOWN

The organization of the legion differed slightly over time, and was greatly reformed and standardized by Gaius Marius at the beginning of the second century CE. An example of a legion might have consisted of 5,000 men each. The legion itself was broken down into ten cohorts of 480 men each. The first cohort contained an additional 200 soldiers and was the elite corps of the legion. Each cohort was in turn comprised of six centuries. The century was comprised of 80 men led by a centurion. In addition, a cavalry of elite Roman soldiers might have supported the legionary foot soldiers.

Each legionary soldier had a significant amount of equipment. A sturdy iron helmet covered his head, complete with neck and cheek guards. Over his tunic, the legionaries wore a *lorica* – body armour consisting of overlapping strips of metal attached to leather straps. The lorica consisted of panels that were lashed together to cover the body and shoulders of the soldier. The legionary also carried a rectangular shield, or *scutum*, made of wood and leather. The shield was curved to wrap around the soldier's body, and was carried

ABOVE The Column of Marcus Aurelius in Rome was built in honour of the emperor's conquests and was completed in 193 CE – 13 years after his death. The spiral relief depicts the Danubian Wars that were waged from 166–180 CE.

using a central boss. The legionary carried javelins, which were used at the outset of engagements, and a short sword known as the *gladius*. The gladius was the primary weapon of the legionary soldier, and was used to stab at the enemy from behind cover of the shield.

Roman soldiers also carried their food and supplies, as well as tools for digging ditches and building fortifications.

NOT QUITE INFALLIBLE

The Roman legions succeeded because of the level of training and skill of the legionaries. As professional soldiers enlisted for 25 years of service, legionaries learned to perform tactical manoeuvres with shocking efficiency, the battle formations moving seamlessly into place. However, they were not always successful. Boudicca defeated the Roman legion, IX Hispana, around 60 CE. The Romans also lost embarrassing battles at Carrhae in 55 BCE, and the Battle of the Teutoburg Forest in 9 CE. Germanic armies under the leadership of Arminius ambushed and destroyed three Roman legions in the Teutoburg Forest east of the River Rhine. This halted Roman advancement into the territory of what is now Germany, inhabited at the time by Germanic tribes.

RIGHT The victory of the Germanic tribes at the Battle of the Teutoburg Forest in 9 CE was a crushing blow to the Roman legions.

DECLINE AND FALL OF ROME C. 300–476

BARBARIAN INVASIONS

WHILE THE FALL OF ROME IS TRADITIONALLY DATED TO 476, WHEN GERMANIC KING ODOACER DEPOSED THE LAST ROMAN EMPEROR, ROMULUS AUGUSTUS, THE PROCESS WAS ACTUALLY MUCH MORE GRADUAL. BY THE END OF THE FIFTH CENTURY, ROME HAD WEAKENED CONSIDERABLY.

The Roman Empire reached its height around the first century CE, during the reign of Trajan. After Trajan, the empire remained prosperous for some time, but gradually began to lose strength and fragment. During the fourth century, the empire split into two halves: east and west. The eastern half of the empire came to be known as the Byzantine Empire, which lasted until the Sack of Constantinople by the Ottoman Turks under Mehmed II in 1453. The western half retained the name of Rome, so while the fall of 'Rome' is dated to 476, this really only refers to the western half.

'BARBARIANS' WITHOUT AND WITHIN

While many attribute the fall of Rome to the incursions of various Germanic tribes, this view is too simplistic. It does not account for the critical changes within the Roman military organization that gradually weakened the empire. Over time, the Romans employed an increasing number of foreign mercenaries to do the work of protecting their borders. Many Germanic leaders served in the Roman army and returned to their own people with significant military experience and knowledge of Roman battle tactics. Alaric, who sacked Rome in 410, had served as commander of Gothic troops in the Roman army before becoming leader of the Visigoths. Alaric's Roman rival, Flavius Stilicho, had Vandal ancestry. By the fifth century, a significant portion of the Roman army was comprised of Germanic warriors.

LEFT Gallic chieftain, Brennus, looks on the women he has taken captive following trhe Battle of the Allia, when Rome was first sacked, in 387 BCE.

During the fourth century, the Germanic peoples began migrating south, pressing upon the Roman Empire from the north. In 378, the Visigoths defeated the Romans at the Battle of Adrianople. After sacking Rome in 410, the Visigoths withdrew and settled in Spain. Rome, however, failed to recover. Attila the Hun stormed into Europe from Asia, threatening Rome. Vandal King, Gaiseric, sacked Rome in 455. In 476, Odoacer took over control of Italy. Odoacer was from an East Germanic tribe called the Sciri, but had been an officer in the Roman army. While the kingship of Odoacer is typically viewed as the end of the Roman Empire, the institutions of Rome continued to function for many years. Rome was sacked once more by Ostrogoths in 546.

There is a saying that 'Rome was not built in a day'. Equally true is that Rome did not fall in a day. The complex organizations and systems of the western Roman Empire gradually disintegrated until Rome itself had fragmented into something new and different.

ABOVE Attila meets Pope Leo the Great in 452.

TOP Oil painting by Johann Peter Theodor Janssen showing Germanic warriors attacking Roman troops.

BATTLE OF POITIERS 732

THE FIGHT FOR EUROPE

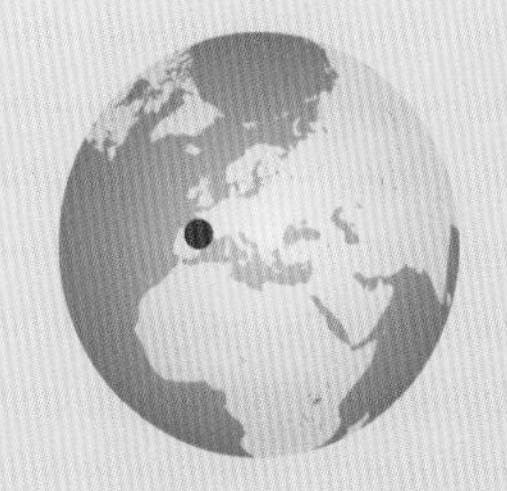

IN THE BEGINNING OF THE EIGHTH CENTURY, THE UMAYYAD EMPIRE EXPANDED WITH ASTONISHING FORCE AND SPEED. IN 711, TARIQ IBN ZIYAD CROSSED THE STRAIT OF GIBRALTAR AND CONQUERED VISIGOTHIC SPAIN. WHO COULD STOP THEIR ADVANCE?

ABOVE Tarik ibn Ziyad led the Umayyad conquest of Spain in 711.

A legend exists that Tariq ibn Ziyad burned all the Umayyad boats after crossing to the Iberian Peninsula from North Africa. There was no turning back: they would achieve either death or victory. Such a strong mentality allowed the Umayyads to conquer territory after territory. By 718, Tariq had conquered most of the Iberian Peninsula and established the Moorish kingdom of Al-Andalus – but the Umayyads did not want to stop there.

A PIVOTAL BATTLE

The Battle of Poitiers – also known as the Battle of Tours – is widely regarded as a pivotal battle in European history. By defeating the Umayyads at Poitiers, the Franks put an end to Umayyad expansion in Europe. Without the victory at Poitiers, the European Middle Ages may very well have looked drastically different. Instead of the Christian kingdoms that developed in France, Germany and England, Western Europe might have become Muslim and fallen under the power of the Umayyad Caliphate. While the halting of Umayyad expansion in Europe cannot be attributed to this battle alone, Poitiers retains an important position in the history of Western Europe.

The battle took place in October 732 somewhere between Poitiers and Tours in modern-day France. The Umayyad forces under Abd al-Rahman advanced towards Poitiers after defeating Odo the Great of Aquitaine. Although Odo had defeated Abd al-Rahman before, the Umayyad forces routed the armies of the King of Aquitaine, and Odo was forced to appeal to an old rival, Charles Martel, for aid. Charles, known as the 'Hammer', was the king of the Franks.

ABOVE The Córdoba Caliphate in Spain was founded by Abd al-Rahman in 755 after the Umayyad expansion was stopped at the Battle of Poitiers.

TOP RIGHT A 19th-century depiction of Charles Martel (Charles the Hammer) at the Battle of Poitiers.

RIGHT This map shows the Battle of Poitiers (Tours) and the Umayyad expansion into what is now France.

Charles the Hammer, recognizing the Umayyad threat, rose up immediately, summoning his Frankish warriors to arms. They marched out to meet the 20,000–30,000 Umayyad soldiers, choosing for themselves a suitable battlefield on which to use Frankish shield-wall tactics to engage their enemy. Abd al-Rahman and his cavalry were defeated soundly by Charles and his forces. Abd al-Rahman himself was killed in the battle, and his men retreated back to Al-Andalus.

CARL THE GREAT 768–814

LEADER OF THE FRANKS

ONE OF THE GREATEST KINGS OF THE MIDDLE AGES IN EUROPE, CARL THE GREAT – MORE COMMONLY KNOWN AS CHARLEMAGNE – ESTABLISHED THE CAROLINGIAN EMPIRE. THROUGH A NUMBER OF CONQUESTS, CHARLEMAGNE EXPANDED THE FRANKISH KINGDOM TO A NEW HEIGHT.

ABOVE Map of Europe showing the extent of Charlemagne's empire.

OPPOSITE LEFT A 16th-century painting of Charlemagne.

OPPOSITE RIGHT Saxon leader, Wittekind, submits to Charlemagne in 785.

Though known for helping lay the foundation of France, and therefore referred to by his French name, Charlemagne, the King of the Franks was a Germanic king and spoke a variant of Old High German. Charlemagne was particularly fond of traditional Germanic poetry, and commissioned collections of these poems to be assembled into books. Though these collections have been lost, we know from other sources that they would have contained a number of heroic and legendary tales. Drawing on the legends of his ancestors for inspiration, Charlemagne himself would attain legendary status and figure as a character in the fictional romances of the later Middle Ages.

SUBDUING THE SAXONS

Charlemagne and his court were devoutly Christian, and waged a heavy and expensive campaign against the peoples of neighbouring Saxony, in modern-day northern Germany. For decades, Charlemagne waged constant war

against the Saxons. The cost and casualties on both sides were high, but the Frankish king refused to concede. In 782, Charlemagne reportedly massacred 4,500 Saxon prisoners in retaliation for a Saxon revolt. This event, known as the Massacre of Verden, only brought on more bloodshed with the Saxons. The wars are often presented in religious terms, and it is likely that Charlemagne himself felt a strong duty to convert the pagan Saxons to Christianity. At length, he succeeded in his ambition, and by 805 Saxony had become Christian and was under Carolingian rule.

THE HOLY ROMAN EMPIRE

Charlemagne expanded the Frankish kingdom east into Lombardy and Bavaria, and west and south into the Iberian Peninsula. Charlemagne's campaigns in the Iberian Peninsula and what is now Spain are perhaps best known from the old French poem, *La Chanson de Roland* (*The Song of Roland*), in which Charlemagne's nephew, Roland, leads a brave and defiant last stand against a Basque army. The poem is based on the Battle of Roncesvalles in 778. Roland refuses to sound his horn and call for aid until it is too late to save his life or the lives of his companions, but he sounds the alarm in time for Charlemagne to arrive and avenge the death of his kinsman.

The territories under his dominion encompassed much of Western Europe, and in 800 Pope Leo III crowned Charlemagne Emperor of the Romans in St Peter's Basilica in Rome. Charlemagne thus became the first Emperor in Western Europe since Romulus Augustus in 476. This was the foundation of the Holy Roman Empire, which would become increasingly significant throughout the Middle Ages.

THE VIKING AGE C.793–1100

FURY OF THE NORTHMEN

BEGINNING WITH THE SACK OF LINDISFARNE IN 793, THE VIKING AGE SAW THE INHABITANTS OF SCANDINAVIA SWEEP ACROSS THE GLOBE IN THEIR AMAZING LONGBOATS IN A DAZZLING TALE OF CONQUEST, EXPLORATION AND DESTRUCTION.

The term *Viking* comes from the Old Norse *vik*, meaning 'creek' or 'inlet'. The Vikings were those who inhabited the creeks and inlets along the sea. Indeed, what made their astonishing expeditions possible was the craftsmanship of their longboats. Capable of holding dozens of men, these longboats had shallow drafts, allowing them to sail up the shallow rivers of Europe, attack, and disappear before anyone could give chase. At the same time – despite not having a keel – these boats could traverse ocean waters. While the Vikings normally navigated along coastal waters, they were able to hit the open seas, striking North Africa, Sicily and even reaching North America around 1000.

HIGHLY TRAINED PIRATES

The Vikings were essentially highly skilled and trained pirates from Scandinavia. Beginning by raiding monasteries and other wealthy, but poorly defended establishments, the Vikings quickly earned the hatred of the rest of Europe through their hit-and-run tactics. Motivated by wealth and fame, the Vikings struck easy targets, but were never ones to back down from a fight. The Vikings conquered huge portions of England, establishing the Danelaw in the east, as well as the great Viking town, Jorvik (now York), in the north. They sailed up the Seine and attacked Paris in the ninth century. Striking throughout Europe, they could scarcely be defeated in battle, and only withdrew when they received the price they demanded.

TOP LEFT The Norse practised ship burials, as seen here in this representation of an early Russian noble funeral.

LEFT A boar, a traditional beast of battle, adorns the sail of this Viking longboat.

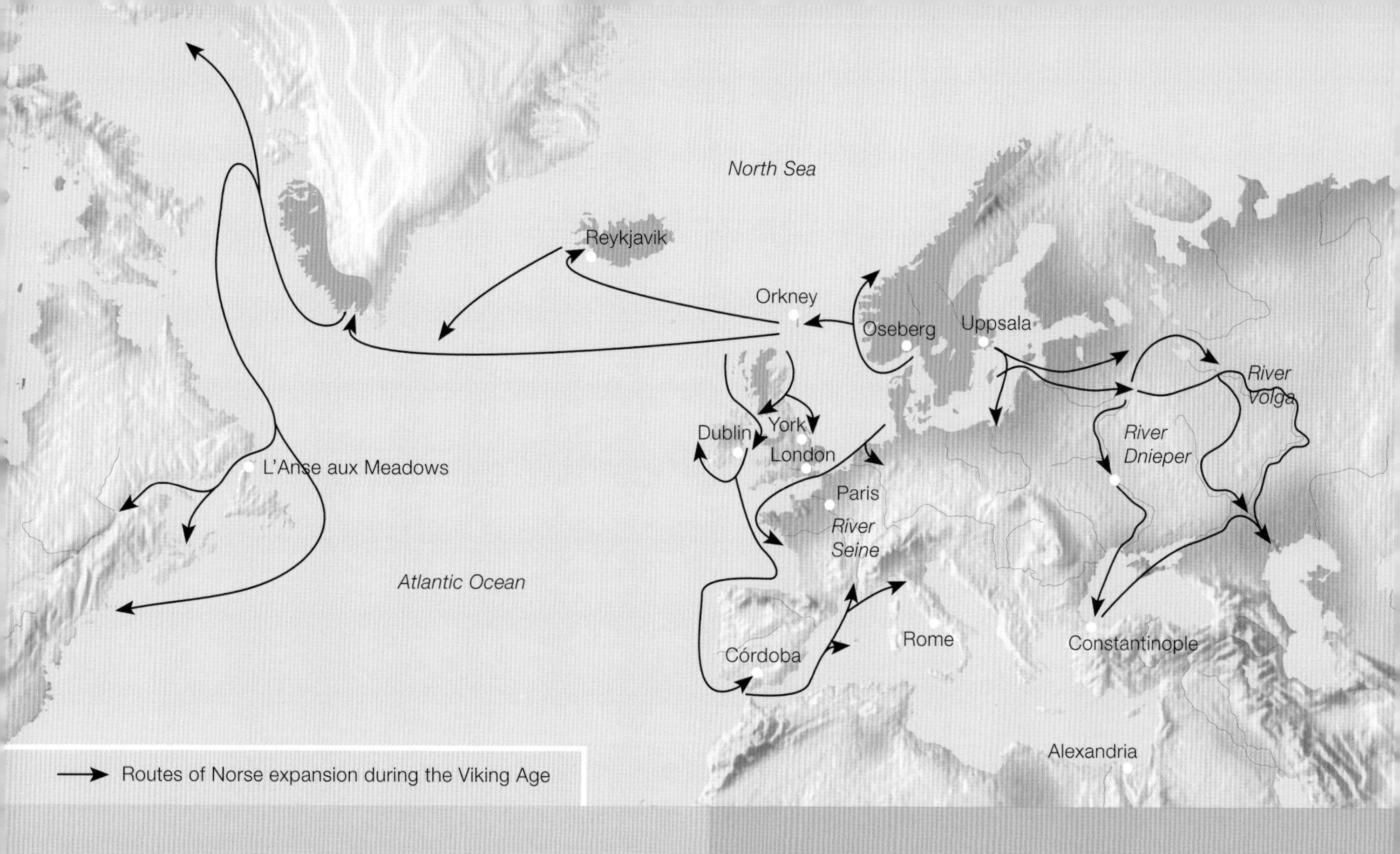

CITY BUILDERS

Despite the amount of destruction the Vikings caused throughout Europe, they also built a great number of settlements we know well today. Dublin in Ireland was originally a Viking settlement. Scandinavians fleeing the wrath of Harold Fairhair in Norway began settling Iceland during the Viking Age, and Eric the Red would later settle Greenland. A tribe of Swedes, known as the Rus, would settle along the River Volga and come to develop a kingdom there, eventually abandoning their Norse language for the local Slavic language. This kingdom would, of course, become Russia. Rollo, a Danish Viking, settled in Northern France after assisting in a siege of Paris. He agreed to protect the land from other Vikings. His dominion became known as Normandy (after the Northmen), and his descendent, William, would conquer England in 1066.

ABOVE Lindisfarne Castle, shown here, was not there in 793 when Vikings sacked the wealthy monastery on the island.

TOP This map shows the routes of the Vikings during the Viking Age. The Norsemen typically adopted the local language and customs of the regions they conquered.

AN ELITE GUARD

Many Vikings, seeking fame and fortune, became mercenaries. The best place for them to hire themselves out as mercenaries was *Miklagarðr*, the Great City – Constantinople. Thousands of Scandinavians travelled to Constantinople to serve in the Byzantine army, so many, in fact, that they formed their own elite guard, known as the Varangian Guard. Armed to the teeth with spears, swords, daggers and axes, they advanced in tight formations with shields interlocked. This shield wall was very hard to break. The Varangians became the bodyguard of the Byzantine emperor, and were known particularly for their use of axes. Deployed throughout the empire, Varangians returned to Scandinavia with a number of treasures.

THE BATTLE OF HASTINGS 1066

CONQUEST OF ENGLAND

THE BATTLE OF HASTINGS IN 1066 WAS A RELATIVELY SMALL MILITARY ENGAGEMENT BETWEEN WILLIAM, THE DUKE OF NORMANDY, AND HAROLD GODWINSON, THE KING OF ENGLAND. YET THIS SMALL BATTLE WOULD DECIDE THE FATE OF NOT ONLY A NATION, BUT ALSO A LANGUAGE.

ABOVE King Harold had to face foes both in the north at Stamford Bridge and in the south at Hastings.

INSET RIGHT The Battle of Stamford Bridge was a decisive English victory.

Upon the death of Edward the Confessor in 1066, a power struggle arose over succession to the throne of England. Edward died childless, yet on his deathbed he named Harold, Earl of Wessex, the next king. Harold was crowned king the next day, but his coronation was not without some controversy. Two other nobles lay claim to the throne: Harald Sigurdsson of Norway and William of Normandy.

TWO BATTLES

Harald Sigurdsson – also known as Harald Hardrada – laid his claim to the throne of England through Harold II's brother, Tostig Godwinson, who invited the Norwegian king to come and challenge Harold's rule. Harold marched north to meet the Norwegian invasion in Yorkshire, where he engaged Harald and Tostig in battle at Stamford Bridge. The Battle of Stamford Bridge on 25 September 1066, was a decisive victory for Harold II of England. Both Harald and Tostig were slain, along with many of the invading army. Despite his victory, Harold had little time to relish it, for he faced a second invasion from the south, and so he turned and marched, with his army, back to the south of England.

ABOVE The famous Bayeux Tapestry tells the story of the Battle of Hastings and the conquest of England by William the Conqueror.

LEFT A stark portrait of William the Conqueror.

William, Duke of Normandy, was a cousin of Edward the Confessor, and staked a legitimate claim to the throne of England. Crossing the English Channel from Normandy, William landed at Pevensey and marched from there with his army of nobles and mercenaries to Hastings. There he met Harold, and they battled it out for the throne of England.

THE BATTLE

Harold arrayed his men in the tight shield-wall formation typical of Anglo-Saxon tactics. Harold and the English forces were on top of the hill at Hastings, while William and his army approached from below. William engaged Harold's forces first with archers, and then with cavalry charges. The tight shield wall of the English soldiers, however, prevented the cavalry charges from being effective, and the English dealt heavy casualties with their spears. William began to retreat. On seeing the Normans quitting the field, the English broke their formation in celebration, only to have William turn and double back on the English army. With their formation broken, the cavalry charges of the Normans destroyed the English defence. Harold was shot in the eye with an arrow during the battle, and the victory left William the sole king of England.

THE ENGLISH LANGUAGE

At this point in history, Harold and the English forces spoke a Germanic language known as Old English. William, though of Norse descent, spoke Old French. After his conquest, the language of government in England became French. Over time, Old English and Old French merged together as languages, creating the language we know today as English.

THE MEDIEVAL CASTLE

THE ICONIC FORTRESS

Few images encapsulate the romantic ideal of medieval knighthood better than a large, stone castle. The castles that we know and love from the medieval period were actually developed and used over a relatively short period of time. Most of the fortifications during the early Middle Ages were made of earth and timber, or were of a small-scale in stone. A number of developments, however, inspired rulers to begin constructing larger, more intricate castles in the eleventh century.

STONE WALLS RISING

Castles first started to be constructed in Europe mostly as the Carolingian Empire collapsed and was replaced by smaller fiefdoms, each with its own feudal lord. Each lord required a fortified residency to protect and govern his territory. Castles therefore started springing up everywhere in Europe. In addition to the practical necessities they addressed, castles quickly became symbols of status and means of displaying wealth and power.

SIEGE ENGINES, SUCH AS TREBUCHETS AND ONAGERS, WERE NECESSARY TO BREACH THE THICK, STONE WALLS OF MEDIEVAL CASTLES.

ABOVE Trebuchet siege machine.

TOP LEFT Dover Castle in Kent, England, was built in the 12th century and is the largest castle in England.

These fortifications in turn created new possibilities for defence and attack, and siege warfare became increasingly important. Powerful trebuchets and onagers were designed to destroy the thick, stone walls of medieval castles. Mines were routinely dug beneath the walls to collapse them. Castle architecture likewise included means of defending against sieges. Narrow slits in castle walls provided an opening for archers to pick off attacking soldiers; 'murder holes' in the ceilings allowed defenders of a castle to pour hot water, wax, or oil on attackers. Moats or walls of up to 6 m (20 feet) thick were added around the perimeter of a castle. Over time, castle design became more intelligent, as did the means of attacking these fortresses.

Castles still dot the European landscape today, from the incredible Caernarfon in North Wales, to the enormous Malbork Castle in Poland. Some in pristine condition, others in ruins, these castles have continued to tantalize the imaginations of all who see them.

THE MOTTE AND BAILEY

Among the more famous castle designs is the motte-and-bailey castle, used widely by the Normans. The 'motte' was a large, steep mound, or hill, on top of which sat the keep. Around the hill was the 'bailey', a wall or enclosure. Sometimes, these motte-and-bailey castles were very simple and relatively small, but they could be built up to colossal proportions. Windsor Castle, in England, is a motte-and-bailey castle. The design allowed them to be defended by a small number of men.

OPPOSITE CENTRE Alcázar is a magnificent castle in Segovia, Spain.

OPPOSITE BELOW Harlech Castle in Wales was built by Edward I in the 13th century.

ABOVE LEFT Burg Eltz near Koblenz, Germany, capitalizes on the natural defensive features of the local topography.

ABOVE RIGHT Tall towers allowed defending knights to see the advance of their enemies from kilometres in the distance.

RECONQUISTA C. 718–1492

RETAKING SPAIN

AFTER THE BERBER LEADER, TARIQ IBN ZIYAD, CROSSED THE STRAIT OF GIBRALTAR IN 711 AND CONQUERED THE IBERIAN PENINSULA, SEVERAL ATTEMPTS FOLLOWED BY CHRISTIAN EUROPEANS TO OUST THE MUSLIM 'MOORS'. THE *RECONQUISTA*, OR RECONQUEST, WOULD TAKE CENTURIES TO COMPLETE.

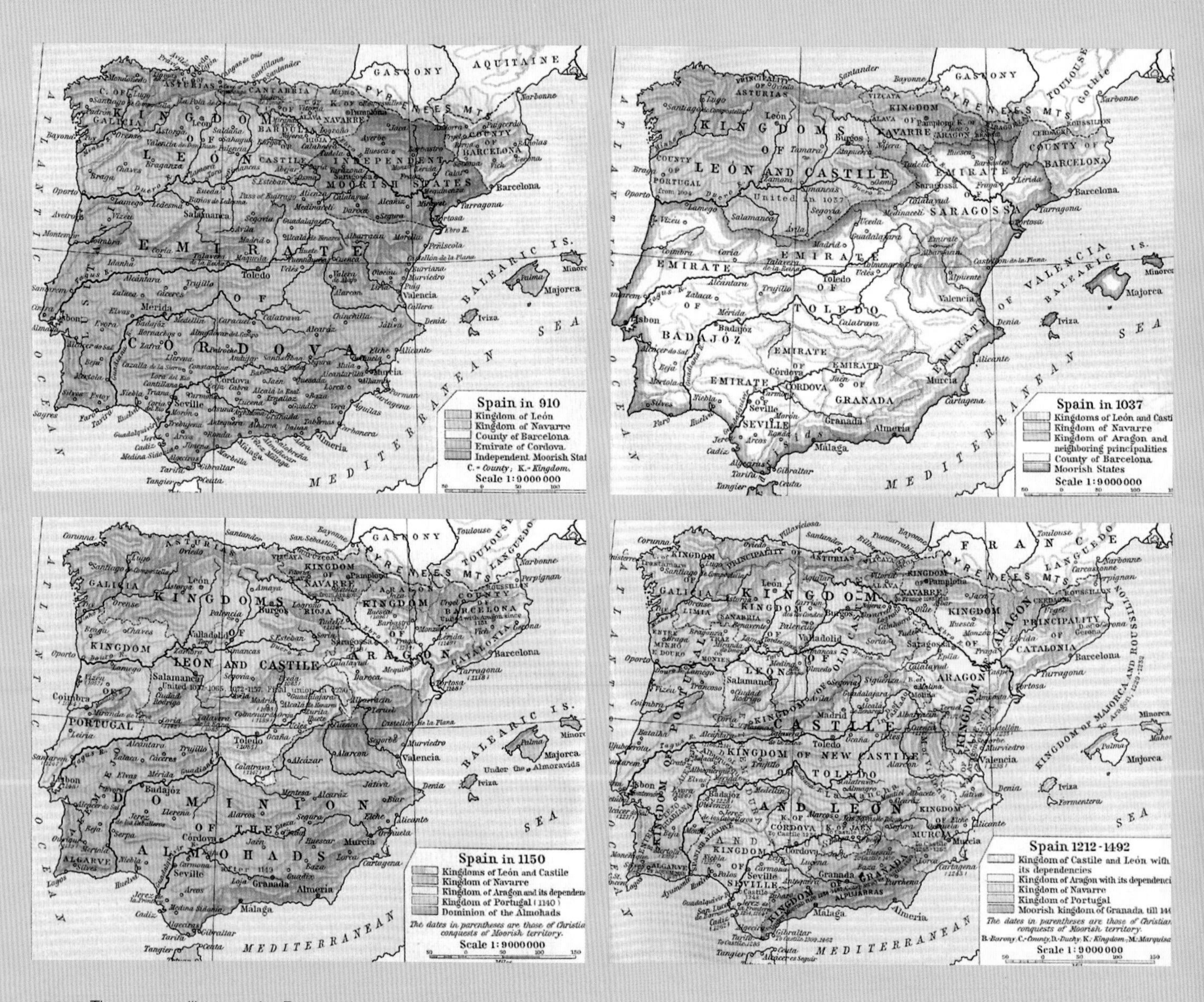

ABOVE These maps illustrate the Reconquista over time. Top left: 910. Top right: 1037. Bottom left: 1150. Bottom right: 1212–1492.

The kingdom of Al-Andalus flourished during the early Middle Ages, and its capital of Córdoba was one of the most prosperous cities in Europe in its day. Arabic learning and scholarship were in many ways superior to that of the Latin church, and many new disciplines and influential texts would enter Europe through the scholarly centres of Al-Andalus. Algebra and various forms of astronomy and science entered Latin Europe through translations of Arabic scholarship. Despite the wealth and prosperity of Al-Andalus – as well as the positive benefits it brought to the rest of Europe – the kingdom was Muslim, and was therefore seen as a threat to the rest of Christian Europe.

ABOVE John II of Castile defeated the forces of Muhammed IX at the Battle of La Higueruela, in 1431.

BELOW Granada finally gave up control to Ferdinand and Isabella in 1492, effectively concluding the Reconquista.

THE BIRTH OF SPAIN AND PORTUGAL

Some scholars date the beginning of the Reconquista to 718, immediately after the establishment of Al-Andalus. More realistically, however, the process began at the end of the eighth century with Charlemagne's battles against the Moors of Spain. Very little headway in the campaign to re-Christianize the Iberian Peninsula can be seen until the eleventh century. The Umayyad Caliphate collapsed in 750, but the kingdom of Al-Andalus continued to flourish, and eventually became the Córdoba Caliphate in 929 CE. The Córdoba Caliphate itself eventually collapsed, fragmenting into a number of smaller kingdoms in 1031. The lack of a centralized power in the Iberian kingdoms facilitated the Reconquista.

In the mid to late eleventh century, Alfonso VI, King of León, begin to attack the *taifa*, or independent principalities, of the former Córdoba Caliphate. After defeating his own brothers, to consolidate the power of León, Castille and Galicia, Alfonso attacked and conquered Toledo, in 1085. Despite the political rivalries, Alfonso had earlier taken refuge at Toledo, and was on good terms with Muslim Moors, despite them not being Christian.

The Almoravids of North Africa came to the aid of the Moors in Al-Andalus, and fought vigorously against Alfonso, defeating him at Zallaqah, in 1086. The Christian kings were not able to respond sufficiently to this new threat, and were temporarily beaten back. As infighting broke out among the Muslim leaders of the Iberian Peninsula, their political unity began to break down, along with their military might. By the beginning of the thirteenth century, the crusader spirit had swept across Europe and in the first half of the century, Alfonso VIII led a crusade against the Muslim kings of Spain. They defeated Córdoba in 1236, Jaén in 1246 and Seville in 1248. By the middle of the thirteenth century, most of the Iberian Peninsula had been 'reconquered' by Christian Europe. The process would be completed when Ferdinand II and Isabella I of Spain took the final Muslim tributary kingdom of Granada in 1492.

EDWARD I (R.1272–1307)

RULING WITH AN IRON FIST

EDWARD I REIGNED OVER ENGLAND DURING THE LAST QUARTER OF THE THIRTEENTH AND INTO THE BEGINNING OF THE FOURTEENTH CENTURIES. A STRONG AND SUCCESSFUL RULER, EDWARD NONETHELESS EARNED HIMSELF MANY ENEMIES THROUGH HIS DOMESTIC POLICIES AND HIS EXPLOITS IN WALES AND SCOTLAND.

ABOVE An early 14th-century manuscript image of Edward I and Eleanor of Castille.

By the end of the thirteenth century, tensions between the Welsh kings of Wales and the Anglo-Saxon kings of England had existed for centuries. In the wars between the two, England had the definitive upper hand, but the Welsh continued to put up staunch resistance. The Treaty of Montgomery, in 1267, recognized the Welsh lord Llywelyn as the Prince of Wales. However, this treaty did not engender lasting peace. When Edward I ascended the throne in 1272, relations between England and Wales were deteriorating. Llywelyn refused to journey to England to swear fealty to Edward. Armed conflict became unavoidable.

WAR IN WALES

Edward I declared war on 12 November 1276. He led a troop of some 15,000 infantry, and nearly 1,000 cavalry into Wales, quickly defeating most of the Welsh lords. Very few of them offered any real resistance, since many suspected Edward I would be victorious, and that it was therefore in their best interests not to oppose him. Llywelyn was pushed back into the mountains of Snowdonia in north Wales, and he was forced to capitulate in 1277, when the Treaty of Aberconwy was signed. This was not, however, the end of armed rebellion in Wales. In 1282, revolts erupted again, and this time the Welsh enjoyed more initial successes, quickly taking control of several English strongholds. Welsh lords, who had formerly allied with England, were dissatisfied with the exactions of the English king, and rose up against him. Edward responded quickly, and by 1283 had quelled the rebellion. These events led to the construction or refortification of the so-called 'Iron Ring' castles in Wales.

ABOVE Caernarfon Castle in Wales is one of the impressive 'Iron Ring' castles built to maintain control over the Welsh.

RIGHT Robert the Bruce of Scotland defeated Edward's son and successor at the Battle of Bannockburn, in 1314.

LEFT Late 13th- or early 14th-century manuscript showing King Edward I with the royal coat of arms on his chest.

The Iron Ring castles are enormous stone fortresses built around Wales for the purpose of subjugating the Welsh.

CAMPAIGNS IN SCOTLAND

In 1292, John Balliol ascended the throne of Scotland. His appointment as king was greatly assisted by the arbitration of Edward I, who proceeded to treat Scotland as a vassal state. Eventually, the nobles of Scotland allied with France in 1295, and Edward invaded in 1296. Edward was a strong military commander, and quickly defeated the Scottish rebels. However, in the following year, 1297, rebellion broke out again led by two of the most famous people in Scottish history: Robert the Bruce and William Wallace. The next several years were filled with fighting, but in 1305 William Wallace was caught and executed. Rising up again in 1306, Robert the Bruce would eventually defeat Edward's successor at the Battle of Bannockburn in 1314. Edward himself died in 1307. Edward is nicknamed 'Longshanks', as well as 'Hammer of the Scots'.

THE HUNDRED YEARS' WAR 1337–1453

BATTLE FOR FRANCE

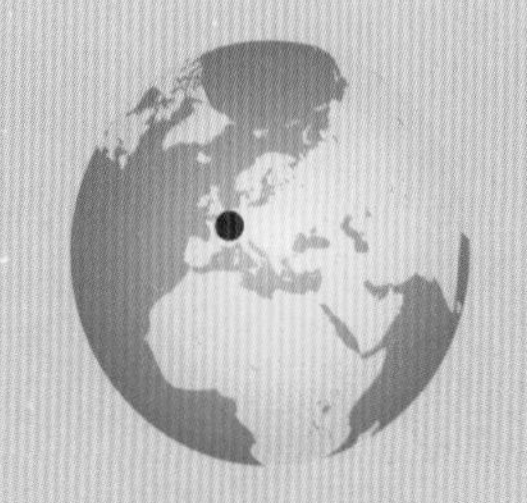

THE HUNDRED YEARS' WAR THAT SPANNED FROM THE FOURTEENTH INTO THE FIFTEENTH CENTURIES INVOLVED CONFLICT LARGELY BETWEEN ENGLAND AND FRANCE OVER SUCCESSION TO THE CROWN OF FRANCE ITSELF. THE FIGHTING WOULD, IN FACT, LAST MORE THAN A CENTURY.

ABOVE The Hundred Years' War was fought over English and French claims to territories in France and to the kingdom of France itself.

After William, Duke of Normandy, conquered England in 1066, the kings of England had various claims to territories in France. While some fighting had existed between English and French before the traditional start of The Hundred Years' War in 1337, the conflict truly began over a dispute about the succession to the throne of France after the death of Charles IV. There were two potential candidates for the next King of France: Philip, Count of Valois, and Edward III, King of England. In addition to being King of England, Edward III was Duke of Guyenne in Aquitaine and Count of Ponthieu. After an assembly of French nobles chose Philip VI as King of France, Philip began working to oust Edward from Guyenne in order to remove him as a future threat. Edward, who at first appeared content with the decision to appoint Philip as king, now began challenging the new monarch of France.

MEDIEVAL WARFARE

Warfare during this period consisted largely of laborious and expensive sieges on the heavily fortified castles of France. In contrast to a pitched battle in an open field, which could be decided within a few hours, medieval sieges dragged on for weeks or months, often resulting in stalemates with no clear victor. Despite several English victories during the early stages of the war, including at Crécy in 1346, Calais in 1347 and Poitiers in 1356, the English were unable to take the crown. Even after Edward's son, the Black Prince, captured King John II of France, son of Philip VI, at the Battle of Poitiers, England effectively only received a hefty ransom. After his third invasion of France, during which Edward III besieged Reims for more than a month, Edward was forced

ABOVE King Edward III of England (r. 1327–1377) began The Hundred Years' War in 1337, by laying claim to the throne of France.

BELOW This bronze relief from France shows the type of plate-mail armour that would have been worn during The Hundred Years' War.

ABOVE Heavily armoured knights storm forward at the Siege of Calais in 1346–1347.

LEFT This 14th-century manuscript illumination shows Edward III awarding Aquitaine to Edward, the Black Prince.

to turn away, and negotiated the Treaty of Brétigny with John II. Edward received a greater share of Aquitaine, but did not become King of France.

The peace did not last long, however, and Charles V of France fought vigorously during his reign (r. 1364 –1380), reconquering much of the territory lost to the English. He took Aquitaine back from the Black Prince, in 1369, and the forces of French military leader, Bertrand du Guesclin, seized most other English territories. The end of the fourteenth and beginning of the fifteenth centuries saw relative peace between England and France.

THE HUNDRED YEARS' WAR 1337–1453

ABOVE The Battle of Poitiers, 1356. Armoured knights joust in the background, while foot soldiers march on each other, and archers harry the enemy in the foreground.

ABOVE RIGHT Mounted knights were the most powerful force on the battlefield in medieval Europe.

BELOW English archers take on the French crossbowmen at the Battle of Crécy in 1346.

THE ENGLISH LONGBOW

One of the most important developments during The Hundred Years' War was the widespread use of the English longbow. At the Battle of Crécy, in 1346, the English archers lined up in a V formation. With a tremendous range, pinpoint accuracy and the ability to fire several arrows a minute, the archers proved incredibly effective against the heavily armoured French forces, especially when compared with the French use of crossbows. The English forces at Crécy numbered probably between 10,000 and 15,000, and were outnumbered roughly two to one. Combining the use of archers with flexible tactics, and forcing the French cavalry

OPPOSITE LEFT A stylized rendition of the Battle of Agincourt. The English archers would have been arranged in a sawtooth pattern.

OPPOSITE RIGHT Joan of Arc is a national hero of France and a canonized saint in the Roman Catholic Church.

to dismount and fight on foot, by digging trenches and placing caltrops on the field, the English won a resounding victory at Crécy.

AGINCOURT

By the beginning of the fifteenth century, use of the English longbow in battle tactics was more developed. At the Battle of Agincourt, in 1415, Henry V successfully used his archers to win a surprising victory over the heavily armoured French knights. Despite being vastly outnumbered, hungry and ill, Henry's men carried the day largely because of their use of the longbow. Arranged in a sawtooth pattern, the archers at Agincourt were able to send a constant stream of arrows down on the French as they approached. In addition to the sheer volume of arrows shot by the archers, the English longbowmen were incredibly accurate, and could target not only individual knights on the battlefield, but also aim to shoot them between the chinks in their armour. By the time they ran out of arrows, the French were in disarray, and the English, putting down their bows, engaged them in hand-to-hand combat.

Outnumbered as many as five to one, the English achieved victory at Agincourt while the French received an embarrassing defeat. As the character of Henry V says in Shakespeare's play bearing his name, 'The fewer men, the greater share of honour'. The use of bows and arrows had formerly been seen as dishonourable, because the combatants did not need to engage in direct contact. The success of the English longbowmen, however, would serve as a precursor to the use of more powerful distance weapons – the firearms that developed in the later Middle Ages.

JOAN OF ARC

One of the heroines at the end of The Hundred Years' War was Joan of Arc. Claiming to have received visions from God instructing her to throw off the oppression of English forces that controlled her homeland, she led French resistance in a number of important engagements, and was sent by King Charles VII as reinforcement to the besieged city of Orléans. Despite the criticism of her contemporaries, Joan was able to lift the siege from Orléans in only nine days. She was subsequently captured by Burgundians, handed over to the English, tried and executed for heresy in 1431. She was only 19 years old when she was burned at the stake. Joan of Arc was beatified in 1909, and is a patron saint of France.

THE BATTLE OF NICOPOLIS 1396

CRUSADE AGAINST THE OTTOMANS

BY THE END OF THE FOURTEENTH CENTURY, THE OTTOMAN EMPIRE HAD BECOME A SIGNIFICANT POWER ON THE DOORSTEP OF EUROPE. CONQUERING ALL OF ANATOLIA, THE OTTOMANS ATTACKED CONSTANTINOPLE AND LED AGGRESSIVE CAMPAIGNS IN THE BALKANS.

In 1395, the Ottomans laid siege to Constantinople under the leadership of Bayezid I (r. 1389–1402). With Anatolia lost, and the Ottomans taking more and more control of the Balkans, Constantinople found itself surrounded by a hostile enemy. Severely weakened, and with little chance against the much more powerful Ottoman forces, the Byzantine emperor, Manuel II, called upon the powers of Western Europe for aid. The force subsequently organized by King Sigismund of Hungary would be the last real crusade of the Middle Ages.

A COALITION OF FORCES

The Europeans who came to the aid of the Byzantine Empire mostly came from France and Burgundy, but also Germany and England, as well as Sigismund's native Hungary. Estimates as to the number of knights who travelled east along the Danube to relieve the Byzantines vary widely, but the force probably numbered between 15,000 and 20,000, with an equal number of combatants on the side of the Ottomans.

BELOW With Anatolia conquered, the Ottomans pressed into Eastern Europe in the 13th century.

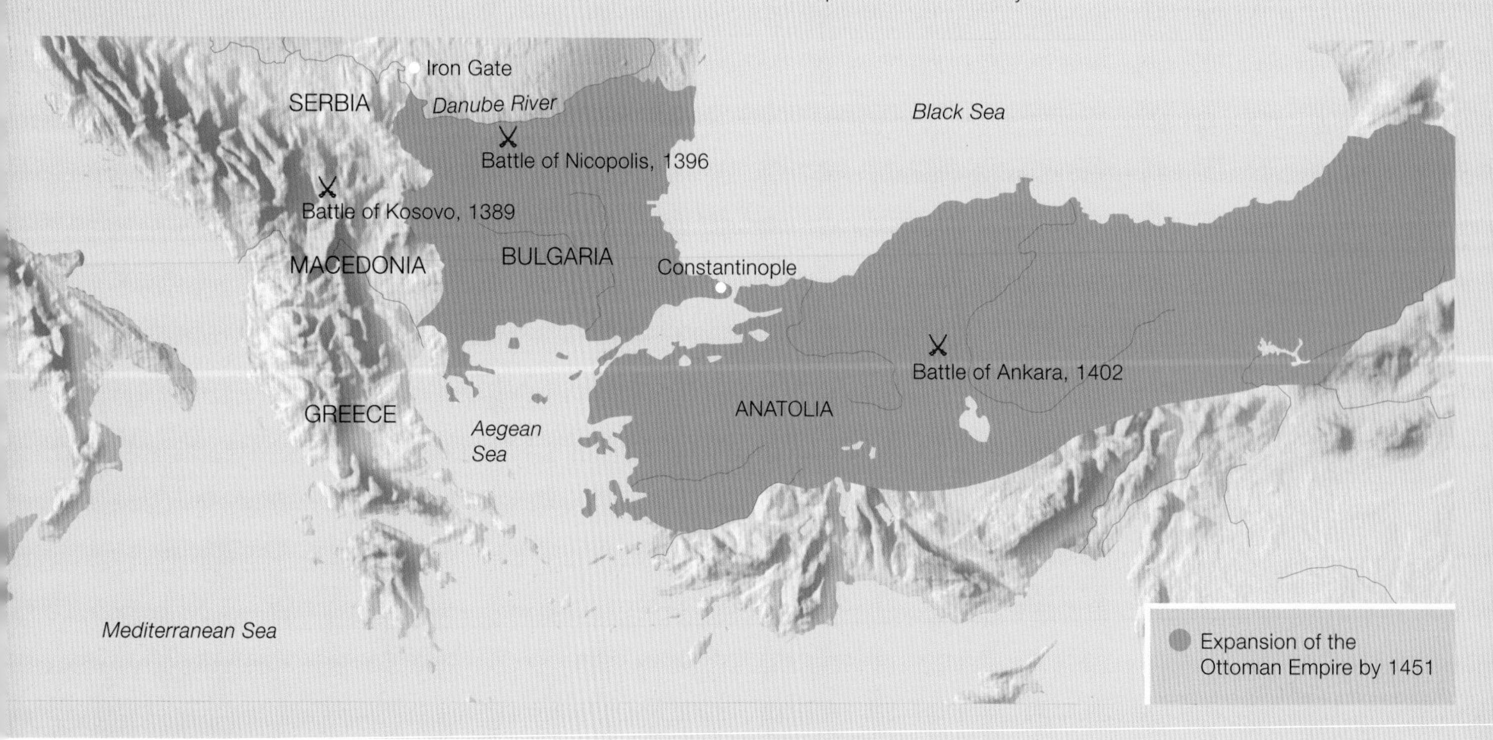

ABOVE Though the Battle of Nicopolis was the last real European crusade, crusaders maintained a presence on the Mediterranean for a long time thereafter. Here, Ottomans finally expel the Knights Hospitaller from Rhodes in 1522.

ABOVE The Battle of Kosovo, or the Battle of Blackbird's Field, fought between the Serbs and Ottomans, in 1389, continues to be remembered as a basis for Serbian identity today.

Advancing eastwards along the River Danube, the coalition of European forces was able to defeat several smaller troops of Ottomans, and establish garrisons along the route. They made their way to Nicopolis, Bayezid's stronghold. Bayezid was not there himself at the time, and the crusader army hoped to surprise the Ottomans. But the Ottoman Sultan brought his army up from Constantinople to assist his forces at Nicopolis. By the time they arrived at Nicopolis, the crusader force had dwindled owing to defections and illness. The main reason for their defeat, however, would lie in their tactical errors.

THE ILL-FATED CHARGE

The battle took place on 25 September 1396. Against the strong objections of Sigismund, the French leader, John of Nevers, decided to charge Bayezid's forces directly. Bayezid had arranged his troops on a nearby hill. While the French were able to scatter the light cavalry that formed the Ottoman's first line of defence, the Sultan was waiting behind this cavalry with a strong additional force that quickly routed the European knights. Sigismund attempted to come to the aid of his allies, but was unable to reach them in time. The battle was a crushing defeat for the Europeans.

LEFT Timur captured Bayezid I at the Battle of Ankara in 1402 and imprisoned him, as seen here. This led to civil war in the Ottoman Empire.

THE WAR OF THE ROSES 1455–1485

BATTLE FOR THE THRONE

AFTER THE DEATH OF KING HENRY V (R. 1413–1422) IN 1422, THE CROWN PASSED TO HIS INFANT SON, HENRY VI. UNLIKE HIS FATHER, THE YOUNGER HENRY PROVED UNABLE TO LEAD EFFECTIVELY, SPAWNING A BATTLE FOR SUCCESSION TO THE THRONE OF ENGLAND.

Two different houses lay claim to the throne of England: Lancaster and York. The Lancastrians occupied the throne since 1399, when Henry Bolingbroke deposed Richard II, and took over as Henry IV. Henry was the son of John of Gaunt, of the House of Plantagenet. John of Gaunt was the son of Edward III. The Yorkists laid their claim to the throne of England through descent from Edward's other children. The heraldic symbol of Lancaster included a red rose, while that of York included a white rose. From this imagery comes the name – 'War of the Roses' – for the Civil War that dominated England during the middle of the fifteenth century.

RIGHT A reconstruction of a 16th-century embroidered book binding, showing the red roses of the Lancastrians and the white roses of the Yorkists.

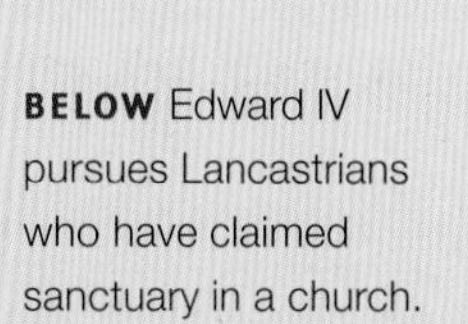

BELOW Edward IV pursues Lancastrians who have claimed sanctuary in a church.

LEFT The Battle of Bosworth Field, in 1485, saw the victory of the Lancastrians and the rise of Henry Tudor.

RIGHT Edward IV of York ruled England from 1461–1470 and again from 1471–1483.

FIGHTING KICKS OFF

The incompetent reign of Henry VI, punctuated by fits of madness, left much of the political power of the country in the hands of his wife, Margaret of Anjou. In 1455, she excluded Richard, Duke of York, from a Great Council, provoking the Duke's wrath and subsequent violence. The first real battle of the War of the Roses was the First Battle of St Albans, fought on 22 May 1455. The battle was fought in St Albans, north of London, and was a resounding victory for York. He defeated the Lancastrians led by Edmund, Duke of Somerset, and captured Henry VI himself. This was an important first step in York's path to rise to the throne of England. The fighting, however, had only just begun.

THE RESULTS

Seeking to deny York his claims to the throne, Margaret of Anjou again tried to remove York from his position of power as Constable of England, gained in the wake of the Battle of St Albans. Once again, this provoked York. Violence erupted, and the Yorkists were successful, installing Edward IV, son of Richard of York, as king. For the next 25 years, the two houses of England would wage war against each other. At the end of the war, the power and kingship passed back to a Lancastrian, Henry Tudor, who would become Henry VII and usher in a time of great prosperity for England, known as the 'Tudor Period'.

RIGHT Henry VI (r. 1422–1461, 1470–1471) was often incapable of rule, and power fell to his wife, Margaret of Anjou.

THE INVINCIBLE ARMADA 1588

NOT SO INVINCIBLE...

BETWEEN 1585 AND 1604, ENGLAND AND SPAIN MET HEAD-ON IN SPORADIC MILITARY ENGAGEMENTS, CLASHING LARGELY OVER DIFFERENCES BETWEEN THE CATHOLIC AND PROTESTANT CHURCHES. THE MOST DECISIVE ENGAGEMENT WAS THE DEFEAT OF THE SPANISH ARMADA IN 1588.

ABOVE Elizabeth I with her hand on a globe and the Spanish Armada in the background.

Also known as the 'Invincible Armada', the Spanish Armada that sailed against England in 1588 would prove to be anything but invincible. Tensions between the two nations had been mounting for a number of years. Elizabeth I (r. 1553–1603), a Protestant, replaced her Catholic predecessor, Mary I (r. 1553–1558) in 1558. Mary had re-established Catholicism in England, an act that Elizabeth promptly undid upon ascension to the throne. Religious tensions between England and Spain played out through, and were exacerbated by, a number of political factors. Philip II of Spain was married to Mary I, and he also controlled the Spanish Netherlands. Elizabeth supported the Dutch revolt against the Spanish, specifically signing the Treaty of Nonsuch, in 1585. English privateers, such as Francis Drake, frustrated Spain by capturing gold being sent back to Europe from the Americas. All of these factors contributed to Philip II sending his Armada to overthrow Elizabeth I in 1588.

RIGHT Sighting of the Spanish Armada off the English coast.

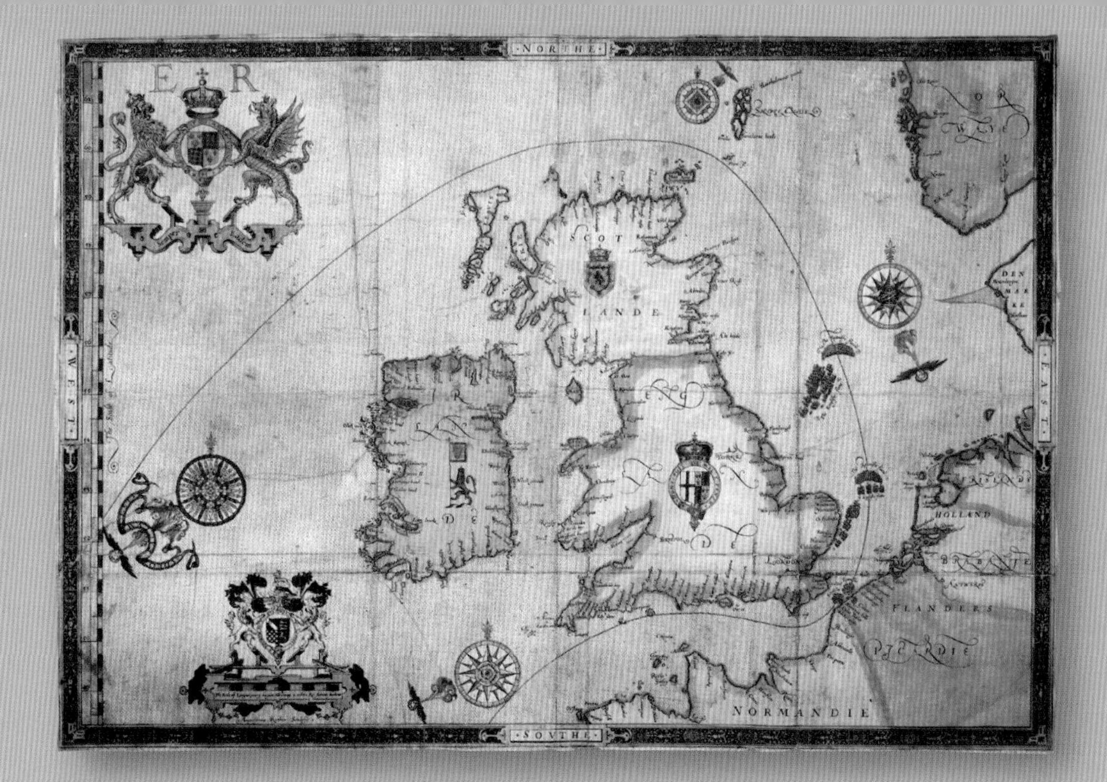

RIGHT This map shows the route of the Spanish Armada through the English Channel, then north up the east coast of England and Scotland.

SUPREMACY OF THE SEAS

Around 130 ships sailed under the command of the Duke of Medina Sidonia, travelling to the Netherlands to meet the Duke of Parma, who would provide an army with which to sail across the English Channel. About 40 of these ships were battleships. The English outnumbered the Spanish in terms of total number of vessels, but had less firepower than the Spanish Armada. The English fleet was comprised of lighter, swifter craft, and was not encumbered by the roughly 19,000 soldiers brought by the Spanish. The Spanish Armada was first sighted off Cornwall, and the English fleet began harrying their Spanish opponents in the English Channel. The Spanish managed to reach Calais and anchored there, but the English sent a series of fireships among the Spanish Armada. Realizing they could not safely wait for Parma's forces, the Spanish sailed to Gravelines in the Netherlands. On 8 August, a fierce battle ensued at Gravelines, and the Spanish were driven back and forced up England's east coast. Unable to turn back, the Spanish fleet had to sail north, rounding Scotland, returning south along the western coast of Ireland. Violent storms in the North Atlantic sank many of the Spanish ships. The English viewed the intervention of the storms as a providential sign of God's will. The English victory also demonstrated the country's burgeoning naval power.

ABOVE This painting shows several key events in the story of the Armada, including the Battle of Gravelines and the lighting of beacons to signal the arrival of the Spanish fleet.

RIGHT The Spanish Armada was supposed to be invincible, yet it was decimated by violent storms in the North Atlantic.

RUSSIANS AND OTTOMANS C.1676–1878

THE RUSSO-TURKISH WARS

BETWEEN THE SEVENTEENTH AND NINETEENTH CENTURIES, RUSSIA AND THE OTTOMAN EMPIRE FOUGHT A NUMBER OF WARS, PRIMARILY OVER TERRITORIES AROUND THE BLACK SEA AND IN WHAT IS NOW EASTERN EUROPE. THESE WARS CONTRIBUTED TO THE DECLINE OF THE OTTOMANS.

RIGHT Ottoman ruler, Suleiman the Magnificent, on top of his mount.

Following the reign of Suleiman the Magnificent (r. 1520–1566), the Ottoman Empire continued to expand until reaching its peak in 1683. At its height, the Ottoman Empire encompassed all of Anatolia, much of the Middle East and North Africa, the area around the Black Sea and the entire Balkan Peninsula, as far north as Hungary, and nearly all the way to Vienna. In 1682, however, a new ruler ascended the throne in Russia: Peter the Great (r. 1682–1725). Under Peter, Russia would exert more and more pressure on the Ottoman Empire, contributing to the empire's decline and eventual collapse.

CENTURIES OF WAR

Conflicts began in the late seventeenth century between Russia and the Ottomans, primarily because the Russians wanted to establish a warm-water port on the Black Sea. At the time, the Ottomans controlled all the territory surrounding the Black Sea, though the strip of land they controlled along the northern border of the sea was relatively narrow. The first Russian attempt in 1676–1681 failed, but the Russians under Tsar Peter the Great were able to capture the fortress of Azov in the war of 1695–1696. Over the next several decades, Peter attempted to throw Ottoman rule off the Slavic peoples of the Balkans. He failed, and was defeated in 1711.

LEFT The Russians defeated the Ottomans at the Siege of Ochakov in 1788.

ABOVE Catherine the Great was Empress of Russia from 1762–1796.

ABOVE Peter the Great was a strong military commander and expanded Russia considerably during his reign.

LEFT The Russians conquered Azov in 1696 under Peter the Great.

The conflict escalated in 1768 during the reign of Catherine the Great (r. 1762–1796). Empress Catherine II imposed policies in Poland that led to revolt. The Ottomans ordered that Russia not interfere in Poland further, and things quickly escalated to large-scale war. Between 1768 and 1774, Russia waged a fierce war against their Turkish enemies, bringing Azov and territories in the Ukraine, the Caucasus and Crimea under their control.

THE FINAL BATTLES

Over the coming century, Russia continued its military engagements with Turkey, taking further territories in the Balkans and around the Black Sea. In 1877, Russia launched the final Russo-Turkish War. Allying with Serbia, Russia helped Bosnia and Herzegovina, as well as Bulgaria, to revolt against Turkish rule. While these Balkan territories received autonomy, they were largely viewed by the rest of Europe as Russian gains.

THE GREAT NORTHERN WAR 1700–1721

THE FALL OF SWEDEN

WHEN CHARLES XII ASCENDED THE THRONE OF SWEDEN IN 1697, HE WAS ONLY 14 YEARS OLD. HIS TENDER AGE APPEARED TO PROVIDE THE PERFECT OPPORTUNITY FOR THE COUNTRIES SURROUNDING SWEDEN ON THE BALTIC TO ATTACK.

By the time war broke out in 1700, Sweden had become a dominant power in Europe. The kingdom covered not only the territory of modern Sweden, but also significant territories on the main continent of Europe along the Baltic Sea. Russia, eager to be able to use the Baltic for trade, coveted these territories. Likewise, Norway and Denmark – then one single kingdom – feared the growing power of their Scandinavian neighbour, and bitterly resented Sweden's capture of Scania (modern Skåne). The kings of Germany and Poland likewise harboured resentments and fears of Sweden.

THE YOUNG EMPEROR

Despite only being 18 years old when the Great Northern War began in 1700, Charles XII commanded the Swedes with surprising skill and ability. Although the coalition was comprised of several foreign powers – essentially including all of Sweden's southern neighbours – the first six years of war were victorious for Sweden under Charles XII. Charles even invaded Saxony to chase after Augustus II of Poland, whom he finally defeated after several years of combat. The coalition had likely underestimated the power and ability of the young king, but though defeated, they were not conquered. The coalition would regroup and attack again, this time with greater force and more carefully crafted strategies.

LEFT Augustus II the Strong of Poland, King Frederick I of Prussia and Frederick IV of Denmark meet in Potsdam, in 1709.

BELOW Peter the Great defeated the Swedish armies of Charles XII at the Battle of Poltava in 1709.

DEFEATS OF CHARLES XII

After being defeated early in the Northern War, Peter spent several years building up his military force, and establishing a navy on the Baltic after founding the city of St Petersburg, in 1703. Charles attacked Russia again in 1707, but this time he was not so lucky. Peter the Great defeated him in 1708 and again in 1709. Charles appealed to the Ottoman Turks, long the enemy of Russia, and received their aid, allowing him to gain an important victory in 1711. However, the Turks did not continue in their assistance, and Russia and the other members of the coalition began taking portions of Sweden's Baltic territories. Charles died in 1718 during an invasion of Norway, leaving the Swedish kingdom to his sister and her husband, Frederick, who became Frederick I of Sweden. Frederick negotiated peace with the coalition, ending the war with the Treaty of Nystad, which granted Russia several concessions along the Baltic. Estonia, Ingria and Livonia now all fell under Russia's dominion.

ABOVE Charles XII (r. 1697–1718) was only 14 years old when he ascended the throne of Sweden.

ABOVE RIGHT Despite the tender age at which he took the throne, Charles XII quickly proved himself an able military leader.

RIGHT Augustus II the Strong was Elector of Saxony from 1694–1733 and King of Poland from 1697–1706 and again from 1709–1733.

WAR OF SPANISH SUCCESSION 1701–1714

DIVIDING FRANCE AND SPAIN

IN 1700, WAR BROKE OUT AMONG THE POWERS OF WESTERN EUROPE REGARDING THE SUCCESSION TO THE SPANISH THRONE. FOURTEEN YEARS OF FIGHTING ENDED IN A PERMANENT SEPARATION BETWEEN THE KINGDOMS OF FRANCE AND SPAIN.

When Charles II of Spain (r. 1665–1700) died in 1700, Philip of Anjou ascended to the throne of the Spanish Empire. Philip was the grandson of Louis XIV of France (r. 1643–1715), and therefore an heir to the throne of France as well. Philip was not the original heir intended. In 1698, several countries signed an agreement that Joseph Ferdinand would be the successor to Charles II, but Ferdinand died the following year, and Archduke Charles was put forward as a replacement. The terms of his appointment were not agreed, however, and Charles II left a will bequeathing his empire to Philip.

YOU CAN'T HAVE IT ALL

In 1700, Spain commanded an enormous empire, comprised of Spain, the Spanish Netherlands, territories in Italy, as well as Spanish territories in Latin America. France likewise controlled significant territories and wealth. The prospect of a single ruler carrying the power of both Spain and France was terrifying to the other countries of Europe. Such a situation would have seriously disrupted the European balance of power. Louis XIV crowned his grandson, Philip, King of Spain on 24 November 1700, and then proceeded

ABOVE Eugene of Savoy was a brilliant military leader alongside the Duke of Marlborough in the wars against the French.

RIGHT Eugene of Savoy at the Battle of Blenheim, in 1704.

RIGHT Claude Louis Hector de Villars defeated Eugene of Savoy at the Battle of Denain, in 1712.

to invade the Spanish Netherlands. A coalition of forces rose up to combat France, forming a Grand Alliance. It was comprised of England, the Dutch Netherlands and the forces of Emperor Leopold of the Holy Roman Empire.

The combined force of France and Spain was a heavy opposition to contend with, but the Alliance's forces were led by the English Duke of Marlborough, an outstanding warrior and strategist. He was aided in his command by Eugene of Savoy. Marlborough quickly expelled the French from the Low Countries and defeated the French at the Battles of Blenheim, in 1704, Ramillies in 1706 and Oudenarde in 1708. In 1711, Marlborough had to return to England; at the same time, French commander, Marshal Claude Louis Hector de Villars began to turn the tide of battle against the Alliance. The war largely came to a close in 1713 with the Treaty of Utrecht. Philip V retained control of Spain as the first Bourbon King, and Louis XIV agreed that France and Spain would not fall under the dominion of a single ruler. Other Spanish territories in Europe were divided among other European powers.

LEFT King Philip V of Spain.

LEFT The Duke of Marlborough's brilliance as a military leader ensured many victories for the Allies early in the war.

THE NAPOLEONIC PERIOD 1799–1815

THE LITTLE CORPORAL

THE END OF THE EIGHTEENTH CENTURY IN FRANCE SAW THE VIOLENT UPHEAVALS OF THE FRENCH REVOLUTION. IN THE WAKE OF THEIR SUCCESS, A NEW MILITARY LEADER WOULD RISE UP WHO WOULD BECOME ONE OF THE GREATEST GENERALS OF ALL TIME – NAPOLEON BONAPARTE.

ABOVE A romantic painting by Jacques-Louis David of Napoleon crossing the Alps in 1800.

Napoleon was born in Corsica, in 1769, to Italian parents of noble birth. Showing great ambition from an early age, Napoleon overcame his early hatred of France, and worked his way up quickly through the ranks of the French military. Napoleon distinguished himself both through his military genius and through his ambition. He was one of history's most power-hungry leaders.

THE BRITISH AND OTTOMANS

In 1796, the Directory of France appointed Napoleon commander-in-chief of the Army of Italy. Over the coming year, Napoleon won several significant victories, effectively bringing France's wars on the continent to a close. After winning several battles in Italy, Napoleon advanced into Austria in 1797, where he was no less successful. Napoleon proceeded to exercise greater command of French forces, as well as significant political influence in France.

With wars on the continent settled for the time being, France's main opponent was now Great Britain, whose

RIGHT The French won an important victory at the Battle of Borodino on 7 September 1812, forcing the Russians to retreat. This was the largest single battle of the Napoleonic advance into Russia, resulting in around 70,000 casualties.

ABOVE A strong Russian soldier attacks one of Napoleon's soldiers in this cartoon illustrating the failed expedition to Russia, in 1812.

LEFT This drawing shows battle formations at the Battle of Austerlitz, in 1805.

BELOW Despite Napoleon's dominance on land, the British defeated the French and Spanish on the seas in the Battle of Trafalgar, in 1805.

BOTTOM Napoleon comes through the Brandenburg Gate in Berlin, in 1806.

advanced Navy was the pinnacle of its day. Deeming a direct invasion of Great Britain unsound, Napoleon proposed attacking Egypt, then under British control. Despite initial impressive victories at Malta and Alexandria, Napoleon's forces were beaten by British commander Horatio Nelson at the Battle of the Nile on 1 August 1798. At the battle, the British managed to sink the 120-gun flagship of Napoleon, *L'Orient*. Napoleon continued his attacks on land, travelling into Syria to do battle against the Ottomans, where his advance was stopped at Acre. His campaign ended in failure.

COUP D'ÉTAT

In 1799, Napoleon returned to France to participate in a coup d'état, overthrowing the French Directory and establishing the French Consulate, of which Napoleon was the first Consul. Napoleon's defeats in Egypt were largely forgotten back in France, and most looked to him with great hope and expectation. The Consulate was effectively a dictatorship, with Napoleon in charge. Napoleon initiated a number of reforms, including within the military, where he significantly restructured the training and organization of soldiers. In 1804, the French Consulate was transformed into the French Empire, and Napoleon was crowned its first Emperor.

THE NAPOLEONIC PERIOD 1799–1815

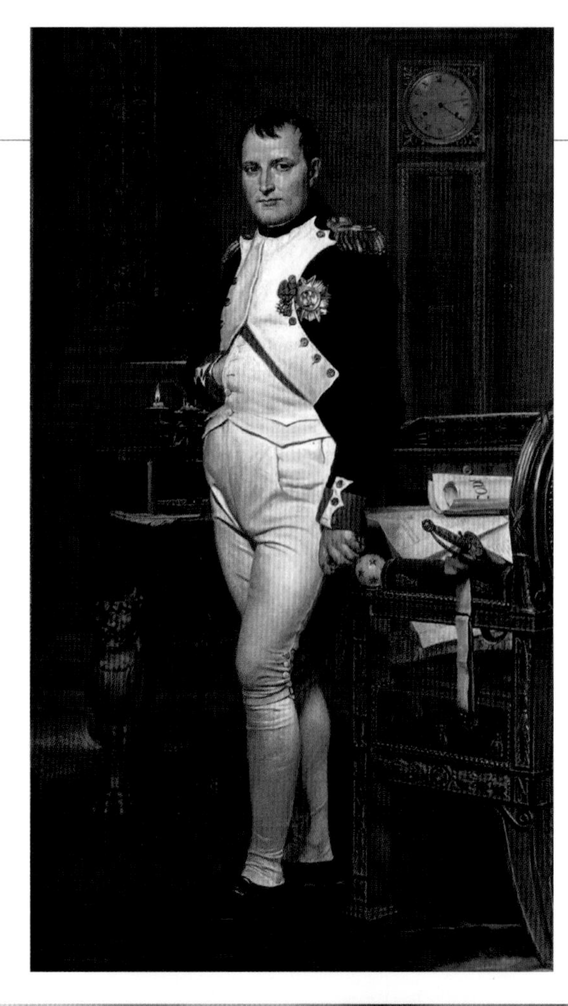

LEFT The famous pose of Napoleon, with his hand tucked inside his jacket.

After becoming emperor in 1804, Napoleon launched several military campaigns throughout Europe. He brought his newly organized military to the field, swiftly proving its efficacy by winning engagement after engagement, even when vastly outnumbered. By 1812, most of Europe lay under Napoleon's control. Ever thirsting for yet greater power, Napoleon set his sights on Russia. This would prove to be disastrous.

Blindly pursuing the Russian army deeper and deeper into Russian territory, Napoleon did not plan for retreat. The Russians lured Napoleon and his army further into their country, using scorched-earth tactics to ensure that the French were unable to replenish their supplies. Napoleon reached Moscow in September 1812, but was unable to secure victory against the Russians. He was forced to retreat, but autumn was upon him and his men, and they had no warm clothing and little food. The rapid onset of the harsh Russian winter decimated Napoleon's troops as they marched back to France, plagued by Russian guerrilla fighters. The campaign in Russia was an utter disaster, with hundreds of thousands of French soldiers lost. Napoleon not only showed that he could be beaten, he also lost the bulk of his fighting force.

RIGHT Another commemoration of the Battle of Borodino, in 1812.

EUROPE CLOSES IN

In the wake of Napoleon's defeats in Russia, the other nations of Europe banded together to form an alliance against France. Napoleon was soundly beaten at the Battle of Leipzig on 16–19 October 1813. The alliance opposing Napoleon then invaded France, taking Paris in 1814. Napoleon abdicated on 6 April, and was exiled to the island of Elba, which was granted him as a sovereign principality. But Napoleon returned to France in 1815, along with a small force, and for the next three months Napoleon contended against the Seventh Coalition, including Great Britain, Austria, Prussia and Russia, all of whom had pledged to put an end to his rule. This period is known as Napoleon's 100 days.

THE BATTLE OF WATERLOO

On 18 June 1815, Napoleon and his Imperial Army were finally defeated at the Battle of Waterloo near Waterloo in modern-day Belgium. At this battle, the forces of the Duke of Wellington and the Prussian army of Gebhard Leberecht von Blücher were initially separated, with Napoleon planning to face off against the Duke of Wellington. However, on 18 June, he delayed attacking to allow the ground to dry. This gave the Prussians enough time to arrive. After Napoleon finally did attack the Duke of Wellington, he soon also had to face the Prussians. Napoleon suffered a crushing defeat at Waterloo, losing roughly a quarter of his men with 25,000 killed. Napoleon was exiled on St Helena where he died in 1821.

ABOVE Napoleon's men battled cold and hunger more than enemy soldiers during their terrible retreat from Russia.

RIGHT The Duke of Wellington helped defeat Napoleon at the Battle of Waterloo in 1815.

BELOW The relative positions of French, British and Prussian troops at the Battle of Waterloo, in 1815.

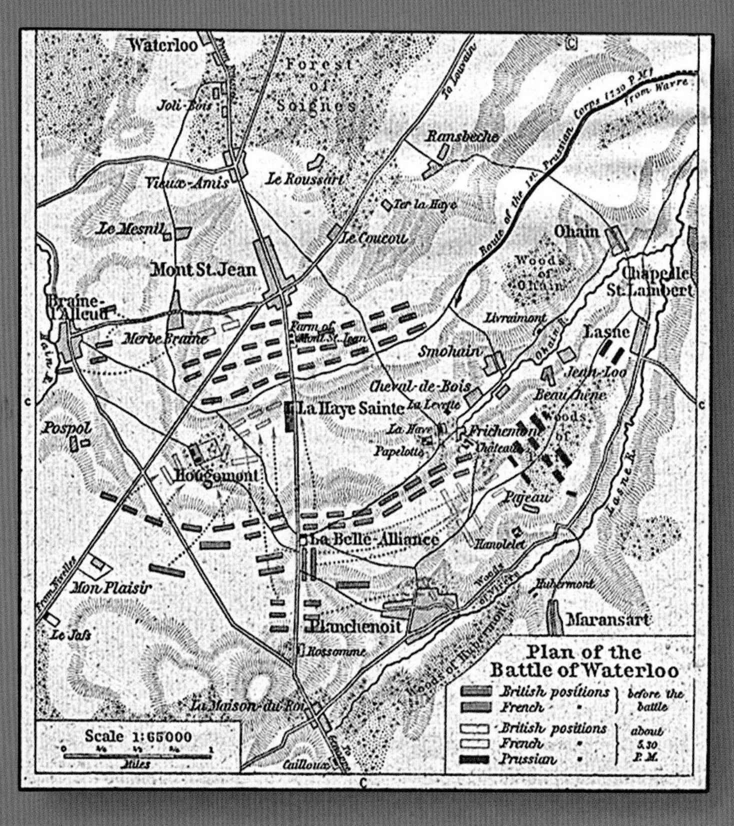

THE CRIMEAN WAR 1853–1856

THE MODERNIZATION OF BATTLE

FOUGHT BETWEEN RUSSIA AND AN ALLIANCE OF THE OTTOMAN EMPIRE, BRITAIN AND FRANCE, THE CRIMEAN WAR WAS A LONG AND BLOODY CONFLICT THAT SAW THE INTRODUCTION OF A NUMBER OF TECHNOLOGIES THAT WOULD CHANGE THE FACE OF WAR ITSELF.

As part of the ongoing Russo-Turkish Wars, the Crimean War in the mid-nineteenth century ultimately did not considerably affect the territorial holdings of the major players in the war. Although having extended to the Baltic, Russia still harboured hopes of a warm-water port along the shores of the Black Sea. The Ottoman Empire had been weakening for some time, and Russia saw an opportunity to strike against its southern neighbour and long-term rival.

BELOW Soldiers transport supplies through the harsh Crimean winter. Dead horses are partially buried by the road.

THE ALLIANCE

Both Britain and France viewed Russia as a potential threat, and wanted to ensure Russia's power and territorial holdings remained limited. Russia was also Eastern Orthodox Christian by religion, and sought to gain control over Christian religious sites in Palestine. Furthermore, Russia was considered the protector of Orthodox Christians within the Ottoman Empire. France began to engage with Russia over the control of religious sites and Christianity within the Ottoman Empire.

ABOVE The Battle of Alma, in 1854, was one of the first battles of the Crimean War.

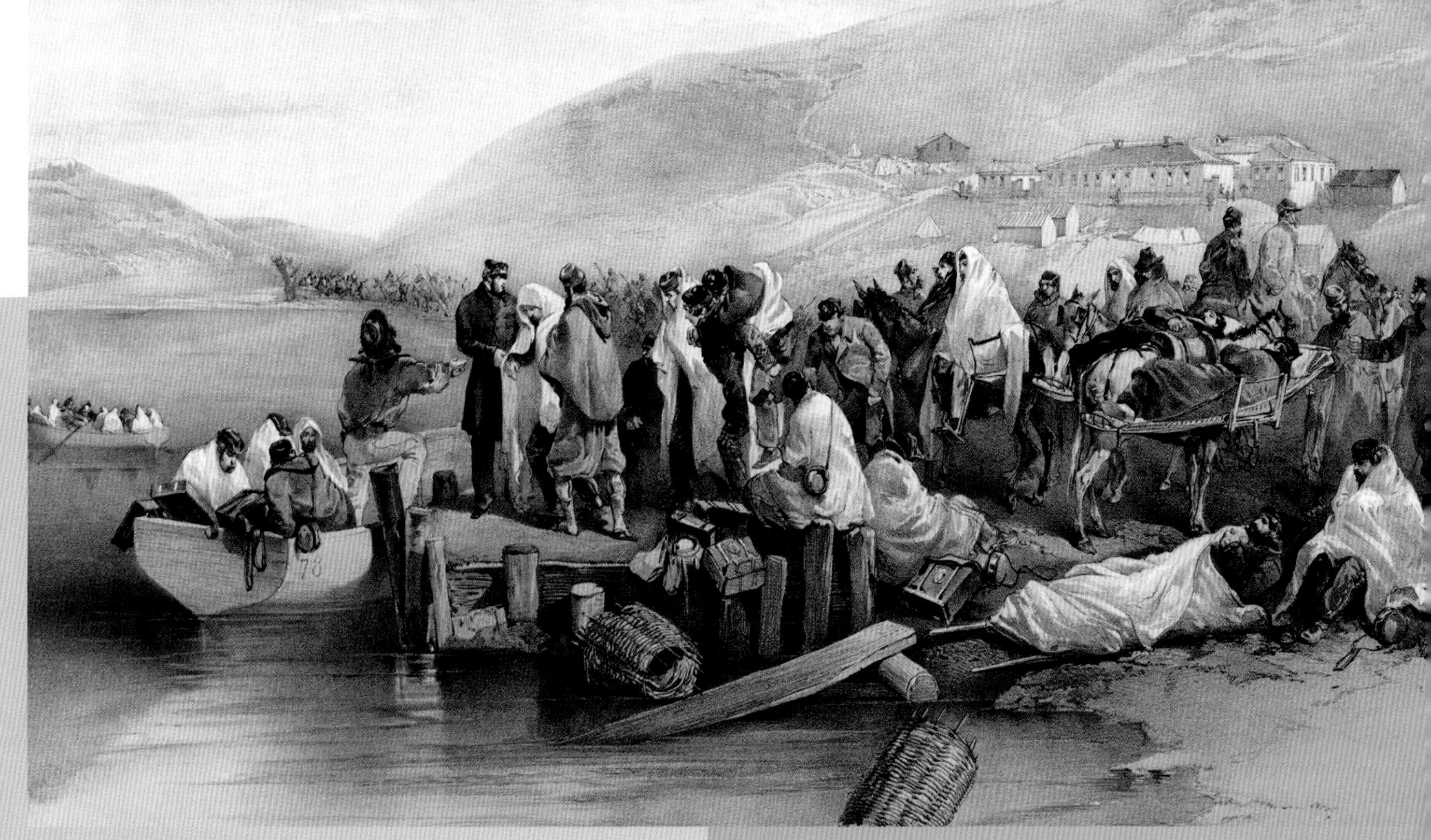

ABOVE Sickness was as deadly as gunfire in the Crimean War.

After Russian troops began pressing south into Ottoman territory in the Balkans during the summer of 1853, the Ottomans declared war in the autumn. Russia proceeded to sink a fleet of Ottoman ships in the Black Sea in an event known as the Battle of Sinope, on 30 November 1853. Britain used this event as an excuse to side with the Ottoman Empire, and declare war on Russia. France, allying with Britain, joined in the declaration.

THE WAR

Much of the fighting took place on the Crimean Peninsula itself. In order to satisfy Austria and avoid war on that front, Russia withdrew from the territories around the Danube, which it had entered in 1853. Britain and France entered the Black Sea early in 1854, declaring war on Russia on 28 March 1854. The war lasted for two years, resulting in approximately half a million deaths. It was concluded by the Treaty of Paris on 30 March 1856. The treaty protected Ottoman integrity, and opened trade along the Danube to all nations. Russia was furthermore forced to relinquish the territory it had gained along the mouth of the Danube.

ABOVE CENTRE The French advance on Malakoff, in 1855, during the Siege of Sevastopol.

ABOVE The Charge of the Light Brigade was an ill-fated charge later immortalized by the English poet Alfred, Lord Tennyson.

THE CRIMEAN WAR 1853–1856

TECHNOLOGICAL ADVANCES

The Crimean War saw the clash of old and new technologies and tactics, often playing out in bloody and devastating ways. A new type of rifle helped the Allies to gain a crushing victory over the Russians at the Battle of Inkerman on 5 November 1854. Most ships during this period were still wooden, but in 1855, a few proto-ironclad ships were used against the Russians for the first time in battle. In order to withstand the blasts of ever increasingly powerful guns and cannons, the French began to cover the outside of their ships with plates of steel or iron. The success of these during the Crimean War led to the development of ironclad warships, which would see their first full use a few years later during the American Civil War.

In addition to new weapon technology, several other new developments affected the Crimean War. New opportunities for transport and communication existed that would change the nature of warfare and battlefield tactics. Railways could transport both soldiers and supplies, and the telegraph could wire intelligence about enemy positions, or be used to coordinate attacks.

CHARGE OF THE LIGHT BRIGADE

One of the most famous events from the Crimean War was in the charge of Britain's Light Brigade on 25 October 1854. Owing to miscommunications, the Light Brigade ended up not pursuing artillery as expected, but rather faced a different artillery in a full-frontal assault. The 670 or so riders managed to reach their goal, suffering heavy losses from the artillery fire as they charged. Despite reaching the artillery,

ABOVE British soldiers of the 13th Light Dragoons during the Crimean War, in 1855.

LEFT The Siege of Sevastopol lasted a year and resulted in more than 200,000 casualties.

RIGHT Burning ships during the Battle of Sinope that started the Crimean War, in 1853.

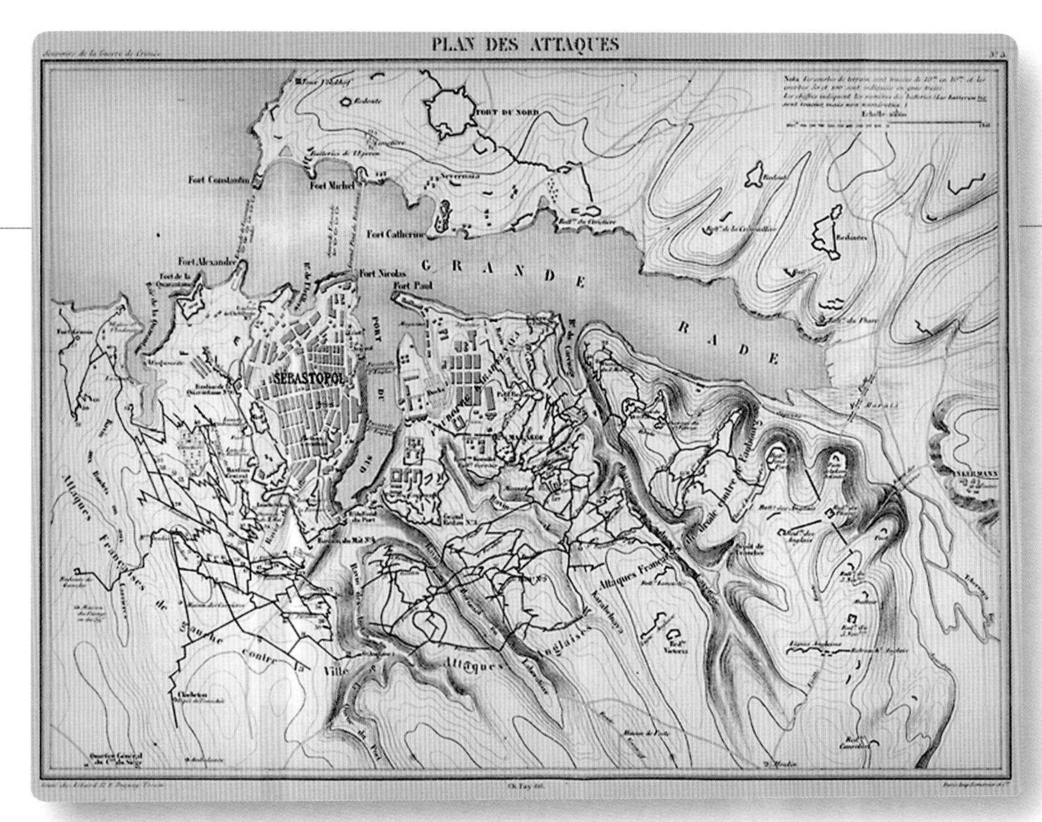

ABOVE A French map showing the plan of attack for French troops (in blue) and British troops (in red) at the Siege of Sevastopol.

ABOVE RIGHT Florence Nightingale was a nurse during the Crimean War and later pioneered standardization of nursing practices.

they were forced to turn back. The event was immortalized by Alfred, Lord Tennyson in his poem, 'The Charge of the Light Brigade'. Old-style cavalry charges were no longer as effective in the face of new firearms and artillery. It would take several decades, however, before charges of this nature would become obsolete.

FLORENCE NIGHTINGALE

In addition to the new technology used in transport, both on land and at sea, as well as in communications and weaponry, the Crimean War was also one of the first major conflicts to be documented and shared with the rest of the world through journalism and media. The Crimean War also saw advancements in battlefield medicine. Among the most famous heroines of the war was Florence Nightingale, a British nurse who cared for wounded soldiers in Turkey. She became known as the 'Lady with the Lamp' for her nightly rounds in the wards. She would go on after the war to standardize nursing practices and establish the Nightingale School of Nursing in 1860.

BATTLE OF KÖNIGGRÄTZ 1866

RISE OF PRUSSIA

IN THE MID-NINETEENTH CENTURY, MUCH OF WHAT IS NOW GERMANY WAS COMPRISED OF INDIVIDUAL DUCHIES AND PRINCIPALITIES. THROUGH THE WORK OF OTTO VON BISMARCK, PRUSSIA UNITED GERMANY, TO THE EXCLUSION OF AUSTRIA.

ABOVE A cartoon from *Puck* showing Otto von Bismarck as the Angel of Peace.

When Frederick VII of Denmark died in 1863, he left in his wake a dispute over succession to the Duchies of Schleswig and Holstein. When Denmark refused to grant German-speaking southern Schleswig to Prussia, Prussia launched the Second War of Schleswig in 1864, ultimately taking both Schleswig and Holstein. Contention between Prussia and Austria over control of the territories, however, escalated into armed conflict.

AUSTRIA VS PRUSSIA

The Prussian armies were led by Helmuth von Moltke, a brilliant military commander serving under Bismarck. The Prussian armies consisted of three main divisions, totalling some 285,000 men. The Austrian army was led by Ludwig August and again totalled approximately 285,000 men. August, unfamiliar with the terrain and having only recently taken up his position as commander, hesitated and failed to attack the Prussian forces while they were still separated.

The battle took place on 3 July 1866, near the town of Sadowa in what is now the Czech Republic. The Austrian forces used muzzle-loading rifles, while the Prussian forces benefited from newer breech-loading rifles, known as the Dreyse needle gun. Despite the technological advantage they had, which allowed them to fire more rapidly, the Prussians soon found themselves losing ground to their Austrian enemies. So far, however, only a portion of the total Prussian army had engaged in the attack. As Austria began to sense that victory was near, another division of Prussian troops arrived and decimated their Austrian opponent. The Austrians lost about 45,000 men, with nearly 6,000 killed and more than 20,000 captured. Prussia lost only 10,000 men, with around 2,000 soldiers dead. The technological advantages of the Prussians' weaponry certainly contributed to the disparity in these figures, especially since the total Prussian force was quite similar to that of Austria.

OUTCOMES

The Battle of Königgrätz was a crushing defeat for Austria, and catapulted Prussia into a newfound position of power. Now controlling the unified German states, Prussia outstripped Austria in terms of political and military power. This victory allowed Prussia to go on to found the German Empire in 1871, with Wilhelm I as Emperor.

ABOVE Field Marshal Helmuth von Moltke commanded the Prussians at Königgrätz.

ABOVE Otto von Bismarck united Germany into an empire under Prussian leadership.

BELOW The chaos of battle at Königgrätz.

WORLD WAR I 1914–1918

THE BALANCE OF POWER

ON 28 JUNE 1914, ARCHDUKE FRANZ FERDINAND OF AUSTRIA WAS ASSASSINATED IN SARAJEVO, BOSNIA AND HERZEGOVINA. THIS SINGLE INCIDENT TRIGGERED A CHAIN REACTION WITHIN EUROPE, QUICKLY ESCALATING INTO A WORLD WAR THAT WOULD COST THE LIVES OF MILLIONS.

TOP The assassination of Archduke Franz Ferdinand precipitated World War I.

ABOVE The single incident in Sarajevo ended up quickly involving the entire European continent and beyond.

Archduke Franz Ferdinand was the heir to the throne of the Austro-Hungarian Empire. He was visiting Sarajevo when he and his wife were assassinated. Bosnia and Herzegovina had been annexed by the Austro-Hungarian Empire, triggering the enmity of Serbia. In an effort to block Serbian interests in Bosnia and Herzegovina, Austria issued an ultimatum with which Serbia could not comply. This triggered the initial declarations of war.

COMPLEX ALLIANCES

Over the preceding century, Europe had carefully constructed an intricate network of alliances in order to maintain a balance of power. No nation was to become too powerful. These alliances, however, would create the rapid escalation of the Archduke's assassination into world war.

Germany had pledged unconditional support of Austria in the wake of the Archduke's assassination. When Austria-Hungary declared war on Serbia on 28 July 1914, it triggered a quick response from Russia, who sided with Serbia. This brought Germany into the war. Germany requested that France remain neutral, but France was allied with Russia, so France mobilized its army. Germany therefore found itself facing a war on two fronts. Deciding it would be best to deal with the threat of France first, Germany advanced through Belgium to strike at France. This in turn brought Britain into the war on the side of the Allied, or Entente, Powers. The Central Powers, consisting of Germany, Austria-Hungary, the Ottoman Empire and Bulgaria, found themselves fighting war on all sides of their territories.

ABOVE A stamp from Bosnia and Herzegovina produced in 1917 to commemorate the deaths of Archduke Franz Ferdinand and his wife, Sophie, the Duchess of Hohenberg, who were killed in Sarajevo, in 1914.

ABOVE A portrait of Archduke Franz Ferdinand.

ABOVE Franz Ferdinand's uniform stained with blood from when he was shot and killed.

TRENCH WARFARE

The Entente Powers stopped the German offensive at the First Battle of the Marne in September 1914. Both sides dug in, and a new type of warfare emerged: trench warfare. Trenches and ditches had been used for centuries, but their use in World War I reached a new level of development. Digging long lines of trenches to escape the bullets whizzing by overhead, armies of both sides hunkered down. The old charges of the past were still used, only now soldiers were mown down by the thousands thanks to new machine guns. Weeks of fighting and thousands of lives only produced centimetres of gain in terms of territory. The only hope of complete success was through attrition, completely wearing down the enemy and his resources.

BELOW The only shelter from the spray of bullets was behind earthworks.

RIGHT British recruitment poster from World War I encouraging men to arms.

BELOW Realist painting by John Singer Sargent of World War I officers.

WORLD WAR I 1914–1918

World War I saw the introduction of several new technologies to the battlefield. Trains, which had been in use for decades, played an important role in transporting both troops and supplies in Western Europe. Russia, however, was unable to mobilize its troops as effectively because of a lack of transport infrastructure. In addition to the train, another form of transport had also emerged: the automobile. In contrast to the horse, which was still used extensively during World War I, trains and automobiles did not tire. The first use of automobiles to transport soldiers in war was at the First Battle of the Marne when 600 taxis from Paris brought 6,000 troops to the battlefield.

In addition to these vehicles on the ground, a new vehicle took to the air. Planes were used on a large scale in battle for the first time in history. Initially used for intelligence gathering and reconnaissance, planes would become increasingly used as weapons themselves, fitted with guns and loaded with bombs. The new skillsets of fighting in the air quickly became much sought after on both sides of the conflict.

LEFT World War I was the first time gas was used widely as a weapon on the battlefield.

ABOVE Painting entitled 'The Charge of the 3rd Light Horse Brigade'.

ABOVE Trench of the Cheshire Regiment in 1916 during the Battle of the Somme.

ABOVE The Tyneside Irish Brigade move forward on the first day of the Battle of the Somme in 1916.

RIGHT A captured Turkish trench in 1915.

CENTRAL VS AXIS POWERS

When war erupted in 1914, the powers of Europe each had extensive colonial holdings abroad. Involvement of these colonies was unavoidable, and they quickly joined in the fight. The resistance of the Central Powers soon faltered abroad, and the battle was brought home to Europe. Troops from all over the globe would come to assist in the fighting.

With Britain and France now at odds with the Ottoman Empire, it was decided that an offensive in Gallipoli would be worth a try. Control of the Dardanelles Strait would make routes to the Black Sea easier, allowing access to Russia. This might help Russia mobilize more of its forces to assist the Allies, who constantly waited for relief from Russian troops.

Most of the troops who fought in the Gallipoli campaign of 1915 were from the Australian and New Zealander Army Corps (ANZAC), as well as from India. After an unsuccessful naval campaign, the British Commonwealth forces landed on 25 April 1915. They met staunch resistance from the Ottomans, but refused to give up. Digging in, and engaging in the trench warfare that came to dominate World War I, the Commonwealth forces fought throughout a difficult and brutally hot summer. After suffering almost a quarter of a million casualties, they decided to withdraw. The withdrawal began in November, and lasted into January 1916. Many equated this retreat with defeat, and considered it illustrative of the Allies' weakness.

RIGHT A boat packed with British soldiers makes its way to Cape Helles in April 1915 during the invasion of Gallipoli. ANZAC forces won fame for their bravery during this offensive.

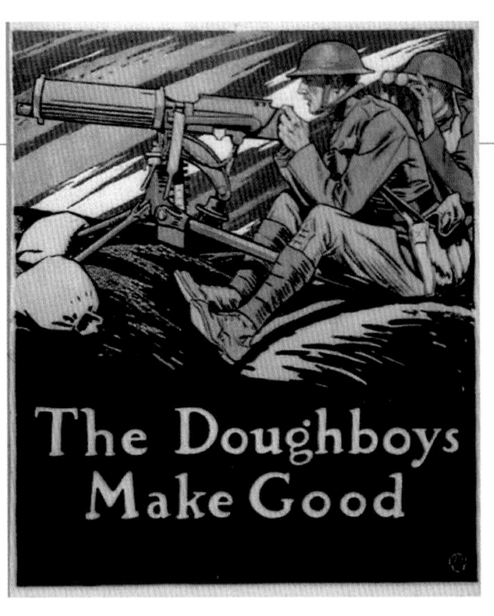

ABOVE Magazine cover from 1917 showing American soldiers operating a machine gun.

ABOVE Painting of the Battle of Vimy Ridge in northern France, 1917.

BELOW The USS *Texas* (BB-35) was launched in 1912, served in both World Wars and is the oldest remaining dreadnought battleship.

BATTLES OF YPRES

The town of Ypres in Flanders was the location of three major battles during World War I. The first occurred soon after the start of the war, when Allied forces reclaimed the city from the Germans. During Christmas 1914, the two sides of the battle engaged in a kind of truce, even exchanging gifts with each other across the trenches. The Second Battle of Ypres began on 22 April 1915, and lasted more than a month. It was one of the first times that gas – chlorine at this point – was used in battle. The Third Battle of Ypres, in November 1917, cost half a million casualties for only a small advance in position. The Germans used mustard gas during this engagement, lending it the nickname 'Yperite'.

THE BATTLE OF VERDUN

In 1916, the Germans launched a massive offensive against the French, who were unprepared for the initial onslaught at Verdun. Recovering quickly, however, the French managed to fend off the German advance after months of heavy fighting. According to some estimates, the Battle of Verdun resulted in almost a million casualties.

ABOVE Map showing the Western Front during World War I.

ABOVE Soldiers rest at a captured fortification during the Battle of Vimy Ridge, 9–12 April 1917.

BATTLE OF JUTLAND

The Battle of Jutland was the only major naval battle of World War I. It was fought on 31 May 1916, in the Skagerrak of the North Sea about 97 km (60 miles) away from Jutland, Denmark. Both British and German fleets spotted each other, and opened fire. The British suffered heavy losses and turned away, only to encounter the Germans again. The British gave fight, and the Germans now turned away, this time encountering more British vessels. The outcome of the battle was inconclusive. Germany claimed it had won because it caused greater damage to the British fleet. Britain, however, retained control of the waters of the North Sea, and therefore staked its claim as the victor.

AMERICA ENTERS THE WAR

After Germany exercised unrestricted submarine warfare, and sank several American merchant ships, the United States entered World War I, declaring war on 6 April 1917. By this point, the Allied forces were deadlocked against the Central Powers. Russia, crumbling from within, was unable to send the aid so much needed in France and elsewhere and disintegrated into civil war. The American troops brought new blood to the fight, significantly boosting the morale of the Allies. Importantly, they also brought tanks, which at last proved an effective means of combating trench warfare. The Germans launched their Spring Offensive in spring 1918, attempting to break British and French resistance before significant American reinforcements arrived. The Germans drove quickly, but were halted, and as more and more American troops poured into Europe to bolster the resistance of the Allies, the Germans finally retreated.

BELOW The British soccer team pose with gas masks before a soccer goalmouth in 1916.

ABOVE World War I saw the dawn of armoured vehicles, like this German tank.

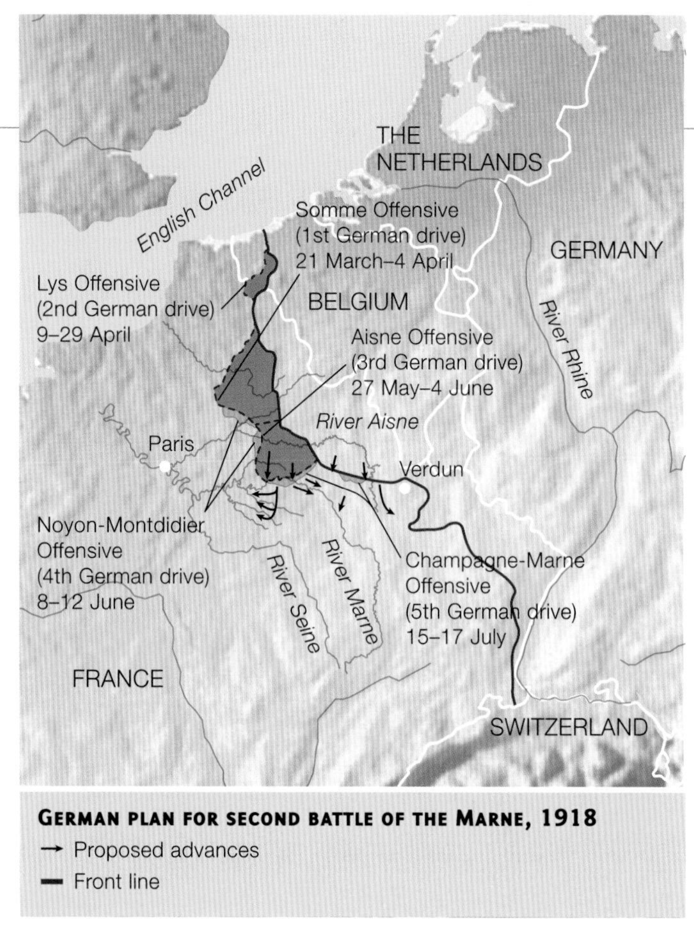

ABOVE The topography of the flatlands around the Marne provided little natural cover.

THE BEGINNING OF THE END

The Second Battle of the Marne in July 1918 was a last-ditch attempt of the Germans to break through the Allied defence in Flanders. By this point, most of the Spring Offensive of German military commander Erich Ludendorff had failed. As thousands of American soldiers poured into the Western Front every day, Germany knew that if it were to win the war it would have to do so quickly.

The Germans began the attack on 15 July, hitting the Allies hard. Despite staunch resistance from a number of scattered divisions, the Germans advanced quickly. Casualties were high on both sides, and the Allies were forced to fall back temporarily. They managed to check the Germans, however, on 17 July, launching a major counteroffensive on 18 July. British, French, Italian and US troops managed to turn the tide of battle and begin pushing the Germans back.

Instrumental to the success of the Allied powers at the Battle of the Marne was their use of tanks, including the Renault FT. Within a few days, they were able to cross the River Marne and begin the long process of driving the Germans back to the Hindenburg Line. The fighting continued until 6 August, only a few months before the close of World War I itself.

RIGHT French soldiers at the First Battle of the Marne, in 1914.

RIGHT The River Marne seen from the air in 1918.

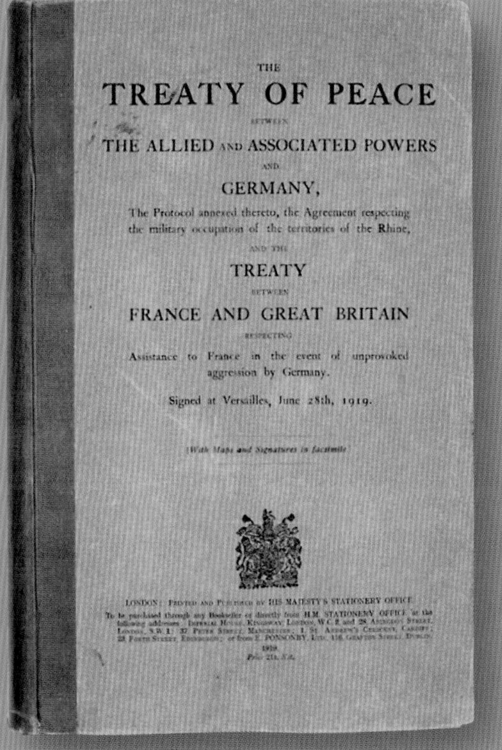

THE

TREATY OF PEACE

BETWEEN

THE ALLIED AND ASSOCIATED POWERS

AND

GERMANY,

The Protocol annexed thereto, the Agreement respecting the military occupation of the territories of the Rhine,

AND THE

TREATY

BETWEEN

FRANCE AND GREAT BRITAIN

RESPECTING

Assistance to France in the event of unprovoked aggression by Germany.

Signed at Versailles, June 28th, 1919.

(With Maps and Signatures in facsimile)

LONDON: PRINTED AND PUBLISHED BY HIS MAJESTY'S STATIONERY OFFICE

ABOVE An English copy of the Treaty of Versailles that ended World War I.

THE GREAT WAR

On the eleventh hour of the eleventh day of the eleventh month in 1918, the Armistice ending World War I was signed. World War I was considered 'The Great War' – the war to end all wars. Nearly ten million were killed in combat, and much of Europe lay in ruins. Even the victors had little to celebrate other than peace, for their resources were depleted and a generation had been killed or scarred. Russia had erupted in revolution and was now plagued by violent civil war. The Treaty of Versailles that ended the war also imposed harsh restrictions on Germany and demanded that reparations be paid to the other nations in Europe. This caused tensions that contributed to the outbreak of World War II.

RIGHT French soldiers of General Henri Gouraud take cover in the ruins of a church at the Second Battle of the Marne.

FLIGHT IN WARFARE

TAKING TO THE SKIES

On 17 December 1903, two American brothers, Wilbur and Orville Wright, completed the first successfully controlled mechanical flight with a human being onboard. This marked the beginning of a new era in which human beings were no longer confined to the ground, but could travel – and also fight – in the skies.

World War I saw the first widespread use of planes on the battlefield. Initially, no one thought to use these planes for combat purposes. Like the balloons that preceded them, they were used for reconnaissance and intelligence gathering. They were also as yet too small to transport troops in any meaningful way – only a couple of passengers could be carried in the early planes. But necessity is the mother of invention, and during World War I both sides soon began using planes for combat purposes. The early aviators were some of the most famous heroes of the war. Even the German 'Red Baron', Manfred von Richthofen, and his so-called 'Flying Circus', earned the respect of Allied powers. When he was finally shot down on 21 April 1918, Allied forces awarded him a full military burial.

LEFT German pilot, Manfred von Richthofen, also known as the 'Red Baron'.

BELOW The North American X-15 fighter plane can reach speeds over 6,440 kmh (4,000 mph).

FAR LEFT Manfred von Richthofen by his famous red airplane, with other members of the 'Flying Circus'.

LEFT World War I poster showing planes and zeppelins.

ADVANCES

Aviation continued to develop swiftly after World War I, and pilots played an even greater role in World War II. Planes also began being used to transport troops and supplies, allowing for much faster deployment and reinforcement. During the Cold War, the Soviet Union and the United States used planes to spy on one another, and satellites began being launched into space. Over the years, fighter planes became more and more refined, as well as faster. Fighter planes nowadays routinely break the speed of sound and sustain supersonic speeds. Modern planes are furthermore capable of incredibly acrobatic manoeuvres and are armed with both guns and missiles. In addition to planes, helicopters – developed in the 1930s – have also become essential components of battle. Capable of lifting straight off the ground, helicopters do not need a runway for take-off or landing, allowing them to be landed in jungle clearings and other areas where planes could not touch down. While not possessing the speed of fighter planes, helicopters offer greater flexibility at lower altitudes.

PILOTLESS FLIGHT

The idea of using pilotless planes for combat has been around for a while, but it wasn't until the 1990s that technological advances began to make this a real possibility. Today, drones are being used more and more, particularly by the US military in Afghanistan under the direction of President Obama. Controlled either by onboard computers or remotely by humans, these drones are equipped with a number of cameras and sensors designed to enable them to gather information and target specific individuals. The use of drones, while avoiding pilot deaths, has come under heavy criticism for the threat it poses to civilians. The US Government claims civilian casualties from drone attacks are low, but several reports contradict these assertions. Concern is warranted for how this new computerized technology will affect how war will be waged in the future.

IN MORE RECENT YEARS, PILOTLESS PLANES, OR DRONES, HAVE COME INCREASINGLY INTO USE. LIKE THE FIRST AIRPLANES, THE FIRST DRONES WERE USED PURELY FOR INFORMATION GATHERING AND RECONNAISSANCE.

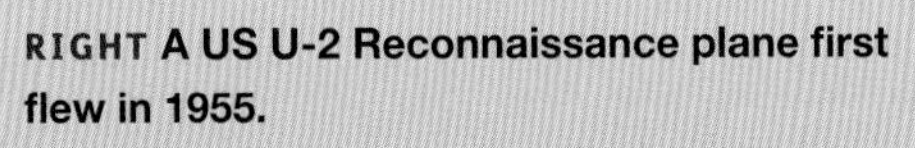

RIGHT A US U-2 Reconnaissance plane first flew in 1955.

REVOLUTION IN RUSSIA 1905–1923

RISE OF THE SOVIETS

THE OPPRESSIVE REGIME OF TSAR NICHOLAS II OF RUSSIA (R. 1894–1917) AND HIS FAILURES TO MODERNIZE RUSSIA SPARKED REBELLION, BEGINNING IN 1905. THE EMBARRASSING DEFEATS OF RUSSIA DURING WORLD WAR I, HOWEVER, WOULD SPARK CIVIL WAR OF ENORMOUS PROPORTIONS.

ABOVE LEFT Alexandra Feodorovna, wife of Tsar Nicholas II.

ABOVE RIGHT Portrait of Tsar Nicholas II.

LEFT Men stand at a barricade in Petrograd in 1917.

LEFT Bolsheviks march through Red Square in Moscow, in 1917.

Russia suffered its first embarrassing defeat at the hands of the Japanese in the Russo-Japanese War of 1904–1905. The defeat was partially due to Russia's failings, and partially due to the impressive military power of the Japanese, who had worked aggressively to modernize all aspects of their fighting force. Unfair working conditions, long working hours and better wages were also a major point of frustration for the Russian public. On 22 July 1905, the imperial troops of Nicholas II gunned down an unarmed demonstration against the Tsar. The day is known as Bloody Sunday. This initial revolt spread, but was eventually quelled. Nonetheless, it was the beginning of revolutionary stirrings that would come into full effect during World War I.

REVOLUTION BREAKS OUT

World War I was a disaster for Russia. Despite having a huge fighting force in terms of manpower, Nicholas II had failed to modernize and industrialize his country sufficiently, and these men did not have the equipment they needed to fight the Central Powers effectively. Without modern systems of transport, they also could not be mobilized. France and Britain kept looking to Russia for aid during the early stages of the war, but that aid did not – and, indeed, could not – materialize. Russia was simply not equipped to handle modern warfare.

In February 1917, strikes and demonstrations broke out in Russia. These escalated into what has become known as the February Revolution, resulting in the abdication of Nicholas II in March. This was not enough, however, to solve the serious problems of the country, including famine and terrible working conditions.

FAR LEFT Grigori Rasputin, a mystic, became involved with the royal family of Russia after being asked to heal the Tsar's son. A highly controversial figure, Rasputin was eventually assassinated.

LEFT This 1920 painting shows the unstoppable force of the Bolsheviks.

LENIN

Sent into exile for his Marxist political activities, Vladimir Lenin returned to Russia following the February Revolution and, as leader of the Bolsheviks, he assisted in organizing the October Revolution, or 'Red October', which overthrew the Russian Provisional Government and laid the groundwork for the establishment of the Soviet Union in 1922. On 3 March 1918, Lenin signed the Treaty of Brest-Litovsk with the Central Powers, giving up several territories along the Baltic to avoid further German hostilities during World War I. Russia, now withdrawn from external wars, disintegrated into an incredibly violent civil war between the Red Army of the Bolsheviks and the anti-communist White Army. In the end, the Bolsheviks prevailed and were able to establish the first constitutionally communist country in the world – the Union of Soviet Socialist Republics (USSR). By the end of the civil war, the country was in ruins, and millions had died from fighting, disease and famine.

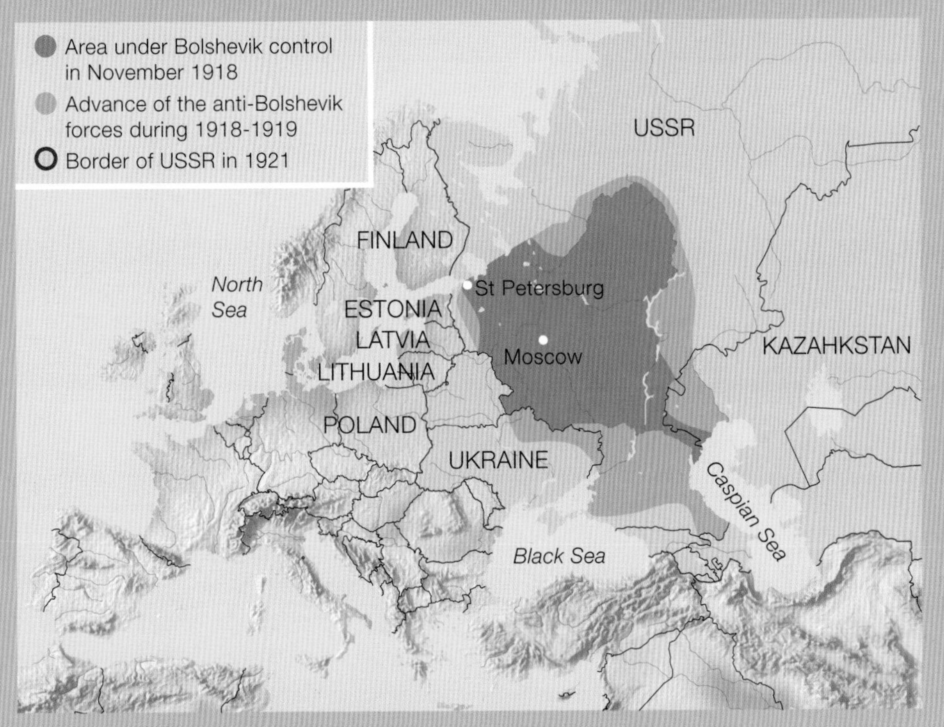

ABOVE Map showing the spread of the Red Army during the Russian Revolution.

ABOVE RIGHT Lenin addresses a crowd in Sverdlov Square, Moscow. Leon Trotsky, first leader of the Red Army, stands on the platform below.

ABOVE *The Pogrom of the Winter Palace* by Lithuanian artist Ivan Vladimirov.

IRISH WAR OF INDEPENDENCE 1919–1921

BREAKING FREE OF BRITAIN

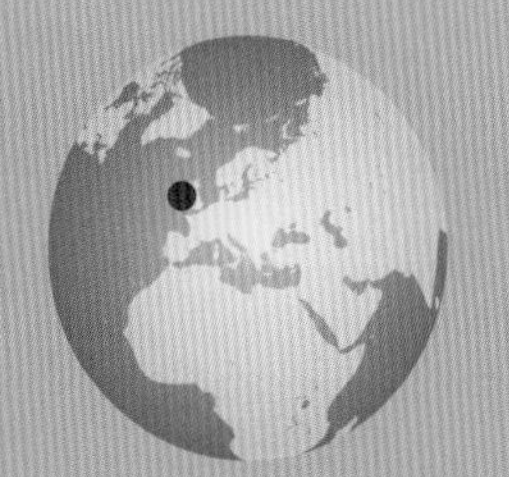

TENSION BETWEEN THE IRISH AND THE ENGLISH WAS CERTAINLY NOT NEW WHEN IRELAND REVOLTED IN 1919 AFTER DECLARING INDEPENDENCE. HOWEVER, THE UPRISING IN 1919 LED TO THE FIRST IRISH INDEPENDENCE IN CENTURIES.

ABOVE An archaic map of Ireland.

ABOVE RIGHT Sean Hogan, an IRA leader, and his 'Flying Column'.

From the time of the Normans, the English exercised control over their island neighbour to the west. For nearly 800 years, England and Ireland had been at odds with each other, even after England took control of Ireland. The early twentieth century saw the great empires of Europe beginning to disintegrate. In the wake of World War I, Britain was exhausted and depleted. Now was the time for Ireland to gain its independence.

SINN FÉIN AND THE IRA

During Easter 1916, the Irish rose up against British rule, hoping to gain independence. They had already been calling for the right to Home Rule for decades. The rebellion was put down and its leaders were executed, but this only provoked additional action a couple of years later.

Out of the Easter uprising of 1916, two organizations emerged: Sinn Féin and the Irish Republican Army (IRA). Sinn Féin, which had existed since 1905, now became a republican political party. The IRA was the militant group that would provide the armed resistance during the Irish War of Independence.

POBLACHT NA H EIREANN.

THE PROVISIONAL GOVERNMENT

OF THE

IRISH REPUBLIC

TO THE PEOPLE OF IRELAND.

IRISHMEN AND IRISHWOMEN In the name of God and of the dead generations from which she receives her old tradition of nationhood, Ireland, through us, summons her children to her flag and strikes for her freedom.

Having organised and trained her manhood through her secret revolutionary organisation, the Irish Republican Brotherhood, and through her open military organisations, the Irish Volunteers and the Irish Citizen Army, having patiently perfected her discipline, having resolutely waited for the right moment to reveal itself, she now seizes that moment, and, supported by her exiled children in America and by gallant allies in Europe, but relying in the first on her own strength, she strikes in full confidence of victory.

We declare the right of the people of Ireland to the ownership of Ireland, and to the unfettered control of Irish destinies, to be sovereign and indefeasible. The long usurpation of that right by a foreign people and government has not extinguished the right, nor can it ever be extinguished except by the destruction of the Irish people. In every generation the Irish people have asserted their right to national freedom and sovereignty; six times during the past three hundred years they have asserted it in arms. Standing on that fundamental right and again asserting it in arms in the face of the world, we hereby proclaim the Irish Republic as a Sovereign Independent State, and we pledge our lives and the lives of our comrades-in-arms to the cause of its freedom, of its welfare, and of its exaltation among the nations.

The Irish Republic is entitled to, and hereby claims, the allegiance of every Irishman and Irishwoman. The Republic guarantees religious and civil liberty, equal rights and equal opportunities to all its citizens, and declares its resolve to pursue the happiness and prosperity of the whole nation and of all its parts, cherishing all the children of the nation equally, and oblivious of the differences carefully fostered by an alien government, which have divided a minority from the majority in the past.

Until our arms have brought the opportune moment for the establishment of a permanent National Government, representative of the whole people of Ireland and elected by the suffrages of all her men and women, the Provisional Government, hereby constituted, will administer the civil and military affairs of the Republic in trust for the people.

We place the cause of the Irish Republic under the protection of the Most High God, Whose blessing we invoke upon our arms, and we pray that no one who serves that cause will dishonour it by cowardice, inhumanity, or rapine. In this supreme hour the Irish nation must, by its valour and discipline and by the readiness of its children to sacrifice themselves for the common good, prove itself worthy of the august destiny to which it is called.

Signed on Behalf of the Provisional Government,

THOMAS J. CLARKE.

SEAN Mac DIARMADA. THOMAS MacDONAGH.

P. H. PEARSE. EAMONN CEANNT.

JAMES CONNOLLY. JOSEPH PLUNKETT.

In 1919, the Irish declared independence and set up their own republic. Hostilities began when IRA members shot and killed two Royal Irish Constabulary Officers. For the next two years, the IRA waged a guerrilla war against the British, who did not know quite how to deal with these types of attacks. Accustomed to the trench warfare of World War I, the tactics of the Irish were not something the British were equipped to deal with. As the British public grew increasingly discontented with further war, being already sick of violence from the Great War, a truce was reached on 11 July 1921. The subsequent Anglo-Irish treaty in December 1921 granted Irish independence. Northern Ireland, however, was given the choice of joining the new Irish Free State or remaining a part of the United Kingdom. It chose the latter, which in turn led to sporadic violence between unionists and nationalists for decades to come.

TOP Michael Collins was Director of Intelligence for the IRA during the War of Independence. He was killed during the Civil War in 1922.

ABOVE Patrick Pearse was one of the leaders of the Easter Rising.

ABOVE RIGHT The proclamation of the Irish Republic from the Easter Uprising.

RIGHT A photo supposedly of the 'Cairo Gang', a group of British Intelligence agents.

SPANISH CIVIL WAR 1936–1939

RISE OF FRANCO SPAIN

BY THE MID-1930S, SPAIN WAS READY FOR REFORM. HIGH UNEMPLOYMENT, FAMINE AND POLITICAL INSTABILITY AND INFIGHTING PLAGUED THE COUNTRY. THIS SET THE STAGE FOR FRANCISCO FRANCO'S RISE TO POWER THROUGH THE SPANISH CIVIL WAR.

Several factions and parties within the Spanish Government campaigned for implementing competing political philosophies. After the elections of 16 February 1936 gave control to the political left, the political right revolted under the leadership of General Francisco Franco. Franco led a coup, which failed, resulting in the subsequent civil war that lasted three years.

A NATION DIVIDED

The two sides of the conflict represented different demographics. The Republicans were mostly farmers, workers and the educated. They held a demographic majority, and therefore succeeded in the elections of 1936. The Nationalists, as the party of Franco was called, were mostly businessmen, staunch Roman Catholics and members of the military. Having the military on Franco's side proved instrumental in his eventual victory, but it also meant that victory would be won by hardfought bloodshed.

The war was an important precursor to World War II. In the polarization of political philosophies, Spain drew other nations into its civil war. Germany and Italy supported Franco, while the Soviet Union and Mexico supported the Republicans. Several countries, including France and Britain, signed a non-intervention agreement in August 1936. While Germany, the Soviet Union and Italy all signed this agreement as well, none of them abided by its terms.

ABOVE LEFT Traditionalist Carlist flag (top) and fascist Falange flag (bottom) from the 1930s.

LEFT General Franco invaded Spain from Morocco and gradually expanded his hold on the country.

NATIONALISTS TAKE OVER

Franco led the invasion of Spain from Morocco and gradually expanded his territory from the southern coast, pushing towards Madrid by the end of 1936, and taking the northern coast during 1937. Soviet support for the Republicans began to dwindle, and with the continued support from Germany, the Nationalists kept acquiring more ground. Disorganization within the Republican resistance also weakened their cause. Gradually, the

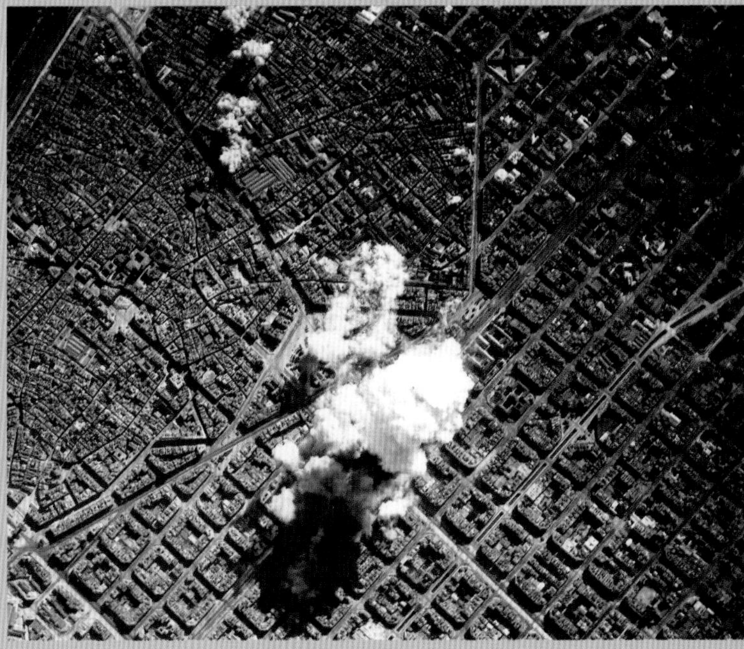

ABOVE Three writers during the Spanish Civil War: Ernest Hemingway (centre), Ilya Ehrenburg (left) and Gustav Regler (right).

TOP RIGHT The Savoia-Marchetti was an Italian three-engine plane used during the Spanish Civil War.

CENTRE RIGHT Smoke rises from bombs hitting Barcelona in 1938.

BELOW RIGHT Guernica in ruins after German bombings.

Nationalists forced the Republicans through a series of retreats. By early 1939, the Republicans were fleeing. The war ended on 28 March 1939, when the Nationalists entered Madrid. As many as half a million people had died in the war. Franco's government and his authoritarian control of Spain would last until his death in 1975. He is known today for his harsh leadership, censoring the public and imprisoning those with contrary political views.

WORLD WAR II 1939–1945

THE LARGEST WAR IN HISTORY

THE HARSH TERMS OF THE TREATY OF VERSAILLES THAT ENDED WORLD WAR I CREATED HUGE UNREST AND HARDSHIP IN GERMANY, FACILITATING ADOLF HITLER'S RISE TO POWER. THE TERMS DESIGNED TO RESTRICT GERMANY, WOULD CONTRIBUTE TO THE ONSET OF THE WORLD'S LARGEST WAR.

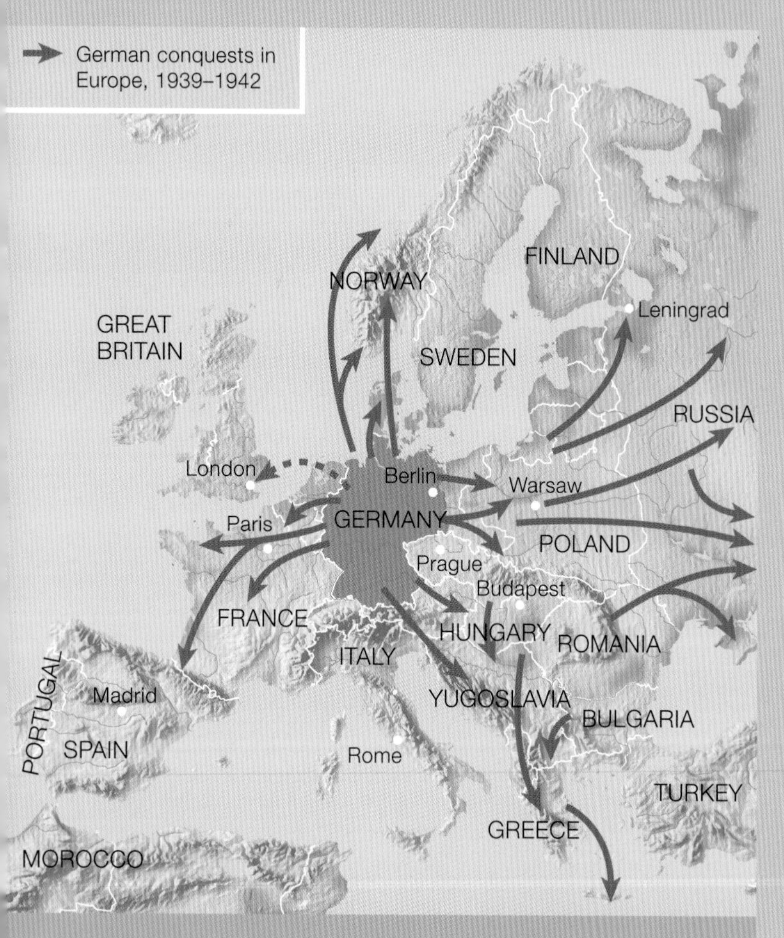

ABOVE The Axis powers faced opponents on all sides.

OPPOSITE TOP The Polish cavalry during the Battle of the Bzura, 9–19 September1939.

Germany's imperial ambitions in World War II differed from their previous incarnations in the ideologies that lay beneath them. World War II became a battle not just between political entities, but one for humanity itself as Adolf Hitler sought to exterminate various groups of people he considered degenerate. These included Jews, homosexuals and Roma or gypsies. Anyone not of 'Aryan' descent could be deemed unworthy of life under his control. It is important to remember, however, that while the atrocities committed by the Nazis during the Holocaust were among the worst of any leader or party in history, World War II was also a political war, and not all Germans who fought in the German army shared Hitler's racism, xenophobia and anti-Semitism.

APPEASEMENT

As Hitler rose to prominence in the 1930s, he began amassing greater and greater power and control for himself and the Nazi party. With World War I having ended only 20 years before, the other powers of Europe were eager to avoid war at all cost. They practised a policy of appeasement when it came to Hitler, allowing him to grow in power rather than standing up against him. However, when Hitler invaded Poland on 1 September, 1939, Britain declared war on Germany. This was effectively the start of World War II in Europe.

Germany's assault on the rest of Europe was well-planned. Before the invasion of Poland, Hitler had made an arrangement with the Soviet Union to divide Poland between them. This ensured Germany would not have to fight the Soviet Union upon invading Poland. Furthermore,

Germany took several important lessons from World War I, and introduced the concept of 'blitzkrieg', or 'lightning war'. This was the practice of using tanks and heavy artillery to plough through an enemy's defences, advancing with as much speed and force as possible in an effort to disable the enemy before any resistance could be organized. He did not want to get bogged down in trench warfare.

On 10 May 1940, Germany invaded Luxembourg, Belgium, the Netherlands and France. The blitzkrieg tactics allowed Germany to conquer the Netherlands in only a few days. By 22 June, Germany controlled most of France. Germany's military was technologically advanced, and its tactics were executed with clockwork precision.

BELOW LEFT British POWs in 1940.

BELOW RIGHT Adolf Hitler poses before the Eiffel Tower. The German advance into France was swift and effective, and marked a high point for Germany in the war.

WORLD WAR II 1939–1945

THE AXIS

The Axis Powers found themselves in a position similar to that of the Central Powers in World War I. Germany, Italy, Bulgaria, Hungary and Romania were the principal Axis Powers in Europe. Once the goodwill between Germany and the USSR had eroded, Germany invaded Russia on 22 June 1941. The Axis Powers now faced opposition from Britain and portions of France in the west, and from Russia in the east. Germany's alliance with Italy, however, may have caused more trouble than it was worth. Italy's defeats in North Africa required Germany to send aid. Field Marshal Erwin Rommel, who had distinguished himself in the invasion of France, was dispatched to North Africa. Further failings by Italy in Greece required German assistance.

Germany advanced through Eastern Europe and into Russia with the same force and speed with which it had in France the year before. Germany came close to reaching Moscow, but by this point the harsh Russian winter was beginning to set in. Like the expedition of Napoleon Bonaparte in 1812, the German advance into Russia could not succeed through the winter. The Soviet Union, meanwhile, was able to begin organizing its resistance. The Battle of Stalingrad, which took place from August 1942 to February 1943, marked a turning point in the war. It was one of the bloodiest battles of all time with well over a million casualties. The Axis defeat at Stalingrad coincided with defeats in North Africa, and Japanese defeats in the Pacific. The Germans were subsequently defeated at the Battle of Kursk in July 1943.

TOP LEFT German soldiers advance through Stalingrad, in October 1942.

TOP RIGHT Smoke and fire amidst the chaos of the Battle of Stalingrad in 1942, one of the bloodiest battles in history.

ABOVE German soldiers on the Eastern Front in 1941.

RIGHT This Russian poster reads, 'To the West!' It shows a Russian soldier destroying a German sign that reads, 'To the East!' Russian dive bombers can be seen in the background.

D-DAY

The beginning of the end for the European theatre of World War II was the Allied invasion of Normandy, France, on 6 June 1944. Owing to the significance of the operation, the day is known as D-Day, or Doomsday. Codenamed Operation Neptune, the Allied invasion was an incredible feat of logistics and planning. An airborne assault preceded the landings on the Normandy beaches. More than 160,000 soldiers landed on the beaches of Gold, Juno, Storm, Utah and Omaha. The American forces who landed at Omaha met the staunchest German resistance, suffering 2,000 casualties during the landing.

The Germans counter-attacked, but the Allied forces under the Supreme Command of Dwight D Eisenhower offered fierce resistance, and managed to establish their beachhead from which they would then push eastwards and inland, driving German forces back.

SO MUCH DEATH

World War II was the largest war in history, with nearly 25 million military deaths, and probably twice that number of civilian deaths. That includes the roughly six million Jews systematically rounded up and killed. Never before in history had killing been refined to such a machine-like process. Only through extreme organization and technological ingenuity was it even possible for the Nazis to actually kill as many civilians as they did. Furthermore, technological advances likewise increased the number of military casualties.

TOP LEFT View from inside one of the landing craft at Normandy on D-Day, 6 June 1944. American soldiers make their way to the beach.

TOP RIGHT Hundreds of paratroopers descend into the Netherlands in September 1944.

ABOVE CENTRE Cold American soldiers queue for food on their way to La Roche-en-Ardenne, Belgium, in January 1945.

ABOVE Emaciated prisoners at Buchenwald concentration camp, in April 1945.

BATTLE OF BRITAIN 1940

Beginning in the summer of 1940, Hitler's Luftwaffe began aerial raids on England, hoping to destroy the Royal Air Force (RAF). Hitler considered Britain vastly inferior to Germany in terms of military strength. At first, however, Hitler did not plan to invade Britain after defeating France. When he decided to start launching aerial attacks on British ships in the English Channel in early July, his forces were relatively ill-equipped to handle the air battles that were about to begin. Britain, meanwhile, braced itself for war.

DANCE IN THE SKY

By August, the Germans had organized and launched their main offensive against Britain's Air Force. Targeting airfields and radar-control stations, the Luftwaffe sought to put the RAF out of commission. The British radar systems, however, were the best of their day, and the forewarning they provided allowed the smaller force of British planes to intercept the attacking Luftwaffe. Germany based its planes across the channel in France, with several times the number of aircraft as Britain. The British, however, had superfast Spitfire planes, which were speedier and more agile than the German planes escorting their bombers. By combining their Spitfire planes with heavier Hurricanes, the British were able to fend off German attacks throughout August. By the end of August, the British had lost about 200 planes; the Germans had lost three times that number.

TOP Documents detailing German plans for the invasion of England.

ABOVE LEFT German bombers fly over the English Channel in 1940.

LEFT This photo shows tracer ammunition from the Spitfire planes used to defend England from German air attacks.

BOMBINGS OF LONDON

In early September, German bombers dropped a few bombs on London, and the British swiftly retaliated by bombing Berlin. Hitler, who did not appear to have any cohesive strategy to defeat Britain in the air, changed his tactics and began bombing British cities, including London, Liverpool, Birmingham, Plymouth, Bristol, amongst others. From 7 September 1940 to 16 May 1941, the Germans continued to bomb British cities in what is known as 'The Blitz'. The shift away from military targets marked an important victory for the RAF in its defence of Britain against the Luftwaffe during the Battle of Britain. Nonetheless, these attacks on civilians put the population of Britain constantly on edge, as the sound of air-raid sirens echoed in the streets. Germany was never able to launch a full invasion of Britain.

TOP LEFT A man scans the sky with binoculars in London. St Paul's Cathedral stands in the background.

TOP RIGHT Another shot of St Paul's Cathedral, this time surrounded by smoking rubble from German bomb blasts.

CENTRE RIGHT Children in East London sit before a pile of rubble left from an air raid.

RIGHT Two women observe the damage of a bombing during 'The Blitz'.

BATTLE OF THE BULGE 1944–1945

In the months following the Allied invasion of Normandy, Allied forces under Dwight D Eisenhower pushed the Germans back, advancing through France and into Belgium. In the autumn, however, their progress began to slow and come to a halt. Suspecting that if he were to succeed in beating the Allies, he would have to do so quickly, Hitler threw much of his remaining resources at a counteroffensive, which began on 16 December. While the Germans enjoyed some initial successes in the battle, driving the Allies back, the expenditure of energy and supplies only catalysed the downfall of the Nazis. Even Hitler's own commanders knew the offensive would not be successful.

THE BATTLE

The Germans outnumbered the American forces more than two to one, with an army of roughly 200,000 strong. As could be expected of a German offensive, it was swift and powerful, with 1,600 artillery pieces deployed over 130 km (80 miles). The offensive was aimed at capturing Antwerp, an important supply port for the Allies, especially for taking shipments from Britain across the Channel. Snow and fog prevented the US Air Force from providing assistance to the troops on the ground. The attack was unexpected, and threw the US troops into confusion. For the first few days of the assault, fighting occurred sporadically throughout the Ardennes Forest, as American soldiers sought to understand the battle formations of the attacking Germans. The Americans, however scattered, refused to give up.

ABOVE LEFT Dwight D Eisenhower was Supreme Commander of the Allied Forces. A five-star general, he would later become the 34th President of the United States.

LEFT The bodies of dead Belgians lie in the street, mown down by German gunfire in December 1944.

OPPOSITE BOTTOM LEFT Entertainer Al Jolson shakes the hand of General George Patton in 1945.

OPPOSITE BOTTOM RIGHT Troops cross the Siegfried Line of German defences in the final stages of the war.

ABOVE A British tank along the River Meuse.

ABOVE A large line of American POWs in December 1944.

THE FINAL TURN

On 22 December, the commander of US troops besieged at Bastogne, Brigadier General Anthony McAuliffe, was presented with two options by the Germans: surrender – or death. His famous official reply to the Germans was simply, 'Nuts!' If anyone were to surrender, it would be the Germans.

By 23 December, American forces had stopped the Germans just a few kilometres short of the River Meuse. The tide began to turn against the Germans once more. Without supplies to continue the push that created the 'bulge' in the Allied lines, the Germans began to crumble. As the weather cleared, the US fighter pilots took to the skies. The American counteroffensive began in early January 1945, and the Germans were forced to retreat.

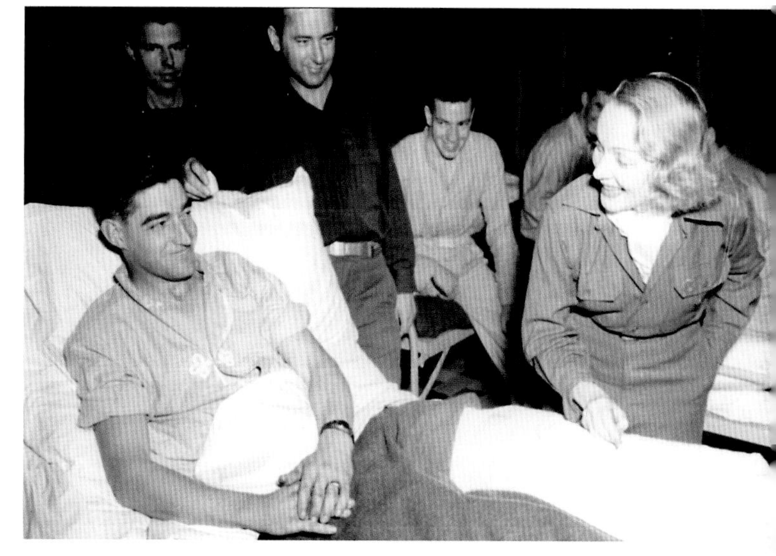

ABOVE Famous actress Marlene Dietrich signs an autograph on the leg cast of an American soldier in Belgium, 1944.

KOSOVO CONFLICT 1998–1999

'ETHNIC CLEANSING'

AS YUGOSLAVIA BROKE UP DURING THE 1990S, TENSIONS ESCALATED IN THE PROVINCE OF KOSOVO BETWEEN ETHNICALLY ALBANIAN MUSLIMS AND ETHNICALLY SERBIAN CHRISTIANS. THE RESULTING WAR SAW EXTENSIVE BLOODSHED AND THE SO-CALLED 'ETHNIC CLEANSING' OF BOTH SERBIANS AND ALBANIANS.

ABOVE Kosovo used to be part of Serbia, and the historic Battle of Kosovo in 1389 is still considered an essential part of Serbian identity.

Kosovo had enjoyed a certain degree of autonomy earlier in the twentieth century, but ethnic tensions between Serbian and Albanian populations had been brewing for a long time. Kosovo holds an important place in Serbian history and identity. It is the location of the 1389 Battle of Kosovo in which the Serbs presented a valiant stand against the invading Ottomans of Murad I. Though unsuccessful against the Ottomans, the Serbs consider the Battle – and therefore the territory – of Kosovo a significant part of their national identity.

START OF WAR

In 1989, Slobodan Milosevic became president of Yugoslavia and began implementing Serbian nationalist policies. Ibrahim Rugova, leader of the Albanians in Kosovo, advocated for peaceful separation and independence from Yugoslavia. Others, however, felt that independence should be gained through military force and formed the Kosovo Liberation Army (KLA). Throughout the 1990s, the KLA launched attacks against Yugoslav security forces and also targeted Serbs. The Federal Republic of Yugoslavia – as well as other countries – considered the KLA to be a terrorist organization. In 1998, as KLA violence against Serbs increased, Milosevic struck against the Albanians of Kosovo.

With the provocations of the KLA as justification, Milosevic invaded. He began a campaign of ethnic cleansing, killing thousands of ethnic Albanians in Kosovo and driving hundreds of thousands away. The conflict, rather than a clash between two political entities, was largely over ethnicity and religion. Instead of aiming to maintain political and military

ABOVE President Slobodan Milosevic meets with Admiral T Joseph Lopez in Belgrade, in 1996, to discuss maintaining peace in the region.

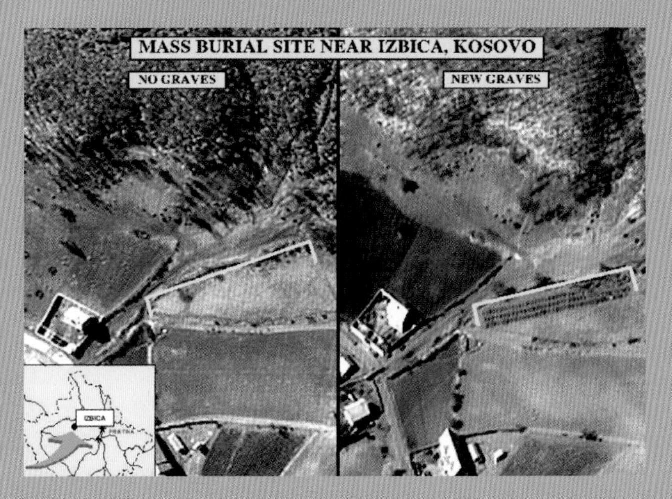

ABOVE These contrasted satellite images show mass graves dug near Izbica in Kosovo after the Izbica Massacre of 1999.

control of Kosovo, Milosevic sought to put down the Kosovo independence movement by killing the ethnic Albanians. At the same time, the KLA continued its attacks against Serbs, both sides committing atrocities. Massacres, kidnappings and murders were common. Perhaps most grotesquely, organ theft – the theft and sale of human organs – was also practised.

NATO INTERVENTION

In June 1998, NATO began its intervention in the war. Peace efforts were thwarted, however, as both sides broke ceasefires and continued fighting. The war eventually came to a close after the NATO bombings of Yugoslavia in spring 1999. Milosevic was arrested in 2001 and subsequently tried for war crimes; he died in prison in 2006. KLA leaders were also indicted for crimes against humanity.

TOP This photo from 1999 shows a charred town wrecked by the Kosovo War. Many scars of the destruction can still be seen across the landscape today.

ABOVE Buildings aflame during the NATO bombings of Yugoslavia.

THE PARADOX OF WAR

After reading such a sweeping account of some of the greatest conflicts in history throughout the world, one can start to see patterns emerge out of the chaos of war. What works? What doesn't? How can wars be won, and how can they be avoided? In each battle and each clash of arms, we can still hear the echoes of those who fell, crying out in horror or rage. We know intellectually that war is a terrible thing, but we are irresistibly drawn to it all the same. This is the great 'paradox of war'.

There are many reasons for fighting: we protect our kinsmen, our ways of life and our resources. We also wage war to obtain better ways of life and more resources. However, as you ponder the examples of war throughout this book, ask yourself: how many of these conflicts could have been avoided if both sides had sought peace?

The truth of the matter is that we as a species love to fight. What tale would be complete without struggle and strife? How dull would the world be without the heroes of battle? As the external reasons for armed conflict disappear in many parts of the world – with advancing technology providing means of distributing food and clean water – our human attachment to war itself becomes clearer and clearer. Only by understanding this fundamental desire for the supreme excitement of battle can we actually work towards attaining peace.

War is changing as technology advances and as the destructive capability with weapons increases. Snipers take out enemies up to 2.4 km (a mile and a half) away; computerized drones can drop bombs without any risk to the lives of the attackers; strength-enhancing exoskeletons will revolutionize the soldier's role on the battlefield. As our capability for destruction increases, so do our efforts to create defensive armour. The technological advancement of both offensive and defensive weaponry will continue to escalate until one day we will perhaps collectively realize what many individuals already have: the only way to win is not to play at all. As the old proverb goes, 'the sparrow never lands where the tiger roams'.

Despite the mechanization and computerization of various aspects of warfare, our humanity remains underneath it all. Let us learn from the successes and failures of what has already been done. War will continue to fascinate us, but it will do so primarily for the bravery and strategic intelligence of men and women who overcome great odds to accomplish seemingly impossible feats.

LEFT The European Parliament in Strasbourg. The European Union won the Nobel Peace Prize in 2012.

ABOVE An unmanned, computerized combat drone is capable of dropping bombs or deploying computerized missiles without requiring an onboard human pilot.

RIGHT Winner of the 2009 Nobel Peace Prize, U.S. President Barack Obama is seen in many parts of the world as an important figure of international peace and diplomacy.

APPENDIX: CHRONOLOGY

3100 BCE	Unification of Egypt
2900–2270 BCE	Kingdom of Sumer
2300 BCE	Sargon the Great
1792–1750 BCE	Hammurabi of Babylon
18th–12th centuries BCE	Kingdoms of the Hittites and Hurrians
1500 BCE–900 CE	Mayan Civilization
1274 BCE	Battle of Kadesh
1200–500 BCE	Olmec Civilization in Mesoamerica
1200–30 BCE	Ancient Greece
911–627 BCE	Assyrian Empire
771–476 BCE	Spring and Autumn Period of China
760 BCE	Nubian Kingdom of Kush conquers Egypt
700 BCE–600 CE	Scythians and Sarmatians
603 BCE	Nebuchadnezzar conquers Judah
600–1 BCE	Expansion of the Celts
575–530 BCE	Cyrus the Great
522–486 BCE	Darius the Great
490 BCE	Battle of Marathon
475–221 BCE	Warring States Period of China
431–404 BCE	Peloponnesian War
336–323 BCE	Alexander the Great
321–297 BCE	Chandragupta Maurya
312–64 BCE	Seleucid Empire
264–146 BCE	Punic Wars
221–206 BCE	Qin Dynasty rules unified China
206 BCE–89 CE	Sino-Xiongnu Wars
100–44 BCE	Julius Caesar
55–36 BCE	Roman-Parthian War
66–135 CE	Jewish-Roman Wars
98–117 CE	Trajan, Emperor of Rome
100–750 CE	Moche Civilization in South America
220–265 CE	Three Kingdoms Period of China
226–671 CE	Sassanid Empire
320–550 CE	Gupta Empire of India
370–453 CE	Huns and Hephthalites branch out from the steppes
400–668 CE	Koguryo Wars with China
476 CE	Traditional date for Fall of Rome
618–907 CE	Tang Dynasty of China
632–750 CE	Rise of the Islamic Empire
718–1492 CE	Reconquista
732 CE	Battle of Poitiers (Tours)
768–814 CE	Charlemagne
793–1100 CE	Viking Age
802–15th century CE	Khmer Empire
9th century CE	Gunpowder invented in China
960–1279 CE	Song Dynasty of China
1066 CE	Battle of Hastings
1096–1272 CE	The Crusades
1162–1227 CE	Mongols storm the world stage
1180–1185 CE	Gempei War forges Japan
1250–1532 CE	Inca Empire
1272–1307 CE	Edward I of England
1258 CE	Mongol Sack of Baghdad
1280 CE	Polynesians settle New Zealand
1289–1292 CE	Mongol Wars in Java
1300–1922 CE	Ottoman Empire
1337–1453 CE	The Hundred Years' War
1396 CE	Battle of Nicopolis
1427–1521 CE	Aztec Empire
1453 CE	Ottoman Sack of Constantinople
1455–1485 CE	War of the Roses
1467–1600 CE	Sengoku Jidai, Warring States in Japan

1468–1591 CE	Songhai Empire
1486–1752 CE	Toungoo Dynasty of Burma
1526–1857 CE	Mughal Empire
1575 CE	Battle of Nagashino
1588 CE	Spanish Armada
1676–1878 CE	Russo-Turkish Wars
1700–1721 CE	Great Northern War
1701–1714 CE	War of Spanish Succession
1701–1896 CE	Ashanti Empire
1747–1792 CE	Ten Great Campaigns of Qianlong
1754–1763 CE	French and Indian War
1775–1783 CE	American Revolution
1782–1810 CE	Kamehameha the Great unifies Hawaii
1791–1804 CE	Haitian Revolution
1799–1815 CE	Napoleon Bonaparte
1804–1835 CE	Black War in Tasmania
1807 CE	Musket Wars begin among the Maori
1809 CE	Wars of Independence begin in South America
1810–1821 CE	Mexican War of Independence
1812–1815 CE	War of 1812
1839–1842 CE	Opium Wars in China
1853–1856 CE	Crimean War
1857–1858 CE	Sepoy Mutiny in India
1861–1865 CE	American Civil War
1866 CE	Battle of Königgrätz
1878–1879 CE	Zulu Wars
1880–1902 CE	South African Wars
1892–1902 CE	Philippine Wars of Independence
1895–1896 CE	First Italo-Ethiopian War
1898 CE	Spanish-American War
1899–1901 CE	Boxer Rebellion in China
1903 CE	Wright Brothers take off
1904–1905 CE	Russo-Japanese War
1905–1923 CE	Russian Revolution
1912–1933 CE	Nicaraguan Civil War
1914–1918 CE	World War I
1918 CE	Second Battle of the Marne
1919–1921 CE	Irish War of Independence
1927–1949 CE	Chinese Civil War
1935–1945 CE	African Theatre of World War II
1936–1939 CE	Spanish Civil War
1939–1945 CE	European Theatre of World War II
1940 CE	Battle of Britain
1941–1945 CE	Pacific Theatre of World War II
1942–1943 CE	Battle of Guadalcanal
1944 CE	D-Day
1944 CE	Battle of the Bulge
1945 CE	Battle of Iwo Jima
1947–present	Indo-Pakistani Wars
1948–present	Arab-Israeli Wars
1950–1953 CE	Korean War
1953–1959 CE	Cuban Revolution
1954–1962 CE	Algerian Revolution
1955–1975 CE	Vietnam War
1983–2009 CE	Sri Lankan Civil War
1990–1993 CE	Rwandan Civil War
1998–1999 CE	Kosovo Conflict
2001 CE	September 11 Attacks
2001–present	Afghanistan War
2003–2011 CE	Iraq War
2011–present	Arab Spring

INDEX

D

E

F

G

INDEX

INDEX

ACKNOWLEDGEMENTS

t: top, r: right, l: left, b: below, c: centre

8–9 shutterstock-gallery-595873p1./Byelikova Oksana | 10–11 Shutterstock/Ed Phillips | 13 shutterstock-gallery-507811p1/ Art Konovalov

AFRICA 19tr Shutterstock/Inna Felker 20bl Bertramz | 22 Punic Thesaurus opticus Titelblatt | 28t Ashanti-African objects in the American Museum of Natural History | 28b Ashanti soulwasher by Claire H | 32–33 Menelik II-Petit Journal | 34–35 Battle of Belmont, Boer War

MIDDLE EAST 47tr Donation of the British Museum/ Eric Gaba | 57b Marie-Lan Nguyen | 53cr Mark Randall Dawson | 56r The Metropolitan Museum of Art (Rogers Fund) | 59t Circle Juan de la Corte/The Burning of Jerusalem by Nebuchadnezzar's Army/Google Art Project | 61br Alireza Shakernia | 64t Luis García | 64b Ad Meskens | 70l Shakko | 94t Shutterstock/Zastolskiy Victor | 97t Shutterstock/Sergey Kamshylin

ASIA 102tl David Schroeter | 103bl Ayelia | 105tl Shutterstock/Philip Lange | 105tr Ayelie | 110t Derzsi Elekes Andor | 112–113b Shutterstock/Fotohunter | 115tl Fanghong | 122l Shutterstock/Zhang Kan | 124l Shutterstock/WitthayaP | 125t Shutterstock/65665828 | 125r Vladimir Renard | 129tl Walters Art Museum | 130 Shutterstock/Stripped Pixel | 135t Shutterstock/ThavomC | 143tl Shutterstock/windmoon | 144l Shutterstock/Antonio Abrignani |146tr Shutterstock/Sam DCruz | 147br Shutterstock/Antonio Abrignani |153t Shutterstock/jorisvo | 162l NARA

OCEANIA 168tl CT Snow | 168bl Metropolitan Museum of Art, gift of Heber R Bishop, 1902
169t 1999_47_63_b [Club, French Polynesia, 19th c.] | 169bl David Hall | 171 National Maritime Museum, Greenwich, London | 174t Art Gallery of South Australia | 176tl http://www.joserizal.ph/images/execution

AMERICAS 184b Michael Wal | 185c Dongringo 185bl Ruben Charles | 185br Frida27Ponce, retouched by Peter Hanula, originally uploaded by User:Madman2001 | 187bl Michel Wal/Mus.es Royaux d'Art et d'Histoire, Brussels | 187r Jami Dwyer, National Museum of Archaeology, Mexico City | 191b Bernard Gagnon | 192 HJPD | 193cl Wolfgang Sauber | 196cr Library of Congress, LC-USZC2-3154 | 187bl Michel Wal/Mus.es Royaux d'Art et d'Histoire, Brussels | 188tr Walters Art Museum | 188br Walters Art Museum | 189c Walters Art Museum | 191b Bernard Gagnon | 192l HJPD | 193cl Wolfgang Sauber | 196cr Library of Congress, LC-USZ62-2258 | 200b AlejandroLinaresGarcia | 204bl Library of Congress | 205b JJ Olmedo | 207bl Library of Congress | 208l Library of Congress, LC-DIG-ppmsca-19211 | 211tl NARA | 211tr NARA | 211b Library of Congress, LC-B8184-7964-A 212r NARA | 213tr Library of Congress cph.3g06550 | 214t Library of Congress cph.3b39563 | 214bl Library of Congress LC-USZ62-63850 | 214br author: ManicalCritic | 215cr Library of Congress 25403 | 215bl NARA | 216l Harris & Ewing, Library of Congress 25355 | 216r NARA | 217br Library of Congress cph.3b48925 | 218b TheMachineStops

EUROPE 222l Shutterstock/0098006 | 223tl, b Walters Art Museum, Baltimore, MD | 226 Shutterstock/1626006 | 227l Giovanni Dall'Orto | 227tr Walters Art Museum, Baltimore, MD | 231l Museum of Fine Arts, Munich | 233b Marcus Cyron, Pergamon Museum, Berlin | 237t Shutterstock/4574061 | 237b Musée des beaux-arts de Lyon | 239b Shutterstock/0285067 | 245b Shutterstock/2010021 | 246 Shutterstock/0096014 | 248b Delaware Art Museum/Photo Ad Meskens | 252cl Shutterstock/LianeM | 252br Shutterstock/Dja65 | 253tl Shutterstock/vagabond54 | 253tr Shutterstock/Adrian Zenz | 274b Shutterstock/Oleg Golovnev | 275tl Shutterstock/Antonio Abrignani | 293tr Library of Congress | 310 Shutterstock-gallery-904822p1./Leonid Andronov | 311r Shutterstock-gallery-143386p1/ Christopher Halloran

The publisher wishes to thank all of the photographers (known and unknown) whose images appear in this book. We apologize in advance for any omissions, or neglect, and will be pleased to make any corrections in future editions.